GW00360379

GREATER DUBLIN

Contents

Tourist & travel information 2

Key to map symbols 3

Key to map pages 4-5

Route planning map 6-7

Main Dublin maps 8-123

Central Dublin map 124-125

Guide to central Dublin 126-145

Index to place names 146

Index to street names 146-176

2 Tourist and travel information

Air

Dublin Airport
Tel: 01 814 1111.
Web: www.dublin–airport.com
Frequent direct flights operate between Dublin and many airports in Britain, Europe and North America. Internal flights are available to Cork, Donegal, Galway, Kerry, Knock, Shannon & Sligo. Aer Arann **Tel: 0818 210210 (R of I), 0800 587 2324 (UK)** www.aerarannexpress.com & Aer Lingus **Tel: 01 886 8888 (R of I), 0845 084 4444 (UK)** www.aerlingus.com operate the internal routes. Other operators flying into Dublin are British Airways **Tel: 1890 626 747 (R of I), 0870 850 9850 (UK)** www.britishairways.com, Flybe **Tel: 1890 925 532 (R of I), 0871 700 0535 (UK)** www.flybe.com, British Midland **Tel: 01 407 3036 (R of I), 0870 6070 555 (UK)** www.flybmi.com & Ryanair **Tel: 01 609 7800 (R of I), 0871 246 0000 (UK)** www.ryanair.com.

The airport is 12km (8 miles) north of the city centre with Dublin Bus operating many services to and from the airport including the 'Airlink' express coach service operating between the airport, the central bus station in Store Street (Bus Áras) and the two mainline rail stations, Connolly and Heuston. It runs every 10 - 15 mins (15 - 20 mins on Sundays) between 05.45 and 23.30 from the airport and between 05.15 and 22.50 from O'Connell Street in the centre of Dublin. **Tel: 01 873 4222** www.dublinbus.ie. 'Aircoach' runs between the airport and Dublin City and South Dublin City stopping at major hotels. The 24 hour service operates every 10-20 minutes except from 24.00 and 05.00 when an hourly service operates. **Tel: 01 844 7118** www.aircoach.ie. 'Aerdart' is a bus service operating every 15 minutes between the airport and Howth Junction DART station.

Services at Dublin airport include Travel Information, Tourist Information and Bureau de Change

Passenger and vehicle ferries

Numerous modern ferries and high-speed services with drive-on drive-off facilities cross the Irish Sea to Dublin from Britain (Liverpool, Mostyn, Holyhead), the Isle of Man and France (Cherbourg).

Irish Ferries (Dublin–Holyhead). **Tel: 01 638 3333 / 0818 300 400** or from UK: **08705 17 17 17.**
Web: www.irishferries.com
Email: info@irishferries.ie

Norse Merchant Ferries (Dublin–Birkenhead). **Tel: 01 819 2999** or from UK: **0870 600 4321.**
Web: www.norsemerchant.com

P & O Irish Sea (Dublin–Liverpool). **Tel: 1800 409 049** or from UK: **0870 24 24 777.**
Web: www.poirishsea.com

Isle of Man Steam Packet Company/Sea Containers (Dublin–Douglas).
Tel: 1800 80 50 55 or from UK: **08705 523 523.**
Web: www.steam–packet.com

Stena Line
(Dún Laoghaire–Holyhead & Dublin–Holyhead).
Tel: 01 204 7777
or from UK: **08705 70 70 70.**
Web: www.stenaline.co.uk
Email: info.ie@stenaline.com

Dublin Port and Dún Laoghaire have bus and taxi services to the city centre although on busy sailings it may be prudent to pre-book a taxi. The ferry terminal at Dún Laoghaire is also linked to the city by the DART rail service with a 20 minute journey time.

Tourist information

Dublin Tourism Centre, Suffolk Street. **Tel: 01 605 7700.** Open: (July and August) Mon–Sat 09.00–19.00, (Sept–June) Mon–Sat 09.00–17.30. Open Sun & bank holidays 10.30–15.00; closed 25 & 26 Dec & 1 Jan. Formerly St. Andrew's Church, the centre provides details of visitor attractions and events in the city as well as acting as a ticket and accommodation bureau. Transport and tour information, exchange facilities and a café are also on hand.
Other tourist information and reservation centres in Dublin (walk-in only) are located at:
Dublin Airport. Open: Mon–Sun 08.00–22.00. Open bank holidays except 25 & 26 Dec & 1 Jan.
Dún Laoghaire Ferry Terminal. Open: Mon–Sat 10.00–18.00, closed 13.00-14.00. Open bank holidays except 25 & 26 Dec & 1 Jan.

Baggott Street Bridge. Open: Mon–Fri 09.30–17.00, closed 12.00-12.30. Closed bank holidays.
For accommodation reservations in Dublin and Ireland contact Ireland Reservations. Tel from within Ireland: **1800 363 626**; from within UK: **008 002 580 2580.**

Official tourism website for Dublin:
Web: www.visitdublin.com
Email: information@dublintourism.ie
or reservations@dublintourism.ie

Irish Tourist Board Website:
Web: www.ireland.ie
Department of Environment, Heritage & Local Government:
Web: www.heritageireland.ie
Email: info@heritageireland.ie

Key to map symbols ③

M1 Motorway / under construction	▣ GSS Garda Síochána (police) station
- - - - - Tunnelled motorway	🅸 Tourist information centre
N6 National primary road	+ Church
N55 National secondary road	■ PO ■ Lib Public service building (appropriate name shown)
R95 Regional road	▭ Leisure / Tourism
Other road	▭ Shopping
:::::::::: Track	▭ Administration / Law
- - - - - - - Ferry	▭ Health / Hospital
Administrative boundary	▭ Education
▬▭▬ Railway / Station	▭ Notable building
JERVIS Dublin Luas tramway / Station	▭ Built up area
⬤ Bus / Coach station	▭ Park / Garden / Sports ground / Public open space
Ⓟ Car park	▭ Cemetery
Lake / River	

```
0        0.25        0.5        0.75        1 km
0                    ¼                    ½ mile
```

Scale 1:15,840 4 inches (10.2cm) to 1 mile / 6.3cm to 1km

Published by Collins
An imprint of HarperCollins*Publishers*
77-85 Fulham Palace Road, Hammersmith, London W6 8JB

www.collins.co.uk

Copyright © HarperCollins*Publishers* Ltd 2005
Collins® is a registered trademark of HarperCollins*Publishers* Limited
Mapping generated from Collins Bartholomew digital databases

Based on Ordnance Survey Ireland by permission of the Government. © Government of Ireland.

Printed in China by South China Printing Co. Ltd.
ISBN 0007202229 Imp 001   SI11942 / NDB

e-mail: roadcheck@harpercollins.co.uk

Moynalvy
Springvalley
Bogganstown
Knockstown
Kilmore
Mullagh
Batterstown
Kilsallagh
Mullinam
Newtown
Coolquoy
N2
Ward
Pinkeen
Kilbride
W
Garadice
Kiltens Gap
Kilclone
Baytownpark
N3
Tulka
Killshane
Ballynare
Rodanstown
Dolanstown
Kilgraigue
Dunboyne
Ballymacoll
Clonee
22 - 23
26 - 27
28 - 2
Kilcock
Rathleek
24 - 25
Corduff
M50
Portgloriam
Laragh
M4
Maynooth
Clonsilla
38 - 39
Blanchardstown
40 - 4
6
Leixlip
66 - 67
Castleknock
56 - 57
Toll
58 - 5
Phoen Park
Taghadoe
Celbridge
68 - 69
N4
Lucan
7
Palmerston
70 - 71
Chapeliz
72 - 7
Baltracey
Rathcoffey
Windgates
Stacumny
Grand Canal
80 - 81
82 - 8
Baybush
Mainham
Straffan
Coolfitch
Hazelhatch
Milltown
Clondalkin
9
Betaghstown
Liffey
Newcastle
Brownsbarn
90 - 91
92 - 9
Kingswood
N7
10
Clane
Rathmore
Ardclough
Saggart
TALLAGHT
M5
Firmount
Athgoe
Oughterard
Rathcoole
102 - 103
104 - 1
Friarstown
Sherlockstown
Redgap
N81
Raheen
Sallins
Kill
Porterstown
Brittas
N7
Johnstown
Thornberry
Kilteel
Monaspick
Cunard
M7
Halverstown
7
Rathmore
8
Naas
Eadestown
Hempstown
Kilbride
Newland
Two Mile House
Mullacash
Tipperkevin
Oldcourt
Liffey
Silliothill
Donode
Blessington
Carnalway

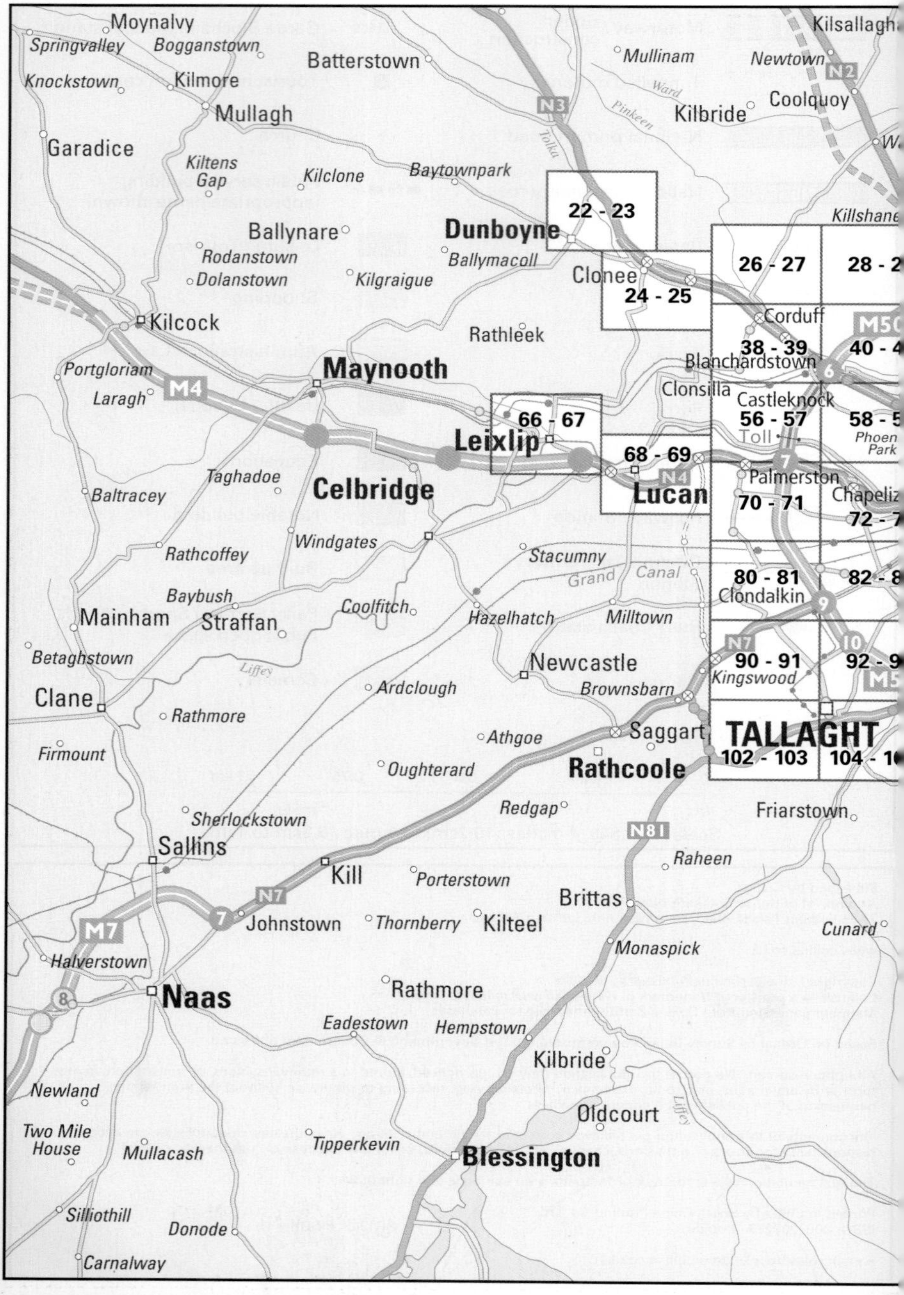

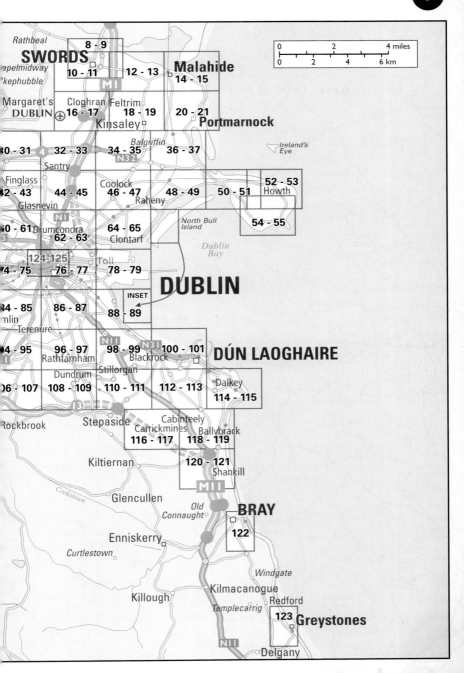

5

Rathbeal

SWORDS
apelmidway
'kephubble

8 - 9
10 - 11   12 - 13   **Malahide**
14 - 15

Margaret's
DUBLIN ✈ 16 - 17
Cloghran *Feltrim*
18 - 19   20 - 21   **Portmarnock**
Kinsaley

Balgriffin
0 - 31   32 - 33   34 - 35   36 - 37

⌐*Ireland's Eye*

Santry

Finglass
2 - 43   44 - 45   *Coolock* 46 - 47   48 - 49   50 - 51   52 - 53 Howth
Raheny

Glasnevin

0 - 61 *Drumcondra*   64 - 65
62 - 63   *Clontarf*

North Bull Island

54 - 55

124-125   *Toll*
4 - 75   76 - 77   78 - 79

Dublin Bay

DUBLIN

INSET
88 - 89

4 - 85   86 - 87
mlin
Terenure

4 - 95   96 - 97   98 - 99   100 - 101   **DÚN LAOGHAIRE**
Rathfarnham   *Blackrock*

Dundrum   *Stillorgan*
06 - 107   108 - 109   110 - 111   112 - 113   *Dalkey*
114 - 115

Rockbrook   *Stepaside*   *Cabinteely*
Carrickmines *Ballybrack*
116 - 117   118 - 119

Kiltiernan   120 - 121
Shankill

Cookstown   *Glencullen*   *Old Connaught*   **BRAY**
122

Enniskerry
Curtlestown

Windgate
Kilmacanogue
Killough   *Redford*
Templecarrig   123 **Greystones**

Delgany

0   2   4 miles
0   2   4   6 km

Route planning map

Scale

| 0 | 5 | 10 | 15 km |
| 0 | 3 | 6 | 9 miles |

Road distances shown in blue
are in miles

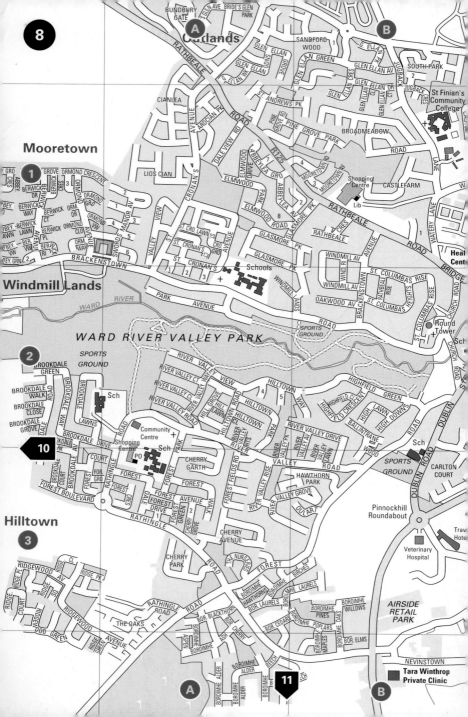

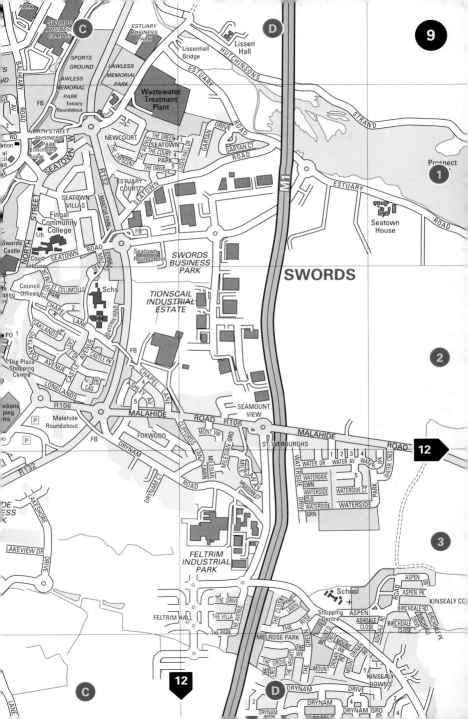

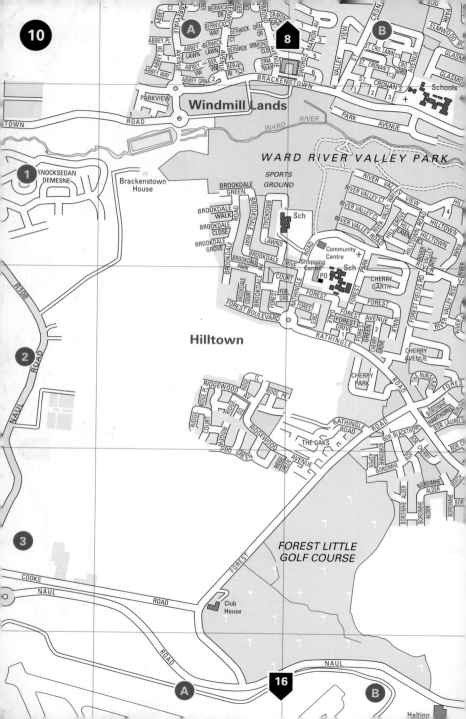

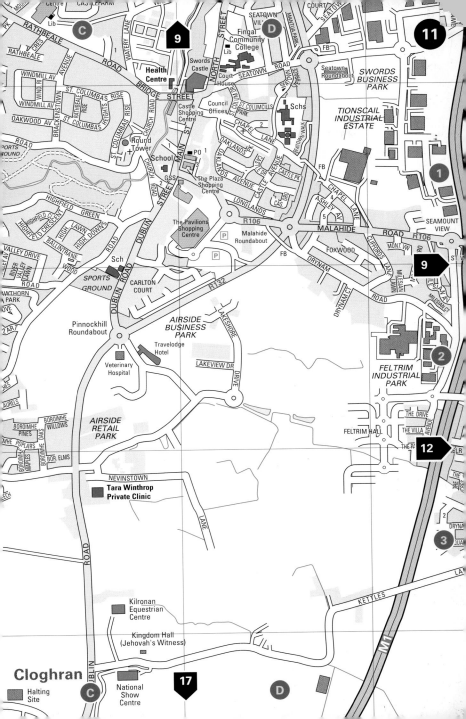

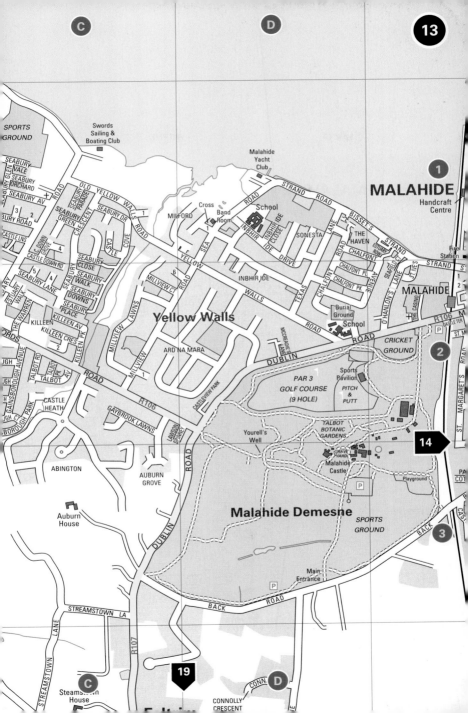

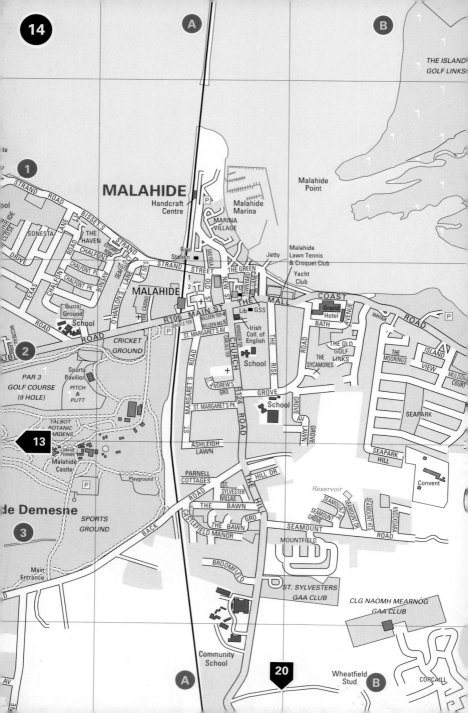

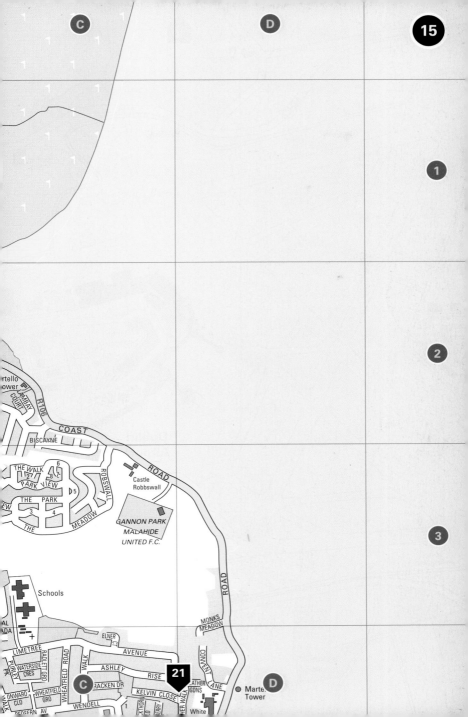

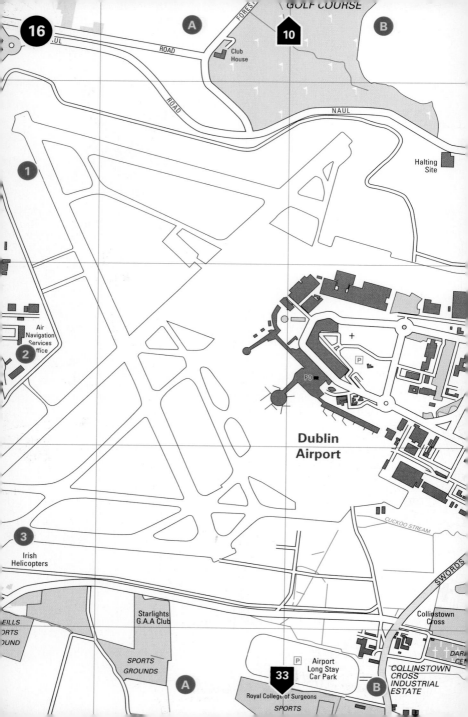

16

A

B

10

GOLF COURSE

FOREST

NAUL

ROAD

ROAD

Club
House

1

Halting
Site

2

Air
Navigation
Services
Office

P

PO

+

**Dublin
Airport**

CUCKOO STREAM

3

SWORDS

Irish
Helicopters

Collinstown
Cross

EILLS
ORTS
UND

Starlights
G.A.A Club

SPORTS
GROUNDS

A

P Airport
Long Stay
Car Park

B

COLLINSTOWN
CROSS
INDUSTRIAL
ESTATE

33

Royal College of Surgeons

SPORTS

DAR
CE

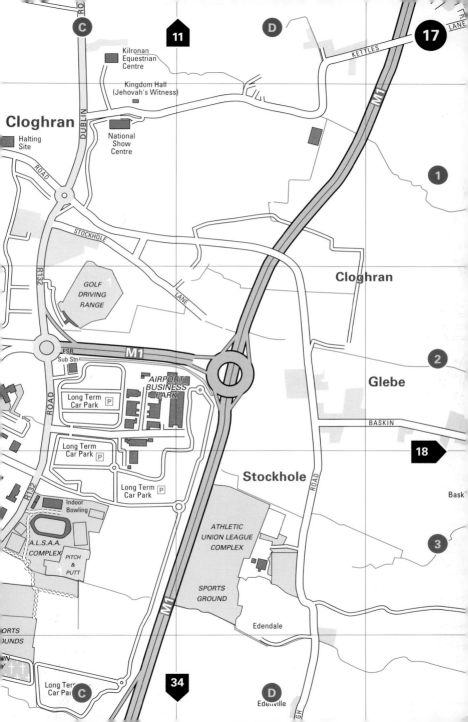

C
11
D
17

Kilronan
Equestrian
Centre

KETTLES

Kingdom Hall
(Jehovah's Witness)

1

Cloghran

Halting
Site

National
Show
Centre

DUBLIN

ROAD

STOCKHOLE

R132

Cloghran

GOLF
DRIVING
RANGE

LANE

M1

2

ESB
Sub Stn

AIRPORT
BUSINESS
PARK

Glebe

BASKIN

Long Term
Car Park
P

18

ROAD

R132

Long Term
Car Park
P

Long Term
Car Park
P

Long Term
Car Park
P

Stockhole

ROAD

GH

Bask

Indoor
Bowling

A.L.S.A.A.
COMPLEX

PITCH
&
PUTT

ATHLETIC
UNION LEAGUE
COMPLEX

3

M1

ORTS
UNDS

SPORTS
GROUND

Edendale

Long Term
Car Park
C

34

D
Edenville

18

A

18

KETTLES

12

FELTRIM

B

M1

Feltrim
Quarry

1

Cloghran

Greenwood

2

Glebe

ASHGROVE

Ballymac

BASKIN

LANE

BASKIN
COTTAGES

17

ckhole

ROAD

Baskin Hill

Emswort

3

dale

Spring Hill

A

35

B

nville

GH

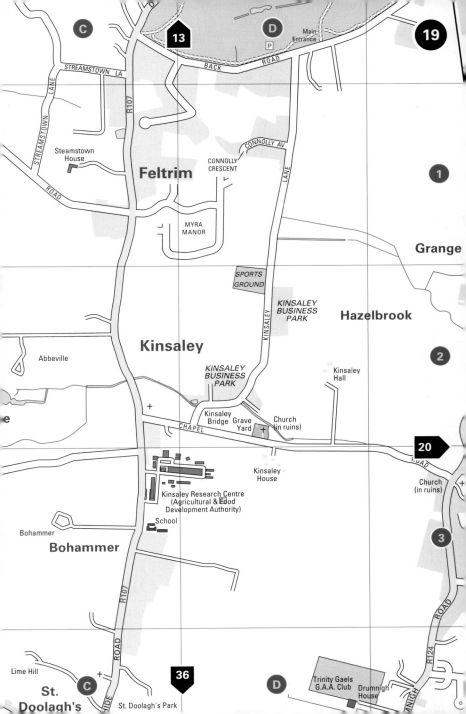

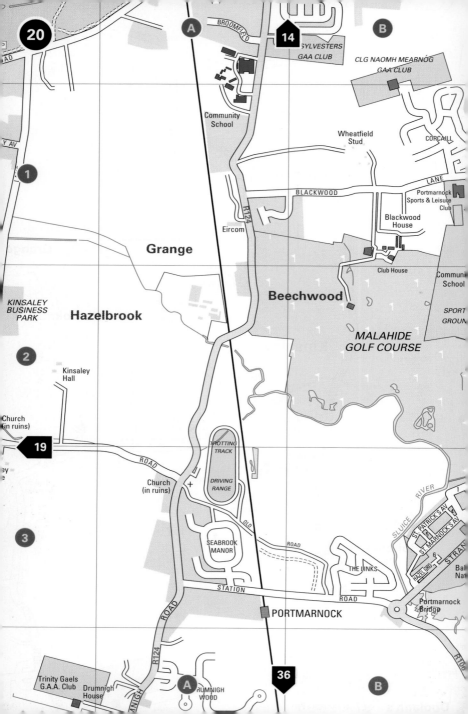

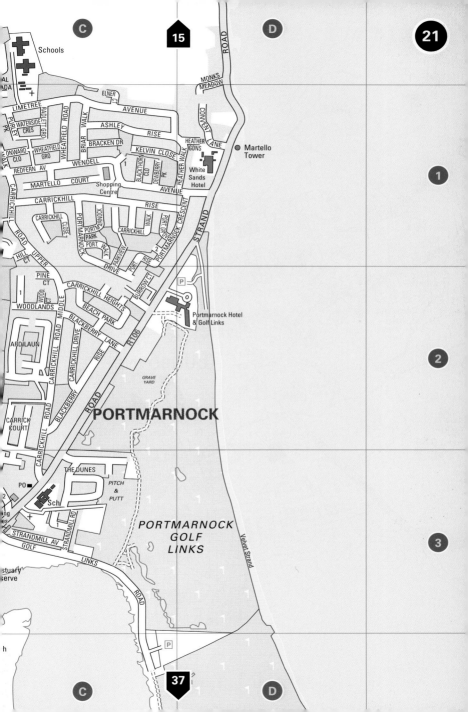

ROAD

MONKS
MEADOW

Schools

ELNER

LIMETREE
PURLEY
PK
WATERSIDE
CRES
RADLETT GDO
WHEATFIELD ROAD
BRIAR WALK
AVENUE
ASHLEY
RISE
BRACKEN DR
HEATHER
GDNS

CONVENT LANE

Martello
Tower

ONWARD
CLO
WHEATFIELD
GRO
WENDELL
KELVIN CLOSE
BLACKTHORN
CLO
NEWBERRY
PK
HEATHER WALK

White
Sands
Hotel

REDFERN AV
MARTELLO COURT
Shopping
Centre
AVENUE

CARRICKHILL
RISE
CARRICKHILL

CARRICKHILL
CLOSE
PORTMARNOCK
PARK
WARNOCK
CARRICKHILL
WALK
PORTMARNOCK CRESCENT
PORTMARNOCK CRESCENT

STRAND

1

HILL
CT
UPPER
PORT
WALK
PORT
DRIVE
PARKVIEW
PORT
RISE
BURROW CT

PINE
CT
CARRICKHILL HEIGHTS
WOOD
1
WOODLANDS

P

CARRICKHILL
ROAD

BEACH
PARK
BLACKBERRY
LANE

Portmarnock Hotel
& Golf Links

ARDILAUN

CARRICKHILL ROAD
CARRICKHILL DRIVE
BLACKBERRY
ROAD
RISE
R106
ROAD

GRAVE
YARD

2

CARRICK
COURT

PORTMARNOCK

CARRICKHILL
ROAD

PO

THE DUNES

PITCH
&
PUTT

Velvet Strand

Sch

STRANDMILL RD

STRANDMILL AV
GOLF
LINKS

**PORTMARNOCK
GOLF
LINKS**

3

stuary
serve

ROAD

h

P

A   B

1

PLUNKETT
HALL

THE COURT
THE AVENUE
THE CLOSE
THE GROVE
THE CRES
THE DRIVE
THE GREEN
THE AVENUE

Pumping
Station

DUNBOYNE
BUSINESS
PARK

R157 ROAD

N3

TOLKA
RIVER

LUTTERELL
HALL

THE DALE

THE PARK

R156

THE LAWN
SUMMERHILL

THE PARK
THE AVENUE
THE DRIVE
THE CRES
THE CLOSE
THE COURT

ROAD

THE PADDOCKS

KILBRINA

THE PADDOCKS

TEMPLE MANOR

GARNETT
HALL

THE DRIVE
THE GROVE

COURTHILL
DRIVE
MEADOW
VIEW

COURT
ST PETER'S
PARK

ST PATRICK'S PARK

NAVAN

OLD FAIR GREEN

OLD FAIR GREEN

CEDAR DR
MAPLE DR
ROSDALE
THE MEADOWS

THE ELMS

CRESCENT
CT

SILVER
BIRCHES

SADLEIR
HALL

GSS

PO

GRAVE
YARD

Hall

Hall

AVONDALE
SQ

MAIN ST

DUNBOYNE

Sch

St. Peter's
College

Comm
Cen

WILLOW

PARK

MILLFARM

ELTON DR

ELTON CT.

ELTON GROVE

NEWTOWN

ROAD

STATION   ROAD

R156

CASTLEVIEW
ESTATE

Hotel

Lib
Community
Service
Centre

ROAD

ROOSKE CT

HAMILTON
HALL

LARCHFIELD

MAYNOOTH

R157

DUNBOYNE
CASTLE

WOODVIEW
HEIGHTS

CONGRESS
HALL

CONGRESS
PARK

BEECHDALE

Dunboyne
Athletic
Club

St. Peter's
Dunboyne

SPORTS
GROUND

CHESTNUT
GROVE

SPORTS
GROUND

2

3

A   B

BRACETOWN
BUSINESS
PARK

Glenmo

1

THE

Gunnocks
House

Merrycourt

2

Loughsallagh
Bridge

ROAD

3

TOLKA RIVER

N3

Dunboyne
Tennis Club

CLONEE

Clonee
Bridge

Clonee

Club
House

R156

PO

BYPASS

ROYAL
MEATH
PITCH
& PUTT
CLUB

NAVAN

ROAD

SUMMERSEAT COURT

Littlepace
Stud

BEECHFIELD

MEADOW

RISE

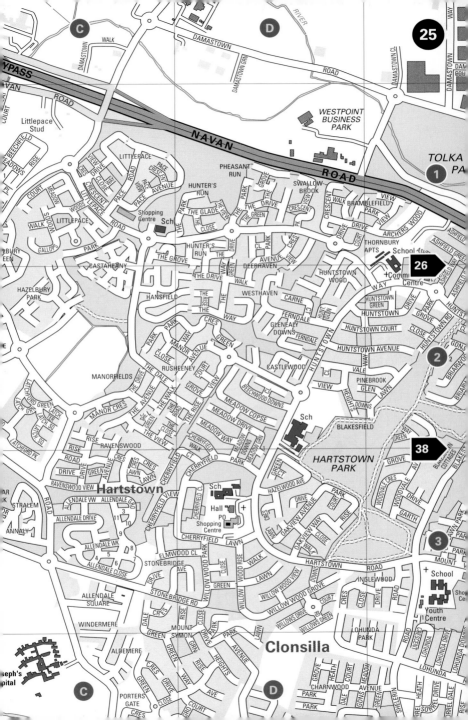

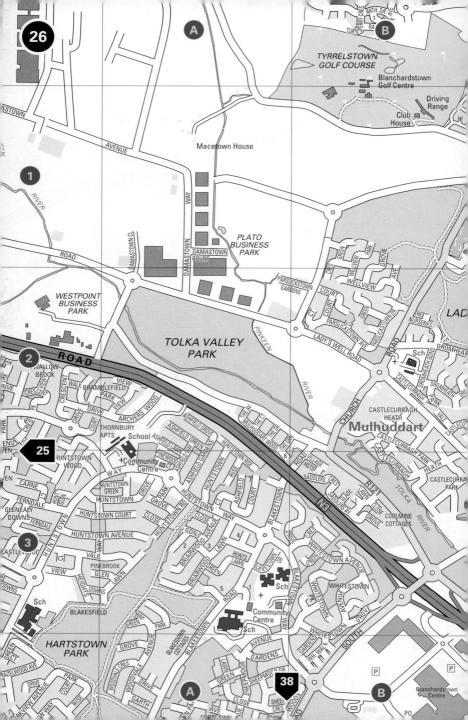

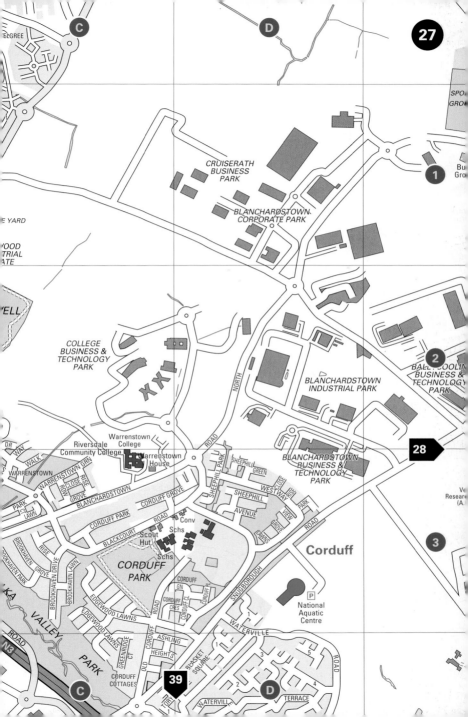

ELGREE

C

D

SPO
GRO

CRUISERATH
BUSINESS
PARK

Bu
Gro

1

BLANCHARDSTOWN
CORPORATE PARK

E YARD

OOD
TRIAL
ATE

ELL

COLLEGE
BUSINESS &
TECHNOLOGY
PARK

BALL...OLIN
BUSINESS &
TECHNOLOGY
PARK

2

BLANCHARDSTOWN
INDUSTRIAL PARK

NORTH

Warrenstown
College

Riversdale
Community College

Warrenstown
House

ROAD

28

DR
WAY

WALK

WARRENSTOWN

WARRENSTOWN GRN

CLOSE
ESE

GROVE

BLANCHARDSTOWN

CORDUFF GROVE

SHEEPHILL PARK

SHEEPHILL
GREEN

SHEEPHILL
AVENUE

WEST WAY

VIEW

RISE

BLANCHARDSTOWN
BUSINESS &
TECHNOLOGY
PARK

Ve
Resear
(A.

PARK
LAWN

CORDUFF PARK

CORDUFF GROVE

ROAD

Conv
Schs

Scout
Hut

BLACKCOURT

GROVE

DAWS

GROVE

ROAD

3

Corduff

BROOKHAVEN PARK

RISE

BROOKHAVEN GROVE

BROOKHAVEN DRIVE

Schs

CORDUFF
PARK

CORDUFF
GN

CORDUFF
CRES

CORDUFF PK

CORDUFF

SNUGBOROUGH

National
Aquatic
Centre

P

ROAD

KA

VALLEY

PARK

EDGEWOOD LAWNS

EDGEWOOD LAWNS

GREENRIDGE
CT

CORDUFF
ROAD

OLD

ASHLING
HEIGHTS

BASKET
SQUARE

WATERVILLE

TERRACE

N3

ROAD

C

39

CORDUFF
COTTAGES

TOB

WATERVILL

D

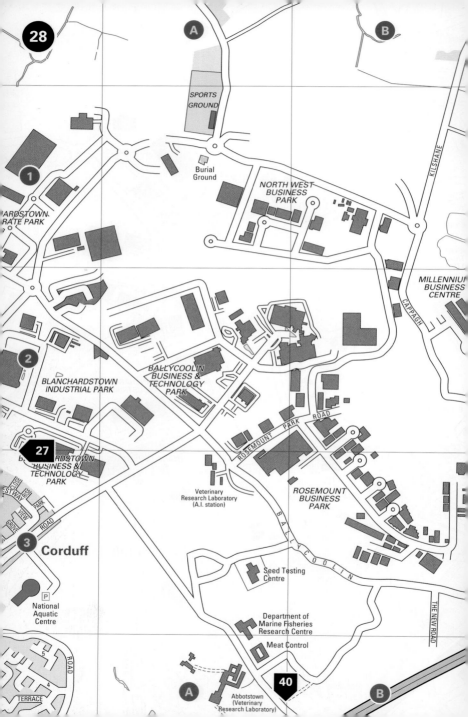

A

B

SPORTS
GROUND

Burial
Ground

NORTH WEST
BUSINESS
PARK

KILSHANE

MILLENNIUM
BUSINESS
CENTRE

CAPPAGH

1

RDSTOWN
RATE PARK

2

BLANCHARDSTOWN
INDUSTRIAL PARK

BALLYCOOLIN
BUSINESS &
TECHNOLOGY
PARK

ROSEMOUNT   PARK   ROAD

ROSEMOUNT
BUSINESS
PARK

27

b. RDSTOWN
BUSINESS &
TECHNOLOGY
PARK

STWAY RISE
VIEW
GROVE
PARK
ROAD

Veterinary
Research Laboratory
(A.I. station)

BALLYCOOLIN

THE NEW ROAD

3 Corduff

P
National
Aquatic
Centre

Seed Testing
Centre

Department of
Marine Fisheries
Research Centre

Meat Control

5

4

ROAD

TERRACE

A

40

B

Abbotstown
(Veterinary
Research Laboratory)

C

D

29

1

Sand & Gravel Quarry

NORTH ROAD

N2

2

Ju

Electricity Station

Grange House

Kildonan House

30

NORTH PARK BUSINESS & OFFICE PARK

NOR ES

ROAD

STADIUM BUSINESS PARK

CAPPOGE COTTAGES

3

NORTH ESTA

PLUNKET

PLUNKETT

AVENUE

PLUNKETT DRIVE

PLUNKETT GRN

BARRY

BARRY PK

CAPPAGH

M50

BARRY PARK

BARRY DR

CAPPAGH

Sch

BARRY PARK

BARRY GRN

BARRY ROAD

KILDONAN ROAD

C **41** Cappagh National Orthopaedic Hospital

D

Sch

AVILA PK

KILDONAN PARK

MELION

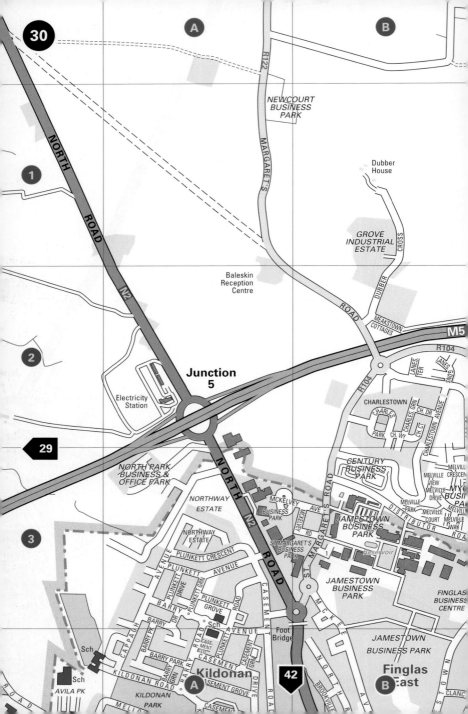

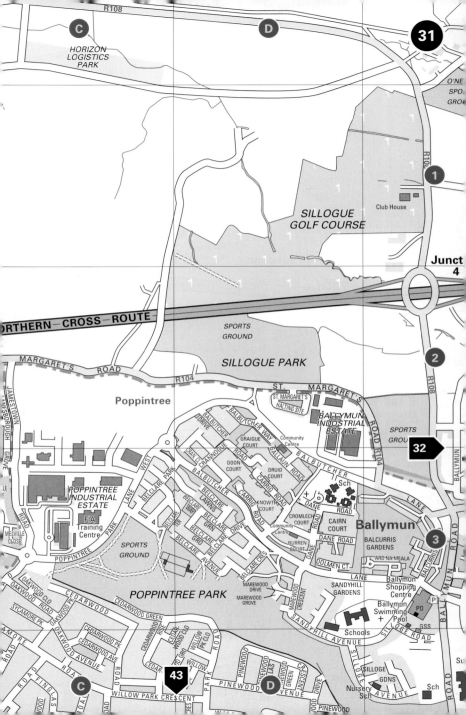

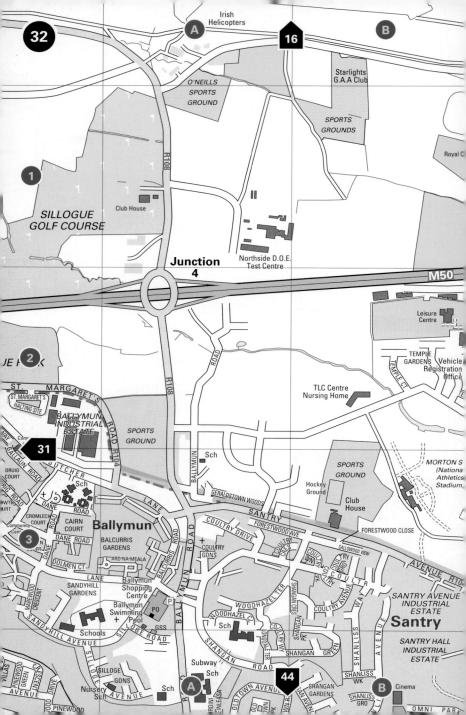

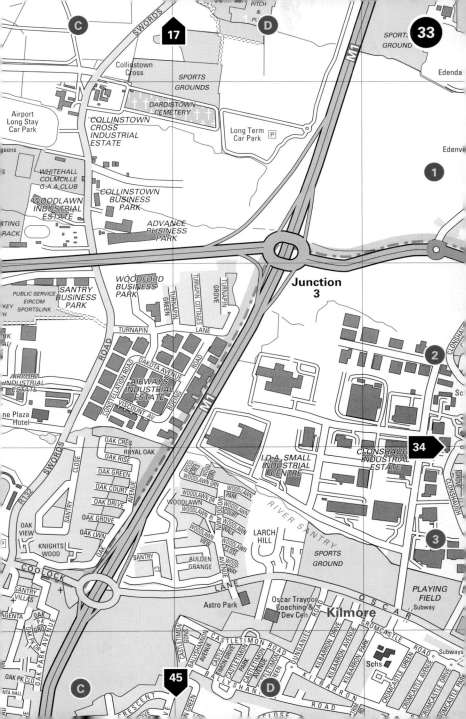

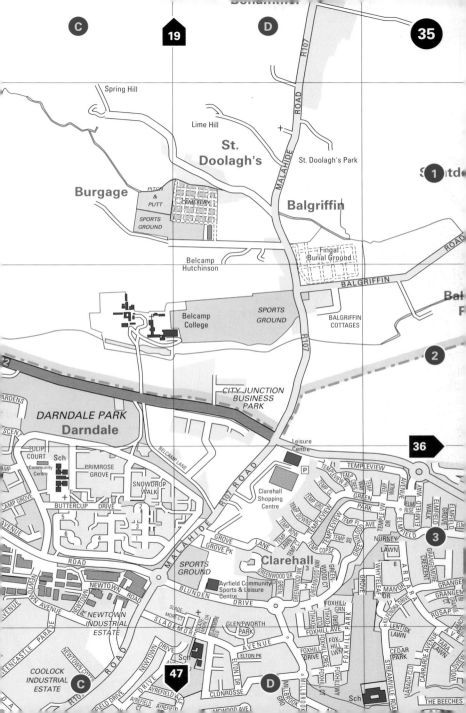

THE LINKS

C

Baldoyle Estuary
Nature Reserve

21

LINKS

D

ROAD

ARNOCK

Portmarnock
Bridge

Murragh

R106

Maynetown

Moyne Lodge

ROAD

MOYNE
PARK

Mayne
Bridge

Stapolin

COAST

ROAD

R106

PORTMARNOCK
OLD
GOLF LINKS

Club
House

1

2

CASTLE ROSSE

CASTLEROSSE CRESENT

STAPOLIN

VIEW

School

GRANGE PARK

LAWNS

GRANGE AVENUE

GRANGE

ROAD

GRANGE CLOSE

GRANGE DRIVE

ALDOYLE
DUSTRIAL
STATE

GRANGE WAY

C

ABBEY

MARIAN PARK

49

SEAGRANGE ROAD

SEAGR

SEACLIFF AVE

P.O.

Racecourse
Shopping Centre

SEAGRANGE AV

SEAGRANGE DR

Youth
Club

SEAGRANGE

PARK

Health
Centre

PARK

ADMIRAL

WILLIE

NOLAN

ROAD

BROOKSTONE RD

Sch

GEORGIAN
HAMLET

DUBLIN

Sch

WBROOK

MEADOWBROOK

AVENUE

MEADOWBROOK PARK

TUSCANY PARK

D

Sch

8

6

COLLEGE STREET

MAIN

STREET

Sch

Grave
Yard

Nursing
Home

TURNBERRY

Community Hall
St. Mary's
Hospital

3

Baldoyle

STRAND

P.O.
Lib

WARRENHOUSE ROAD

WARREN
GREEN

ROAD

MOYCLARE
DRIVE

MOYCLARE
PARK

MOYCLARE
AVE

MOYCLARE ROAD

BURROWFIELD

ROAD

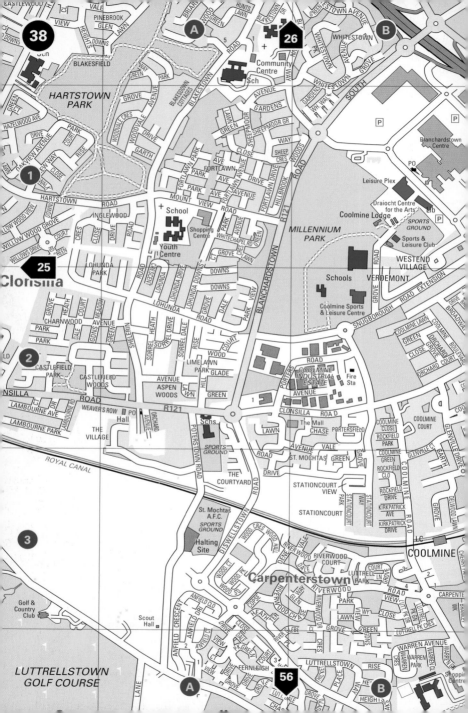

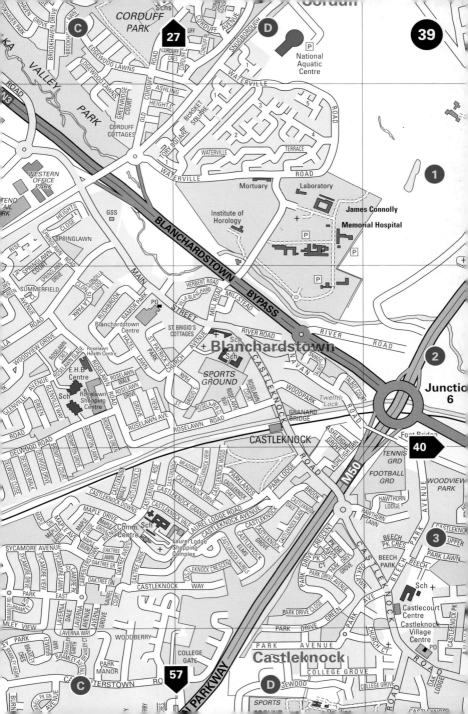

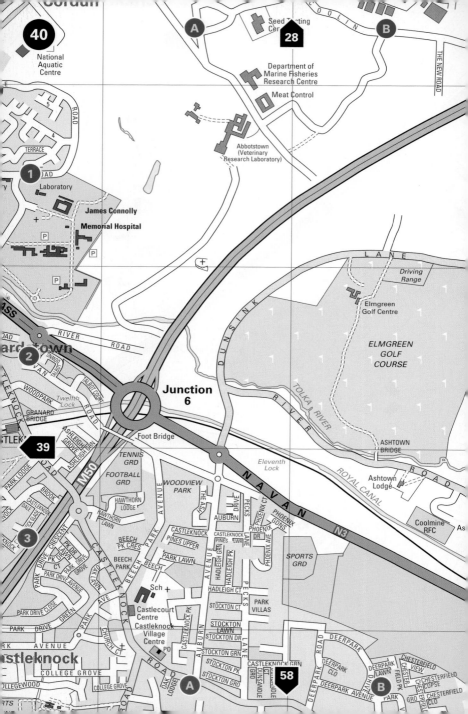

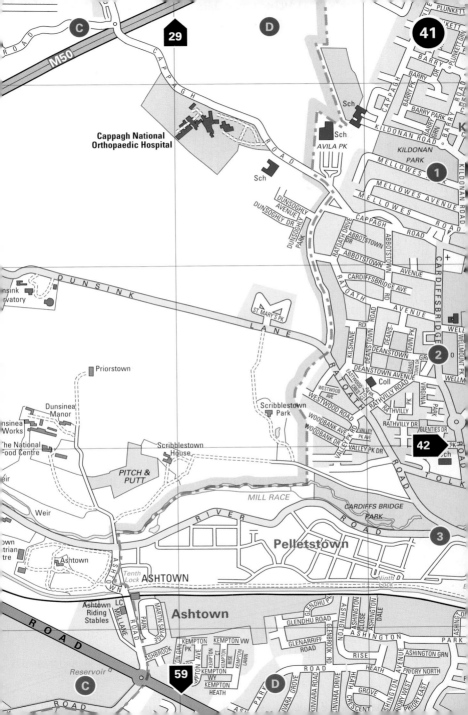

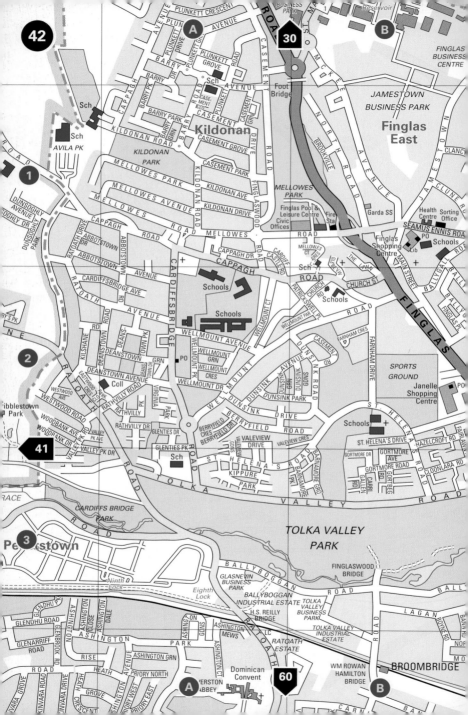

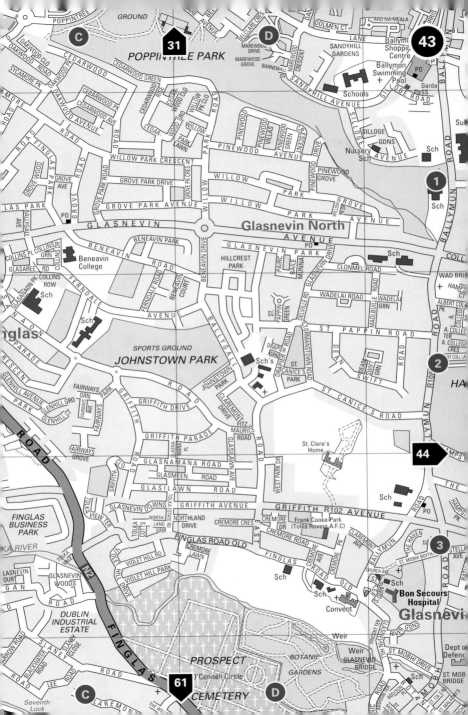

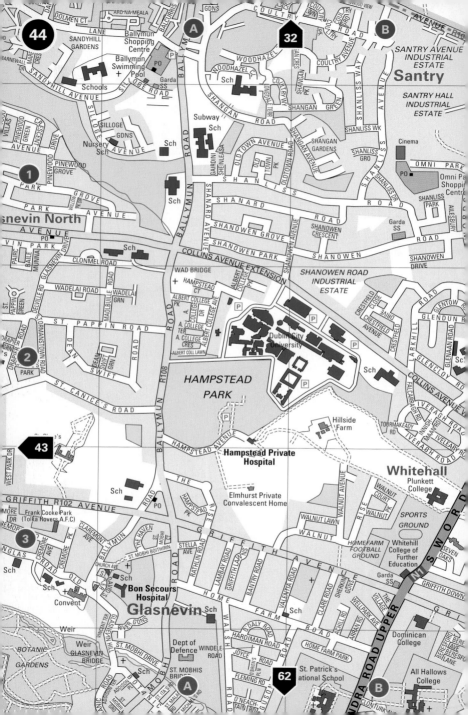

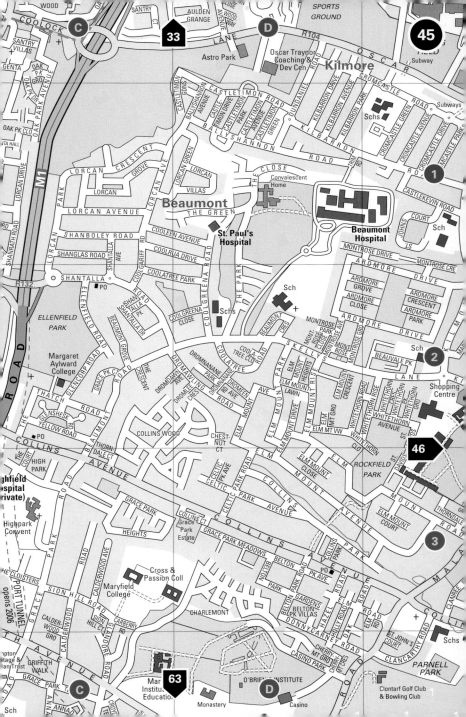

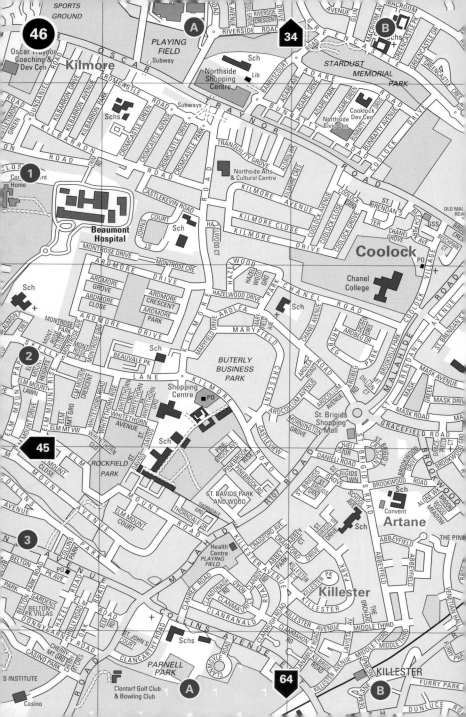

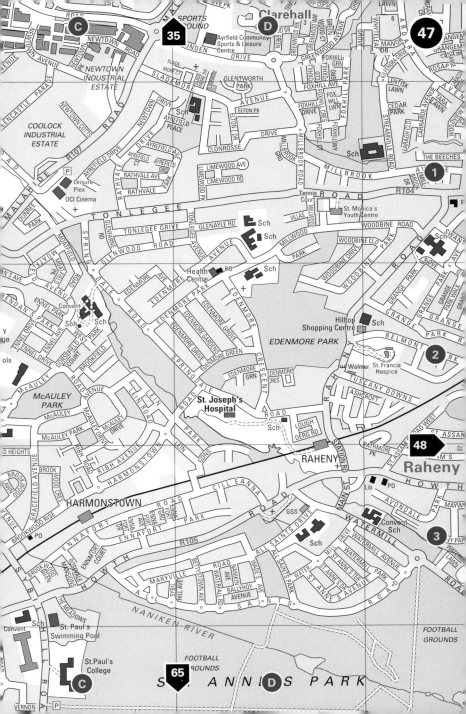

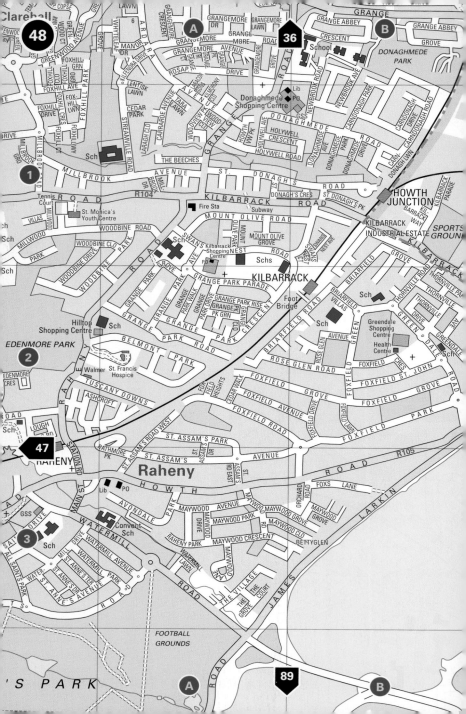

50

Baldoyle

A

B

Cush Point

Sutton G.C.
Club House

PO
Lib

Grave
Yard

Nursing
Home

DUBLIN

Sch

Sch

COLLEGE STREET

MAIN
STRAND
STREET

WARRENHOUSE ROAD

TURNBERRY

WARREN
GREEN

MOYCLARE
DRIVE

MOYCLARE ROAD

MOYCLARE AVE

MOYCLARE CLO.

MOYCLARE
PARK

MEADOWBROOK AVENUE

MEADOWBROOK

BOOKSTONE RD

BURROWFIELD ROAD

JAMES
McCORMACK
GARDENS

STATION

ROAD

SUTTON
GOLF COURSE

Suncroft

SUTTON

1

Sch

SUTTON

SUTTON
PARK

RAILWAY
AVENUE

BALDOYLE ROAD

SEAFIELD
CT.

THE
CRES.

BINN

EADAR

THE
COURT
VIEW

Sch

Sutton

SUTTON
PARK
LAWNS

ROAD

R105

BARRACK
CEMETERY

LC

LC

LC

LAUDERS LA.

GOLF LINKS

Sutton Cross
Shopping Centre

P

PO

DUBLIN

GREENFIELD

BURROW

R

SPORTS
GROUND

CHURCH ROAD

Marine
Hotel

S U T T O N   S T R A N D

2

SUTTON CREEK

◀ **49**

OURSE

3

A

B

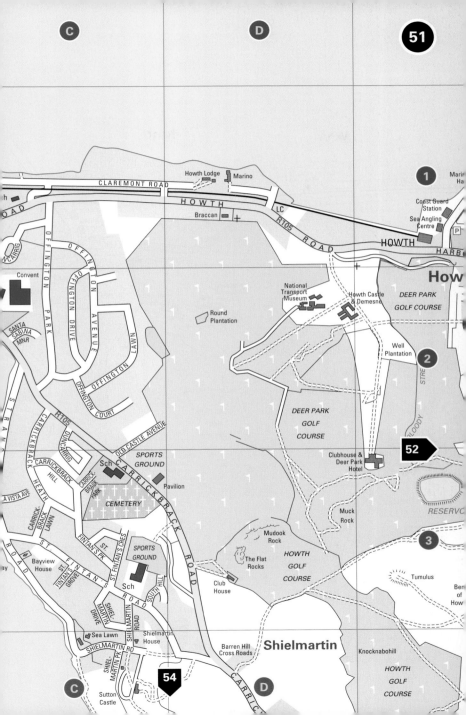

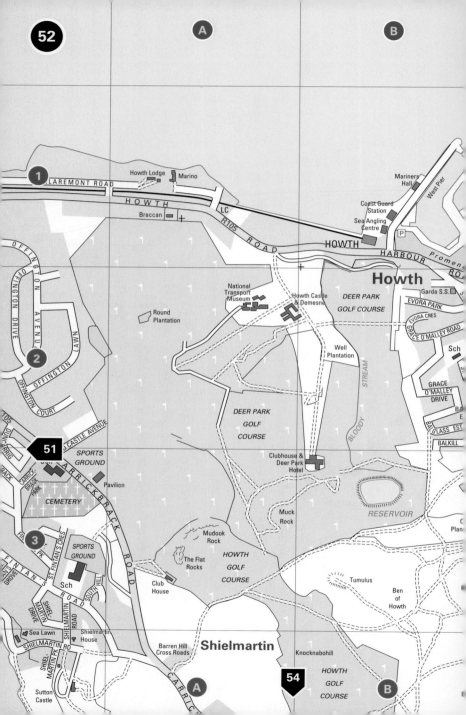

A

B

HOWTH

1

CLAREMONT ROAD

Howth Lodge

Marino

Mariners Hall

West Pier

HOWTH

Braccan

LC

R105 ROAD

Coast Guard Station

Sea Angling Centre

P

HOWTH

HARBOUR RD

Promenade

Howth

Garda S.S.

OFFINGTON AVENUE

OFFINGTON DRIVE

OFFINGTON LAWN

Round Plantation

National Transport Museum

Howth Castle & Demesne

DEER PARK GOLF COURSE

EVORA PARK

EVORA CRES

GRACE O'MALLEY ROAD

2

OFFINGTON COURT

Well Plantation

BLOODY STREAM

Sch

GRACE O'MALLEY DRIVE

BALLGLASS EST

BALKILL

R105

DUNGRIRRIG

51

CASTLE AVENUE

SPORTS GROUND

CARRICKBRACK ROAD

DEER PARK GOLF COURSE

Clubhouse & Deer Park Hotel

RESERVOIR

CARRICK BRACK PARK

Pavilion

CEMETERY

Muck Rock

3

FINTAN'S GROVE

ST FINTAN'S CRES

SPORTS GROUND

Sch

SOUTH HILL

Mudook Rock

The Flat Rocks

HOWTH GOLF COURSE

Tumulus

Ben of Howth

SHIEL MARTIN DRIVE

SHIELMARTIN ROAD

Sea Lawn

Shielmartin House

SHIELMARTIN RD

Barren Hill Cross Roads

Shielmartin

Knocknabohill

SHIEL MARTIN PK

Sutton Castle

CARRICK

A

54

HOWTH GOLF COURSE

B

East Pier

P
Martello
Tower

BALSCADDEN BAY

Health
Centre
BALSCADDEN ROAD
P
Puck's Rocks

Lib

ASGARD PK.
KILROCK ROAD
NASHVILLE PARK
Kilrock
Nose
of
Howth

NASHVILLE RD

CROSSTREES

THORMANBY
COWBOOTER LANE

ASGARD ROAD

CLIFF WALK (Fingal Way)

THORMANBY LAWNS

CANNON ROCK VIEW UPPER

CLIFF RD

Cannon Rock
Cottage

DUNGRIFFAN ROAD

MARINERS COVE

WOODCLIFF HEIGHTS

CASANA VIEW

ROAD

GREYS LANE

Rookstown

THORMANBY LODGE

Green
Ivy

THORMANBY WOODS

Highfield

Ashville

Bearna

WINDGATE ROAD

Oakley Park

Piper's
Gut

KITESTOWN ROAD   R105

NEW ROAD

WINDGATE RISE

ROAD

Fox Hole

CLIFF WALK

The
Haven

BAILEY GRN RD.

CK ROAD

White
Water

Old Baily
Cottage

C   D   m Bed

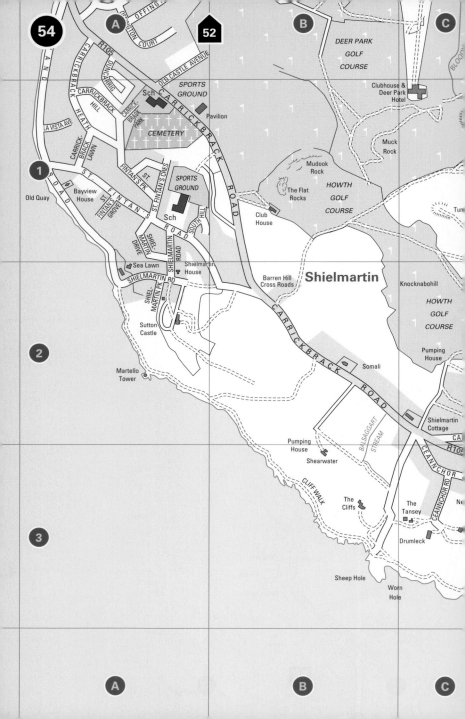

GRACE
PETERS
TER
SEAVIEW
BALGLASS
ESTATE
BALGLASS ESTATE
BALKILL PK

CROSSTREE
BALGLASS RD
BALKILL RD
THORMANBY
MEADOWBOOTER LANE

ASH RD
CANNON ROCK VIEW
UPPER
CLIFF RD
MARINERS
COVE

Cannon Rock Cottage

CLIFF WALK (Fingal Way)

THORMANBY
LAWNS

DUNGRIFFAN ROAD

BEANN EADAIR
G.A.C.(RUGBY
GROUND)

WOODCLIFF
HEIGHTS

CASANA VIEW

THORMANBY ROAD

Green Inn

Old
Plantation

Pav

GREYS LANE

Rookstown

THORMANBY WOODS

THORMANBY LODGE

Highfield

Bearna

Piper's
Gut

Ashville

Highfield

Oakley Park

Loughoreen Hills

WINDGATE ROAD

ROAD

KITESTOWN ROAD

R105

The
Haven

CLIFF WALK

Fox Hole

Black
Linn

NEW ROAD

WINDGATE RISE

ROAD

BAILEY GRN RD

Highroom Bed

Black Heath

CARRICKBRACK ROAD

White
Water

P

Old Baily
Cottage

Cloghereen

Lough Leven

2

Gaskin's Leap

Whitewater
Brook

Carraigbreac
House

ROAD

Roxborn

THORMANBY ROAD

Webb's Castle
Rock

Convent

Earlscliffe

CLIFF WALK

Danes
Hollow

Broad Strand

Lion's Head

3

DOLDRUM BAY

The Needles or Candlesticks

Baily
Lighthouse

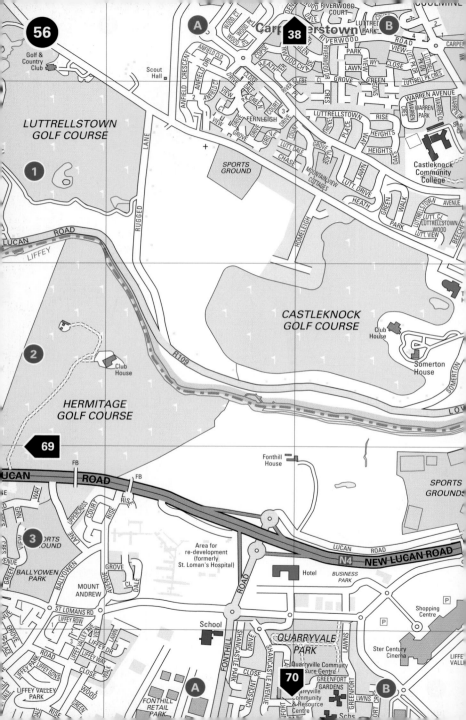

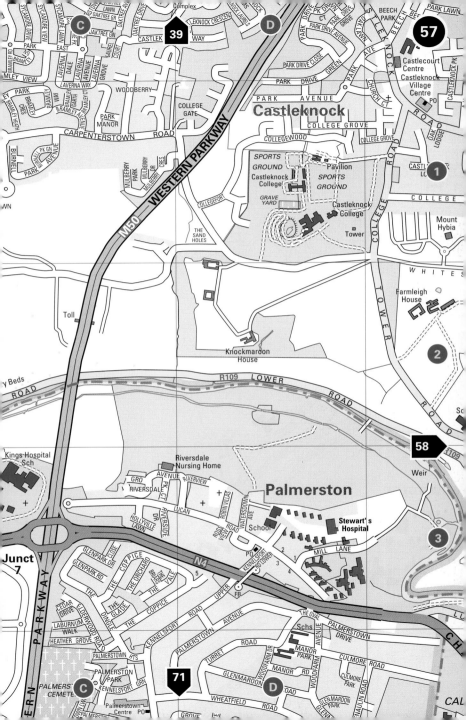

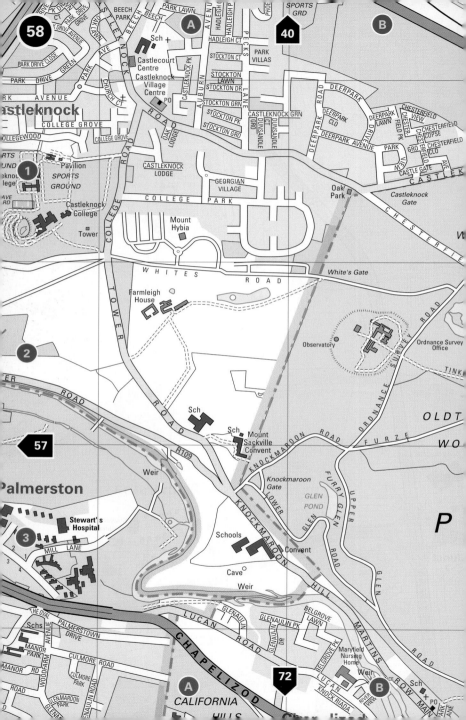

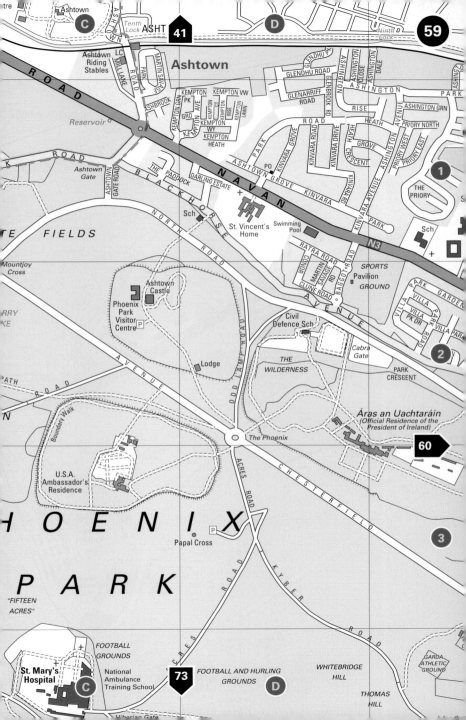

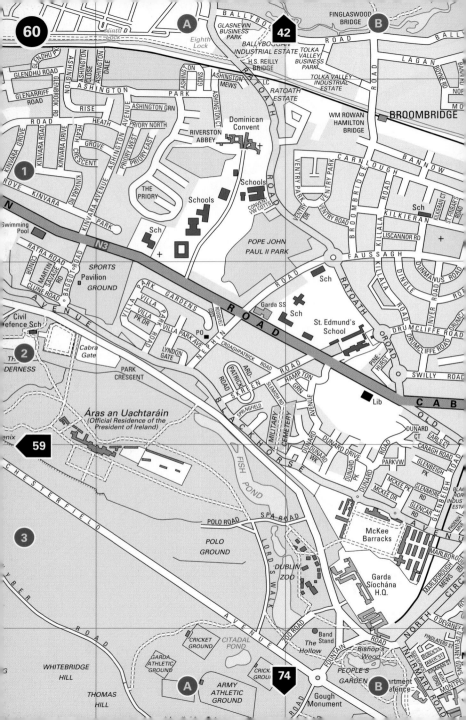

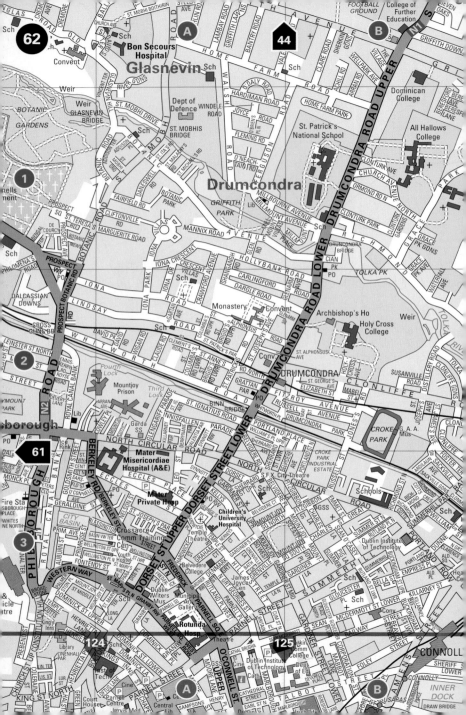

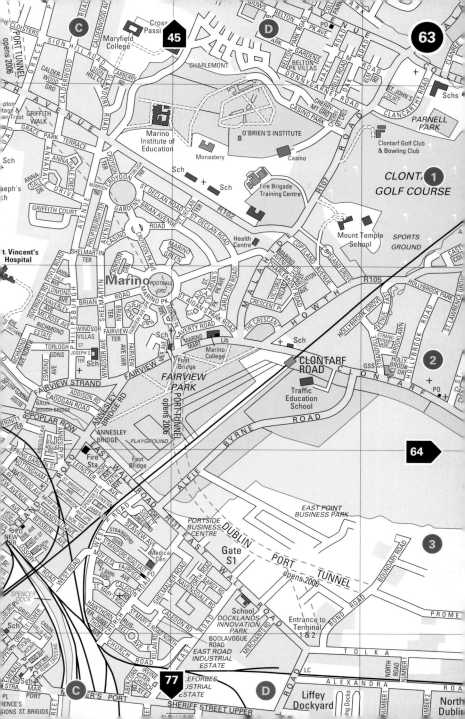

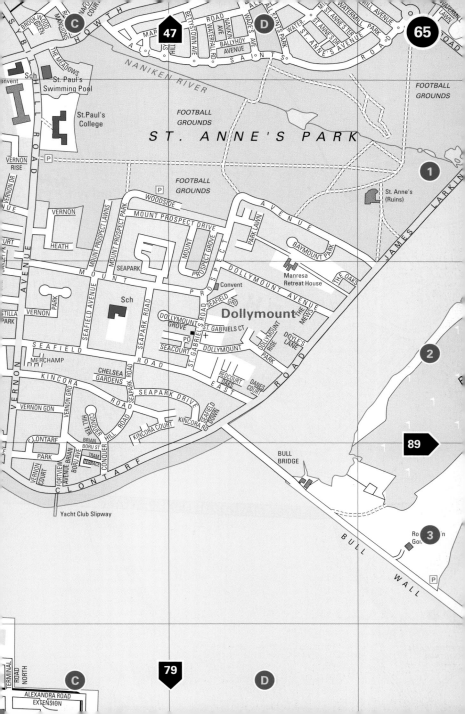

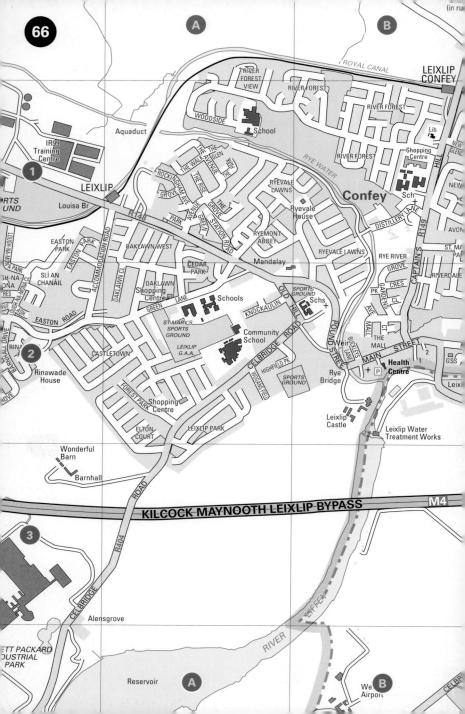

A

B

ROYAL CANAL

LEIXLIP
CONFEY

RIVER
FOREST
VIEW

RIVER FOREST

RIVER FOREST

WOODSIDE

School

RIVER FOREST

Aquaduct

Lib

IR99
Training
Centre

THE AIGLEN
THE
AVENUE
THE
PARK

RYE WATER

Shopping
Centre

1

ROCKINGHAM AVE
THE WALK
THE RISE
THE
GROVE

RYEVALE
LAWNS

Confey

Sch

LEIXLIP

GROV

STATION ROAD

Ryevale
House

NEW

Louisa Br

R148

PARK

THE
GREEN
THE
AVENUE

RYEMONT
ABBEY

RYEVALE LAWNS

DISTILLERY LANE

R149

AVON

EASTON
PARK

EASTON
PARK

ACCOMMODATION ROAD

OAKLAWN WEST

Mandalay

RYE RIVER

ST. MA
PA

CAPTAIN'S

GROVE
CRES

SLÍ AN
CHANÁIL

CEDAR
PARK

PK
GARDENS

RIVERDALE

OAKLAWN CL

OAKLAWN
Shopping
Centre

Schools

SPORTS
GROUND

Schs

CL

AVE

THE
MALL

EASTON ROAD

GREEN
LANE

KNOCKAULIN

OLD
HILL
ROAD

Ct

THE MALL

STREET

BARNHALL DRIVE

CASTLETOWN

ST. MARY'S
SPORTS
GROUND

LEIXLIP
G.A.A.

POUND STREET

Weir
Lane

BUCKLEY'S
LANE

MAIN

Health
Centre

GSS

2

CELBRIDGE ROAD

HIGHFIELD PK

P

Leix

Rinawade
House

FOREST PARK

Shopping
Centre

WIGANS FIELD

SPORTS
GROUND

Rye
Bridge

Leixlip
Castle

Leixlip Water
Treatment Works

ELTON
COURT

LEIXLIP PARK

Wonderful
Barn

Barnhall

ROAD

KILCOCK MAYNOOTH LEIXLIP BYPASS

M4

3

R404

CELBRIDGE

RIVER LIFFEY

Alensgrove

ETT PACKARD
DUSTRIAL
PARK

RIVER

CELBR

Reservoir

A

We
Airport

B

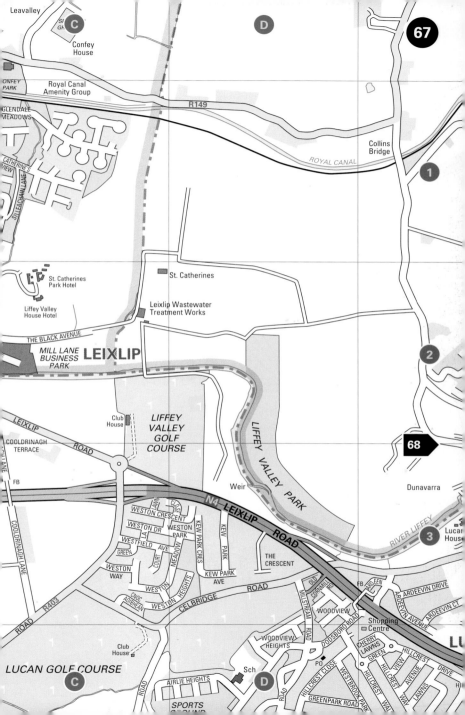

Leavalley

C Confey House

SI GA

CONFEY PARK

Royal Canal Amenity Group

GLENDALE MEADOWS

ST. CATHERINE'S VIEW

SLEACHAN LANE

R149

D

Collins Bridge

ROYAL CANAL

67

1

St. Catherines

St. Catherines Park Hotel

Liffey Valley House Hotel

Leixlip Wastewater Treatment Works

THE BLACK AVENUE

MILL LANE BUSINESS PARK

LEIXLIP

2

LEIXLIP

COOLDRINAGH TERRACE

ROAD

FB

COOLDRINAGH LANE

Club House

LIFFEY VALLEY GOLF COURSE

LIFFEY VALLEY PARK

Weir

68

Dunavarra

RIVER LIFFEY

3 Lucan House

N4 LEIXLIP ROAD

WESTON CRESCENT

LAWN CLOSE

WESTON DR

WESTON PARK

KEW PARK CRES

KEW PARK

KEW PARK AVE

THE CRESCENT

WESTFIELD AVE

GREEN

COURT

MEADOW

WESTON WAY

WESTON HEIGHTS

CNOC AOIBHEAN

WESTON

CELBRIDGE ROAD

CORMILL RD

MILLSTREAM ROAD

DODSBORO ROAD

FB

GREEN

ARDEEVIN DRIVE

ARDEEVIN AVENUE

ARDEEVIN CT

Woodview

Shopping Centre

R403

ROAD

Club House

LUCAN GOLF COURSE

C

AIRLIE HEIGHTS

WOODVIEW HEIGHTS

PO

Sch

D

SPORTS

ROAD

HILLCREST CLOSE

WESTBROOK PARK

GREENPARK ROAD

CHERRY LAWNS

GREEN

HILLCREST VIEW

HILLCREST AVENUE

HILLCREST WAY

HILLCREST LAWNS

HILLCREST DRIVE

LU

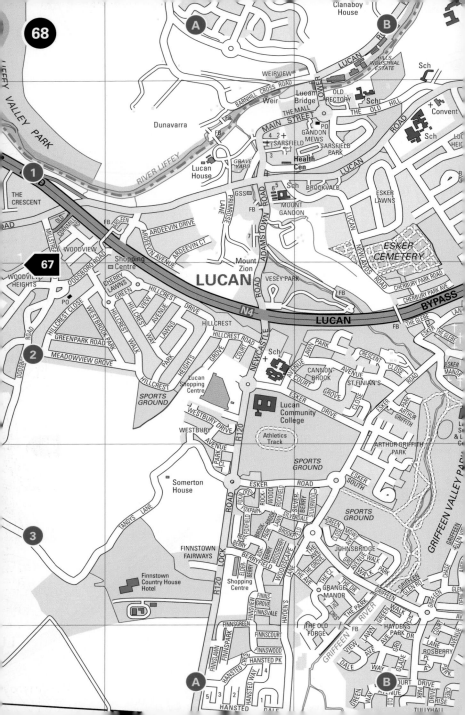

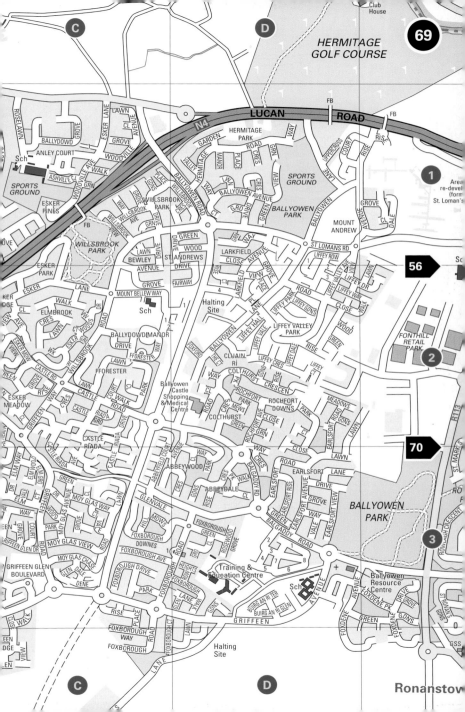

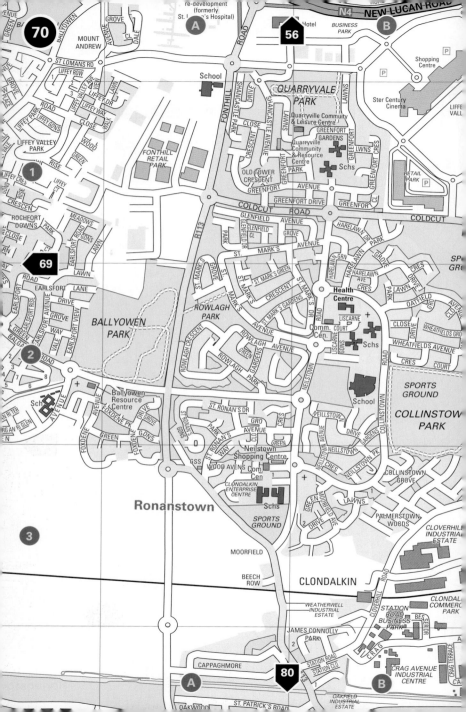

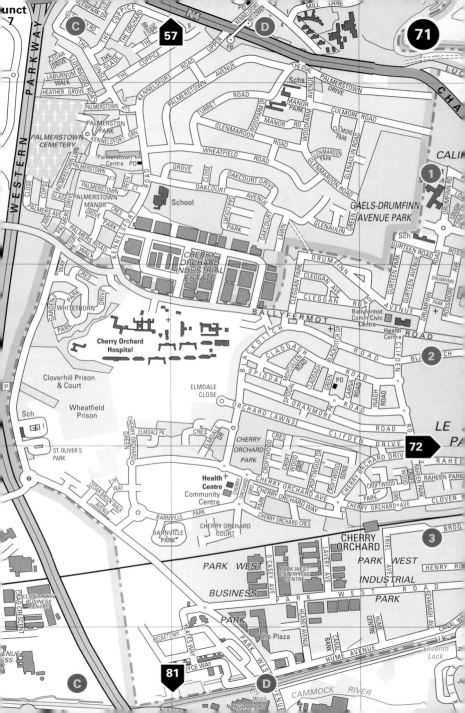

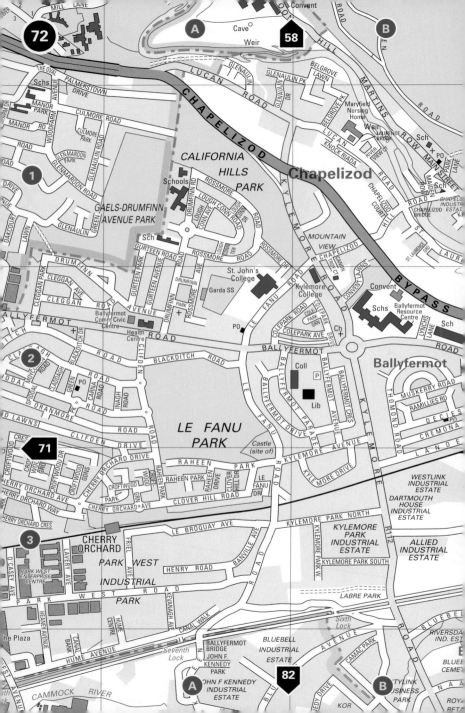

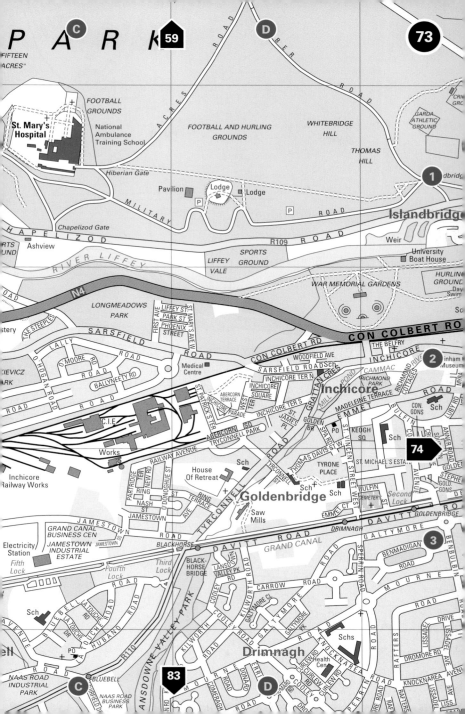

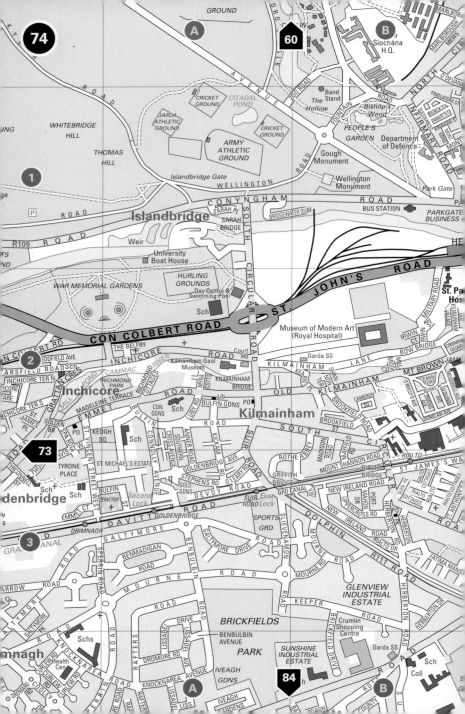

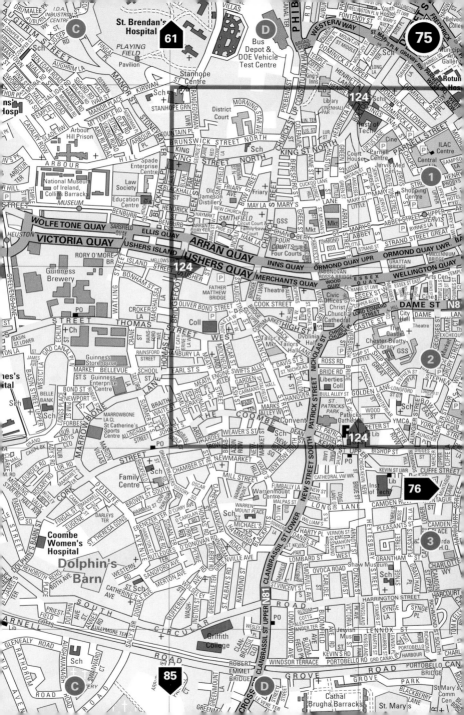

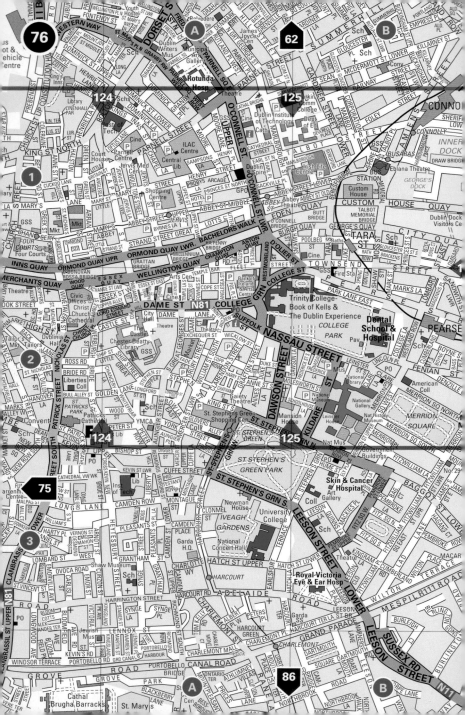

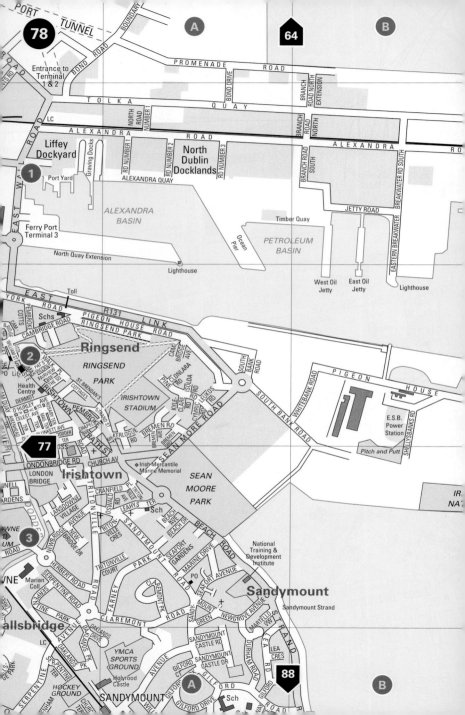

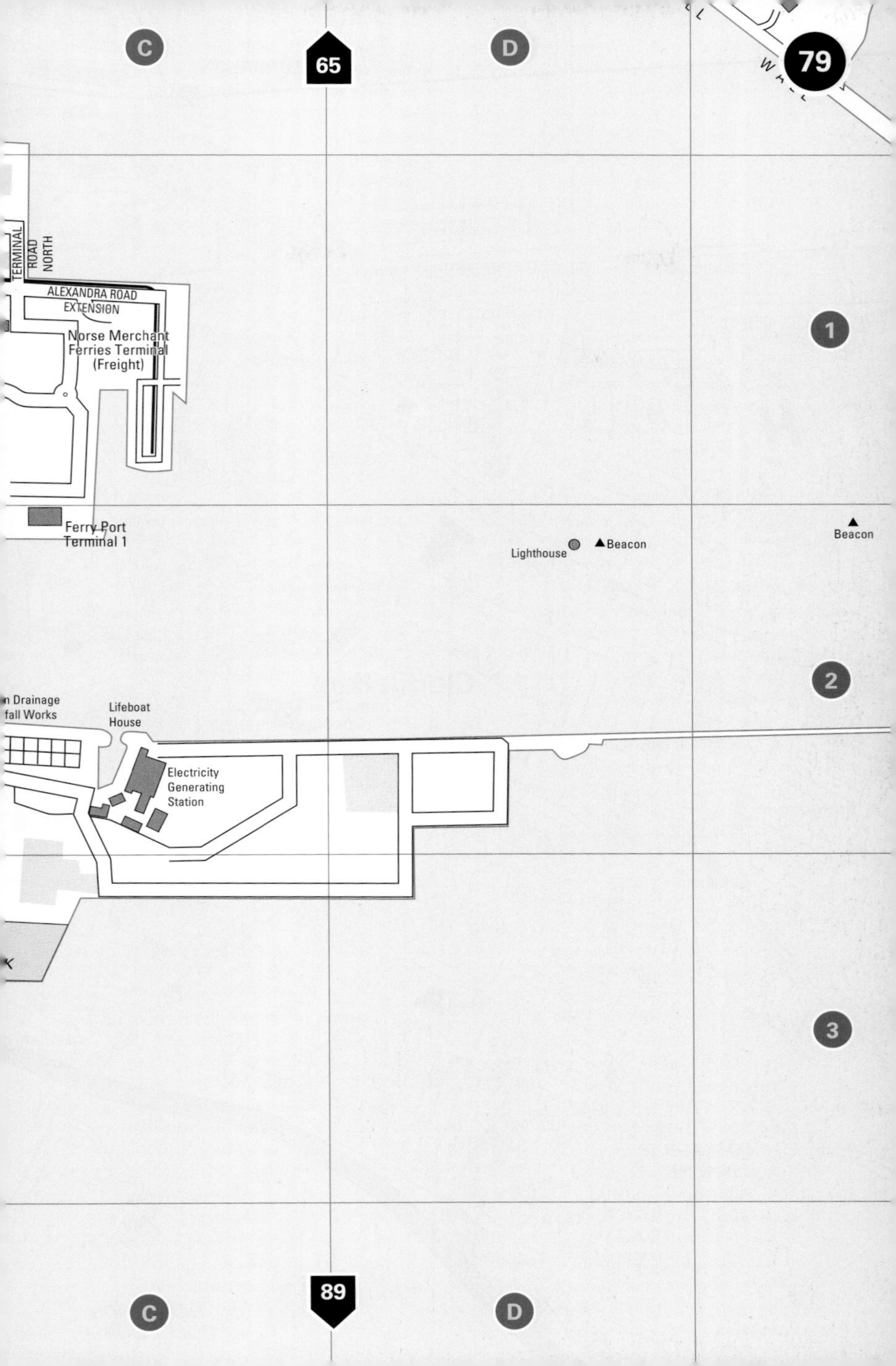

TERMINAL ROAD NORTH

ALEXANDRA ROAD
EXTENSION

Norse Merchant
Ferries Terminal
(Freight)

Ferry Port
Terminal 1

Lighthouse ● ▲ Beacon

▲
Beacon

1

2

Drainage
fall Works

Lifeboat
House

Electricity
Generating
Station

3

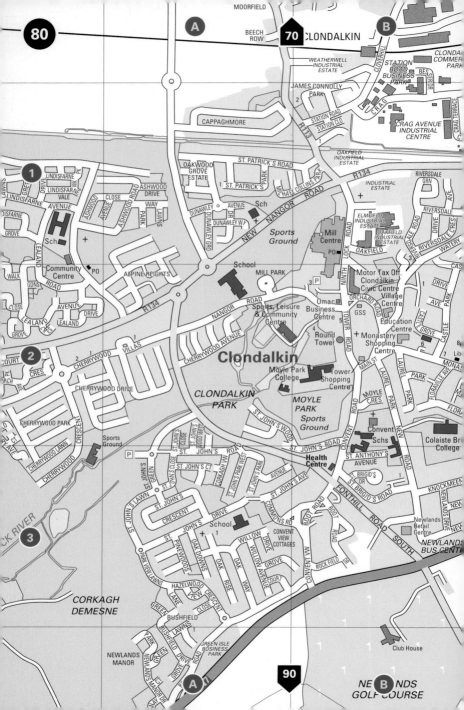

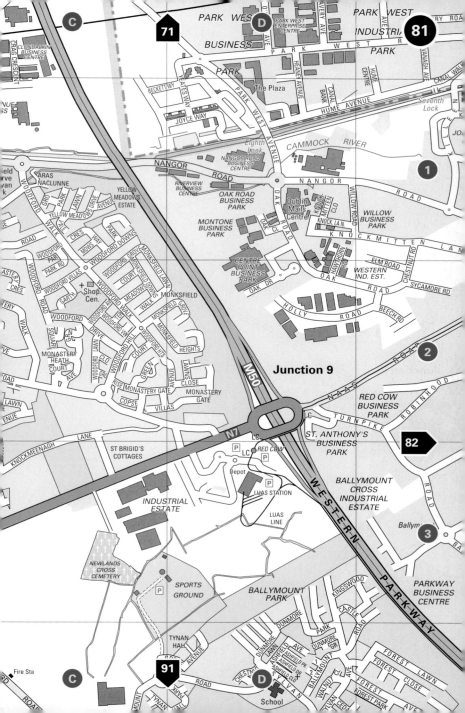

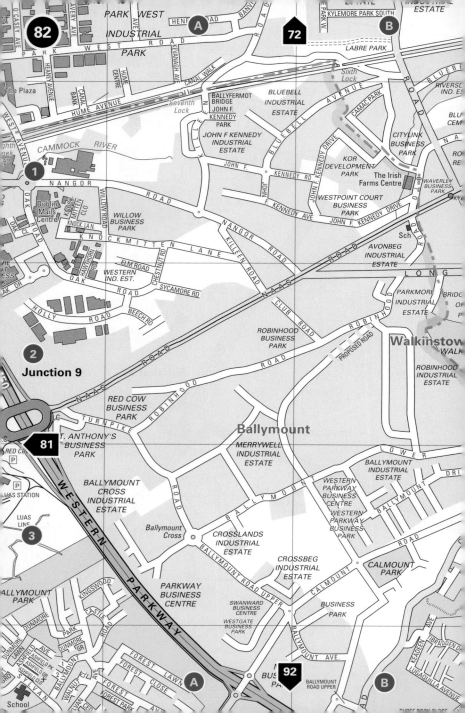

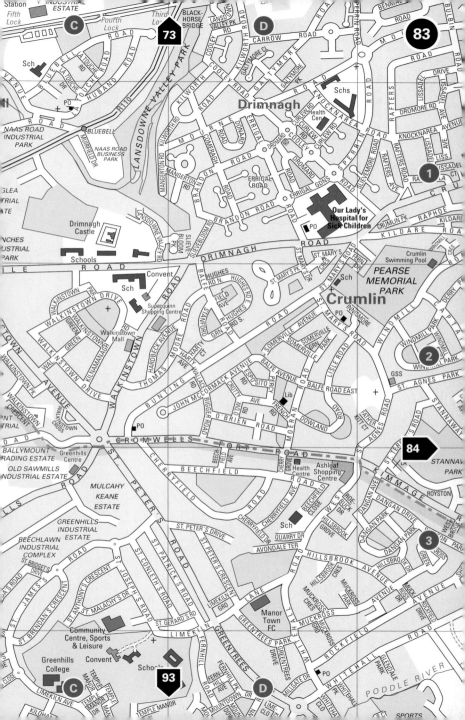

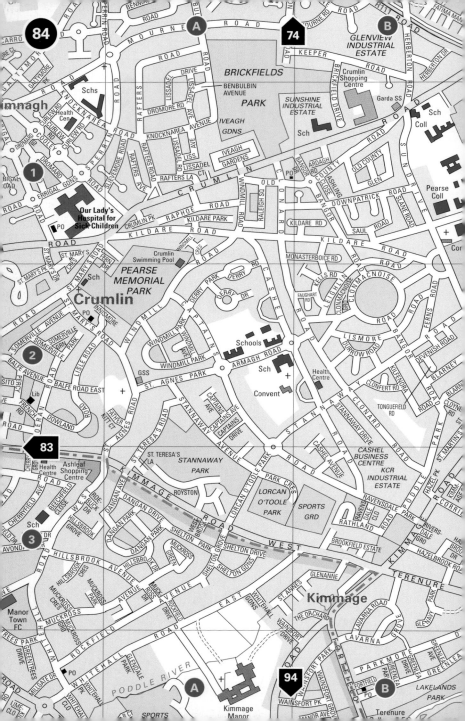

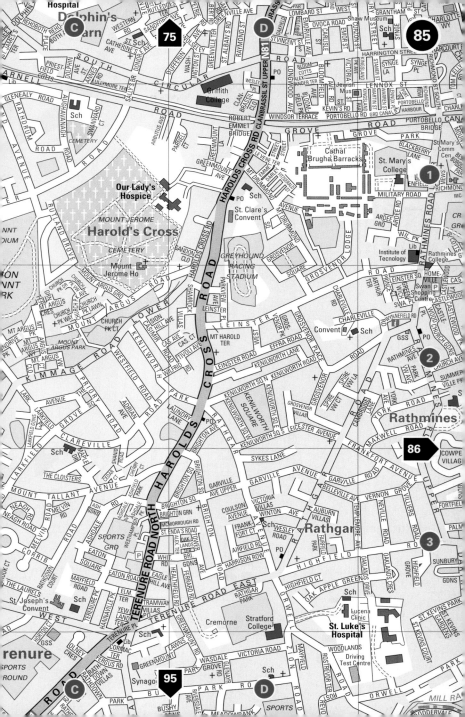

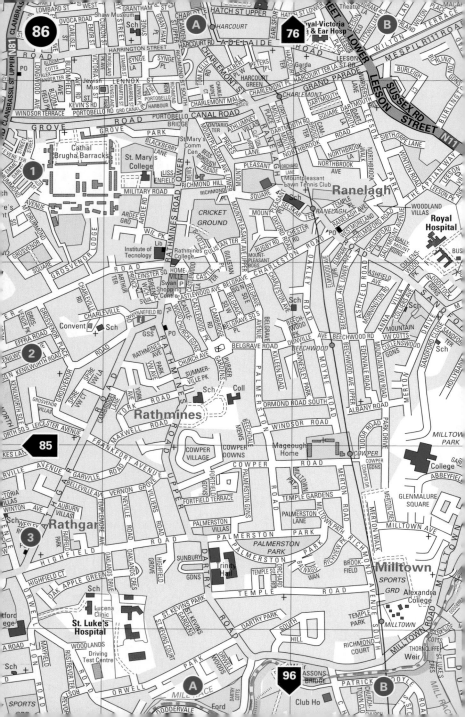

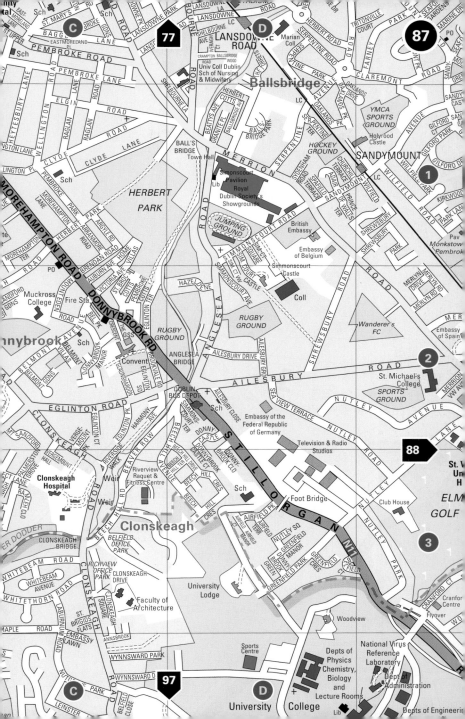

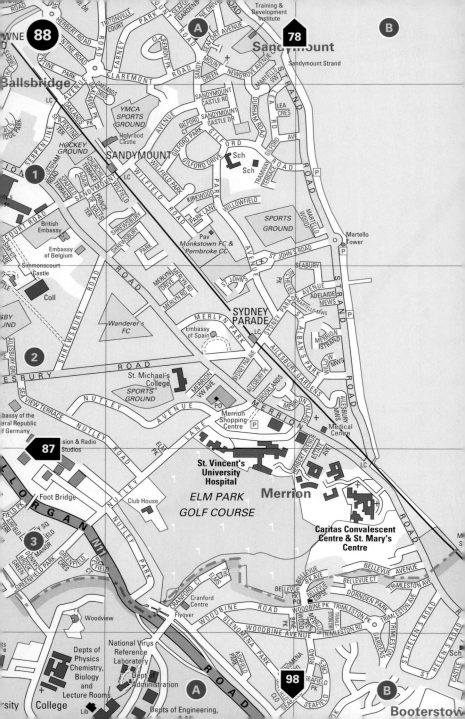

WATER...

WOOD...

ROAD

THE VILLAGE

THE GROVE

THE COURT

JA...

FOOTBALL
GROUNDS

North

JAMES LARKIN ROAD

St. Anne's
(Ruins)

Interpretive
& Visitors
Centre

P

i

1

ROYAL DUBLIN GOLF COURSE

2

3

BOOTERSTOWN

P

AVENUE

C

99

D

School

Martello Tower

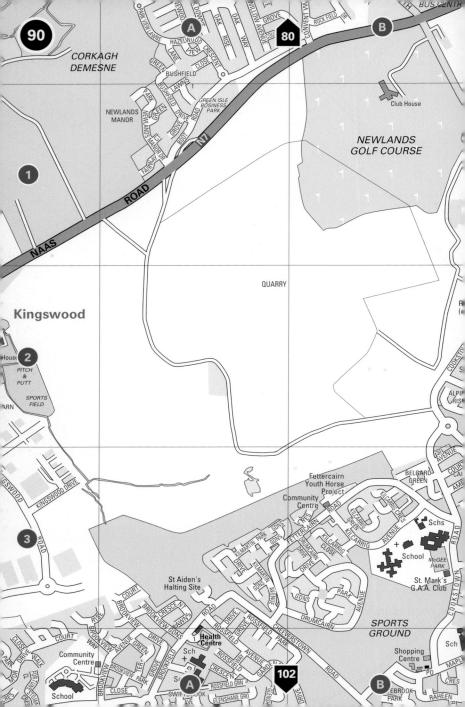

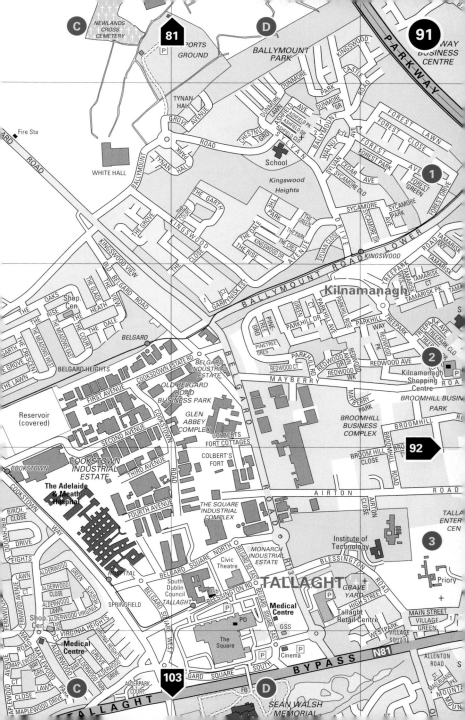

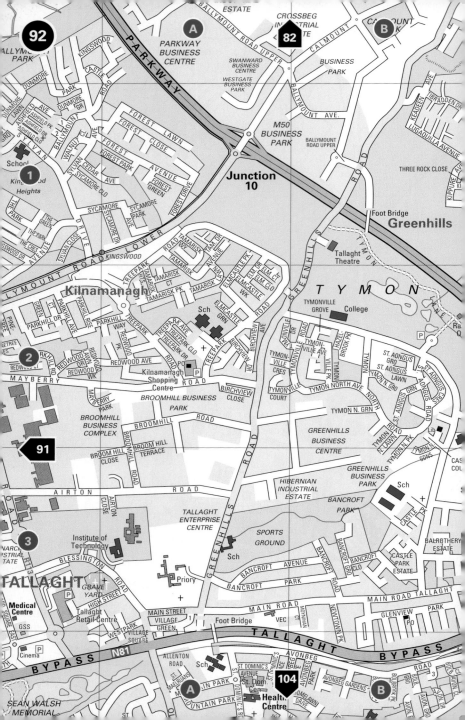

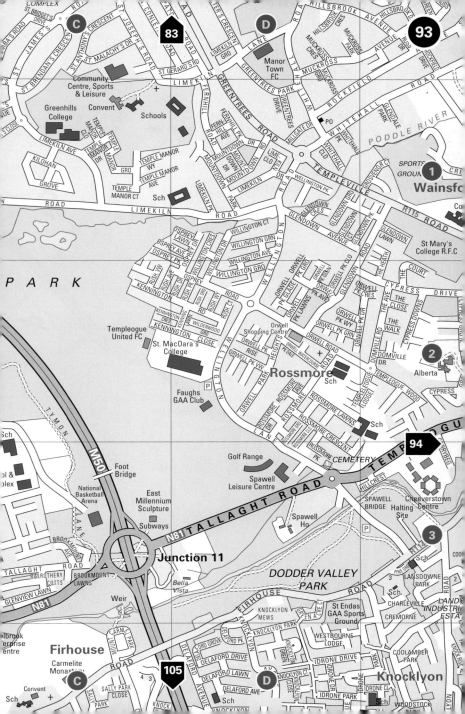

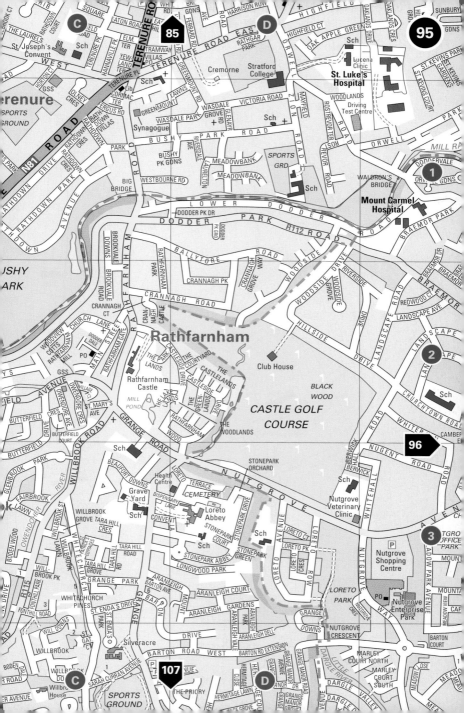

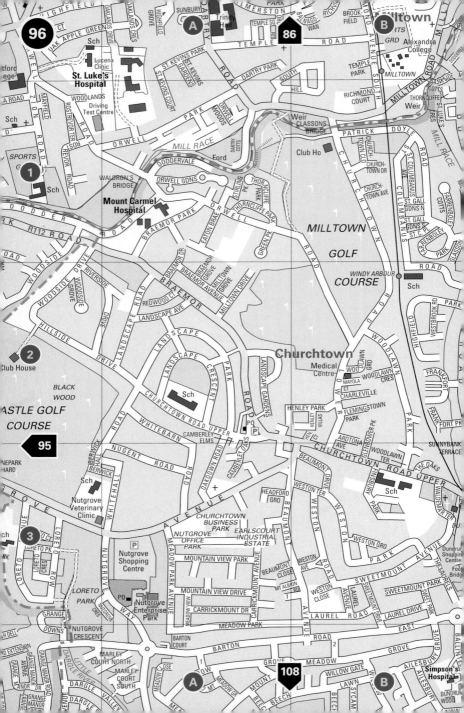

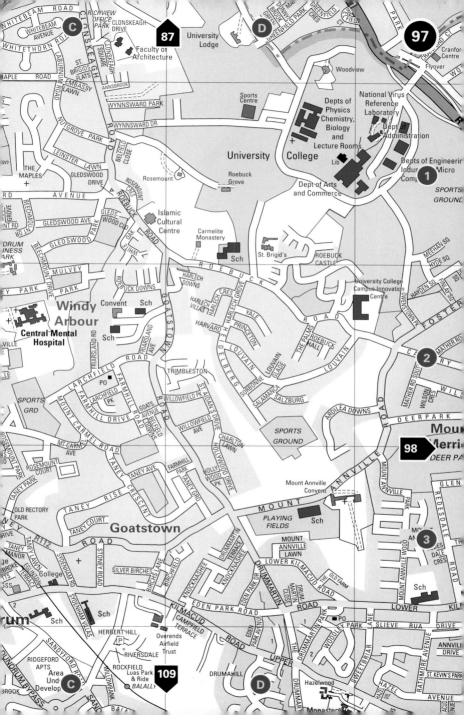

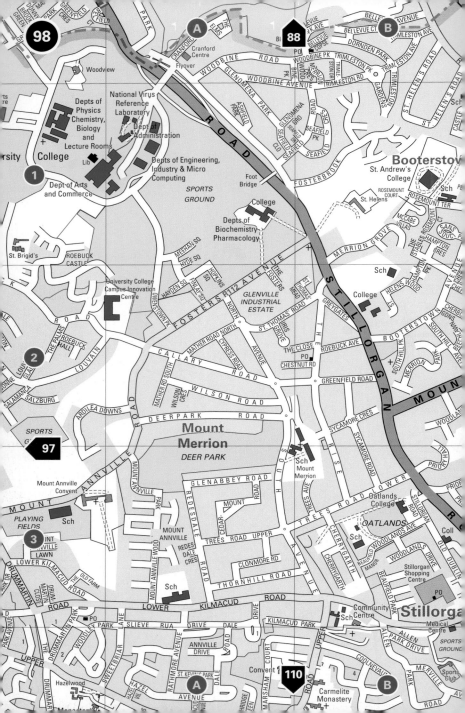

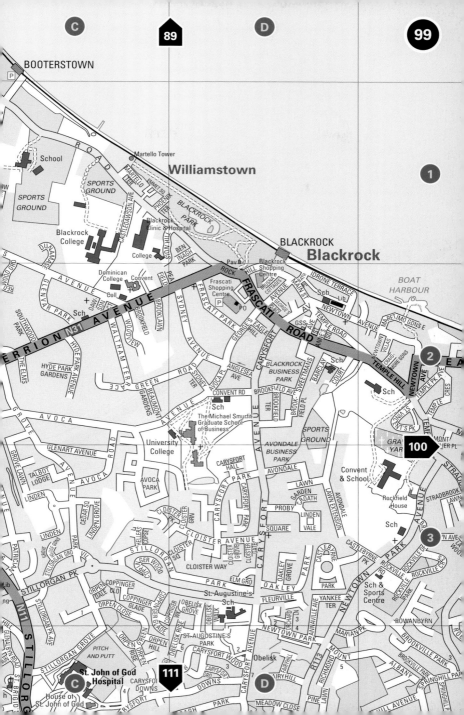

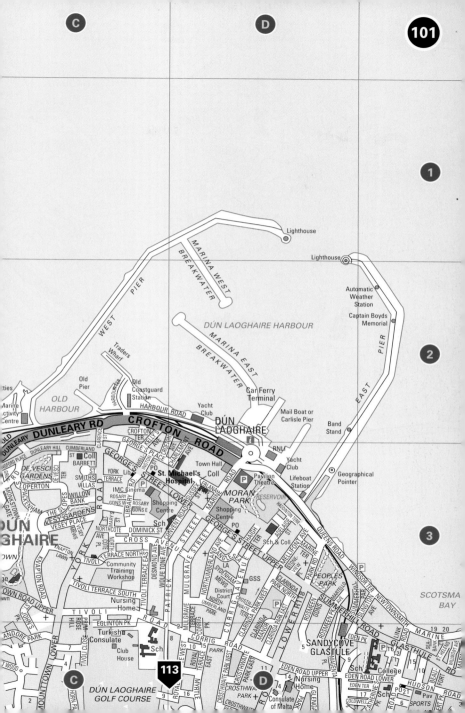

1

Lighthouse

Lighthouse

Automatic
Weather
Station

Captain Boyds
Memorial

MARINA WEST BREAKWATER

WEST PIER

DÚN LAOGHAIRE HARBOUR

2

MARINA EAST BREAKWATER

EAST PIER

Traders
Wharf

Old
Pier

Old
Coastguard
Station

Car Ferry
Terminal

Band
Stand

ties

Marine
Activity
Centre

OLD
HARBOUR

HARBOUR ROAD

Yacht
Club

Mail Boat or
Carlisle Pier

DÚN
LAOGHAIRE

DUNLEARY RD   CROFTON ROAD

DUNLEARY HILL

CROFTON
TER

RNLI

Geographical
Pointer

CLARENCE ST

GEORGE'S PLACE

Cumberland
St

DE VESCI
GARDENS

THE SLOPES

VESEY PLACE

VESEY GARDENS

VESEY MEWS

Coll
BARRETT
ST

SMITHS
VILLAS

YORK
TERRACE

IMC
Cinema

ROSARY
GDNS

WILLOW
BANK

GEORGE'S STREET LOWER

CHARLESTON

Town Hall

Yacht
Club

Lifeboat
Station

3

Lib
Sch
ROSARY
GDNS E

CHRISTON ST

Shopping
Centre

FRIANAN

St. Michael's
Hospital

Coll

Pavilion
Theatre

MORAN
PARK

RESERVOIR

HUDDSTON TER

QUEEN'S ROAD

NORTHCOTE
AVE

DOMINICK ST

CROSS
AVENUE

Community
Training
Workshop

KNAPTON
LAWN

KNAPTON
ROAD

YORK ROAD

TIVOLI

TERRACE NORTH

TIVOLI TERRACE EAST

DESMOND AVE

WOLFE TONE AVE

CONVENT RD

GEORGE'S STREET UPPER

PATRICK ROAD

MULGRAVE STREET

NORTHUMBERLAND AVE

GEORGE'S ST

MELLIFONT AVE

MARINE AVE

PARK RD

CLARINDA PARK WEST

PEOPLES
PARK

WINDSOR TER

NEWTOWNSMITH

TIVOLI TERRACE SOUTH

Nursing
Home

TIVOLI

TIVOLI
ROAD

TIVOLI CLOSE

HILL

ROSE

EGLINTON PK

Turkish
Consulate

Club
House

Sch

Nursing
Home

SANDYCOVE
GLASTHULE

ST. JOHN'S

ANDORE PARK

PKS

OWN ROAD UPPER

LA
MEWS

SYDENHAM

District
Court
NORTH

CROSTHWAITE
PARK NORTH

CORRIG ROAD

CORRIG

MULGRAVE
ROAD

CORRIG
AVENUE

ROYAL TER EAST

ROYAL TER WEST

CROSTHWAITE PARK WEST

UMBERLAND
PARK

CROSTHWAITE
PARK EAST

CLARINDA PARK NORTH

CLARINDA
PARK EAST

CLARINDA
ROAD

MAGENTA

LOWER ROAD

RISMORE

ROSMEEN GDNS

EDEN PK

SUMMERHILL ROAD

ADELAIDE ST

Sch & Coll

GSS

TINNAHINCH TER

MARTELLO TER

College

EDEN ROAD UPPER

Nursing
Home

Consulate
of Malta

EDEN ROAD LOWER

EDEN TER

MAGENTA PL

COLDWELL

GLENGEARY

HUDSON ROAD

ST

SPORTS

Pav

19 20

GLASTHULE

MARINE ROAD

SCOTSMA
BAY

DÚN
AGHAIRE

DÚN LAOGHAIRE
GOLF COURSE

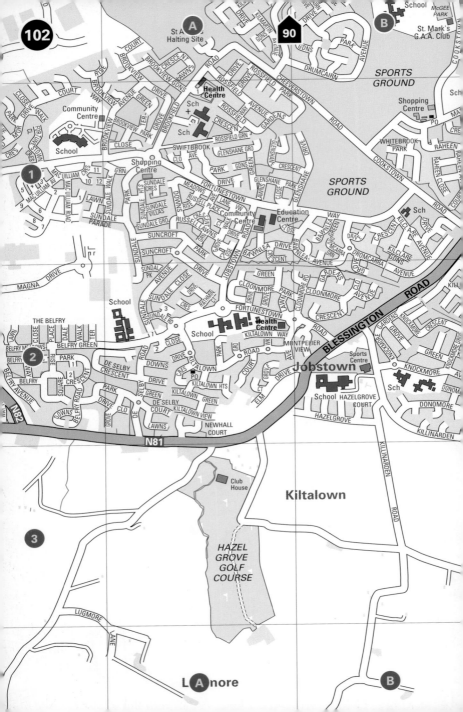

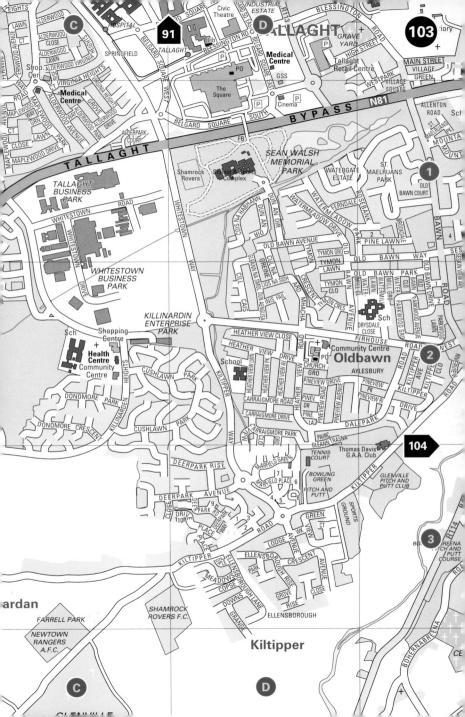

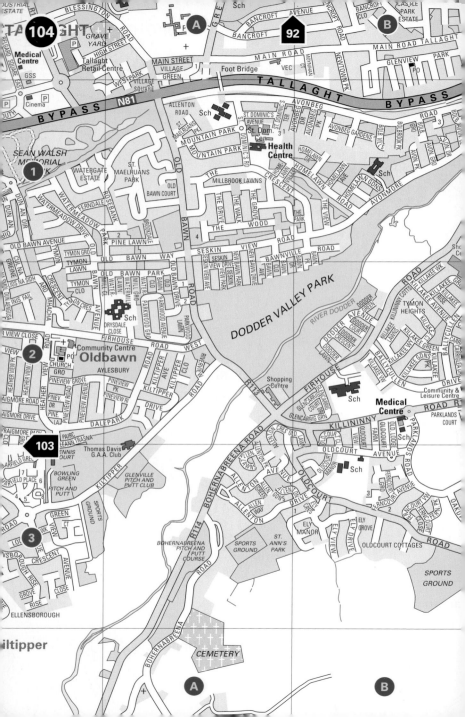

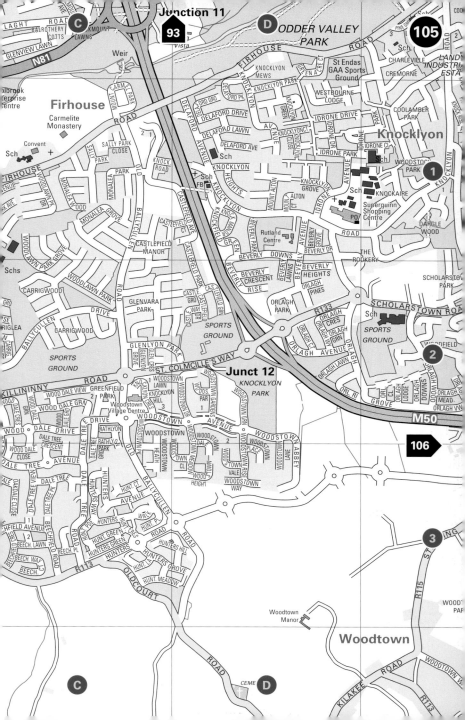

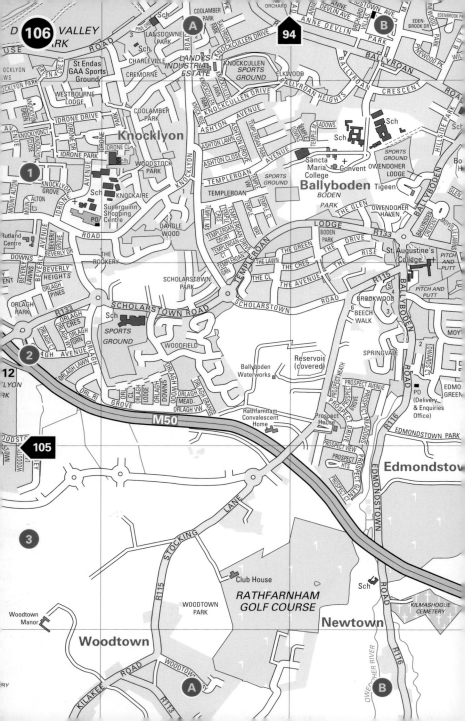

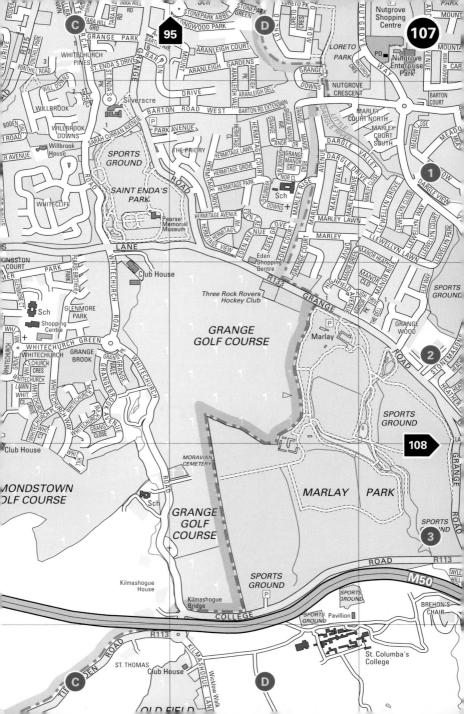

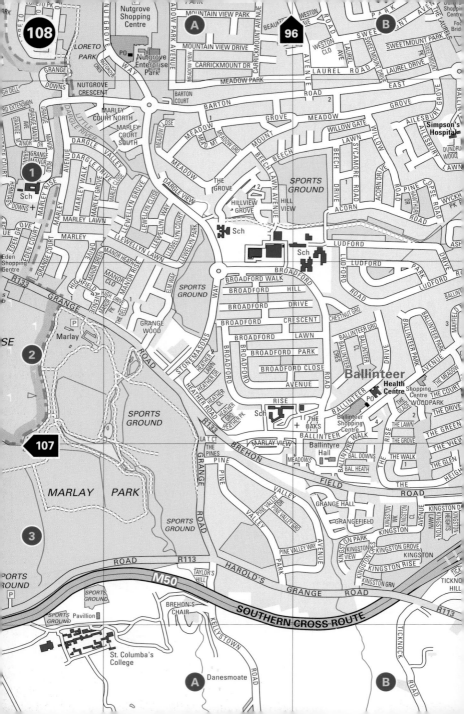

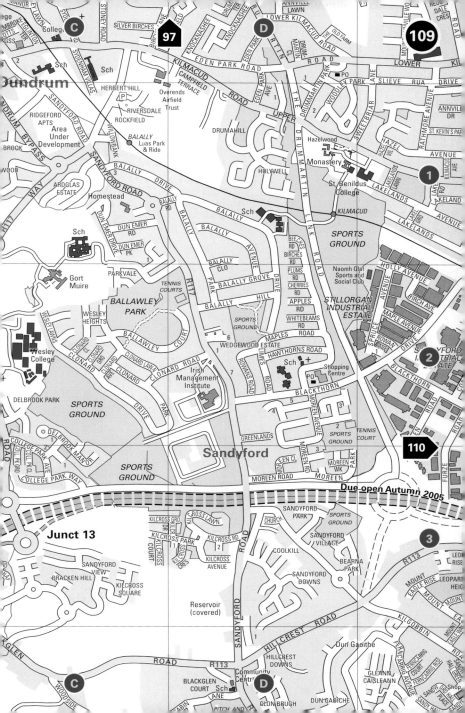

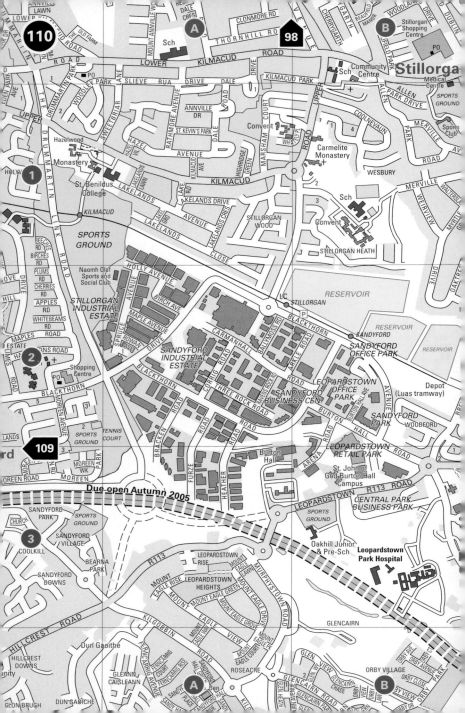

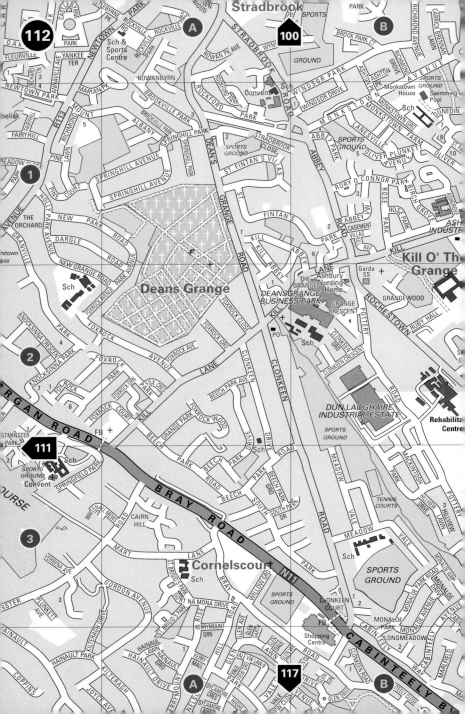

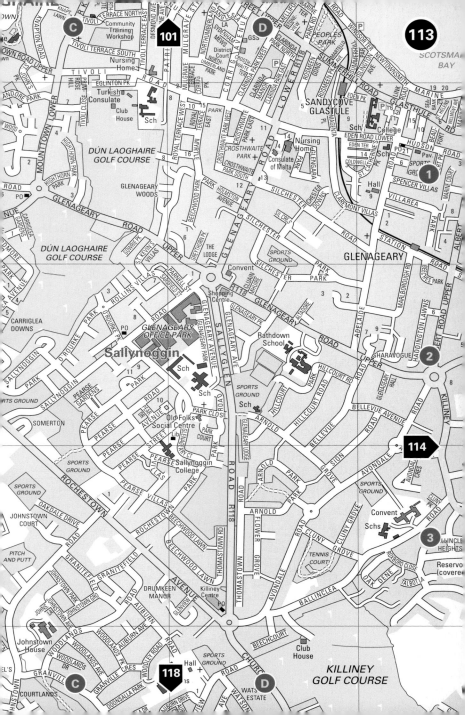

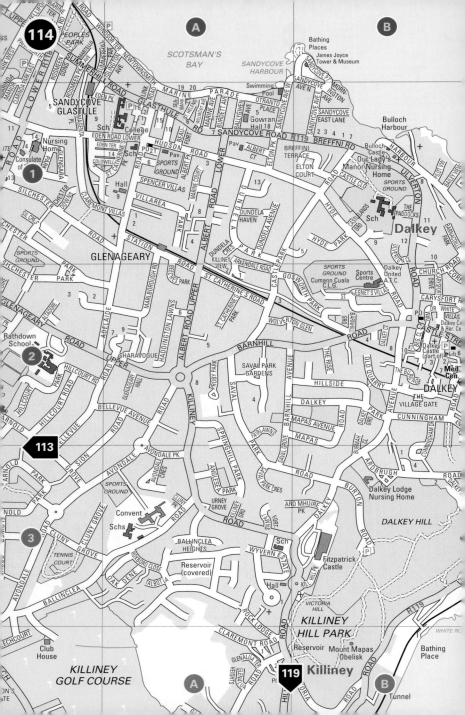

1

2

3

ce

Schs

Loreto
Abbey School

SPORTS
GROUNDS

MAIDEN ROCK

Pier

Martello
Tower

Coliemore
Harbour

LAMB ISLAND

MUGLINS

DALKEY SOUND

Promontory
Fort
+

Martello
Tower

DALKEY ISLAND

KNOCK-NA-CREE
GROVE

NA-CREE

Tunnel

SORRENTO
PARK

SORRENTO ROAD

SORRENTO
POINT

HAWK CLIFF

KNOCK-NA-CREE ROAD

NERANO ROAD

MOUNT SALUS ROAD

VICTORIA ROAD

COLIEMORE ROAD

GREEN RD

DALKEY SOUND

HEANY AVE

BICKFORT AVENUE

ROAD

DRIVE

LORETO AVENUE

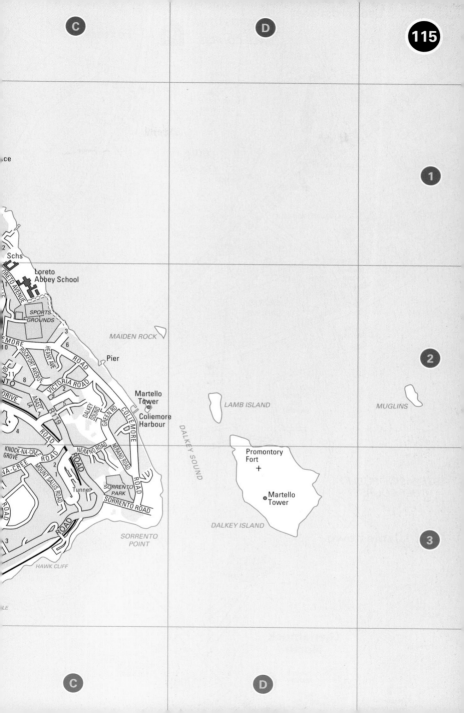

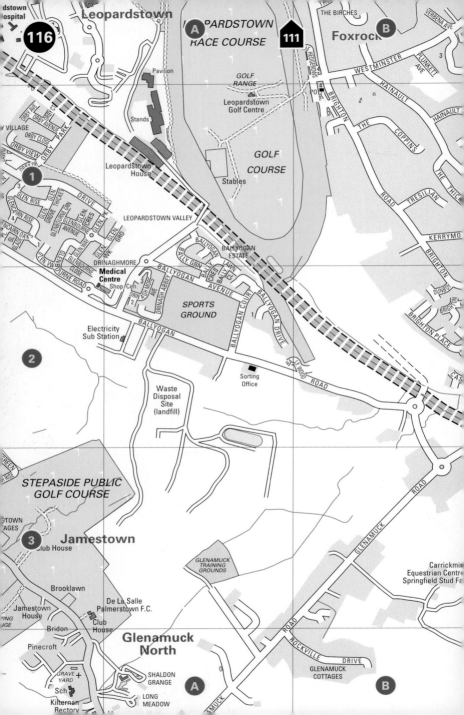

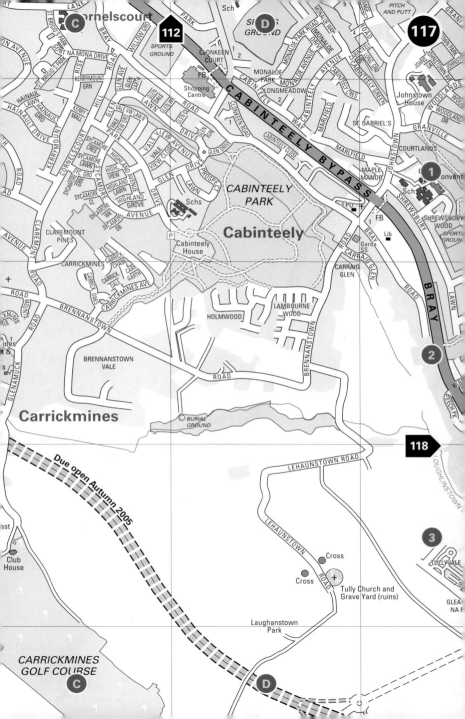

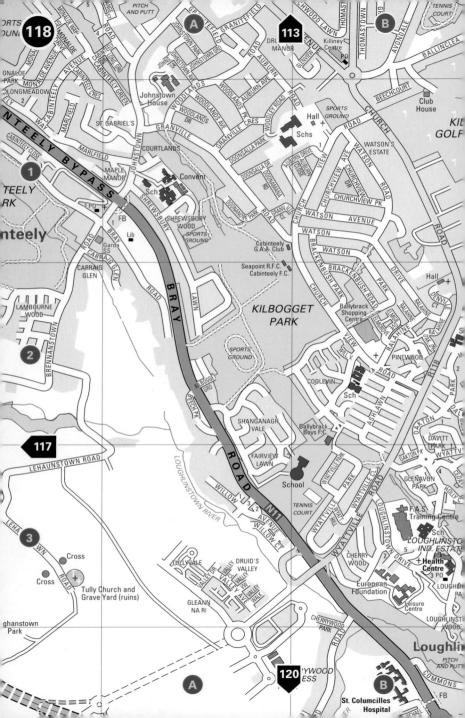

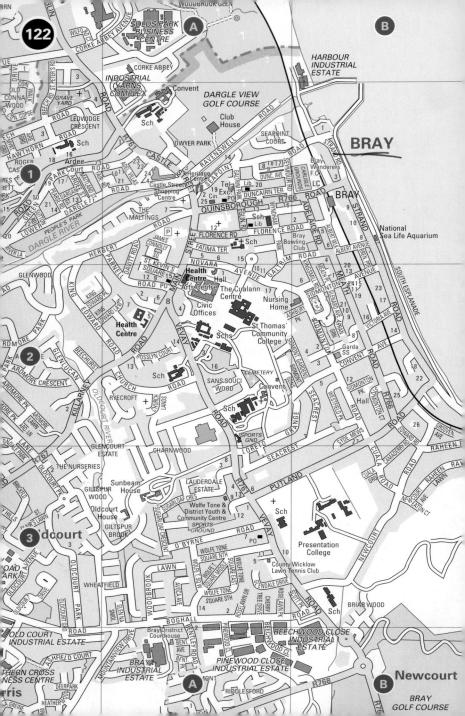

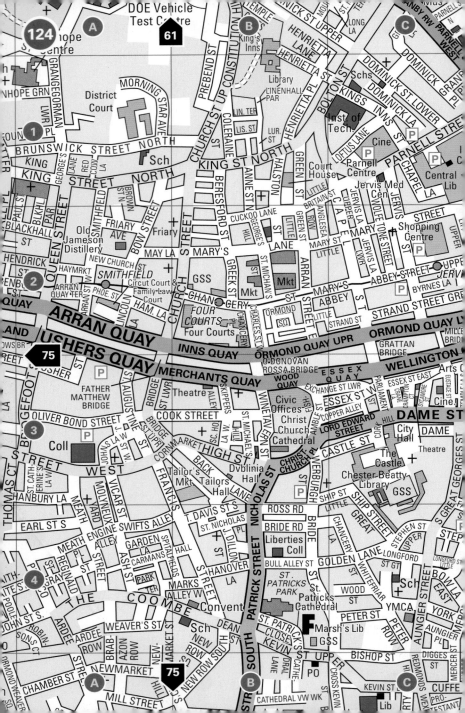

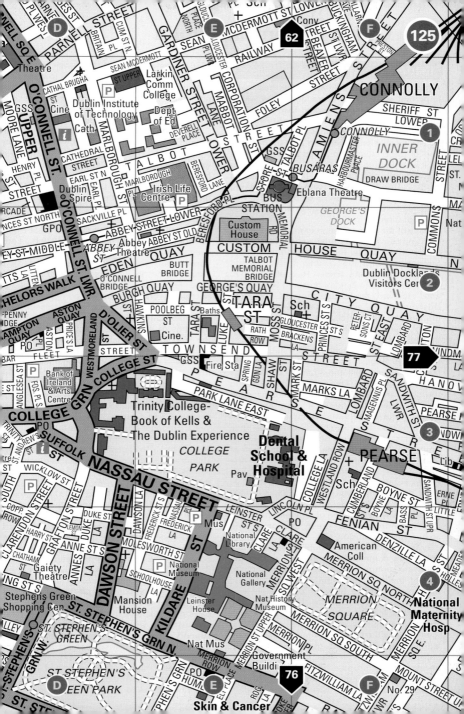

Guide to central Dublin

History

The ford over the River Liffey has been important since Celtic times and there was a thriving Christian community here from the 5thC, following their conversion by St Patrick in AD448. Marauding Vikings landed here in AD840, established a garrison port by the Dark Pool or Dubbh Linn, and within a few years had built a fortified town on the high ground above the estuary. Originally a base for raiding sorties, Dublin soon became a flourishing trading port as well, until Viking dominance was curtailed following a defeat by Brian Boru at the Battle of Clontarf in 1014.

Many of the Vikings had inter-married with the Irish and converted to Christianity but they were finally driven out by the Anglo-Normans under Strongbow, who took Dublin by storm and executed the Viking leader Hasculf. In 1170 Henry II arrived in Dublin, defeated Strongbow and received the submission of the Irish chieftains on the site of College Green. Henry granted the city by charter to the citizens of Bristol, thereby establishing English authority in Ireland.

The city and surrounding area, established as the seat of English government and protected by an enclosing wall and strategic castles, was known as The Pale. Frequently attacked during the 12thC and 13thC by the Irish clans based in the Wicklow Mountains, it was assaulted unsuccessfully by Edward Bruce in 1316. The city witnessed the crowning of Lambert Simnel, pretender to the English throne, in Christ Church in 1486. Unmoved by the rebellion of 'Silken' Thomas Fitzgerald in 1534, the inhabitants remained loyal to the English crown, supporting King Charles during the Civil Wars. Parliamentarians captured Dublin in 1647 and at this time the city was in decline. Following the Restoration of Charles I, however, Dublin underwent a great economic and architectural expansion.

By the end of the 17thC Dublin had become a flourishing commercial centre and during the following century the city was transformed into one of the most beautiful Georgian cities in Europe. The 'Wide Streets Commission' was established in 1757 and in 1773 the Paving Board was formed. New, elegantly spacious streets and squares were planned and palatial town houses built. In 1783 the Irish Parliament led by Henry Grattan was granted a short-lived autonomy but there was growing political unrest, which erupted in the unsuccessful uprising of 1798. Lord Edward Fitzgerald died of wounds sustained resisting arrest and in 1800 the detested Act of Union was established and the fortunes of the city began to wane.

With government now in London, few of the noblemen required their fine mansions and many returned to their country estates or left for London. Bitterness increased; in 1803 the Lord Chief Justice was assassinated and Robert Emmet, the leader of an abortive insurrection, was hanged. The newspaper The Nation was established by Charles Gavan Duffy in 1842, the heyday of the Repeal Movement. Daniel O'Connell was elected Lord Mayor in 1841 but only three years later he was interned in Richmond Gaol for campaigning for the repeal of the Union and the restoration of Grattan's 'Irish Parliament'. In 1873 the first great Home Rule Conference was held and in 1879 the Land League was formed, whose leaders, including Parnell and Davitt, were imprisoned as a consequence. In 1882 the new Chief Secretary, Lord Frederick Cavendish, and his Under Secretary were assassinated in Phoenix Park by the Invincibles, a new terrorist organisation.

As the campaign for Home Rule gathered momentum, the Gaelic League, which started the Irish literary renaissance, was established by Douglas Hyde and Eóin MacNeill in 1893. Conceived as a means of reviving interest in the Irish language and traditional Irish life, the Gaelic League was also responsible for a remarkable literary revival resulting in the formation of the Abbey Theatre in 1904, where plays by J M Synge, Sean O'Casey and W B Yeats, amongst others, were performed.

In 1905 the Sinn Fein movement was formed, in 1909 the Irish Transport and General Workers Union was set up under the leadership of James Connolly, and in 1913 there was a massive strike, paralysing the city. The Irish Volunteers came into being in 1914, largely to combat the Ulster Volunteers who had been raised by Edward Carson in January 1913 to defend the right of Ulster to remain united with Great Britain. In 1916 the Irish Volunteers seized the General Post Office in Lower O'Connell Street as their headquarters and the Easter Rising had begun. It was quickly crushed, but so brutally that public conscience, clearly appalled, overwhelmingly elected Sinn Fein at the general election of December 1918 with Eamon de Valera as the new president.

Whilst the Dublin faction was openly in support of the guerrilla bands operating across the country, the Ulster Unionists set up their own provisional government, and the ambushes and assassinations which characterised the Anglo-Irish War, featuring the notorious Black and Tans, began in bloody

earnest. The war ended in the truce of July 1921. Despite the ratification of the Irish Free State in January 1922, a large and dissatisfied faction of leaders in the Irish movement took up arms against their former comrades and seized the Four Courts, which they held for two months. The subsequent shelling ordered by the new Dublin Government destroyed much of O'Connell Street but by the 1930s Dublin was emerging as a modern capital city and most of the public buildings had been restored.

Visiting Dublin

Passports

Citizens of the European Union need either a valid national identity card or passport to enter the Republic of Ireland. It is recommended that visitors from the UK bring a passport as a means of identification. Nationals of other countries require a passport and may require a visa. Enquiries should be made with a travel agent or Irish Embassy before travelling. The address of the Irish Embassy in London is 17 Grosvenor Place, SW1X 7HR.

Tel: 020 7235 2171 & (020 7225 7700 Passport/Visa)

Web: www.irlgov.ie

Banks

In February 2002 the Irish Punt (IEP) was withdrawn from circulation and the Euro (€) became the Irish unit of currency.

Banks open Monday–Friday from 10.00–16.00 and in Dublin most branches remain open until 7.00 on Thursdays. Major banks have 24 hour ATM machines which accept Plus and Cirrus symbols. Most credit cards, including all those with the Eurocard symbol, are widely accepted in shops, petrol stations, restaurants and hotels. Personal cheques from banks outside the Republic of Ireland are not accepted in the country without prior arrangement.

Bureaux de Change

Banks and Bureaux de Change generally offer the best exchange rates, although post offices, hotels, travel agents and some department stores offer exchange facilities.

There is a Bureau de Change at Dublin Airport and Dún Laoghaire ferry terminal. Dublin Airport also has a 24 hour Bank of Ireland foreign currency note exchanger and multi-currency Pass machines. Foreign exchange facilities are also to be found at the central bus station (Busárus) and Connolly railway station.

Language

English is spoken by everyone in Ireland. The country is officially bilingual with Irish (Gaelic) also spoken.

Customs and excise

The Republic of Ireland is a member of the European Union and, in accordance with EU regulations, travellers within the Community can import 90 litres of wine, 110 litres of duty paid beer and 800 cigarettes without question. Duty free sales of goods amongst European community members are now abolished. There are restrictions on taking certain food items into Ireland and checks should be made beforehand with the Irish Embassy or travel agent. Pets may not be brought into the country unless travelling from the UK, all other animals entering the country have to undergo quarantine.

Emergency

If you are involved in an emergency and require the services of the Police, Fire Brigade, Ambulance Service, or Coastguard, dial 999.

Medical treatment

Visitors to Ireland from European Community countries are entitled to free treatment by a general practitioner, medicines on prescription and treatment on a public ward in a hospital. British citizens need only show some form of identification such as a passport or driving licence to the doctor or hospital and request treatment under the EU health agreement. Visitors from other EU countries need to present form E111 (available from social security offices prior to departure). Health Insurance is recommended for visitors from outside the EU. No inoculations are required for travellers to Ireland.

Disabled visitors

The Irish Wheelchair association can offer advice and can arrange wheelchair hire. Tel: 01 818 6400 (Mon–Fri 09.00–17.00).
Web: www.iwa.ie

Irish Rail publishes a 'Guide for Mobility Impaired Passengers' which details the accessibility of all railway and DART stations. Obtainable at all manned stations or from the Access and Liaison officer, tel: 01 703 2634. Most of the Dublin Bus fleet is low floor easy access, and the buses run by Bus Éireann – Ireland's national bus company – are largely wheelchair accessible. Discounts on many ferry sailings from Britain are available to disabled drivers who wish to take their own car to Ireland. Drivers should contact the Disabled Drivers' Association or Motor Club in Britain to obtain the relevant form. This form should then be sent to the ferry company.

Phones

Most calls are dialled direct with cheaper call charge rates between 18.00 and 08.00 Mon–Fri

and all day Saturday, Sunday and bank holidays. The dialling code for Dublin is 01 and so for calls within Dublin omit 01 at the beginning of a number. To dial Dublin from abroad dial the access code for Ireland (00353) plus the area code for Dublin (01) but omit the zero. For directory enquiries, including Northern Ireland, dial 11811; for Great Britain or International numbers dial 11818. For operator assistance dial 10 (Ireland and UK) or 114 for the international operator. Card phones are cheaper than payphones and are widely available. Callcards are obtainable at post offices, newsagents and supermarkets. Mobile phones can be brought into Ireland but visitors need to ensure their phone company has a roaming agreement with the Irish network operators.

Transport

Driving

Driving is on the left-hand side of the road in Ireland as in the UK; at roundabouts give way to traffic from the right. All drivers and front seat passengers must wear seat belts, and rear belts if they are fitted. Children under twelve must have a suitable restraint. Helmets are compulsory for motorcyclists. The maximum speed limit is 97kph (60mph) outside urban areas and the motorway speed limit is 110kph (70mph). In urban areas the limit is usually 50kph (30mph). There are on-the-spot fines for speeding and drink driving laws are strict. Parking infringements are taken seriously and illegally parked cars in Dublin City are liable to be clamped or towed away to the Corporation pound with a recovery charge payable.

Distances and speed limits are now both measured in kilometres (speed limit signs changed on 20th January 2005). Place names are generally in English and Irish. Unleaded petrol and diesel are widely available. Recorded weather information is available for Dublin by calling the Meteorological Service Tel: 1550 123 854. There is a charge for this call.

Car hire

Car hire is readily available in Dublin, although in July and August there is a high demand and it is best to book in advance. You must have held a full licence for 2 years and be under 70 and over 23. Some companies make exceptions to this but charges may be higher. A full valid driving licence of your country of residence (which you must have held for at least two years without endorsements) must be presented at the time of hiring.

Most international car rental companies have offices in Dublin and cars can also be hired at the airport and Dún Laoghaire ferry terminal. The cost of hire will depend on the type of car and time of year and it is worthwhile shopping around. It is important, however, to check the insurance details and ensure Collision Damage Waiver is included. A deposit is usually payable at the time of booking or before you drive away. Fly-drive or rail-sail-drive packages arranged by travel agents or the air and ferry companies can be an economical and easy way of hiring a car.

Public transport

Dublin is linked with the cities and towns of Ireland by a network of rail and bus services overseen by Córas Iompair Éireann (CIE), which is Ireland's National Transport Authority. The CIE organises Iarnód Éireann (Irish Rail), Bus Éireann (Irish Bus) and Dublin Bus. Bus and rail timetables can be bought at most newsagents. Unlimited use period tickets are available for use on rail and/or bus services.

Bus and coach travel

Dublin Bus (Bus Átha Cliath) operates the public bus services in Dublin and the surrounding area. Pre-paid tickets can be bought for periods of time ranging from one day to one month and are good value for money. They can be bought at any of the many bus ticket agencies in the city, from the CIE information desk at Dublin Airport or at Dublin Bus head office at 59 O'Connell Street Upper. Many routes operate an exact fare only policy. Dublin Bus also operates late night services (Nitelink) to most suburban areas on Thursdays, Fridays and Saturdays, links to the ferry ports and railway stations, and also sightseeing tours.

Open Mon–Sat 09.00–19.00.

Tel: 01 872 0000 or 01 873 4222

Web: www.dublinbus.ie has details of routes, timetables, and special tickets.

National bus services between Dublin, Dublin Airport and other major cities and towns are provided by Irish Bus (Bus Éireann) and many private companies. Bus Éireann also operate combined bus and ferry services between Britain and Ireland.

Dublin Bus Station (Bus Áras), Store Street.

Tel: 01 836 6111

Web: www.buseireann.ie

Scheduled daily hop-on hop-off city sightseeing tours are operated by Gray Line, Guide Friday and City Sightseeing. Buses depart every 10-20 minutes from 09.30-17.30; also available are seasonal half and full day excursions further afield including to Newgrange and the Boyne Valley, Powerscourt Gardens, Glendalough and

Vicklow. 3 & 4 day trips to Kerry and Dingle are also available. Information and tickets from the Desk 1 at the Dublin Tourism Centre, Suffolk Street.
Tel: 01 605 7705
Web: www.irishcitytours.com
Email: info@irishcitytours.com

Taxis

Taxis are available at taxi ranks or by phoning one of the many radio-linked taxi companies. There are numerous taxi ranks including ones in O'Connell Street, Dame Street, and St. Stephen's Green West.
Taxi companies are listed in the Golden Pages classified telephone directory.

Rail travel

Dublin Connolly and Dublin Heuston are the two mainline railway stations and Irish Rail (Iarnród Éireann) operates an excellent service to most towns and cities in Ireland. Irish rail also operates the suburban rail network in Dublin and DART (Dublin Area Rapid Transit) with 26 stations between Howth on the north of Dublin Bay to Bray in the south.
Tel: 01 850 366222
Web: www.irishrail.ie

Bike hire

Tracks Bikes, Botanic Road, Glasnevin.
Tel: 01 850 0252

Irish Cycling Safaris, Belfield Bike Shop, University College Dublin.
Tel: 01 260 0749

Lost property

Enquire at the nearest police station or:
Dublin Airport. Open Mon–Fri 07.00-22.30.
Tel: 01 814 5555

Dublin Bus. Open Mon–Fri 08.45–17.00.
Tel: 01 703 1321

Irish Bus. Open Mon–Fri 09.00–17.00.
Tel: 01 703 2489

Irish Rail (Connolly Station). Open Mon–Fri 9.00–17.00. **Tel: 01 703 2358**

Irish Rail (Heuston Station). Open Mon–Fri 9.00–17.00. **Tel: 01 703 2102**

Places of interest

Arbour Hill Cemetery, Arbour Hill.
The leaders of the Easter Rising are buried here.
Bank of Ireland, College Green.
Designed by Sir Edward Lovett Pearce in 1729, it was later enlarged by James Gandon and Robert Parke between 1785–1794. Originally the Parliament House, the first of a series of great public buildings erected in 18thC Dublin, it was

taken over by the Bank of Ireland in 1804. A statue of Henry Grattan, leader of the Irish parliament of 1782, stands outside on the lawn of College Green. Two huge 18thC tapestries commemorating the Siege of Londonderry and the Battle of the Boyne hang in the oak-panelled chamber of the former House of Lords.
There are guided tours of the House of Lords on Tuesdays at 10.30, 11.30, and 13.45.
Admission free. Disabled access.
Tel: 01 671 1488

Bank of Ireland Arts Centre, Foster Place.
An arts centre which presents classical concerts and recitals and houses an interactive museum. The museum illustrates the history of the adjoining College Green buildings where many of the dramatic events of Irish history were played out in the Irish parliament. The museum also reflects the role played by the Bank of Ireland in the economic and social development of Ireland.
Open Tues-Fri 9.30–16.00, Sat 10.00-16.00.
Disabled access.
Tel: 01 671 1488

Belvedere House, North Great George's Street.
One of the best 18thC mansions in Dublin. Taken over by Jesuit Belvedere College in 1841; James Joyce went to school here between 1893–1898. Not open to the public.

Casino, off Malahide Road, Marino.
A miniature 18thC neo-classical masterpiece designed by Sir William Chambers and recently restored. Casino means 'small house'. It was built as a pleasure house beside Marino House (now demolished), Lord Charlemont's country residence, for the enormous sum of £60,000. It is a compact building, remarkably containing 16 rooms, with many interesting architectural features. The interior circular hall, ringed by columns, is crowned by a coffered dome. The graceful roof urns disguise chimneys while the columns conceal drainpipes.
Open Daily (May-Oct) 10.00-17.00 (18.00 Jun-Sept); (Nov-Apr) Sat & Sun 12.00-16.00 (17.00 Apr). Closed January. Access by guided tour only. Last tour leaves 45 mins before closing. Access to interior by stairway.
Tel: 01 833 1618

City Hall, Dame Street.
Completed in 1779, this fine building was designed as The Royal Exchange. Subsequent use included a prison and corn exchange before being taken over by the city in 1852. Presently used by Dublin City Council. It features a beautiful Corinthian coffered dome and portico.

The archives include the original charter of 1171 in which Henry II granted Dublin to the citizens of Bristol.
Open Mon-Sat 10.00-17.15, Sun 14.00-17.00.
Tel: 01 222 2204
Web: www.dublincity.ie/cityhall

Custom House Visitor Centre, Custom House Quay.

The Custom House, with a magnificent long river frontage, is an architectural masterpiece designed by James Gandon and completed in 1791. Exhibits relate to James Gandon and the history of the Custom House itself, with illustrations of how the building was restored after it was gutted by fire in 1921. The building is best viewed from the south bank of the River Liffey.
Open: Wed-Fri (Nov-16 Mar) & Mon–Fri (17 Mar-Nov) 10.00–12.30, Sat & Sun 14.00–17.00. Disabled access by prior arrangement.
Tel: 01 888 2538

Drimnagh Castle, Long Mile Road.

Ireland's only castle with a flooded moat. This Norman castle has a fully restored Great Hall, medieval undercroft and 17thC style formal garden.
Open (Apr–Sept) Wed, Sat, Sun 12.00–17.00; (Oct–March) Wed, Sun 12.00–17.00. Last tour 16.15. Open at other times by appointment.
Tel: 01 450 2530
Email: drimnaghcastle@eircom.net

Dublin Castle, off Dame Street.

The Castle was originally built between 1204-1228 as part of Dublin's defensive system. The Record Tower is the principal remnant of the 13thC Anglo-Norman fortress and has walls 5 metres (16ft) thick but what remains today is largely the result of 18thC and 19thC re-building. It now contains the Garda (Police) Museum. The 15thC Bermingham Tower was once the state prison where Red Hugh O'Donnell was interned in the 16thC; it was rebuilt in the 18thC. The State Apartments, Undercroft and ornate Chapel Royal are open to the public. The State Apartments, dating from the British Administration, were once the residence of the English Viceroys and are now used for Presidential Inaugurations and state receptions. Within these apartments are the magnificent throne room and St Patrick's Hall, 25 metres (82ft) long with a high panelled and decorated ceiling. In the undercroft can be seen the remains of a Viking fortress, part of the original moat, and part of the old city wall.
The Chester Beatty Library exhibits art treasures from around the world.
Open: Mon–Fri 10.00–17.00, Sat & Sun 14.00–17.00. Access by guided tour only. Disabled access/toilets.
Tel: 01 677 7129
Web: www.dublincastle.ie
Email: info@dublincastle.ie

Dublin Experience, Trinity College.

A film about the story of Dublin which is shown every hour in the Trinity College Arts Building.
Open daily from late May to late Sep 10.00–17.00. Last showing 17.00.
Tel: 01 608 1688

Dublin Writers Museum, Parnell Square.

Tracing the history of Irish literature from its earliest times to the 20thC, this museum is a celebration of this literary heritage. Writers and playwrights including Jonathan Swift, George Bernard Shaw, Oscar Wilde, W B Yeats, James Joyce and Samuel Beckett are brought to life through personal items, portraits, their books and letters. There is also a room dedicated to children's authors. The museum is housed in a restored 18thC Georgian mansion with decorative stained-glass windows and ornate plaster-work.
Open Mon–Sat 10.00–17.00 (18.00 Jun-Aug) Sun 11.00–17.00. Disabled access to ground floor. Last entry 45 mins before closing.
Tel: 01 872 2077
Email: writers@dublintourism.ie

Dvblinia, Christ Church, St. Michael's Hill.

A multi-media recreation of Dublin life in medieval times from the Anglo-Norman arrival in 1170 to the dissolution of the monasteries in 1540. There is a scale model of the medieval city, a life size reconstruction of a merchant's house, and numerous Viking and Norman artefacts from excavations at nearby Wood Quay. The building is the old Synod Hall and is linked to Christ Church Cathedral by an ornate Victorian pedestrian bridge.
Open Mon-Fri 10.00-17.00 (Oct-Mar 11.00-16.00) Sat & Sun 10.00-16.00. Disabled access.
Tel: 01 679 4611
Web: www.dublinia.ie
Email: marketing@dublinia.ie

Dublin Zoo, Phoenix Park.

The Zoo is well known for its captive-breeding programme and is committed to the conservation and protection of endangered species. The 'big cats', living in enclosures which simulate their natural habitats, include lions, tigers, jaguars and snow leopards. Attractive gardens surround two natural lakes where pelicans, flamingos, ducks and geese abound, while the islands in the lakes are home to chimps, gibbons, spider monkeys and orang-utans. A recent development 'Fringes of the

rctic' has provided a state of the art enclosure or the polar bears and is home to wolves, arctic oxes and snowy owls. After the acquisition of more land, the zoo doubled in size in 2000 and an African Plains area has been developed providing greater space and freedom for giraffe, hippo, rhino and other African animals and birds. The city farm and pets' corner provide encounters with Irish domestic animals. Other attractions include a zoo train, discovery centre, open: Mon–Sat 09.30–17.00, Sun 10.30–17.00. last admission 16.00. Closes at dusk in winter.

Tel: 01 474 8900

Web: www.dublinzoo.ie

Email: info@dublinzoo.ie

Dunsink Observatory, Castleknock, Dublin 15.

Founded in 1783, it is one of the oldest observatories in the world and houses the astronomy section of the School of Cosmic Physics. Public open nights are held on the first and third Wednesdays of each month from October to March inclusive at 20.00. Requests for tickets for the open nights must be made by post to the Observatory.

Tel: 01 838 7911

Web: www.dunsink.dias.ie

Email: cwoods@dunsinkdias.ie

Four Courts, Inns Quay.

Originally designed by James Gandon in 1785, it was partially destroyed by a fire in 1922 in the struggle for Irish independence but restored again by 1932. The Four Courts has a 137 metre (450ft) river frontage and the building is fronted by a Corinthian portico with six columns. The square central block with circular hall is crowned by a copper-covered lantern-dome. Housed here are the Irish Law Courts and Law Library.

Tel: 01 888 6457/6460

Web: www.courts.ie

Email: schooltours@courts.ie

Fry Model Railway, Malahide Castle, Malahide.

Covering 233 square metres (2,500sq.ft) this is one of the world's largest working miniature railways and is a delight for children and adults alike. Besides the track, the railway has stations, bridges, trams, buses and barges and includes the Dublin landmarks of Heuston station and O'Connell Bridge. On display are the hand constructed models of Irish trains by Cyril Fry, draughtsman and railway engineer, who made them from the 1930s until his death in 1974. Perfectly engineered, the models represent the earliest trains to those of more modern times.

Situated in the grounds of Malahide Castle, 13km (8 miles) north of Dublin city centre. Open (Apr-Sept) Mon-Sat 10.00-17.00, Sun & public holidays 14.00–18.00; Closed 13.00-14.00 and Oct-Mar.

Tel: 01 846 3779

Web: www.malahidecastle.com

Email: fryrailway@dublintourism.ie

GAA Museum, Croke Park.

The Gaelic Athletic Association (GAA) is Ireland's largest sporting and cultural organisation and is dedicated to promoting the games of hurling, Gaelic football, handball, rounders and camogie. The museum is at Croke Park, home of Irish hurling and football, and traces the history of Gaelic sports and their place in Irish culture right up to the present day. Interactive exhibits allow visitors the chance to try out the skills of the games for themselves. National trophies and sports equipment are also on display.

Open Mon-Sat 09.30-17.00, Sun 12.00-17.00. Last admission 1/2 hour before closing. All groups must be pre-booked.

Tel: 01 819 2323

Web: www.gaa.ie/museum

Email: gaamuseum@crokepark.ie

Heraldic Museum, Kildare Street.

Part of the National Library of Ireland, the museum illustrates the uses of heraldry with displays of coat of arms and banners and a collection of heraldic glass, seals, stamps, and coins.

Open Mon-Wed 10.00-20.30; Thurs-Fri 10.00-16.30; Sat 10.00-12.30. Admission is free.

Tel: 01 603 0311

Email: herald@nli.ie

General Post Office, O'Connell Street.

Designed by Francis Johnston and completed in 1818. A century later the GPO became the headquarters of the 1916 Easter Rising and the Proclamation of the Irish Republic was read from the steps by Patrick Pearse. Bullet marks can still be seen on the pillars. Badly damaged in 1922 in the fight for independence, it was restored in 1929. A bronze sculpture, The Death of Cúchulainn by Oliver Sheppard, stands within the building.

Tel: 01 705 7000

Email: customer.service@anpost.ie

Guinness Storehouse, St. James's Gate.

The story of Guinness is told from its beginnings in 1759, how it is made and the advertising campaigns used to make it internationally famous. Housed in St James's Gate Brewery and spread over six floors, on the highest of which can be found the bar 'Gravity',

from which a 360° view of Dublin can be enjoyed. Open July-Aug 9.30-20.00; Sept-June 9.30-17.00. Disabled access.
Tel: 01 408 4800
Web: www.guinnessstorehouse.com
Email: guinness-storehouse@guinness.com

Ha'penny Bridge, Crampton Quay.
An elegant arching narrow cast-iron pedestrian bridge spanning the Liffey; it was first opened in 1816 and the name derives from the toll once charged.

Irish Jewish Museum, Walworth Road
Opened by President Herzog of Israel in 1985, exhibits relate to the Jewish community in Ireland including synagogue fittings and the reconstruction of a typical Dublin Jewish kitchen of 100 years ago.
Open (May-Sept) Sun, Tues, Thurs 11.00-15.30; (Oct-Apr) Sun 10.30-14.30. Admission is free.
Tel: 01 490 1857

Irish Museum of Modern Art, Military Road, Kilmainham.
Opened in the 17thC Royal Hospital building and grounds in 1991, the museum is an important institution for the collection of modern and contemporary art. A wide variety of work by major established 20thC figures and that of younger contemporary artists is presented in an ever changing programme of exhibitions, drawn from the museum's own collection and from public and private collections world-wide.
Open Tues-Sat 10.00-17.15, Sun & some bank holidays 12.00-17.15. Admission is free.
Tel: 01 612 9900
Web: www.modernart.ie
Email: info@imma.ie

James Joyce Centre, North Great George's Street.
A museum in a restored Georgian town house, built in 1784, devoted to the great novelist and run by members of his family. Dennis J Maginni, dancing master in Joyce's novel Ulysses, ran his dancing school from this house. The library contains editions of Joyce's work and that of other Irish writers as well as biographical and critical writing. There is a set of biographies of real Dublin people fictionalised in Ulysses, and also the door from the house occupied by the central character of the novel, Leopold Bloom and his wife Molly. The centre hosts readings, lectures and debates on all aspects of Joyce and his literature and conducts guided city tours.
Open Tues-Sat 09.30-17.00.
Tel: 01 878 8547
Web: www.jamesjoyce.ie
Email: info@jamesjoyce.ie

James Joyce Museum, Sandycove.
The museum is housed in the Martello Tower which Joyce used as the setting for the opening chapter of Ulysses, his great work of fiction which immortalised Dublin. Joyce stayed here briefly in 1904 and the living room and view from the gun platform remains much as he described it in the novel. The museum collection includes personal possessions, letters, photographs, first editions and items that reflect the Dublin of Joyce. Situated 13km (8 miles) south of Dublin city centre, the tower was one of 15 defensive towers built along Dublin Bay in 1804 to withstand a threatened invasion from Napoleon.
Open (Mar-Oct) Mon-Sat 10.00-17.00, Sun 14.00-18.00. Closed 13.00-14.00.
Tel: 01 280 9265
Email: joycetower@dublintourism.ie

Kilmainham Gaol, Inchicore Road, Kilmainham.
Built as a gaol in 1796, Kilmainham is now dedicated to the Irish patriots imprisoned there from 1792-1924, including Emmet and his United Irishmen colleagues, the Fenians, the Invincibles and the Irish Volunteers of the Easter Rising. Patrick Pearse and James Connolly were executed in the prison yard and Eamon de Valera, later Prime Minister and then President of Ireland, was one of the last inmates. After its closure in 1924 Kilmainham re-opened as a museum in 1966. It is one of the largest unoccupied gaols in Europe with tiers of cells and overhead catwalks. Access is by guided tour only and features an exhibition and audio visual show on the political and penal history of the gaol.
Open daily (May-Sept) 09.30-17.00; (Oct-Mar) Mon-Fri 09.30-16.00, Sun 10.00-17.00. Disabled toilets. Tours for visitors with special needs by prior arrangement.
Tel: 01 453 5984

King's Inns, Henrietta Street.
The Dublin Inns of Court is a glorious classical building, partly built to the plans of James Gandon at the end of the 19thC. The library was founded in 1787 and contains a large legal collection with about 100,000 books. The courtyard opens into Henrietta Street, where Dublin's earliest Georgian mansions remain.
Web: www.kingsinns.ie

Leinster House, Kildare Street.
Originally a handsome town mansion designed by Richard Castle for the Duke of Leinster in 1745; it has been a Parliament House since 1922. The Dáil Éireann (House of Representatives) and Seanad Éireann (Senate) sit here. The

ouse has two contrasting facades: an mposing formal side facing Kildare Street while rom Merrion Square the building has more of he appearance of a country residence. Anybody wanting a tour of Irish Parliament nust contact their respective embassy in Dublin vhere arrangements can be made. Advance notice is required.

Tel: 01 618 3000

Malahide Castle, Malahide.

Originally built in 1185, it was the seat of the albot family until 1973 when the last Lord albot died; the history of the family is detailed n the Great Hall alongside many family portraits. Malahide also has a large collection of Irish portrait paintings, mainly from the National Gallery, and is furnished with fine period furniture. Within the 100 hectares (250 cres) of parkland surrounding the castle is the albot Botanic Gardens, largely created by Lord Milo Talbot between 1948 and 1973. The grounds include walled gardens and a shrubbery with a collection of southern hemisphere plants. Malahide is situated 13km 8 miles) north of Dublin city centre.

Open Mon-Sat 10.00-17.00; Sundays & Bank Holidays 11.00-17.00 (18.00 Apr-Oct); Closed 3.00-14.00. Combined tickets with Fry Model Railway are available.

Tel: 01 846 2184

Web: www.malahidecastle.com

Email: malahidecastle@dublintourism.ie

Mansion House, Dawson Street.

Built in 1705, this Queen Anne style house has been the official residence of the Lord Mayor of Dublin since 1715. The first Irish parliament assembled here in 1919 to adopt Ireland's Declaration of Independence and ratify the 1916 Proclamation of the Irish Republic. Not open to he public.

National Museum of Ireland, Archaeology and History, Kildare Street.

Houses a fabulous collection of national antiquities including prehistoric gold ornaments, and outstanding examples of Celtic and medieval art. The 8thC Ardagh Chalice and Tara Brooch are amongst the treasures. The entire history of Ireland is reflected in the museum with 'The Road to Independence exhibition' illustrating Irish history from 1916–1921. Additionally, there is an Ancient Egypt exhibition.

Open Tues-Sat 10.00-17.00, Sun 14.00-17.00. Admission is free. A Museumlink bus linking the sites of the National Museum operates regularly throughout the day.

Tel: 01 677 7444

Web: www.museum.ie

National Museum of Ireland, Decorative Arts and History (Collins Barracks), Benburb Street.

Ireland's museum of decorative arts and economic, social, political and military history, based in the oldest military barracks in Europe. Major collections include Irish silver, Irish country furniture, and costume jewellery and accessories. The work of museum restoration and conservation is explained and the Out of Storage gallery provides visitors with a view of artefacts in storage.

Open Tues-Sat 10.00-17.00; Sun 14.00-17.00. Admission is free. Full disabled access. A Museumlink bus linking the 3 sites of the National Museum operates regularly throughout the day.

Tel: 01 677 7444

Web: www.museum.ie

National Museum of Ireland, Natural History, Merrion Street.

First opened in 1857 and hardly changed since then, the museum houses a large collection of stuffed animals and the skeletons of mammals and birds from both Ireland and the rest of the world. The exhibits include three examples of the Irish Great Elk which became extinct over 10,000 years ago and the skeleton of a Basking Shark. Fascinating glass reproductions of marine specimens, known as the Blaschka Collection, are found on the upper gallery.

Open Tues-Sat 10.00-17.00; Sun 14.00-17.00. Admission is free. A Museumlink bus linking the 3 sites of the National Museum operates regularly throughout the day.

Tel: 01 677 7444

Web: www.museum.ie

National Print Museum, Haddington Road.

Situated in the former Garrison Chapel in Beggars Bush Barracks, the museum illustrates the development of printing from the advent of printing to the use of computer technology with a unique collection of implements and machines from Ireland's printing industry.

Open Mon-Fri 09.00-17.00, Sat & Sun and Bank Holidays 14.00-17.00.

Tel: 01 660 3770

National Sea Life Centre, Bray.

Features marine life from the seas around Ireland including stingrays, conger eels, and sharks; also freshwater fish from Irish rivers and streams. A touch pool gives children the opportunity to pick up small creatures such as starfish, crabs and sea anemones. By way of contrast is the fascinating 'Danger in the Depths' tank with many sea creatures from

around the world which have proved harmful or fatal to humans.

Open (May-Sept) Mon-Fri 10.00-18.00, Sat & Sun 10.00-18.30; (Oct-Apr) Mon-Fri 11.00-17.00, Sat & Sun 11.00-18.00.

Tel: 01 286 6939

National Transport Museum, Howth.

A collection of buses, trams, trucks, tractors and fire engines, some dating back to 1880, along with other memorabilia from the transport industry.

Open (Jun–Aug) Mon–Fri 10.00–17.00, Sat & Sun 14.00–17.00; (Sept–May) Sat & Sun only 14.00–17.00. Bank holidays 14.00–17.00.

Tel: 01 848 0831

Web: www.nationaltransportmuseum.org
Email: info@nationaltransportmuseum.org

National Wax Museum, Granby Row.

Over 300 life-size wax figures of well-known people and personalities from the past and present ranging from Eamon De Valera to Elvis Presley. Also a dimly lit Chamber of Horrors.

Open: Mon–Sat 10.00–17.30, Sun 12.00–17.30.

Tel: 01 872 6340

Newbridge House, Donabate.

Built in 1737 for Archbishop Charles Cobbe, and still the residence of his descendants, Newbridge has one of the most beautiful period manor house interiors in Ireland and is set within 142 hectares (350 acres) of parkland. A fully restored 18thC farm lies on the estate together with dairy, forge, tack room, and estate worker's house. Situated 19km (12 miles) north of Dublin.

Open (Apr–Sept) Tues–Sat 10.00–17.00, Sun & bank holidays 14.00–18.00; (Oct–Mar) Sat, Sun & bank holidays 14.00–17.00.

Tel: 01 843 6534

Newman House, St Stephen's Green.

Newman House is made up of two splendid Georgian mansions, No 85 and No 86, which were once part of the buildings of the Catholic University of Ireland and named after Cardinal Newman, the first rector of the university. They are now owned by University College Dublin. No 86 was built in 1765 for Richard Whaley MP with marvellous stucco by Robert West, the house has also been owned by the celebrated gambler Buck Whaley. The smaller house, No 85, was designed by Richard Castle in 1739 with beautiful plasterwork by the Swiss La Franchini brothers and includes the Apollo Room with a figure of the god above the mantle. Gerald Manley Hopkins was Professor of Classics here at the end of the 19thC and his study is on view. Also open to the public is a classroom furnished as it would have been when James Joyce was a

pupil here from 1899–1902. A guided tour explains the history and heritage of the house and how it was restored.

Open (Jun, Jul, Aug) Tues–Fri 12.00–17.00.

Tel: 01 716 7422

Number 29, Lower Fitzwilliam Street.

This elegant four-storey house has been restored and furnished exactly as it would have been between 1790–1820 by any well-to-do middle class family. Everything in the house is authentic with period items from the National Museum. The wallpaper was hand-made for Number 29 using 18thC methods. Among the rooms in the house are a kitchen, pantry, governess' room, nursery and boudoir.

Open Tues–Sat 10.00–17.00, Sun 14.00–17.00. Closed for about 2 weeks preceding Christmas.

Tel: 01 702 6165

Old Jameson Distillery, Bow Street, Smithfield Village.

The art of Irish Whiskey making shown through an audio-visual presentation, working model of the distilling process, and guided tour of the old distillery which was in use between 1780–1971.

Open daily 09.00–17.30 (tours only). Disabled access.

Tel: 01 807 2355

Pearse Museum, St. Enda's Park, Grange Road, Rathfarnham.

Housed in the former school run by nationalist Patrick Pearse from 1910–1916, it includes an audio-visual presentation and a nature study room with displays on Irish flora and fauna. Pearse was executed in 1916 for his part in the Easter Rising.

Open (Feb-Apr) 10.00-17.00; (May-Aug) 10.00-17.30; (Sept-Oct) 10.00-17.00; (Nov-Jan) 10.00-16.00; closed 13.00-14.00. Admission is free. Disabled access to ground floor/toilet.

Tel: 01 493 4208

Powerscourt Centre, South William Street.

A lively three storey centre of craft shops, galleries, boutiques and cafés, converted from Powerscourt Townhouse, a classical style mansion designed by Robert Mack and built between 1771–74. It features the original grand wooden staircase and finely detailed plasterwork.

Web: www.powerscourtcentre.com

Powerscourt House & Gardens, County Wicklow.

First laid out in the 1740s, the 18 hectare (45 acre) gardens, perhaps the finest in Ireland, include sweeping terraces cut into a steep hillside, statues and ornamental lakes.

spectacular Italian style stairway leading down to the main lake was added in 1874. Secluded Japanese gardens with bamboo and walled gardens are also notable and there is a huge variety of trees and shrubs. The house suffered a serious fire in 1974 and is no longer lived in. Visitors may walk through the old ballroom, and an exhibition area illustrates the history of the construction of the house and there are models of some of the rooms as they would have been before the fire. The house dates back to the 18thC when in 1731 architect Richard Castle was commissioned by Richard Wingfield to transform the medieval Powerscourt Castle into a grand Palladian style mansion; the castle walls were used to form the main structure and the central courtyard was converted into an entrance hall. Powerscourt is in the foothills of the Wicklow mountains, 19km (12 miles) south of Dublin.
Open daily 09.30–17.30.
Tel: 01 204 6000
Web: www.powerscourt.ie

Phoenix Park Visitor Centre, Phoenix Park.
The visitor centre illustrates the history and wildlife of the park with an audio-visual display, a variety of fascinating exhibits and temporary exhibitions. Adjoining the centre is a restored medieval tower house, Ashtown Castle. On Saturdays there are free guided tours to the Irish President's House which is situated in the Park.
Open: (Jun–Sept) 10.00-18.00; (Apr–May) 09.30-17.30; (Nov–Mar) Sat & Sun only 09.30-16.30. Last admission 45 minutes before closing. Toilet for people with disabilities.
Tel: 01 677 0095

Rathfarnham Castle, Rathfarnham.
Dating from around 1583, this castle has 18thC interiors by Sir William Chambers and James Stuart and is presented to visitors as a castle undergoing conservation. There is a toilet for people with disabilities but restricted access to the castle.
Open daily from May–Oct 09.30–17.00 (last tour 16.30).
Tel: 01 493 9462

Royal Hospital, Military Road, Kilmainham.
The Royal Hospital was built as a home for army pensioners and invalids by Charles I, and continued in use for almost 250 years. Designed by Sir William Robinson in 1684, it has a formal facade and large courtyard and bears similarities to Les Invalides in Paris and The Royal Hospital in Chelsea. The restored building has one of Dublin's finest interiors and houses

the Irish Museum of Modern Art in which there is an audio-visual presentation "The Story of the Royal Hospital Kilmainham". The grounds, including a formal garden, are open to the public.
Tel: 01 612 9900

Shaw Birthplace, Synge Street.
This delightful Victorian terrace home was the birthplace of one of Ireland's four Nobel prize-winners for literature, George Bernard Shaw. Restored to give the feeling that the Shaw family is still in residence, the home provides an insight into the domestic life of Victorian Dubliners.
Open (May–Sept) Mon–Fri 10.00–17.00, Sat & Sun 14.00–17.00. Closed 13.00–14.00.
Tel: 01 872 2077
Email: shawhouse@dublintourism.ie

Tara's Palace – Dolls House, Malahide.
The centrepiece of this museum is the one-twelfth size scale model house reflecting the splendour of 18thC Irish mansions. Conceived by Ronald and Doreen McDonnell in 1980, it was ten years in the making. Irish craftsmen paid meticulous attention to detail, with unique miniature furniture and paintings adorning the walls. The museum also has rare pieces of porcelain, miniature glass and silver. Dolls houses of the 18thC and 19thC are displayed, together with dolls and antique toys.
Open (Apr–Sept) Mon–Sat 10.00–17.00, Sun and bank holidays 14.00–18.00; (Oct–Mar) Sat, Sun and bank holidays 14.00–17.00. Closed all year 13.00–14.00.
Tel: 01 846 3779

Temple Bar
Named after a 17thC landowner, Sir William Temple, this charming neighbourhood is Dublin's cultural quarter. With its narrow cobbled streets running close to the Liffey, Temple Bar is full of character and home to many artists and musicians. The area has been regenerated in recent years and boasts a wide variety of cultural venues and events and an eclectic mix of studios, galleries, shops, markets and eating-places. Modern architecture now blends with the historic. Many free open-air events take place in summer at Meeting House Square and Temple Bar Square, including circus acts, concerts and the outdoor screening of films. Temple Bar is bounded by the south quays of the Liffey, Dame Street, Westmoreland Street and Fishamble Street.
Temple Bar Information Centre, 12 Essex Street East.
Tel: 01 677 2255
Web: www.temple–bar.ie
Email: info@templebar.ie

The Chimney, Smithfield Village.
Originally built in 1895, this 53 metre (175ft) chimney which belonged to the Jameson Whiskey Distillery now provides a 360 degree panoramic viewpoint over the city. A glass walled lift takes visitors up the side of the chimney to two viewing galleries at the top.
Open daily 10.00–17.30.
Tel: 01 817 3800

Trinity College, College Green.
The original Elizabethan college was founded in 1592 but the present building was largely built between 1755–1759. The cruciform complex surrounding cobbled quadrangles and peaceful gardens has an impressive 91 metre (300ft) Palladian facade designed by Henry Keene and John Sanderford. One of the most notable features within the main college square is the 30 metre (98ft) Campanile or bell tower built in 1853 by Sir Charles Lanyon. The oldest surviving part of the college is the red brick apartment building from 1700 known as The Rubrics. Originally a Protestant College, Catholics did not start entering Trinity until the 1970s. The Library has over a million books and a magnificent collection of early illuminated manuscripts, including the famous Book of Kells; areas open to the public include the Colonnades, the Treasury, and the Long Room Library. Edmund Burke, Oliver Goldsmith and Samuel Beckett are among famous former Trinity College students.
Web: www.tcd.ie

Waterways Visitor Centre, Grand Canal Quay.
A modern centre built on piers over the Grand Canal, housing an exhibition about Ireland's inland waterways. Working models of various engineering features are displayed and there is an interactive multimedia presentation.
Open (Jun–Sept) daily 09.30–17.00; (Oct–May) Wed–Sun 12.30–17.00. Last admission 45 minutes before closing. Access to ground floor for people with disabilities.
Tel: 01 677 7510

Cathedrals and churches

Augustinian Church, Thomas Street.
Designed by E W Pugin and G C Ashlin in 1862, it has a mountainous exterior with lofty side aisles to the nave and a 49 metre (160ft) high tower crowned by a spire.

Christ Church Cathedral, Christchurch Place.
The Cathedral was established by Strongbow and Archbishop Laurence O'Toole in 1173 on the site of the cathedral founded around 1030 by the Norse King Sitric Silkenbeard. Lambert Simnel, pretender to the English throne, was crowned here as Edward VI in 1487. It was extensively restored between 1871–78 by George Edmund Street and is one of the best examples in Ireland of early Gothic architecture. The medieval crypt is one of the oldest and largest in Ireland.
Open Mon-Fri 09.45-17.00, Sat & Sun 10.00-17.00.
Tel: 01 677 8099
Web: www.cccdub.ie
Email: welcome@cccdub.ie

Franciscan Church, (Adam and Eve's) Merchants Quay.
Designed by Patrick Byrne in 1830.

St. Ann's Church, Dawson Street.
Designed by Isaac Wells in 1720 with a Romanesque-style facade added by Sir Thomas Deane in 1868. Much of the colourful stained glass dates back to the mid 19thC. Wooden shelves behind the altar were once used to take bread for distribution to the poor. Music recitals are held in the church.
Tel: 01 676 7727

St. Audoen's Church, High Street.
Dublin's only surviving medieval parish church with a 12thC font and portal. The bell tower, restored in the 19thC, has three 15thC bells. The guild chapel has an exhibition on the importance of the church in the life of the medieval city. Dublin's only surviving city gate known as St. Audoen's Arch, stands nearby.
Open Jun–Sept 09.30 (10.15 on Sun)–16.45. Toilet for people with disabilities and church partly accessible.
Tel: 01 677 0088

St. Audoen's RC Church, High Street.
Designed by Patrick Byrne in 1841–47, it has a monumental, cliff-like exterior with a huge Corinthian portico added by Stephen Ashlin in 1898.

St. George's, Temple Street.
This neo-classical church was designed by Francis Johnston in 1802 and has a 61 metre (200ft) high steeple modelled on St. Martin-in-the-Fields, London.

St. Mary's Church, Mary Street.
A handsome galleried church designed by Thomas Burgh in 1627. Wolfe Tone, leader of the United Irishmen, was baptised here in 1763 and Sean O'Casey in 1880.

St. Mary's Abbey, Meetinghouse Lane.
Established originally as a Benedictine foundation in 1139, it became Cistercian eight years later. Until the 16thC it was one of the largest and most important monasteries in

Ireland. The remains include a fine vaulted Chapter House of 1190 and there is an interesting exhibition about the history of the abbey.
Open mid June–mid Sept, Wed and Sun 10.00–17.00. Last admission 45 minutes before closing.
Tel: 01 872 1490

St. Mary's Pro-Cathedral, Marlborough Street.
A Greek Doric style building with the interior modelled on the Church of St. Philippe de Roule in Paris, designed by John Sweetman and built between 1815–1825. St. Mary's is Dublin's most important Catholic Church and is used on State occasions. Tenor John McCormack was once a member of the Palestrina choir that sings a Latin mass every Sunday at 11.00.
Open Mon-Fri 07.30-18.45, Sat 07.30-19.15, Sun 09.00-13.45 and 17.30-19.45.
Tel: 01 874 5441
Web: www.procathedral.ie

St. Michan's Church, Church Street.
Founded in 1095 as a Viking parish church, largely rebuilt in 1685 and restored in 1828. Famous for the 17thC mummified bodies in the crypt which are preserved with skin and hair because of the dry atmosphere created by the limestone walls. Handel is thought to have played on the organ which dates from 1724.
Open (March/April–Oct) Mon–Fri 10.00–12.45 and 14.00-16.45; (Nov–March) Mon–Fri 12.30–15.30; all Saturdays 10.00–12.45. Vaults closed on Sundays.
Tel: 01 872 4154

St. Patrick's Cathedral, St. Patrick's Close.
The National Cathedral of the Church of Ireland, it was built in the late 12thC on the site of the pre-Norman parish church of St. Patrick. It gained and lost cathedral status more than once in its chequered history and Cromwellian soldiers stabled horses here in the Civil War. Architect John Semple added a spire in 1749 and St. Patrick's was fully restored in the 19thC with finance from the Guinness family. The massive west tower houses the largest ringing peel of bells in Ireland. The cathedral is full of memorial brasses, busts and monuments to famous Irishmen. Jonathan Swift was Dean here from 1713–1745; there are memorials to Swift and his beloved Stella (Esther Johnson) and Swift's pulpit contains his writing table and chair, and portrait.
Usually open daily 09.00–17.00. Wheelchair access by arrangement.
Tel: 01 453 9472
Web: www.stpatrickscathedral.ie
Email: admin@stpatrickscathedral.ie

St. Saviour's, Dominick Street.
Designed by J J McCarthy in 1858, this extravagant French style Gothic edifice has a bold west door under a triangular hood, crowned by a large rose window.

St. Stephen's (Pepper Canister), Mount Street Crescent.
This handsome neo-classical church, designed by John Bowden in 1824, has a Greek style portico.

St. Werburgh's Church, Werburgh Street.
Originally the site of an Anglo-Norman foundation, the present church was built in 1715–19 and rebuilt in 1759 following a fire. St. Werburgh's was the Chapel Royal until 1790. Lord Edward Fitzgerald, one of the leaders of the 1798 rebellion, is buried in the vaults.

Whitefriar Street Carmelite Church, Aungier Street.
19thC church standing on the site of a 16thC Carmelite Priory. The remains of Saint Valentine are buried here and there is a 15thC oak statue of the Virgin and Child, thought to be the only surviving Pre-reformation statue of its kind.
Tel: 01 475 8821

Libraries

Central Catholic Library, Merrion Square.
Of religious and general interest, with a large Irish section.
Open Mon–Fri 11.00–18.00, Sat 11.00–17.30.
Tel: 01 676 1264
Web: www.catholiclibrary.ie

Central Library, Ilac Centre.
Tel: 01 873 4333.
Enquiries about other Dublin City Public Libraries (lending, reference and special collections).
Tel: 01 674 4800
Web: www.iol.ie/dublincitylibrary
Email: dublinpubliclibraries@dublincity.ie

Chester Beatty Library, Dublin Castle, Dame Street.
Reopened in 2000 in a purpose designed home in the Clock Tower building of Dublin Castle, the library is a treasure of manuscripts, books, prints and textiles collected by American scholar Sir Alfred Chester Beatty. It has some of the rarest original manuscripts still in existence. The collection reflects the art of manuscript production and printing from many parts of the world and from early to modern times with picture scrolls, jade books and woodblock prints from the Far East, around 4,000 Islamic manuscripts, and fine books, bindings and

manuscripts from Western Europe. With many Early Christian papyri, the library is a major resource for the study of the Old and New Testaments.
Open Mon-Fri 10.00–17.00, Sat 11.00–17.00, Sun 13.00–17.00. Oct-Apr closed Mondays. Admission is free.
Tel: 01 407 0750
Web: www.cbl.ie
Email: info@cbl.ie

Genealogical Office, Kildare Street.
Part of the National Library, the genealogical office offers a service to assist in the task of tracing family history, familiarising people with the relevant records and procedures.
Open Mon–Fri 10.00–17.00, Sat 10.00–12.30.
Tel: 01 603 0200

Gilbert Library, Pearse Street.
Books and manuscripts relating to Dublin which were accumulated by 19thC Dublin historian Sir John T Gilbert and now in the care of Dublin Corporation. The collection includes rare early Dublin newspapers, 18thC bindings, Irish Almanacs, manuscripts of the municipal records of the City of Dublin and the records of the Dublin guilds.
Tel: 01 674 4800

Goethe Institute Library, Merrion Square.
German cultural information centre and library.
Open Tues-Thurs 12.00–20.00, Fri 10.00-14.30, Sat 10.00-13.30.
Tel: 01 661 1155

Irish Architectural Archive, Merrion Square.
Open Tues–Fri 10.00-17.00.
Tel: 01 663 3040

Marsh's Library, St Patrick's Close.
Given to the city by Archbishop Narcissus Marsh and opened in 1701, this is Ireland's oldest public library containing many rare books still in their original carved bookcases. The building was designed by Sir William Robinson who was also the architect of the Royal Hospital, Kilmainham. To prevent the theft of rare books readers were locked in wire cages and three of these cages survive.
Open Mon-Fri 10.00-17.00 (closed 13.00-14.00); Sat 10.30-13.00; closed Tuesdays.
Tel: 01 454 3511
Web: www.marshlibrary.ie
Email: keeper@marshlibrary.ie

National Library of Ireland, Kildare Street.
Offers over half a million books, a vast collection of maps, prints and manuscripts and an invaluable collection of Irish newspapers and periodicals. The impressive Victorian building has been home to the Library since 1890, and there is a large domed reading room. Holds temporary exhibitions on Irish writers and books.
Open: Mon–Wed 10.00–21.00, Thurs–Fri 10.00–17.00, Sat 10.00–13.00.
Tel: 01 603 0200
Web: www.nli.ie
Email: info@nli.ie

National Photographic Archive,
Meeting House Square.
Only established in 1998, it has over 600,000 photographs recording people, political events, and scenes of Irish cities, towns and countryside. Images from the collection are always on view. There is also a reading room and darkrooms.
Open: Mon–Fri 10.00–17.00. Sat 10.00-14.00 (exhibition only) Admission is free. Disabled access/toilet.
Tel: 01 603 0374
Web: www.nli.ie/fr_arch.htm
Email: photoarchive@nli.ie

Royal Irish Academy Library, Dawson Street.
One of the largest collections of ancient Irish manuscripts in the country with one usually on display together with a small exhibition. Access may be restricted depending on Royal Academy meetings and large groups need to make a prior arrangement to visit.
Open Mon–Fri 10.00–17.00. Admission is free.
Tel: 01 676 2570

Trinity College Library, College Green.
The oldest and most famous of Dublin's libraries dating from the late 16thC. Entitled to receive a copy of every book published in Ireland, the library also contains an extensive collection of Irish manuscripts including the Book of Kells, a beautifully illuminated copy of the gospels written on vellum in Latin around the year AD800. The Book of Kells is now bound in four volumes and two are always on display in the Treasury, one open at a major ornamental page and the other to show two pages of script. An exhibition explains how the Book of Kells and other manuscripts such as the Book of Durrow (AD675) and Book of Armagh (AD807) were created and illustrates monastic life in the 8thC. The impressive Old Library or Long Room Library is lined with marble busts of scholars and is nearly 64 metres (210ft) long. It rises two storeys with a high barrel vaulted ceiling and contains over 200,000 of the college's books.

Open Mon–Sat 09.30–17.00; Sun 09.30–16.30 (Jun–Sept), Sun 12.00–16.30 (May–Oct). Last admission 30 minutes before closing.
Tel: 01 608 2308
Web:www.tcd.ie

Arts centres, galleries, and concert halls

Douglas Hyde Gallery, Trinity College.
Showing mainly temporary exhibitions of contemporary art.
Tel: 01 608 1116
Web: www.douglashydegallery.com
Email: dhgallery@tcd.ie

Gallery of Photography, Meeting House Square.
Exhibitions of contemporary photography. Roof terrace has views over the square.
Tel: 01 671 4654
Web: www.irish-photography.com
Email: gallery@irish–photography.com

Hugh Lane Municipal Gallery of Modern Art, Parnell Square North.
19thC and 20thC paintings, mainly Impressionist works, bequeathed by Sir Hugh Lane who was drowned in the Lusitania in 1915, form the nucleus of this collection. The Lane Collection is split with the Tate Gallery in London; each half is alternated between the galleries every 5 years. There is an extensive range of Irish and international paintings, sculpture and stained glass and the acquisition of contemporary work is ongoing. Included is the London studio of Dublin-born artist Francis Bacon, which was carefully dismantled and reconstructed here. Regular 'Sundays at Noon' Concerts are held at the gallery (apart from July and August) with everything from early music to commissioned new works; the music is often arranged to complement one of the temporary exhibitions. The classical building which houses the gallery, Charlemont House, was designed by William Chambers in 1763 for James Caulfield, later 1st Earl Charlemont. It was reconstructed in 1929 to house the Lane Collection and opened in 1933.
Open Tues–Thurs 09.30–18.00, Fri & Sat 09.30–17.00, Sun 11.00–17.00. Admission free except for special exhibitions. Disabled access.
Tel: 01 874 1903
Web: www.hughlane.ie
Email: info@hughlane.ie

National Concert Hall, Earlsfort Terrace.
Home of the National Symphony Orchestra of Ireland, but also a venue for international artists and orchestras, jazz, contemporary and traditional Irish music. The classical building was designed for the Great Exhibition of 1865, then became the centrepiece of University College Dublin before opening as Ireland's National Concert Hall in 1981.
Booking office open Mon–Sat 10.00–19.00. Disabled access/toilet.
Tel: 01 417 0000
Web: www.nch.ie (online booking)
Email:info@nch.ie

National Gallery of Ireland, Merrion Square.
Paintings by illustrious 20thC European artists such as Morrisot, Bonnard, Picasso and Monet hang in the National Gallery as well as the work of Old Masters including Titian, Caravaggio, Rembrandt and Vermeer. There is the National Collection of Irish art, a room dedicated to the work of Jack B Yeats, English paintings, and over 250 sculptures. William Dargan organised the 1853 Dublin Exhibition on this site and used the proceeds to found the collection; his statue stands on the lawn.
Open Mon–Sat 09.30–17.30, Thurs 09.30-20.30, Sun 12.00–17.30. Admission free. Disabled access/toilet.
Tel: 01 661 5133
Web: www.nationalgallery.ie
Email: info@ngi.ie

Royal Dublin Society, Ballsbridge.
Venue for large events including craft and antiques fairs and Ideal Homes exhibitions.
Tel: 01 668 0866
Web: www.rds.ie

Royal Hibernian Academy Gallagher Gallery, Ely Place.
Showing both traditional and innovative work from both Irish and international artists.
Tel: 01 661 2558
Web: www.royalhibernianacademy.com
Email: www.rhagallery@eircom.net

Solomon Gallery, Powerscourt Centre.
One of Ireland's leading contemporary art galleries, situated in an 18thC Georgian townhouse.
Open Mon–Sat 10.00–17.30. Admission free.
Tel: 01 679 4237
Web: www.solomongallery.com
Email: info@solomongallery.com

Temple Bar Gallery and Studios, Temple Bar.
A large complex with studios and exhibition spaces.
Tel: 01 671 0073
Web: www.templebargallery.com
Email: info@templebargallery.com

Temple Bar Music Centre, Curved Street.
Live music venue with recording and rehearsal studios.
Tel: 01 677 0647
Web: www.tbmc.ie
Email: info@tbmc.ie

Taylor Galleries, Kildare Street.
Contemporary art gallery, mainly Irish, with the emphasis on painting and sculpture.
Tel: 01 676 6055

The Ark, Eustace Street.
A cultural centre for children with a child-size theatre.
Tel: 01 670 7788
Web: www.ark.ie
Email: boxoffice@ark.ie

Parks and gardens

Garden of Remembrance, Parnell Square East.
The Garden of Remembrance, opened in 1966, is dedicated to all those who died in the cause of Irish Freedom. There is a sculpture by Oisín Kelly representing the Irish legend, "Children of Lir".
Open (Oct-Mar) 09.30-1600, (Apr-Sept) 08.30-18.00.
Tel: 01 874 3074 (garden) or 01 647 2498 (head office)

Iveagh Gardens, Clonmel Street.
Designed by Ninian Niven in 1863, this is one of the least known and most tranquil of Dublin's parks. Features include a rustic grotto, cascade, fountains, maze, archery grounds, wilderness and woodlands.
Opening according to daylight hours.
Tel: 01 475 7816

Marlay Park, Rathfarnham.
This large park situated at the foot of the Dublin Mountains contains areas of woodland, a large pond, nature trail and model railway.

National Botanic Gardens, Glasnevin.
Established in 1795, these magnificent gardens occupy an area of 20 hectares (49 acres) and contain a fabulous collection of plants, shrubs and trees. Many of the plants come from tropical Africa and South America and are housed in large Victorian glasshouses. Features include a rose garden, rockery and wall plants, herbaceous borders, vegetable garden and arboretum.
Open Summer Mon-Sat 09.00-18.00, Sun 10.00-18.00; Winter Mon-Sat 10.00-16.30, Sun 10.00-16.30. Shorter opening hours for glasshouses. Admission is free. Toilet for people with disabilities, and gardens largely accessible.
Tel: 01 857 0909

Phoenix Park
Phoenix Park, covering over 712 hectares (1,76 acres), is Europe's largest enclosed city park. It name is thought to derive from the Irish meaning "clear water" and a spring does rise in the park. Enclosed by an 11km (7 mile) long stone wall, the park was laid out in the mid 18thC and was the scene of the Phoenix Park murders in 1882, when the Chief Secretary and the Under-Secretary for Ireland were assassinated. A more recent event was when the Pope celebrated mass in the park in front of 1 million people; a 27 metre (90ft) steel cross marks the spot. The park includes a number of buildings, the most important of which is Áras an Uachtaráin; the Viceroy's Lodge built in 1751 but later becoming the official house of the President of Ireland when Dr Douglas Hyde moved there in 1938. Other important buildings are the American ambassador's residence and the Ordnance Survey Office. A 60 metre (205 ft) high obelisk, erected in 1817, is a memorial to the Dublin-born Duke of Wellington. The People's Garden by the main entrance on Parkgate Street is laid out with ornamental planting in ribbon borders, much as it would have been in Victorian times. Dublin Zoo is in the south-east corner. The open space covered by playing fields and paths, known as Fifteen Acres but actually covering more than 200, was used in the 18thC as a duelling ground. Phoenix Park is open to the public at all times but the People's Gardens usually close at sunset.

St. Anne's Park, Dollymount.
Once part of the Guinness family estate, the park covers over 110 hectares (270 acres) and is wooded with oak, pine, beech, chestnut and lime. There is a lovely rose garden, opened in 1975.

St. Enda's Park, Grange Road, Rathfarnham.
The park surrounds the Pearse Museum and includes a walled garden, riverside walks and waterfall. Open daily from 10.00, closing time varies according to daylight hours. Limited access for people with disabilities.

St. Stephen's Green
In the heart of the city, St Stephen's Green was originally an open common but was enclosed in 1663. Opened to the general public in 1877, it is laid out as a public park with flowerbeds, an ornamental pond and several sculptures. There is a garden for the visually impaired and there are summer lunchtime concerts.
Open daily 08.00 (Sun & bank Holidays 10.00); closes according to daylight hours.
Tel: 01 475 7816

War Memorial Garden, South Circular Road, Islandbridge.
Dedicated to the memory of the Irish soldiers who died in the First World War, these gardens include a sunken rose garden and herbaceous borders. They were designed by Sir Edward Lutyens. The names of the 49,400 soldiers who died between 1914–1918 are contained in the granite bookrooms in the gardens, access to which is only by arrangement with the management.
Open Mon–Fri 08.00, Sat & Sun 10.00; closes according to daylight hours.
Tel: 01 677 0236 (gardens)
Tel: 01 647 2498 (head office)

Theatres

Abbey Theatre, Lower Abbey Street.
Ireland's National Theatre, founded by Lady Gregory and W B Yeats in 1904. The Abbey quickly became world renowned, staging plays by J M Synge and Sean O'Casey, and played a significant role in the renaissance of Irish culture. It also provoked controversy in Dublin and even riots. The present theatre was built in 1966 to replace the previous building which had been destroyed by fire. The Abbey stages classic Irish plays, while the Peacock theatre downstairs presents new and experimental drama.
Tel: 01 878 7222
Web: www.abbeytheatre.ie
Andrews Lane Theatre and Studio, Andrews Lane.
A wide variety of works shown both in the theatre and studio.
Tel: 01 679 5720
Web: www.andrewslane.com
Civic Theatre, Tallaght.
New theatre staging everything from drama to variety shows
Tel: 01 462 7477
Web: www.civictheatre.ie
Focus Theatre, Pembroke Place, Pembroke Street.
Small theatre presenting the classics and new writing.
Tel: 01 676 3071
Gaiety Theatre, South King Street.
Restored Victorian building and Dublin's oldest theatre, founded in 1837. Drama, opera (Opera Ireland have two seasons a year), ballet, musicals, pantomime, comedy.
Tel: 01 677 1717
Web: www.gaietytheatre.net

Gate Theatre, Cavendish Row.
Modern Irish and classical drama, also international plays. Founded in 1928.
Tel: 01 874 4045
Web: www.gate-theatre.ie
Lambert Puppet Theatre, Clifton Lane, Monkstown.
Tel: 01 280 0974
Web: www.lambertpuppettheatre.com
Olympia Theatre, Dame Street.
Comedy, drama, pantomime, musicals, concerts.
Tel: 0818 719330
Peacock Theatre, Lower Abbey Street.
New and experimental work.
Tel: 01 878 7222
Project Arts Centre, 39 East Essex Street.
Moved in 2000 into new custom designed building with performance and gallery space; generally innovative new work and everything from drama and visual arts to talks and events.
Tel: 01 881 9613
Web: www.project.ie
Email: info@project.ie
Samuel Beckett Theatre, Trinity College.
Trinity College School of Drama theatre with a variety of student productions during term and touring companies at other times. Venue for Festival Fringe events.
Tel: 01 608 2461
The Point, North Wall Quay.
Theatre and concert venue including ballet.
Tel: 01 836 3633
Sugar Club, Lower Leeson Street.
Multimedia theatre with wide range of entertainment; drama, film, cabaret, comedy, music, events.
Tel: 01 678 7188
Web: www.thesugarclub.com

The Dublin Theatre Festival, held at many venues throughout the city, runs for two weeks every October.
Tel: 01 677 8439, Box office 01 677 8899
Web: www.dublintheatrefestival.com
The Fringe Festival which presents theatre, dance and the visual arts is held for three weeks, commencing in September.
Tel: 01 872 9433
Web: www.fringefest.com

Cinemas

Most cinemas offer cheaper seats before 5pm.
IMC, Dún Laoghaire,
Tel: 01 280 7777. 12 screens.

Irish Film Institute, Eustace Street,
Art house with 2 screens and restaurant converted from old Quaker meeting house. New Irish films and film seasons. The Irish Film Archive, library and special events.
Tel: 01 679 3477.
Web: www.irishfilm.ie
Email: info@irishfilm.ie

Omniplex, Santry, **Tel: 01 842 8844.** 11 screens.

Ormonde Cinema, Stillorgan,
Tel: 01 278 0000. 7 screens.

Savoy Cinema, O'Connell Street Upper,
Tel: 01 874 6000. 6 screens.

Screen Cinema, D'Olier Street,
Tel: 01 672 5500. 3 screens.

Ster Century, Liffey Valley Shopping Centre, Fonthill Road
Tel: 01 605 5700. 14 screens.

UCI Cinema, Blanchardstown,
Tel: 01 8222 624. 9 screens.

UCI Cinema, Coolock,
Tel: 01 848 5122. 10 screens.

UCI Cinema, Tallaght,
Tel: 01 459 8400. 12 screens.

UGC Cinemas, Parnell Street,
Tel: 01 872 8444. 17 screens.
The largest cinema in Ireland.

Shopping

Opening hours are generally 09.00–18.00 Mon–Sat. Many city centre shops and shopping centres remain open until 20.00 or 21.00 on Thursdays and Fridays and open 12.00–18.00 on Sundays.
The main city centre shopping areas are around Grafton Street and Nassau Street to the south of the Liffey and around Henry Street (off O'Connell Street) to the north of the river. Both Grafton Street and Henry Street are pedestrianised. Many up-market and international designer stores can be found in Grafton Street, while shops around Henry Street are generally less expensive. The Temple Bar area has a number of craft and specialist shops.

Department stores

Arnotts, Henry Street, **Tel: 01 872 1111.**

Brown Thomas, Grafton Street,
Tel: 01 605 6666.

Clery and Co, O'Connell Street Lower,
Tel: 01 878 6000.

Debenhams, Jervis Centre, **Tel: 01 878 1222.**

Dunnes Stores, Henry Street, **Tel: 01 671 4629.**

Guiney & Co, Talbot Street, **Tel: 01 878 8835.**

Marks & Spencers, Grafton Street,
Tel: 01 679 7855.

Penneys Stores, Mary Street, **Tel: 01 872 7788.**

Roches Stores, Henry Street, **Tel:01 873 0044.**

Shopping centres

Dún Laoghaire Shopping Centre, Marine Road,
Tel: 01 280 2981.

Ilac Centre, Henry Street, **Tel: 01 704 1460.**

Irish Life Shopping Mall, Abbey Street,
Tel: 01 704 1452.

Jervis Shopping Centre, Jervis Street,
Tel: 01 878 1323.

Powerscourt Centre, South William Street,
Tel: 01 679 4144.

St. Stephen's Green Centre, Tel: 01 478 0888.
There are also shopping centres at Clondalkin (Liffey Valley), Blanchardstown, and Tallaght on the outskirts of Dublin.

Markets

Blackrock, Sat, Sun & bank holidays 11.00–17.30 (bric-a-brac, china and antiques).
Tel: 01 283 3522

George's Street Market Arcade (second hand clothes, jewellery, records).
Tel: 01 280 8683

Liberty Market (clothes, fabrics, household goods), Meath Street.
Tel: 01 280 8683

Moore Street Market, Mon–Sat (flower, fruit and vegetables), off Henry Street.

St. Michan's Street Vegetable Market (fruit, vegetables, fish and flowers).

Temple Bar Square. Food market is open every Saturday from 09.30–18.00 selling organic fruit and vegetables, bread, cheeses, oysters, and smoked fish. Book Market is open on Saturdays from 09.30.
Tel: 01 677 2255

Sport and leisure

International sports venues:
Athletics – Croke Park.
Tel: 01 836 3222

Gaelic Football and Hurling – Croke Park.
Tel 01 836 3222

Rugby and Soccer – Lansdowne Road, Ballsbridge.
Tel: 01 668 4601

Golf (18-hole golf clubs):
Balcarrick Golf Club, Donabate, 16km (10m) north of city centre.
Tel: 01 843 6957

Ballinascorney, 13km (8m) south west of city centre.
Tel: 01 451 6430

Beaverstown Golf Club, Donabate, 16km (10m) north of city centre.
Tel: 01 843 6439

Blanchardstown Golf Centre, Mulhuddart, 13km (8m) north west of city centre.
Tel: 01 821 2054

Castle Golf Club, Rathfarnham, 6km (4m) south of city centre.
Tel: 01 490 4207

Citywest Golf Resort, Saggart, 16km (10m) south west of city centre.
Tel: 01 401 0500

Corballis Golf Links, Donabate,16km (10m) north of city centre.
Tel: 01 843 6583
Web: www.golfdublin.com
Email: corballislinks@golfdublin.com

Deerpark Hotel and Golf Courses, Howth, 14km (9 m) north east of city centre.
Tel: 01 832 2624
Web: www.deerpark–hotel.ie
Email: sales@deerpark.iol.ie

Druids Glen, Newmountkennedy, 32km (2m) south east of city centre.
Tel: 01 287 3600
Web: www.druidsglen.ie
Email: info@druidsglen.ie

Edmondstown, Rathfarnham, 11km (7m) south of city centre.
Tel: 01 493 1082
Email: info@edmondstowngolfclub.ie

Elmgreen Golf Centre, Castleknock, 8km (5m) north west of city centre.
Tel: 01 820 0797
Web: www.golfdublin.com
Email: elmgreen@golfdublin.com

Elm Park, Donnybrook, 5km(3m) south of city centre.
Tel: 01 269 3438
Email: office@elmparkgolfclub.ie

Forrest Little Golf Club, Cloghean, 9km (6m) north of city centre, near to airport.
Tel: 01 840 1183

Grange Castle, Clondalkin, 8km (5m) south west of city centre.
Tel: 01 464 1043
Web: www.grange-castle.com

Grange Golf Club, Rathfarnham, 6km (4m) south of city centre.
Tel: 01 493 2889

Hermitage Golf Club, Lucan, 11km (7m) west of city centre.
Tel: 01 626 8491

Howth Golf Club, Sutton, 14km (9m) north east of city centre.
Tel: 01 832 3055
Web: www.howthgolfclub.ie
Email: manager@howthgolfclub.ie

Island, Corballis, Donabate, 14km (9m) north of city centre.
Tel: 01 843 6462
Web: www.theislandgolfclub.com
Email: info@theislandgolfclub.com

Luttrellstown Castle, Castleknock, 10 km (6 m) west of city centre.
Tel: 01 808 9988
Email: golf@luttrellstown.ie

Malahide Golf Club, 13km (8m) north of city centre. Tel: 01 846 1611
Web: www.malahidegolfclub.ie
Email: malgc@clubi.ie

Portmarnock Golf Club, 11km (7m) north east of city centre.
Tel: 01 846 2968
Web: www.portmarnockgolfclub.ie
Email: emer@portmarnockgolfclub.ie

Portmarnock Hotel and Golf Links, 11km (7m) north east of city centre.
Tel: 01 846 1800
Email: golfres@portmarnock.com

Royal Dublin Golf Club, Dollymount, 5km (3m) north east of city centre.
Tel: 01 833 6346
Web: www.theroyaldublingolfclub.com
Email: info@theroyaldublingolfclub.com

St. Anne's Golf Club, Dollymount, 5km (3m) north east of city centre.
Tel: 01 833 6471
Web: www.stanneslinksgolf.com
Email: info@stanneslinksgolf.com

St. Margaret's Golf Club, 11km (7m) north of city centre.
Tel: 01 864 0400
Web: www.stmargaretsgolf.com
Email: info@stmargaretsgolf.com

Swords Open Golf Course, 13km (8m) north of city centre.
Tel: 01 840 9819/890 1030

Greyhound racing
Greyhound racing is one of Ireland's leading spectator sports. Meetings are held at:

Shelbourne Park Stadium, Ringsend, (Wed, Thurs, Sat at 20.00).
Tel: 01 668 3502
Web: www.shelbournepark.com

Harold's Cross Stadium, (Mon, Tues & Fri at 20.00).
Tel: 01 497 1081

Horse racing

There are two racecourses on the outskirts of Dublin:

Leopardstown.
10km (6 miles) south of Dublin. National Hunt and Flat racing with 22 meetings including 4 day Christmas National Hunt Festival.
Tel: 01 289 3607
Web: www.leopardstown.com
Email: info@leopardstown.com

Fairyhouse.
19km (12 miles) north west of Dublin. Home of the Irish Grand National.
Tel: 01 825 6167
Web: www.fairyhouseracecourse.ie
Email: info@fairyhouseracecourse.ie

Sailing

The Irish Sailing Association, Dún Laoghaire, for information on sailing, windsurfing and powerboating in the Dublin area and elsewhere in Ireland.
Tel: 01 280 0239
Web: www.sailing.ie

Sports centres

Aughrim Street, Tel: 01 838 8085
Glin Road, Coolock, **Tel: 01 847 8177**

Swimming pools

Ballymun, Town Centre, **Tel: 01 842 1368**
Coolock, Northside Shopping Centre, **Tel: 01 847 7743**
Crumlin, Windmill Road, **Tel: 01 455 5792**
Finglas, Mellowes Road, **Tel: 01 864 2584**
Markievicz Pool, Townsend Street, **Tel: 01 672 9121**
Rathmines, Lower Rathmines Road, **Tel: 01 496 1275**
Sean, McDermott Street, **Tel: 01 872 0752**

Help and advice

Embassies

Apostolic Nunciature, Navan Road. Tel: 01 838 0577
Argentina, Ailesbury Drive. Tel: 01 269 1546
Australia, Fitzwilton House, Wilton Terrace. Tel: 01 676 1517
Austria, Ailesbury Road. Tel: 01 269 4577
Belgium, Shrewsbury Road. Tel: 01 269 2082
Brazil, Harcourt Street. Tel: 01 475 6000
Britain, Merrion Road. Tel: 01 205 3700
Bulgaria, Burlington Road. Tel: 01 660 3293
Canada, St. Stephen's Green. Tel: 01 478 1988
China, Ailesbury Road. Tel: 01 269 1707

Czech Republic, Northumberland Road. Tel: 01 668 1135
Denmark, St. Stephen's Green. Tel: 01 475 6404
Egypt, Clyde Road. Tel: 01 660 6566
Finland, St. Stephen's Green. Tel: 01 478 1344
France, Ailesbury Road. Tel: 01 260 1666
Germany, Trimleston Avenue. Tel: 01 269 3011
Greece, Pembroke Street Upper. Tel: 01 676 7254
Hungary, Fitzwilliam Place. Tel: 01 661 2902
India, Leeson Park. Tel: 01 497 0843
Iran, Mount Merrion Avenue. Tel: 01 288 0252
Israel, Pembroke Road. Tel: 01 668 0303
Italy, Northumberland Road. Tel: 01 660 1744
Japan, Merrion Centre. Tel: 01 202 8300
Korea, Clyde Road. Tel: 01 660 8800
Mexico, Ailesbury Road. Tel: 01 260 0699
Morocco, Raglan Road. Tel: 01 660 9449
Netherlands, Merrion Road. Tel: 01 269 3444
Nigeria, Leeson Park. Tel: 01 660 4366
Norway, Molesworth Street. Tel: 01 662 1800
Poland, Ailesbury Road. Tel: 01 283 0855
Portugal, Knocksinna Road. Tel: 01 289 4416
Romania, Ailesbury Road. Tel: 01 269 2852
Russian Federation, Orwell Road. Tel: 01 492 3492
Slovakia, Clyde Road. Tel: 01 660 0008
South Africa, Earlsfort Terrace. Tel: 01 661 5553
Spain, Merlyn Park. Tel: 01 269 1640
Sweden, Dawson Street. Tel: 01 671 5822
Switzerland, Ailesbury Road. Tel: 01 269 2515
Turkey, Clyde Road. Tel: 01 668 5240
USA, Elgin Road. Tel: 01 668 8777

Health centres and pharmacies

Grafton Street Centre, Open Mon, Tues & Thurs 08.30-18.15, Wed 09.30-18.15, Fri 08.30-17.45. **Tel: 01 671 2122**

Mercer's Medical Centre, Stephen Street Lower, Open: Mon–Thurs 09.00–17.30, Fri 09.00–16.30. **Tel: 01 402 2300**

O'Connell's Late Night Pharmacy, O'Connell Street Lower, Open daily Mon-Fri 07.30-22.00, Sat 08.00-22.00, Sun 10.00–22.00. **Tel: 01 873 0427**

Garda Síochána (Police)
City centre Garda stations:
Pearse Street station, Tel: 01 666 9000
Store Street station, Tel: 01 666 8000

Dublin Metropolitan Area Headquarters, Harcourt Square,
Tel: 01 666 6666

Greater Dublin Area Headquarters, Phoenix Park,
Tel: 01 666 0000

Dún Laoghaire station, Tel: 01 666 5000
Web: www.garda.ie

Post Offices
General Post Office, O'Connell Street. Open Mon–Sat 08.00-20.00.
Tel: 01 705 8833
Web: www.anpost.ie

Post offices are usually open Mon–Fri 09.00–17.30 (closed 13.00–14.15) and from 09.00–13.00 on Saturdays.

Welfare organisations
Citizens Information Centre (Comhairle), 13a O'Connell Street Upper.
Tel: 01 809 0633

Samaritans, 112 Marlborough Street.
Tel: 01 872 7700 or callsave 1850 609 090
Web: www.samaritans.org

Social Welfare Services, Store Street.
Tel: 01 874 8444

Tourist Victim Support Service, Garda Headquarters, Harcourt Square.
All referrals must go through the Garda.
Open: Mon–Sat 10.00–18.00, Sun 12.00–18.00.
Tel: 01 478 5295
Web: www.victimsupport.ie/tourist.html
Email: info@touristvictimsupport.ie

Hospitals

The Adelaide & Meath Hospital Incorporating the National Children's Hospital, Tallaght.
Tel 01 414 2000

Beaumont, Beaumont Road. **Tel: 01 809 3000**

Blackrock Clinic (private), Rock Road.
Tel: 01 283 2222

Bon Secours Private Hospital, Glasnevin.
Tel: 01 837 5111

Cappagh National Orthopaedic, Cappagh Road.
Tel: 01 834 1211

Dental Hospital, Lincoln Place, **Tel: 01 612 7200**

James Connolly Memorial Hospital, Blanchardstown.
Tel: 01 646 5000

Mater Misericordiae, Eccles Street.
Tel: 01 803 2000

Mater Private, Eccles Street. **Tel: 01 885 8888**

National Maternity, Holles Street.
Tel: 01 661 0277

Our Lady's Hospital for Sick Children, Crumlin.
Tel: 01 409 6100

Rotunda Hospital, Parnell Square.
Tel: 01 873 0700

Royal Victoria Eye and Ear, Adelaide Road.
Tel: 01 678 5500

St. James's, James's Street, **Tel: 01 410 3000**

St. Mary's Hospital, Phoenix Park.
Tel: 01 677 8132

St. Michael's, George's Street Lower, Dún Laoghaire. **Tel: 01 280 6901**

St. Patrick's, James's Street.
Tel: 01 249 3200

St.Vincent's (Private), Merrion Row.
Tel: 01 269 4533

Artane	46	B3	Cornelscourt	112	A3	Howth	52	B2	Raheny	48	A3
Ashtown	41	C3	Crumlin	83	D2	Inchicore	73	D2	Ranelagh	86	B1
Balgriffin	35	D1	Dalkey	114	B1	Irishtown	77	D3	Rathfarnham	95	C2
Balgriffin Park	36	A2	Darndale	35	C2	Islandbridge	74	A1	Rathgar	85	D3
Ballinteer	108	B2	Deans Grange	112	A2	Jobstown	102	B2	Rathmichael	120	A2
Ballsbridge	87	D1	Dollymount	65	D2	Kilbarrack	49	C2	Rathmines	86	A2
Ballyboden	106	B1	Dolphin's Barn	75	C3	Kildonan	42	A1	Ringsend	77	D2
Ballybrack	119	C2	Donaghmede	36	B2	Kildonan	42	A1	Ronanstown	70	A3
Ballyfermot	72	B2	Donnybrook	87	C2	Killester	46	B3	Rossmore	93	D2
Ballymacartle	18	B2	Drimnagh	83	D1	Killinardan	102	B3	Saintdoolaghs		
Ballymount	82	A2	Drumcondra	62	A1	Killincarrig	123	C3	(east)	36	A1
Ballymun	32	A3	Drumnigh	36	B1	Killiney	119	D1	St. Doolagh's		
Beaumont	45	C1	Dublin Airport	16	B2	Kill O' The Grange	112	B1	(west)	35	D1
Beechwood	20	A2	Dunboyne	22	A2	Kilmainham	74	A2	Sallynoggin	113	C2
Blackrock	99	D1	Dundrum	97	C3	Kilmore	33	D3	Sandyford	109	D3
Blanchardstown	39	D2	Dún Laoghaire			Kilnamanagh	91	D2	Sandymount	78	A3
Bluebell	82	B1	(Dunleary)	101	C3	Kimmage	84	B3	Santry	32	B3
Bohammer	19	C3	Dunleary			Kinsaley	19	C2	Shankill	121	C2
Booterstown	98	B1	(Dún Laoghaire)	101	C3	Kitaltown	102	A3	Shielmartin	54	B2
Bray	122	B1	Edmondstown	106	B3	Knocklyon	106	A1	Snugborough	36	B2
Burgage	35	C1	Feltrim	19	C1	Leixlip	67	C2	Stapolin	37	C2
Cabinteely	117	D1	Finglas	43	C2	Leopardstown	110	B3	Stillorgan	98	B3
Cabra	61	C2	Finglas East	42	B1	Loughlinstown	120	B1	Stockhole	17	D3
Carpenterstown	38	A3	Firhouse	105	C1	Lucan	68	A2	Stradbrook	100	A3
Carrickmines	117	C2	Foxrock	111	D3	Malahide	14	A1	Sutton	50	A1
Castleknock	57	D1	Galloping Green	111	C1	Malahide Demesne	13	D3	Swords	12	A1
Chapelizod	72	B1	Glasnevin	44	A3	Marino	63	C2	Tallaght	91	D3
Churchtown	96	A2	Glasnevin North	43	D1	Maynetown	37	C1	Templeogue	94	A2
Clarehall	35	D3	Glebe	18	A2	Merrion	88	A3	Terenure	95	C1
Cloghran	17	C1	Goatstown	97	C3	Milltown	86	B3	Wainsfort	94	A1
Cloghran (locality)	17	D2	Goldenbridge	73	D3	Monkstown	100	B3	Walkinstown	82	B2
Clondalkin	80	A2	Grange	20	A1	Mount Merrion	98	A2	Whitehall	44	B3
Clonee	23	D3	Greenhills	92	B1	Mulhuddart	26	B2	Willbrook	94	B3
Clonshaugh	34	B1	Greenwood	18	B2	Newtown	106	B3	Williamstown	99	D1
Clonskeagh	87	C3	Greystones	123	D1	Oldbawn	103	D2	Windmill Lands	10	A1
Clontarf	64	A2	Harold's Cross	85	C1	Palmerston	57	D3	Windy Arbour	97	C2
Confey	66	B1	Hartstown	25	C3	Pelletstown	41	D3	Yellow Walls	13	C2
Coolock	46	B1	Hazelbrook	19	D2	Phibsborough	61	D2			
Corduff	27	D3	Hilltown	10	A2	Poppintree	31	C2			
						Portmarnock	21	C2			

Index to street names

General abbreviations

All	Alley	Dr	Drive	Junct	Junction	S	South
Av	Avenue	Dws	Dwellings	La	Lane	Sch	School
Ave	Avenue	E	East	Lo	Lodge	Sq	Square
Bk	Bank	Ex	Exchange	Lwr	Lower	St.	Saint
Bldgs	Buildings	Ext	Extension	Mans	Mansions	St	Street
Boul	Boulevard	Fld	Field	Mkt	Market	Sta	Station
Br	Bridge	Flds	Fields	Ms	Mews	Ter	Terrace
Bri	Bridge	Fm	Farm	Mt	Mount	Vil	Villa, Villas
Cem	Cemetery	Gdn	Garden	N	North	Vw	View
Cen	Central,	Gdns	Gardens	No	Numbers	W	West
	Centre	Gra	Grange	Par	Parade	Wd	Wood
Cl	Close	Grd	Ground	Pas	Passage	Wds	Woods
Clo	Close	Grn	Green	Pk	Park	Wk	Walk
Coll	College	Gro	Grove	Pl	Place	Yd	Yard
Cotts	Cottages	Ho	House	Prom	Promenade		
Cres	Crescent	Hosp	Hospital	Rd	Road		
Ct	Court	Hts	Heights	Ri	Rise		

District abbreviations

Abb.	Abberley	Clond.	Clondalkin	Grey.	Greystones	Manor.	Manorfields
B'brack	Ballybrack	Clons.	Clonsilla	Jobs.	Jobstown	Mulh.	Mulhuddart
B'mun	Ballymun	Collins.	Collinstown	Kill.	Killiney	Palm.	Palmerston
Bald.	Baldoyle	Cool.	Coolmine	Kilsh.	Kilshane	Port.	Portmarnock
Balg.	Balgriffin	Corn.	Cornelscourt	Kilt.	Kiltipper	Sally.	Sallynoggin
Black.	Blackrock	D.L.	Dún Laoghaire	Kins.	Kinsaley	Sandy.	Sandyford
Boot.	Booterstown	Deans Gra	Deans Grange	Leix.	Leixlip	Shank.	Shankill
Cabin.	Cabinteely	Dunb.	Dunboyne	Leo.	Leopardstown	Still.	Stillorgan
Carp.	Carpenterstown	Fox.	Foxrock	Lou.V.	Louisa Valley	Will.	Willbrook
Carrick.	Carrickmines	G'geary	Glenageary	Lough.	Loughlinstown		
Castle.	Castleknock	Gra M.	Grange Manor	Mala.	Malahide		

Some streets are not named on the map due to insufficient space. In some of these cases the nearest street that does appear on the map is listed in *italics*. In other cases they are indicated on the map by a number which is listed here in **bold**.

A

Name	Page	Grid
Abberley	119	C3
Abbey Cotts		
off Abbey St Upr	124	C2
Abbey Ct *Dublin 5*	46	B3
Abbey Ct 1 *D.L.*	112	B1
Abbeydale	69	D3
Abbeydale Cl	69	D3
Abbeydale Cres	69	D3
Abbeydale Gdns	69	D3
Abbeydale Ri	69	D3
Abbeydale Wk	69	D3
Abbeyfield *Dublin 5*	46	B3
Abbeyfield *Dublin 6*	86	B3
Abbeyfield Ct	69	D3
Abbeylea Av	8	A1
Abbeylea Cl 7	8	A1
Abbeylea Dr 2	8	B1
Abbeylea Grn	8	A1
Abbey Pk *Dublin 5*	46	A3
Abbey Pk *Dublin 13*	49	C1
Abbey Pk *D.L.*	112	B1
Abbey Rd	112	B1
Abbey St	53	C2
Abbey St Lwr	125	D2
Abbey St Mid	125	D2
Abbey St Old	125	E2
Abbey St Upr	124	C2
Abbey Thea		
off Abbey St Lwr	125	D2
Abbey Vw	112	B1
Abbeywood	69	C3
Abbeywood Av	69	D3
Abbeywood Cl	69	D3
Abbeywood Cres	69	D3
Abbeywood Pk	69	D3
Abbeywood Way	69	D3
Abbotstown Av (Ascal Bhaile An Abba)	41	D1
Abbotstown Dr	41	D1
Abbotstown Rd	42	A1
Abercorn Rd	77	C1
Abercorn Sq	73	D2
Abercorn Ter *Dublin 7*	61	C3
Abercorn Ter *Dublin 8*	73	D2
Aberdeen St	74	A1
Abington	13	C3
Achill Rd *Dublin 9*	62	B1
Achill Rd *Lough.*	119	C3
Acorn Dr	108	B1
Acorn Rd	108	B1
Acres Rd	59	D3
Adair	87	D1
Adam Ct		
off Grafton St	125	D4
Adamstown Rd	68	A1
Adare Av	46	A1
Adare Dr	46	B1
Adare Grn	46	B1
Adare Pk	46	B1
Adare Rd	34	B3
Addison Pl	62	A1
Addison Rd	63	C2
Addison Ter	62	A1
Adelaide Ms	88	B2
Adelaide Rd *Dublin 2*	76	A3
Adelaide Rd *Bray*	122	A1
Adelaide Rd *D.L.*	113	D2
Adelaide St	101	D3
Adelaide Ter *Dublin 8*		
off Brookfield St	74	A1
Adelaide Ter 1 *D.L.*	114	A1
Adelaide Ter *Bray*	122	A1
Adelaide Vil 2 *D.L.*	114	A1
Admiral Ct 7	37	D3
Admiral Pk	37	D3
Adrian Av	85	C2
Advance Business Pk	33	C1
Aideen Av	84	B3
Aideen Dr	84	B3
Aideen Pl	84	B3
Aikenhead Ter	77	D2
Ailesbury	44	B1
Ailesbury Cl	87	D2
Ailesbury Dr	87	D2
Ailesbury Gdns	88	A2
Ailesbury Gro *Dublin 4*	87	D2
Ailesbury Gro *Dublin 16*	108	B1
Ailesbury Lawn	108	B1
Ailesbury Ms	88	B2
Ailesbury Pk	88	A2
Ailesbury Rd	87	D2
Ailsbury Gro	108	B1
Ailsbury Lawn	108	B1
Airfield Ct	87	D3
Airfield Manor	87	D3
Airfield Pk	87	D3
Airfield Rd	85	D3
Airfield Ter	87	D3
Airport Business Pk	17	C2
Airport Ind Est	33	C2
Airside Business Pk	11	C2
Airside Retail Pk	11	C2
Airton Cl	92	A3
Airton Rd	91	D3
Airways Ind Est	33	C2
Albany Av	100	B3
Albany Ct	119	C3
Albany Rd	86	B2
Albert Av	122	B1
Albert Coll Av	44	A2
Albert Coll Cres	44	A2
Albert Coll Dr	44	A2
Albert Coll Lawn	44	A2
Albert Coll Pk	44	A2
Albert Coll Ter	44	A2
Albert Ct	114	A1
Albert Ct E	77	C2
Albert Pk	114	A1
Albert Pl		
off Inchicore Rd	74	A2
Albert Pl E	77	C2
Albert Pl W	76	A3
Albert Rd Lwr	114	A2
Albert Rd Upr	114	A2
Albert Vil		
off Albert Pl W	76	A3
Albert Wk	122	B1
Albion Ter		
off Inchicore Rd	74	A2
Aldborough Par	63	C3
Aldborough Pl	62	B3
Aldborough Sq	62	B3
Alden Dr	48	B1
Alden Pk	49	C1
Alden Rd	48	B1
Alder Ct 1	21	C1
Alderpark Ct	103	C1
Alders, The	100	A3
Alderwood Av	103	C1
Alderwood Cl	91	C3
Alderwood Ct	103	C1
Alderwood Dr	103	C1
Alderwood Grn	91	C3
Alderwood Gro	103	C1
Alderwood Lawn	91	C3
Alderwood Pk	103	C1
Alderwood Ri	91	C3
Aldrin Wk	46	A1
Alexander Ter *Dublin 1*	77	C1
Alexander Ter *Dublin 8*	75	D3
Alexander Ter 1 *Bray*	122	A2
Alexandra Quay	78	A1
Alexandra Rd	77	D1
Alexandra Rd Extension	79	C1
Alexandra Ter *Dublin 3*		
off Clontarf Rd	65	C3
Alexandra Ter *Dublin 6*	85	D3
Alexandra Ter (Dundrum) *Dublin 14*	96	B3
Alfie Byrne Rd	63	D3
Allendale Cl	25	C3
Allendale Copse	25	C3
Allendale Dr	25	C3
Allendale Elms 6	25	C3
Allendale Glen 3	25	C3
Allendale Grn	25	C3
Allendale Gro	25	C3
Allendale Heath 7	25	C3
Allendale Lawn 10	25	C3
Allendale Pl 5	25	C3
Allendale Ri 11	25	C3
Allendale Sq	25	C3
Allendale Ter 8	25	C3
Allendale Vw	25	C3
Allendale Wk	25	C3
Allen Pk Dr	110	B1
Allen Pk Rd	110	B1
Allenton Av	104	A3
Allenton Cres	104	A3
Allenton Dr	104	A3
Allenton Gdns	104	A3
Allenton Grn	104	A3
Allenton Lawns	104	A3
Allenton Pk	104	A2
Allenton Rd	104	A1
Allenton Way	104	A3
All Hallows Coll	62	B1
All Hallows La off		
Drumcondra Rd Upr	62	B1
Allied Ind Est	72	B3
Allingham St	75	C2
All Saints Dr	47	D3
All Saints Pk	47	D3
All Saints Rd	47	C3
Alma Pl	100	B3
Alma Rd	100	A2
Almeida Av		
off Brookfield St	74	B2
Almeida Ter		
off Brookfield St	74	B2
Alone Wk	46	B3
Alpine Hts	80	A2
Alpine Ri	90	B3
Altadore	113	D2
Altona Ter	61	C3
Alverno	64	A2
Amber Vale	90	B3
Amiens St	125	F1
Anastasia La	115	C2
Anfield Cl	38	A3
Anfield Cres	56	A1
Anfield Dr	56	A1
Anfield Lawn 1	56	A1
Anfield Vw 2	56	A1
Anglesea Av	99	D2
Anglesea Br	87	D2
Anglesea Fruit Mkt		
off Green St Little	124	B2
Anglesea La	101	D3
Anglesea Pk	114	A3
Anglesea Rd	87	D2
Anglesea Row	124	C2
Anglesea St	125	D3
Anley Ct	69	C1
Annabeg 1	118	B2
Annadale Av	63	C1
Annadale Cres	63	C1
Annadale Dr	63	C1
Annagh Ct 1	39	D1
Annaly	25	D3
Annaly Rd	61	C2
Annamoe Dr	61	C2
Annamoe Par	61	C3
Annamoe Pk	61	C3
Annamoe Rd	61	C2
Annamoe Ter	61	C3
Anna Vil	86	B2
Annaville Av	111	D1
Annaville Gro	97	C2
Annaville Pk		
off Annaville Gro	97	C2
Anne Devlin Av	94	B3
Anne Devlin Dr	94	B3
Anne Devlin Pk	94	B3
Anne Devlin Rd	94	B3
Anner Rd	74	A2
Annes La	125	D4
Annesley Av	63	C2
Annesley Br	63	C2
Annesley Br Rd	63	C2
Annesley Pk	86	B2
Annesley Pl	63	C2
Anne St N	124	B1
Anne St S	125	D4
Annsbrook	97	C2
Annville Dr	110	A1
Appian Way, The	86	A2
Apples Rd	109	D2
Aran Av	119	C3
Aran Cl	119	C3
Aran Dr	119	C3
Aranleigh Ct	95	D3
Aranleigh Dell	107	D1
Aranleigh Gdns	95	D3
Aranleigh Mt	95	D3
Aranleigh Pk	95	D3
Aranleigh Vale	95	D3
Áras An Uachtaráin	59	D2
Aras Naclunne	81	C1
Aravon Ct 8	122	B2
Arbour Hill	75	C1
Arbour Pl	75	C1
Arbour Ter	75	C1
Arbutus Av	85	C1
Arbutus Pl	75	C1
Arcade	125	D2
Archers Wd	26	A1
Arches, The 11	119	C3
Ardagh Av	111	D1
Ardagh Cl 1	111	D1
Ardagh Ct	111	C1
Ardagh Cres	111	C1
Ardagh Dr	111	D1
Ardagh Gro	111	C1
Ardagh Pk	111	C1
Ardagh Pk Rd	111	D1
Ardagh Rd	84	B1
Ardara Av	36	A3
Ardbeg Cres	46	B2
Ardbeg Dr	46	B2
Ardbeg Pk	46	B2
Ardbeg Rd	46	B2
Ardbrugh Cl 1	114	B3
Ardbrugh Rd	114	B3
Ardbrugh Vil 2	114	B3
Ardcian Pk	8	A1
Ardcollum Av	46	A2
Ardee Gro	86	A1
Ardeen	68	A1
Ardee Rd	86	A1
Ardee Row	124	A4
Ardee St	124	A4
Ardeevin Av	68	A1
Ardeevin Ct	68	A1
Ardeevin Dr	68	A1
Ardeevin Rd	114	B2
Ardenza Pk		
off Seapoint Av	100	A2
Ardenza Ter	100	A2
Ardglas Est	109	C1
Ardilaun	21	C2
Ardilaun Rd	62	B3
Ardilea Downs	97	D2
Ardlea Rd	46	A2
Ard Lorcain	111	C1
Ard Lorcain Vil 1	111	C1
Ardlui Pk	111	D1
Ardmeen Pk	111	D1
Ard Mhacha	103	D2
Ard Mhuire Pk	114	A3
Ardmore Av	61	C3
Ardmore Cl	45	D2
Ardmore Cres	46	A2
Ardmore Dr	45	D2
Ardmore Gro	45	D2
Ardmore Pk *Dublin 5*	46	A2
Ardmore Pk *D.L.*	113	C1
Ard Na Mara	13	C2
Ard Na Meala	32	A3
Ardpatrick Rd	60	A2
Ard Ri Pl		
off Ard Ri Rd	75	C1
Ard Ri Rd	75	C1
Ardtona Av	96	B2
Arena Rd	110	B3
Argyle Rd	87	C1
Arkendale Ct 1	114	A2
Arkendale Rd	114	A1
Arkendale Wds 2	114	A2
Arkle Rd	110	A2
Arkle Sq 1	110	B3
Arklow St	61	C3
Armagh Rd	84	A2
Armstrong St		
off Harolds Cross Rd	85	D1
Arnold Gro	113	D2
Arnold Pk	113	D3
Arnott St	75	D3
Arran Ct 2	39	C1
Arran Grn	122	B2
Arranmore Av	62	A2
Arranmore Rd	87	C1
Arran Quay	124	A2
Arran Quay Ter	124	A2
Arran Rd	62	B1
Arran St E	124	B2
Arran St W	124	A2
Arthur Griffith Pk	68	A2
Arundel	100	B3
Ascal An Charrain Chno (Nutgrove Av)	95	D3
Ascal Bhaile An Abba (Abbotstown Av)	41	D1
Ascal Bhaile Thuaidh (Ballyhoy Av)	47	D3
Ascal Dun Eanna (Ennafort Av)	47	C3

Name	Page	Grid
Ascal Measc (Mask Av)	46	B2
Ascal Phairc An Bhailtini (Villa Park Av)	60	A2
Ascal Ratabhachta (Ratoath Av)	41	D2
Asgard Pk	53	C2
Asgard Rd	53	C2
Ash, The	40	A3
Ashberry	68	A3
Ashbrook *Dublin 3*	64	A1
Ashbrook *Dublin 7*	59	C1
Ashbury Pk	122	A2
Ashcroft	47	D2
Ashdale (Templeogue)	85	C3
Ashdale Cl	12	A3
Ashdale Gdns	85	C3
Ashdale Pk	85	C3
Ashdale Rd *Dublin 6W*	85	C3
Ashdale Rd *Swords*	12	B3
Ashfield (Templeogue)	94	A3
Ashfield Av *Dublin 6*	86	B2
Ashfield Av *Dublin 24*	91	D1
Ashfield Cl *Dublin 6W* off Ashfield	94	A2
Ashfield Cl *Dublin 24*	91	D1
Ashfield Ct	26	A3
Ashfield Dr	91	D1
Ashfield Gdns	26	A3
Ashfield Grn	26	A2
Ashfield Gro	26	A2
Ashfield Lawn	26	A2
Ashfield Pk (Templeogue) *Dublin 6W* off Ashfield	94	A3
Ashfield Pk (Terenure) *Dublin 6W*	85	C3
Ashfield Pk *Dublin 24*	91	D1
Ashfield Pk *Boot.*	98	A1
Ashfield Pk 7 *Mulh.*	26	A3
Ashfield Rd (Ranelagh)	26	A3
Ashfield Way	26	A3
Ashford Cotts off Ashford St	61	C3
Ashford Pl off Ashford St	61	C3
Ashford St	61	C3
Ashgrove *Dublin 24*	91	C3
Ashgrove *D.L.*	112	B1
Ashgrove Ind Est	112	B1
Ashgrove Ter 1	97	C3
Ashington Av	60	A1
Ashington Cl	41	D3
Ashington Ct	60	A1
Ashington Dale	42	A3
Ashington Gdns	60	A1
Ashington Grn	60	A1
Ashington Ms	42	A3
Ashington Pk	59	D1
Ashington Ri	41	D3
Ash Lawn *Dublin 16*	108	B1
Ashlawn *B'brack*	118	B2
Ashleaf Shop Cen	83	D3
Ashleigh Grn	39	D3
Ashleigh Gro	39	D2
Ashleigh Lawn	14	A3
Ashley Av	11	D1
Ashley Gro 5	11	D1
Ashley Gro 4	11	D1
Ashley Ri	21	C1
Ashling Cl	84	B1
Ashling Hts	39	C1
Ash Pk Av	68	B3
Ash Pk Ct	69	C3
Ash Pk Gro	69	C2
Ash Pk Heath	69	C2
Ash St	124	A4
Ashton Av	106	A1
Ashton Cl	106	A1
Ashton Gro	106	A1
Ashton Lawn	106	A1
Ashton Pk	100	B3
Ashtown Gate Rd	59	C1
Ashtown Gro	59	D1
Ashtown Rd	41	C3
Ashtown Sta	41	C3
Ashurst	119	C3
Ashville Cl	69	C1
Ashwood Dr	80	A1
Ashwood Lawns	80	A1
Ashwood Pk	80	A1
Ashwood Rd	80	A1
Ashwood Way	80	A1
Aspen Dr	12	B2
Aspen Pk 1 *D.L.*	113	C2
Aspen Pk *Swords*	12	B2
Aspen Rd	12	A2
Aspen Wds	38	A2
Aspen Wds Av	38	A2
Aspen Wds Lawn	38	A2
Assumpta Pk	120	B3
Aston Pl	125	D2
Aston Quay	125	D2
Athgoe Dr	121	C2
Athgoe Rd	121	C2
Athlumney Vil	86	A1
Atmospheric Rd 3	114	A2
Aubrey Gro	121	C2
Aubrey Pk	121	C2
Auburn Av *Dublin 4*	87	C2
Auburn Av *Dublin 15*	58	A1
Auburn Av *Cabin.*	118	A1
Auburn Cl *Dublin 15* off Auburn Dr	40	A3
Auburn Cl *Cabin.*	118	B1
Auburn Dr *Dublin 15*	40	A3
Auburn Dr *Cabin.*	118	A1
Auburn Grn off Auburn Dr	40	A3
Auburn Gro	13	C3
Auburn Rd *Dublin 4* off Auburn Av	87	C2
Auburn Rd *Cabin.*	113	C2
Auburn St	61	C3
Auburn Vil	85	D3
Auburn Wk	61	C3
Aughavanagh Rd	85	C1
Aughrim La	61	C3
Aughrim Pl	61	C3
Aughrim St	61	C3
Aughrim Vil off Aughrim St	61	C3
Augustine Vil 1	122	B2
Aulden Gra	33	D3
Aungier Pl	124	C4
Aungier St	124	C4
Austins Cotts off Annesley Pl	63	C2
Avalon 1	116	B1
Ave Maria Rd	75	C3
Avenue, The *Dublin 6W*	94	A2
Avenue, The (Ballinteer) *Dublin 16*	108	B2
Avenue, The (Ballyboden) *Dublin 16*	106	A2
Avenue, The (Lutterell Hall) *Dunb.*	22	A1
Avenue, The *Gra M.*	68	B3
Avenue, The *Kins.*	15	C3
Avenue, The *Lou.V.*	66	A1
Avenue, The 4 *Mala.*	15	C3
Avenue, The *Manor.*	25	C2
Avenue, The *Mulh.*	26	A2
Avenue, The *Swords*	9	C1
Avenue Rd	75	D3
Avila Apartments 2	111	D1
Avila Pk	41	D1
Avoca Av *Black.*	99	C3
Avoca Av *Bray*	122	A2
Avoca Pk	99	C3
Avoca Pl	99	D2
Avoca Rd	99	C3
Avonbeg Ct 1	104	A1
Avonbeg Dr	104	B1
Avonbeg Gdns	104	B1
Avonbeg Ind Est	82	B1
Avonbeg Pk	104	B1
Avonbeg Rd	104	B1
Avondale Av	61	D3
Avondale Business Pk	99	D2
Avondale Ct 4	114	A1
Avondale Cres	114	A3
Avondale Lawn	99	D3
Avondale Lawn Extension	99	D3
Avondale Pk *Dublin 5*	48	A3
Avondale Pk *Dalkey*	114	A3
Avondale Rd *Dublin 7*	61	D3
Avondale Rd *Dalkey*	114	A3
Avondale Sq	22	A2
Avondale Ter	83	D3
Avonmore	111	C2
Avonmore Av 1	104	B1
Avonmore Cl	104	B1
Avonmore Dr	104	B1
Avonmore Gro	104	B1
Avonmore Pk	104	B1
Avonmore Rd	104	B1
Aylesbury	104	A2
Ayrefield Av	47	C1
Ayrefield Cl	47	C1
Ayrefield Dr	47	C1
Ayrefield Gro	47	C1
Ayrefield Pl	47	C1

B

Name	Page	Grid
Bachelors Wk	125	D2
Back La *Dublin 8*	124	B3
Back La 3 *Dublin 13*	37	D3
Back Rd	13	D3
Baggot Cl off Baggot St Lwr	76	B3
Baggot Ct	77	C3
Baggot La	59	D2
Baggot Rd	59	D2
Baggot St Lwr	76	B3
Baggot St Upr	77	C3
Baggot Ter off Blackhorse Av	59	D2
Bailey Grn Rd	55	D2
Bailey Vw	114	B1
Balally Av	109	D1
Balally Cl	109	D1
Balally Dr	109	C1
Balally Gro	109	D2
Balally Hill	109	D2
Balally Pk	109	D1
Balally Rd	109	C1
Balally Ter 1	109	D2
Balbutcher Dr	31	D2
Balbutcher La	31	D3
Balbutcher La	31	D3
Balbutcher Way	31	D2
Balcurris Gdns	32	A3
Balcurris Rd	32	A3
Baldoyle Ind Est	49	C1
Baldoyle Rd	50	A1
Balfe Av	83	D2
Balfe Rd	83	D2
Balfe Rd E	83	D2
Balfe St off Chatham St	125	D4
Balgaddy Rd	69	D3
Balglass Est	52	B2
Balglass Rd	53	C2
Balgriffin	35	D1
Balgriffin Cotts	35	D2
Balgriffin Pk	35	D2
Balkill Pk	52	B2
Balkill Rd	53	C3
Ballawley Ct	109	C2
Ballinclea Hts	114	A3
Ballinclea Rd	113	D3
Ballinteer	108	B2
Ballinteer Av	108	B2
Ballinteer Cl	108	B2
Ballinteer Ct 2	108	B2
Ballinteer Cres	108	B2
Ballinteer Dr	108	B2
Ballinteer Gdns	108	B2
Ballinteer Gro	108	B2
Ballinteer Pk	108	B2
Ballinteer Rd	108	B1
Ballinteer Shop Cen	108	B2
Ballintrane Wd	11	C1
Ballintyre Downs	108	B3
Ballintyre Heath	108	B3
Ballintyre Meadows	108	A3
Ballintyre Wk	108	B3
Ballintyre Wds 4	108	B2
Ball's Br	87	D1
Ballsbridge Av	87	D1
Ballsbridge Pk	87	D1
Ballsbridge Ter off Ballsbridge Av	87	D1
Ballsbridge Wd	77	D3
Ballyboden Cres	106	B1
Ballyboden Rd *Dublin 14*	106	B1
Ballyboden Rd *Dublin 16*	106	B1
Ballyboggan Ind Est	42	A3
Ballyboggan Rd	42	B3
Ballybough Av off Spring Gdn St	63	C3
Ballybough Br	63	C2
Ballybough Ct off Spring Gdn St	63	C3
Ballybough Rd	62	B3
Ballybrack	119	C2
Ballybrack Shop Cen	118	B2
Ballybride	120	B3
Ballybride Rd	120	B2
Ballycoolin Business & Tech Pk	28	A2
Ballycoolin Rd	28	A3
Ballycullen Rd	104	B2
Ballycullen Dr	105	C2
Ballydowd Dr	69	C2
Ballydowd Gro	69	C1
Ballydowd Manor	69	C2
Ballyfermot Av	72	B2
Ballyfermot Cres	72	B2
Ballyfermot Dr	72	B2
Ballyfermot Par	72	A2
Ballyfermot Rd (Bothar Baile Thormod)	72	A2
Ballygall Av	43	C1
Ballygall Cres	42	B2
Ballygall Par	42	B2
Ballygall Pl	43	C2
Ballygall Rd E	43	C2
Ballygall Rd W	42	B2
Ballygihen Av	114	A1
Ballygihen Vil 5	114	A1
Ballyhoy Av (Ascal Bhaile Thuaidh)	47	D3
Ballymace Grn	94	A3
Ballymanagin La 1	80	B1
Ballymoss Par 2	110	B3
Ballymoss Rd	110	A2
Ballymount Av *Dublin 12*	92	B1
Ballymount Av *Dublin 24*	92	B1
Ballymount Cross	82	A3
Ballymount Cross Ind Est	81	D3
Ballymount Dr	82	B3
Ballymount Ind Est	82	B3
Ballymount Lwr Rd	82	A3
Ballymount Rd	81	D3
Ballymount Rd Ind Est	82	B2
Ballymount Rd Upr	82	A3
Ballymount Trd Est	83	C3
Ballymun Ind Est	31	D2
Ballymun Rd	44	A3
Ballymun Shop Cen	32	A3
Ballyneety Rd	73	C2
Ballyogan Av	116	A1
Ballyogan Cl	116	A1
Ballyogan Ct	116	A2
Ballyogan Cres	116	A1
Ballyogan Dr	116	A2
Ballyogan Est	116	A1
Ballyogan Grn	116	A1
Ballyogan Lawn	116	A1
Ballyogan Rd 1	116	A2
Ballyogan Wd	116	A2
Ballyolaf Manor 1	109	C1
Ballyowen Av	69	D1
Ballyowen Castle Shop & Med Cen	69	C2
Ballyowen Cres	69	D1
Ballyowen Ct	69	D1
Ballyowen Dr	69	D1
Ballyowen Grn	69	D1
Ballyowen Gro	69	D1
Ballyowen La	69	D1
Ballyowen Lawn	69	D1
Ballyowen Vw	69	D1
Ballyowen Way	69	D1
Ballyroan Ct 1	94	A3
Ballyroan Cres	94	B3
Ballyroan Hts	106	A1
Ballyroan Pk	94	A3
Ballyroan Rd	94	A3
Ballyshannon Av	45	D1
Ballyshannon Rd	45	D1
Ballytore Rd	95	D1
Balnagowan	86	B3
Balrothery Cotts	93	C3
Balrothery Est	92	B3
Balscadden Rd	53	C2
Bancroft Av	92	A3
Bancroft Cl	92	B3
Bancroft Gro	92	B3
Bancroft Pk	92	A3
Bancroft Rd	92	B3
Bangor Dr	84	B1
Bangor Rd	84	B1

Bank of Ireland 125 D3
Bankside Cotts 96 B1
Bannow Rd 60 B1
Bann Rd 42 B3
Bantry Rd 44 A3
Bantry Sq **4** 39 D1
Banville Av 72 A3
Barclay Ct 99 D2
Bargy Rd 63 D3
Barnacoille Pk 114 B1
Barnamore Cres *off Barnamore Gro* 42 B3
Barnamore Gro 42 B3
Barnamore Pk 42 B3
Barnewall Dr 31 D3
Barnhill Av 114 A2
Barnhill Cross Rd 68 A1
Barnhill Gro 114 B2
Barnhill Lawn **1** 114 B2
Barnhill Pk **4** 114 A2
Barnhill Rd 114 A2
Barnville Pk 71 C3
Barrett St 101 C3
Barrow Rd 61 C1
Barrow Sta 77 C2
Barrow St 77 C2
Barry Av 30 A3
Barry Dr 30 A3
Barry Grn 42 A1
Barry Pk 42 A1
Barry Rd 42 A1
Barryscourt Rd 46 A1
Barton Av 95 C3
Barton Ct 108 A1
Barton Dr 95 C3
Barton Rd E 108 A1
Barton Rd Extension 107 D1
Barton Rd W (Willbrook) 107 C1
Bartra Rock **6** 114 B1
Basin St Lwr 75 C2
Basin St Upr 75 C2
Basin Vw Ter 61 D3
Baskin Cotts 18 B2
Baskin La 18 A2
Bass Pl 125 F4
Bath Av *Dublin 4* 77 D3
Bath Av *Mala.* 14 B2
Bath Av Gdns 77 D3
Bath Av Pl 77 D3
Bath La 62 A3
Bath Pl 99 D2
Bath St 77 D2
Bawn, The 14 A3
Bawn Gro, The 14 A3
Bawnlea Av 102 B1
Bawnlea Cl 102 A1
Bawnlea Cres 102 A1
Bawnlea Dr 102 A1
Bawnlea Grn 102 B1
Bawnville Av 104 A2
Bawnville Cl 104 A2
Bawnville Dr 104 B1
Bawnville Pk 104 B1
Bawnville Rd 104 A1
Baymount Pk 65 D1
Bayshore La 119 C3
Bayside Boul N 49 C1
Bayside Boul S 49 C1
Bayside Pk 49 C1
Bayside Sq E 49 C1
Bayside Sq N 49 C1
Bayside Sq S 49 C1
Bayside Sq W 49 C1
Bayside Sta 49 D1
Bayside Wk 49 C1
Bayswater Ter **7** 114 B1
Bayview *Dublin 4* *off Pembroke St* 77 D2
Bayview **2** *Bray* 122 A1
Bayview *Lough.* 119 C3
Bayview Av 63 C3
Bayview Cl 119 C3
Bayview Ct 119 C3
Bayview Cres 121 C1
Bayview Dr 121 C1
Bayview Glade **1** 121 C1
Bayview Glen **4** 121 C1
Bayview Grn 119 C3
Bayview Gro 121 C1
Bayview Lawn 119 C3
Bayview Pk 119 C3
Bayview Ri **3** 121 C1
Beach Av 78 A3
Beach Dr 78 A3
Beach Pk 21 C2
Beach Rd 78 A3
Beach Vw 49 C2
Beaconsfield Ct *off The Belfry* 74 A2
Bearna Pk 109 D3
Beattys Av 87 D1
Beaufield Manor 98 B3
Beaufield Pk 98 B3
Beaufort 114 A1
Beaufort Downs 95 C3
Beaumont Av 96 A3
Beaumont Cl 96 A3
Beaumont Cres 45 D2
Beaumont Dr 96 B3
Beaumont Gdns 99 C2
Beaumont Gro 45 C2
Beaumont Rd 45 C2
Beau Pk Av 36 B3
Beau Pk Cres 36 B3
Beau Pk Rd 36 B3
Beau Pk Row 36 B3
Beau Pk Sq 36 B3
Beau Pk St 36 B2
Beau Pk Ter 36 B3
Beauvale Pk 46 A2
Beaver Row 87 C3
Beaver St 62 B3
Beckett Way 81 C1
Bedford Row *off Temple Bar* 125 D3
Beechbrook Gro **7** 36 A3
Beechcourt 118 B1
Beechdale 22 B3
Beechdale Ms 86 A2
Beech Dr 108 B1
Beeches, The *Dublin 13* 48 A1
Beeches, The **6** *Dublin 14* 95 C3
Beeches, The **12** *Abb.* 119 C3
Beeches, The *Black.* 100 B3
Beeches Pk 114 A2
Beeches Rd 109 D1
Beechfield 24 B1
Beechfield Av *Dublin 12* 83 D3
Beechfield Av *Dublin 24* 105 C3
Beechfield Cl *Dublin 12* 83 D3
Beechfield Cl **1** *Dublin 24* 105 C3
Beechfield Cl **1** *Dunb.* 24 B1
Beechfield Ct *Dublin 24* 105 C3
Beechfield Ct **1** *Clons.* 24 B2
Beechfield Cres 105 C3
Beechfield Dr 24 B1
Beechfield Grn **2** 24 B1
Beechfield Haven **1** 121 C2
Beechfield Hts **2** 24 B2
Beechfield Lawn *Dublin 24* 105 C3
Beechfield Lawn **1** *Clons.* 25 C1
Beechfield Manor 121 C2
Beechfield Meadows 24 B1
Beechfield Pk **2** 105 C3
Beechfield Pl *Dublin 24* 105 C3
Beechfield Pl *Clons.* 25 C1
Beechfield Ri 25 C1
Beechfield Rd *Dublin 12* 83 D3
Beechfield Rd *Dublin 24* 105 C3
Beechfield Rd (Hartstown) *Clons.* 24 B2
Beechfield Vw 24 B1
Beechfield Way *Dublin 24* 105 C3
Beechfield Way *Clons.* 24 B1
Beech Gro *Boot.* 98 B1
Beech Gro *Lucan* 68 B1
Beech Hill *off Beech Hill Rd* 87 C3
Beech Hill Av 87 D2
Beech Hill Cres 87 D3
Beech Hill Dr 87 D2
Beech Hill Rd 87 C3
Beech Hill Ter 87 D3
Beech Hill Vil *off Beech Hill Ter* 87 D3
Beech Lawn *Dublin 16* 108 A1
Beechlawn *Boot.* 98 B2
Beech Lawn Av 108 A1
Beechlawn Ind Complex 83 C3
Beechmount Dr 97 C1
Beech Pk *Dublin 15* 40 A3
Beech Pk *Cabin.* 118 A2
Beech Pk *Lucan* 68 B1
Beech Pk Av *Dublin 5* 46 B1
Beech Pk Av *Dublin 15* 40 A3
Beech Pk Av *Deans Gra* 112 A2
Beechpark Ct 46 B1
Beech Pk Cres 40 A3
Beech Pk Dr 112 A3
Beech Pk Gro 112 A3
Beech Pk Lawn 40 A3
Beech Pk Rd 112 A2
Beech Rd *Dublin 12* 82 A2
Beech Rd **3** *Shank.* 121 C3
Beech Row **3** *Clond.* 80 B2
Beech Row (Ronanstown) *Clond.* 70 A3
Beechview **1** 106 B2
Beech Wk 106 B2
Beechwood Av Lwr 86 B2
Beechwood Av Upr 86 B2
Beechwood Cl *Bray* 122 A3
Beechwood Cl *Manor.* 25 D2
Beechwood Downs 25 D2
Beechwood Gro **1** 113 D1
Beechwood Lawn 113 D3
Beechwood Pk *Dublin 6* 86 A2
Beechwood Pk *D.L.* 113 D1
Beechwood Rd 86 B2
Belcamp Av 35 C3
Belcamp Cres 34 B2
Belcamp Gdns 34 B2
Belcamp Grn 35 C3
Belcamp Gro 35 C3
Belcamp La 35 C3
Belclare Av 31 D3
Belclare Cres 31 D3
Belclare Dr 31 D3
Belclare Grn 31 D3
Belclare Gro 31 D3
Belclare Lawns 31 D3
Belclare Pk 31 C3
Belclare Ter 31 C3
Belclare Way 31 D3
Belfield Cl 97 C1
Belfield Ct 87 D3
Belfield Downs 97 C2
Belfield Office Pk 87 C3
Belfry, The 74 A2
Belfry Gro 102 A2
Belgard Cl **1** 91 D2
Belgard Grn 90 B3
Belgard Hts 91 C2
Belgard Ind Est 91 D2
Belgard Rd 91 D2
Belgard Sq E 91 D3
Belgard Sq N 91 C3
Belgard Sq S 103 D1
Belgard Sq W 91 C3
Belgrave Av 86 A2
Belgrave Pl 86 A2
Belgrave Rd *Dublin 6* 86 A2
Belgrave Rd *Black.* 100 A2
Belgrave Sq E *Dublin 6* 86 A2
Belgrave Sq E *Black.* 100 B3
Belgrave Sq N *Dublin 6* 86 A2
Belgrave Sq N *Black.* 100 A2
Belgrave Sq S *Dublin 6* 86 A2
Belgrave Sq S *Black.* 100 A2
Belgrave Sq W *Dublin 6* 86 A2
Belgrave Sq W *Black.* 100 A2
Belgrave Ter *Black.* *off Belgrave Rd* 100 A2
Belgrave Ter **9** *Bray* 122 B2
Belgrave Vil **10** 122 B2
Belgrove Lawn 58 B3
Belgrove Pk 72 B1
Belgrove Rd 64 B2
Bella Av *off Bella St* 62 B3
Bella St 62 B3
Belle Bk 75 C2
Belleville Av 85 D3
Bellevue 75 C2
Bellevue Av *Boot.* 88 B3
Bellevue Av *Dalkey* 113 D2
Bellevue Copse 88 B3
Bellevue Ct 88 B3
Bellevue Pk *Boot.* 88 A3
Bellevue Pk *Grey.* 123 C2
Bellevue Pk Av 88 B3
Bellevue Rd *Dalkey* 113 D3
Bellevue Rd *Grey.* 123 C2
Bellmans Wk *off Ferrymans Crossing* 77 C1
Belmont 111 C2
Belmont Av 87 C2
Belmont Ct *off Belmont Av* 87 C2
Belmont Gdns 87 C2
Belmont Grn 111 C1
Belmont Gro 111 C1
Belmont Lawn 111 C1
Belmont Pk *Dublin 4* 87 C2
Belmont Pk *Dublin 5* 48 A2
Belmont Vil 87 C2
Belton Pk Av 45 D3
Belton Pk Gdns 45 D3
Belton Pk Rd 45 D3
Belton Pk Vil 45 D3
Belton Ter **3** 122 A1
Belvidere Av 62 A3
Belvidere Ct 62 A3
Belvidere Pl 62 A3
Belvidere Rd 62 A2
Belview Bldgs *off School St* 75 C2
Belvue 90 B3
Benbulbin Av 84 A1
Benbulbin Rd 74 A3
Benburb St 124 A2
Beneavin Ct 43 C2
Beneavin Dr 43 D2
Beneavin Pk 43 C1
Beneavin Rd 43 C1
Ben Edar Rd 61 C3
Bengal Ter 61 D1
Ben Inagh Pk 99 D1
Benmadigan Rd 74 A3
Benson St 77 D2
Benson St Enterprise Cen 77 C2
Bentley Rd 122 A3
Beresford 62 B1
Beresford Av 62 B1
Beresford La *Dublin 1* 125 E1
Beresford La *Dublin 9* 62 B1
Beresford Pl 125 E2
Beresford St 124 B1
Berkeley Rd 61 D2
Berkeley St 62 A3
Berkeley Ter 77 C3
Berryfield 68 A3
Berryfield Cres 42 A2
Berryfield Dr 42 A2
Berryfield Rd 42 A2
Berwick 95 D3
Berwick Hall 95 D3
Berystede *off Leeson Pk* 86 B1
Bessborough Av 63 C3
Bessborough Par 86 A1
Besser Dr 70 B3
Bethesda Pl *off Dorset St Upr* 62 A3
Bettyglen 48 B3
Bettysford **7** 80 B2
Bettystown Av 47 D3
Beverly Av 105 D2
Beverly Cres 105 D2
Beverly Downs 105 D1
Beverly Dr 105 D1
Beverly Gro 105 D1
Beverly Hts 105 D2
Beverly Lawns 105 D2
Beverly Pk 105 D1
Beverly Ri 105 D2
Bewley 69 C1
Bewley Av 69 C2
Bewley Dr 69 C1
Bewley Gro 69 C2
Bewley Lawn 69 C1
Big Br 95 C1

150

Name	Page	Grid
Bigger Rd	83	D2
Binn Eadair Vw	50	A1
Binns Br	62	A2
Birch Av	110	A2
Birch Dale **2** *D.L.*	113	C2
Birch Dale **1** *Fox.*	111	D3
Birchdale Cl	12	B2
Birchdale Dr	12	B2
Birchdale Pk	12	B2
Birchdale Rd	111	D3
Birches, The	109	D1
Birches Rd	97	D3
Birchfield	112	B1
Birchgrove	97	C3
Birchs La	92	A2
Birchview Av	92	A2
Birchview Cl	92	A2
Birchview Ct		
off Treepark Rd	92	A2
Birchview Dr	92	A2
Birchview Hts		
off Birchview Dr	92	A2
Birchview Lawn		
off Birchview Av	92	A2
Birchview Ri		
off Birchview Dr	92	A2
Birchwood Cl	91	C3
Birchwood Dr	91	C3
Birchwood Hts	91	C3
Bird Av	97	C3
Biscayne	15	C2
Bishop St	76	A3
Bisset's Strand	13	D1
Black Av, The	67	C2
Blackberry La *Dublin*	86	A1
Blackberry La *Port.*	21	C2
Blackberry Ri	21	C2
Blackcourt Rd	27	C3
Blackditch Dr	71	D2
Blackditch Rd	72	A2
Blackhall Par	124	A2
Blackhall Pl	75	C1
Blackhall St	124	A2
Blackheath Av	64	B2
Blackheath Ct	65	C2
Blackheath Dr	64	B2
Blackheath Gdns	64	B2
Blackheath Gro	64	B2
Blackheath Pk	64	B2
Blackhorse Av	60	A2
Blackhorse Br	73	D3
Blackhorse Gro	60	B3
Blackhorse Ind Est	60	B3
Blackpitts	75	D3
Blackrock Business Pk	99	D2
Blackrock Coll	99	C1
Blackrock Shop Cen	99	D1
Blackrock Sta	99	D1
Black St	74	B1
Blackthorn Av	110	A2
Blackthorn Cl *Port.*	21	C1
Blackthorn Cl **1** *Still.*	110	A2
Blackthorn Ct **3**	109	D2
Blackthorn Dr	109	D2
Blackthorn Grn **4**	109	D2
Blackthorn Gro **2**	109	D2
Blackthorn Rd	110	A2
Blackwater Rd	61	C1
Blackwood	24	B2
Blackwood Cl	24	B3
Blackwood Cres	24	B2
Blackwood Dr	24	B2
Blackwood La	20	B1
Blackwood Lawn	24	B2
Blackwood Ms	24	B2
Blackwood Pk	24	B3
Blackwood Pl	24	B3
Blakesfield	25	D2
Blakestown Cotts	38	A1
Blakestown Dr	26	A3
Blakestown Rd	38	A1
Blakestown Way	26	B3
Blanchardstown Business & Tech Park	27	D3
Blanchardstown Bypass	39	C1
Blanchardstown Cen	38	B1
Blanchardstown Corporate Pk	27	D1

Name	Page	Grid
Blanchardstown Ind Pk	27	D2
Blanchardstown Rd N	27	C3
Blanchardstown Rd S	38	A2
Blarney Pk	84	B2
Blasket Sq	39	D1
Blessington Ct		
off Blessington St	62	A3
Blessington Rd		
Dublin 24	91	D3
Blessington Rd *Jobs.*	102	B2
Blessington St	61	D3
Bloom Cotts	75	D3
Bloomfield Av (Donnybrook)		
Dublin 4	86	B1
Bloomfield Av		
Dublin 8	75	D3
Bloomfield Pk	85	D1
Bluebell Av	72	B3
Bluebell Ind Est	82	A1
Bluebell Rd	83	C1
Blunden Dr	35	D3
Blythe Av		
off Church Rd	77	C1
Boden Dale	107	C1
Boden Mill **2**	106	B2
Boden Pk	106	B1
Boden Wd	95	C3
Boeing St	33	C2
Boghall Rd	122	A3
Bohernabreena Rd	104	A3
Bolbrook Av **2**	104	B1
Bolbrook Cl	104	B1
Bolbrook Dr **3**	104	B1
Bolbrook Enterprise Cen	105	C1
Bolbrook Gro	104	B1
Bolbrook Pk	104	B1
Bolbrook Vil	124	C1
Bolton St	78	A1
Bond Dr	63	D3
Bond Rd	75	C2
Bond St	75	C2
Bonham St	77	D1
Boolavogue Rd	98	B1
Booterstown Av	98	B3
Booterstown Pk	98	B3
Booterstown Sta	89	C3
Boot Rd	80	B3
Boroimhe Alder	10	B3
Boroimhe Ash	10	B3
Boroimhe Aspen	10	B2
Boroimhe Beech	10	B3
Boroimhe Birches	10	B2
Boroimhe Blackthorn	10	B2
Boroimhe Cedars	10	B2
Boroimhe Cherry	10	B2
Boroimhe Elms	11	C3
Boroimhe Hawthorns	10	B2
Boroimhe Laurels	10	B2
Boroimhe Maples	11	C3
Boroimhe Oaks	11	C3
Boroimhe Pines	11	C2
Boroimhe Poplars	11	C2
Boroimhe Willows	11	C2
Botanic Av	62	A1
Botanic Gdns	61	D1
Botanic Ms	61	D1
Botanic Pk	62	A1
Botanic Rd	61	D2
Botanic Vil		
off Botanic Rd	62	A1
Bothar An Easa (Watermill Rd)	47	D3
Bothar Baile Thormod (Ballyfermot Rd)	72	A2
Bothar Chille Na Manac (Walkinstown Rd)	83	C2
Bothar Cloiginn (Cleggan Rd)	71	D2
Bothar Coilbeard (Con Colbert Rd) *Dublin 8*	74	A2
Bothar Coilbeard (Con Colbert Rd) *Dublin 10*	73	D2
Bothar Dhroichead Chiarduibh (Cardiffsbridge Rd)	42	A1
Bothar Drom Finn (Drumfinn Rd)	72	A2
Bothar Loch Con (Lough Conn Rd)	72	A1
Bothar Phairc An Bhailtini (Villa Park Rd)	60	A2

Name	Page	Grid
Bothar Raitleann (Rathland Rd)	84	B3
Boundary Rd	64	A3
Bow Br	74	B2
Bow La E	124	C4
Bow La W	74	B2
Bow St	124	A2
Boyne La	125	F4
Boyne Rd	42	B3
Boyne St	125	F3
Brabazon Cotts **4**	122	A1
Brabazon Row	75	D3
Brabazon Sq		
off Gray St	124	A4
Brabazon St		
off The Coombe	124	A4
Bracetown Business Pk	23	C1
Brackenbush Pk	118	B1
Brackenbush Rd	118	B2
Bracken Dr	21	C1
Bracken Hill	109	C3
Bracken Rd	110	A3
Brackens La	125	F2
Brackenstown Av	11	C1
Braemor Av	96	A2
Braemor Dr	96	A2
Braemor Gro	96	A2
Braemor Pk	96	A1
Braemor Rd	96	A2
Brainborough Ter *off South Circular Rd*	75	C2
Braithwaite St	75	C2
Bramblefield	25	D1
Bramblefield Ct	25	D1
Bramblefield Cres	25	D1
Bramblefield Dr	25	D1
Bramblefield Pk	25	D1
Bramblefield Vw	26	A2
Bramblefield Wk	25	D1
Bramley Av	57	C1
Bramley Ct	57	C1
Bramley Cres	57	C1
Bramley Garth	57	C1
Bramley Grn	39	C3
Bramley Gro	39	C3
Bramley Heath	57	C1
Bramley Pk	56	B1
Bramley Rd	39	C3
Bramley Vw	39	C3
Bramley Wk	38	B3
Bramley Way	57	C1
Branch Rd N	78	B1
Branch Rd N Extension	78	B1
Branch Rd S	78	B1
Brandon Rd	83	D1
Bray	122	A2
Bray Head Ter **1**	122	A2
Bray Rd *Cabin.*	118	A2
Bray Rd *Corn.*	112	A3
Bray Sta	122	B1
Breakwater Rd S	78	B1
Breffni Ter	114	B1
Breffni Rd	114	B1
Breffni Ter	114	A1
Bregia Rd	61	C2
Brehon Fld Rd	108	A2
Brehon's Chair	108	A3
Bremen Av	78	A2
Bremen Gro	78	A2
Bremen Rd	78	A2
Brendan Behan Ct *off Russell St*	62	B3
Brendan Rd	87	C2
Brennans Par	122	B1
Brennans Ter **7**	122	B1
Brennanstown Rd	117	D2
Brennanstown Vale	117	C2
Brewery Rd	110	B2
Brian Av	63	C1
Brian Boru Av	65	C3
Brian Boru St	65	C2
Brian Rd	63	C2
Brian Ter	63	C2
Briarfield Gro	48	B2
Briarfield Rd	48	A2
Briarfield Vil	48	B2
Briars, The	57	C3
Briar Wk	21	C1
Briar Wd	122	B3
Briarwood Av	26	A3
Briarwood Cl	26	A3
Briarwood Gdns	26	A3
Briarwood Grn	26	A3
Briarwood Lawn	26	A3
Briarwood Pk **2**	26	A3

Name	Page	Grid
Briarwood Rd **3**	26	A3
Brickfield Dr	74	B3
Brickfield La	75	C3
Bride Rd	124	B4
Brides Glen Rd	120	A1
Bride St	124	B4
Bridgecourt Office Pk	82	B2
Bridgefoot St	124	A3
Bridge St *Dublin 4*	77	D2
Bridge St *Swords*	8	B1
Bridge St Lwr	124	A3
Bridge St Upr	124	A3
Bridgeview **1**	71	C2
Bridgewater Quay	74	A1
Brighton Av *Dublin 3*	63	D2
Brighton Av *Dublin 6*	85	D3
Brighton Av *Black.*	100	B3
Brighton Av *Carrick.*	116	B2
Brighton Cotts **2**	116	B1
Brighton Ct	116	B2
Brighton Gdns	85	D3
Brighton Grn	85	C3
Brighton Hall	116	B2
Brighton Lo **3**	116	B1
Brighton Pl	116	B2
Brighton Rd *Dublin 6*	85	D3
Brighton Rd *Fox.*	116	B1
Brighton Sq	85	D3
Brighton Ter **7**	114	A1
Brighton Vale	100	A3
Britain Pl	62	A3
Britain Quay	77	D2
Broadford Av	108	A2
Broadford Cl	108	A2
Broadford Cres	108	A2
Broadford Dr	108	A2
Broadford Hill	108	A2
Broadford Lawn	108	A2
Broadford Pk	108	A2
Broadford Ri	108	A2
Broadford Rd	108	A2
Broadford Wk	108	A2
Broadmeadow	8	B1
Broadmeadow Rd	8	B1
Broadstone	61	D3
Broadstone Av *off Phibsborough Rd*	61	D3
Broadway Dr	38	B3
Broadway Gro	38	B3
Broadway Pk	38	B3
Broadway Rd	38	B3
Brompton Ct	39	C3
Brompton Grn	39	C3
Brompton Gro	39	C3
Brompton Lawn	39	C3
Brookdale	104	A1
Brookdale Av	10	A3
Brookdale Cl	10	A3
Brookdale Ct	10	A3
Brookdale Dr	10	A3
Brookdale Grn	10	A3
Brookdale Gro	10	A3
Brookdale Lawns	10	A3
Brookdale Pk	10	A3
Brookdale Rd	10	A3
Brookdale Wk	10	A3
Brookdale Way	10	A3
Brookdene	121	C3
Brookfield *Dublin 5*	47	C3
Brookfield *Dublin 6*	86	B1
Brookfield *Black.*	99	C1
Brookfield Lucan	68	A1
Brookfield Av *Black.*	99	D1
Brookfield Av **25** *Bray*	122	A2
Brookfield Ct **1**	84	B3
Brookfield Est	84	B3
Brookfield Pl	99	D1
Brookfield Rd *Dublin 8*	74	B3
Brookfield Rd *Dublin 24*	102	A1
Brookfield St	74	B3
Brookfield Ter	99	D1
Brookhaven Dr	27	C1
Brookhaven Gro	27	C1
Brookhaven Pk	27	C1
Brookhaven Ri	27	C1
Brooklands	88	A2
Brooklawn *Dublin 3*	64	A2
Brooklawn *Black.*	99	C1
Brooklawn *Lucan*	68	A1
Brooklawn Av	100	A3
Brooklawn Wd	100	A3
Brookmount Av	93	C3

Brookmount Lawns
  off Tallaght Rd 93 C3
Brookpark 68 A3
Brook Pk Ct 100 B3
Brookstone La 4 37 D3
Brookstone Rd 37 D3
Brookvale 68 B1
Brookvale Downs 95 C1
Brookvale Rd *Dublin 4* 87 C2
Brookvale Rd
  Dublin 14 95 C2
Brookview Av 102 A1
Brookview Cl 102 A1
Brookview Ct 90 A3
Brookview Cres 90 A3
Brookview Dr 90 A3
Brookview Gdns 90 A3
Brookview Grn 102 A1
Brookview Gro 102 A1
Brookview Lawns 90 A3
Brookview Pk 102 A1
Brookview Ter 102 A1
Brookville 42 B1
Brookville Cres 46 B1
Brookville Pk (Artane)
  Dublin 5 46 B2
Brookville Pk (Coolock)
  Dublin 5 47 C1
Brookville Rd *D.L.* 112 A1
Brookwood 106 B3
Brookwood Av 46 B3
Brookwood Cres 47 C3
Brookwood Dr 46 B3
Brookwood Glen 47 C3
Brookwood Gro 46 B3
Brookwood Hts 46 B3
Brookwood Lawn 47 C3
Brookwood Meadow 46 B3
Brookwood Pk 46 B3
Brookwood Ri 47 C3
Brookwood Rd 46 B3
Broombridge Rd 60 B1
Broombridge Sta 60 B1
Broomfield 14 A3
Broomfield Ct 121 C1
Broomhill Business
  Complex 91 D2
Broomhill Business Pk 92 A2
Broom Hill Cl 91 D3
Broomhill Rd 92 A2
Broom Hill Ter 92 A2
Brown St N 124 A1
Brown St S 75 C3
Brunswick Pl
  off Pearse St 77 C2
Brunswick St N 124 A1
Brusna Cotts 99 D1
Buckingham St Lwr 62 B3
Buckingham St Upr 62 B3
Buckleys La 66 B2
Buirg An Ri Glen 69 D3
Buirg An Ri Ter 69 D3
Bulfin Gdns 74 A2
Bulfin Rd 74 A2
Bulfin St 74 A3
Bull All St 124 B4
Bullock Steps 8 114 B1
Bunratty Av 46 B1
Bunratty Dr 46 B1
Bunratty Rd 46 A1
Bunting Rd 83 C2
Burdett Av 114 A1
Burgage, The 114 B2
Burgess La
  off Haymarket 124 A2
Burgh Quay 125 D2
Burke Pl 74 B2
Burleigh Ct 76 B3
Burlington Gdns 76 B3
Burlington Rd 86 B1
Burmah Cl 114 B3
Burnaby Hts 123 C3
Burnaby Manor 123 D2
Burnaby Ms 123 D2
Burnaby Rd 123 D2
Burnaby Wds 123 D3
Burnell Pk Av 57 C1
Burnell Pk Grn 57 C1
Burren Ct 31 D3
Burris Ct
  off School Ho La W 124 B3
Burrow Ct 21 C2
Burrowfield Rd 50 A1
Burrow Rd 50 A1
Burton Hall Av 110 B2

Burton Hall Rd 110 B2
Burton Rd 114 B3
Bushfield 80 A3
Bushfield Av 87 C2
Bushfield Dr 80 A3
Bushfield Grn 80 A3
Bushfield Gro 90 A1
Bushfield Lawns 90 A1
Bushfield Pl 86 B1
Bushfield Ter 86 B2
Bushy Pk Gdns 95 C1
Bushy Pk Rd 95 C1
Buterly Business Pk 46 A2
Butt Br 76 B1
Buttercup Cl 1 35 C3
Buttercup Dr 35 C3
Buttercup Pk 2 35 C3
Buttercup Sq 3 35 C3
Butterfield Av 94 B2
Butterfield Cl 94 B3
Butterfield Ct 95 C2
Butterfield Cres 94 B3
Butterfield Dr 95 C3
Butterfield Gro 94 B2
Butterfield Meadow 94 B2
Butterfield Orchard 95 C3
Butterfield Pk 94 B3
Byrnes La 124 C1

C

Cabinteely 117 D1
Cabinteely Av 117 D1
Cabinteely Bypass 117 D1
Cabinteely Cl 117 D1
Cabinteely Ct 4 112 B3
Cabinteely Cres 112 B3
Cabinteely Dr 112 B3
Cabinteely Grn 112 B3
Cabinteely Pk 2 117 D1
Cabinteely Way 112 B3
Cabra Dr 61 C2
Cabra Gro 61 C2
Cabra Pk 61 D2
Cabra Rd 60 B2
Cadogan Rd 63 C2
Cairn Ct 31 D3
Cairn Hill 112 A3
Cairnwood 90 B3
Cairnwood Av 90 B3
Cairnwood Ct 90 B3
Cairnwood Grn 90 B3
Calderwood Av 45 C2
Calderwood Gro 45 C3
Calderwood Rd 63 C1
Caledon Rd 63 C3
Callary Rd 98 A2
Calmount Rd 82 B3
Camac Pk 82 B1
Camac Ter
  off Bow Br 74 B2
Camaderry Rd 122 B3
Camberley Elms 96 A2
Camberley Oaks 96 A3
Cambridge Av 78 A3
Cambridge La 85 D2
Cambridge Rd
  Dublin 4 77 D2
Cambridge Rd (Rathmines)
  Dublin 6 77 D2
Cambridge Sq 77 D2
Cambridge Ter 86 B1
Cambridge Vil
  off Belgrave Rd 86 A2
Camden Lock
  off South Docks Rd 77 D2
Camden Mkt
  off Camden St Lwr 76 A3
Camden Pl 76 A3
Camden Row 76 A3
Camden St Lwr 76 A3
Camden St Upr 76 A3
Cameron Sq 74 A2
Cameron St 75 C3
Campbell's Ct
  off Little Britain St 124 B1
Campbells Row
  off Portland St N 62 B3
Campfield Ter 109 D1
Canal Bk 81 D1
Canal Rd 86 A1
Canal Ter 73 C3
Canal Turn 80 B1
Canal Wk 72 A3
Cannonbrook 68 B2

Cannonbrook Lawn 68 B2
Cannonbrook Pk 68 B2
Cannon Rock Vw 53 C2
Canonbrook Av 68 A2
Canonbrook Ct 68 A2
Canon Lillis Av 63 C3
Canon Mooney Gdns
  off Cambridge Rd 77 D2
Canon Troy Ct 72 B1
Capel St 124 C1
Cappagh Av 42 A1
Cappagh Dr 42 A1
Cappaghmore 80 A1
Cappagh Rd 42 A1
Cappoge Cotts 29 C3
Captains Av 84 A2
Captains Dr 84 A2
Captain's Hill 66 B2
Captains Rd 84 A2
Caragh Rd 60 B3
Cara Pk 34 B2
Carberry Rd 45 C3
Cardiff Br
  off Phibsborough Rd 61 D3
Cardiff Castle Rd 42 A1
Cardiffsbridge Av 41 D2
Cardiffsbridge Gro
  off Cappagh Rd 42 A1
Cardiffsbridge Rd
  (Bothar Dhroichead
  Chiarduibh) 42 A1
Cardiffs La 77 C2
Cards La
  off Townsend St 125 E2
Caritas Convalescent Cen
  & St. Mary's Cen 88 B3
Carleton Rd 63 D2
Carlingford Par 77 C2
Carlingford Pl
  off Carlingford Par 77 C2
Carlingford Rd 62 A2
Carlisle Av 87 C1
Carlisle St 75 D3
Carlisle Ter 2 *D.L.* 113 D1
Carlisle Ter *Mala.* 14 A2
Carlton Ct *Dublin 3* 64 A2
Carlton Ct *Swords* 11 C2
Carlton Ms
  off Shelbourne Av 77 D3
Carlton Ter 5 122 A1
Carlton Vil 6 122 A1
Carmanhall Rd 110 A2
Carmans Hall 124 A4
Carmelite Cen 87 C1
Carmelite Monastery
  Dublin 14 97 D1
Carmelite Monastery
  Still. 110 B1
Carna Rd 71 D2
Carndonagh Dr 48 B1
Carndonagh Lawn 48 B1
Carndonagh Rd 48 B1
Carne Ct 25 D2
Carnew St 61 C3
Carnlough Rd 60 B2
Caroline Row
  off Bridge St 77 D2
Carpenterstown Av 39 C3
Carpenterstown Pk E 38 B3
Carpenterstown Rd 57 C1
Carraig Glen 117 D1
Carraig Grennane 119 C2
Carraigmore Cl 103 D2
Carraigmore Dr 103 D2
Carraigbridge Pk 103 D2
Carraigmore Pk 103 D2
Carraigmore Rd 103 D2
Carraigmore Vw 103 D2
Carraroe Av 48 A1
Carrickbrack Heath 51 C2
Carrickbrack Hill 51 C3
Carrickbrack Lawn 51 C3
Carrickbrack Pk 51 C3
Carrickbrack Rd 51 C3
Carrick Brennan Lawn 100 B3
Carrickbrennan Rd 100 B3
Carrick Ct 21 C2
Carrickhill Cl 21 C1
Carrickhill Dr 21 C1
Carrickhill Hts 21 C2
Carrickhill Ri 21 C1
Carrickhill Rd 21 C3
Carrickhill Rd Mid 21 C2
Carrickhill Rd Upr 21 C1

Carrickhill Wk 21 C1
Carrick Lawn 1 109 D1
Carrickmines 117 C2
Carrickmines Av 117 C2
Carrickmines Chase 117 C1
Carrickmines Dale 117 C2
Carrickmines Garth 117 C2
Carrickmines Little 117 C2
Carrickmines Oaks 117 C2
Carrickmount Av 96 A3
Carrickmount Dr 96 A3
Carrick Ter 74 B3
Carrigallen Dr
  off Carrigallen Rd 42 B3
Carrigallen Pk
  off Carrigallen Rd 42 B3
Carrigallen Rd 42 B3
Carriglea 105 C2
Carriglea Av *Dublin 24* 104 B2
Carriglea Av *D.L.* 113 C2
Carriglea Ct *Dublin 24* 105 C2
Carriglea Ct 1 *D.L.* 113 C1
Carriglea Downs
  Dublin 24 104 B2
Carriglea Downs *D.L.* 113 C2
Carriglea Dr 104 B2
Carriglea Gdns 113 C1
Carriglea Gro 104 B2
Carriglea Ind Est 83 C1
Carriglea Ri 104 B2
Carriglea Vw 104 B2
Carriglea Wk 105 C2
Carrig Rd 31 D3
Carrigwood 105 C2
Carrow Rd 73 D3
Carysfort Av 99 D2
Carysfort Downs 111 C1
Carysfort Dr 114 B2
Carysfort Gro 111 D1
Carysfort Hall 99 D3
Carysfort Pk 99 D3
Carysfort Rd 114 B2
Carysfort Wd 111 D1
Casana Vw 53 C3
Casement Cl 42 A1
Casement Dr 42 A1
Casement Grn 42 A1
Casement Gro 42 A1
Casement Pk 42 A1
Casement Rd (Finglas S)
  Dublin 11 42 B2
Casement Rd (Finglas W)
  Dublin 11 42 A1
Casement Vil 112 B1
Cashel Av 84 B2
Cashel Business Cen 84 B3
Cashel Rd 84 A2
Casimir Av 85 C2
Casimir Ct 85 D2
Casimir Rd 85 C2
Casino Pk 63 D1
Casino Rd 63 C1
Castaheany 25 C2
Castilla Pk 65 C2
Castle Av *Dublin 3* 64 B2
Castle Av *Clond.* 80 B2
Castle Av *Swords* 11 D1
Castlebrook 109 C1
Castlebyrne Pk 99 D3
Castle Cl *Clond.* 80 B1
Castle Cl *Dublin 3* 64 A1
Castle Ct 2 *Dublin 16* 109 C1
Castle Ct *Boot.* 98 B1
Castle Cl *Lough.* 119 C3
Castle Cove 2 *Dalkey* 114 B2
Castle Cove *Mala.* 13 C1
Castle Cres 6 80 B2
Castlecurragh Heath 26 B2
Castlecurragh Pk 26 B2
Castlecurragh Vale 26 B2
Castledawson Av 99 C1
Castle Down Cft 4 13 C1
Castle Down Gro 13 C1
Castle Down Rd 13 C1
Castle Dr *Clond.* 80 B2
Castle Dr *Swords* 11 D1
Castle Elms 46 B1
Castle Fm *Shank.* 121 C3

Name	Location	Page	Grid
Castlefarm	Swords	8	B1
Castlefarm Wd		121	C3
Castlefield Av		105	C1
Castlefield Ct		105	C1
Castlefield Dr		105	D2
Castlefield Grn		105	D2
Castlefield Gro		105	D2
Castlefield Lawn 1		105	D1
Castlefield Manor Dublin 24		105	C1
Castlefield Manor Mala.		14	A3
Castlefield Pk		105	D1
Castlefield Ter		123	C3
Castlefield Way		105	D2
Castleforbes Ind Est		77	D1
Castleforbes Rd		77	D1
Castle Gate	Dublin 15	58	B1
Castlegate	Shank.	120	A3
Castle Golf Course		95	D2
Castlegrange Av		8	B1
Castlegrange Cl 1		9	C1
Castlegrange Hts 5		8	B1
Castlegrange Hill 2		9	C1
Castlegrange Rd		9	C1
Castlegrange Way		8	B1
Castle Gro	Dublin 3	64	B1
Castle Gro	Clond.	80	B2
Castle Gro	Swords	11	D1
Castlekevin Rd		46	A1
Castleknock Av		39	D3
Castleknock Brook		39	D3
Castleknock Cl		39	C3
Castleknock Coll		57	D1
Castleknock Cres		39	D3
Castleknock Dale		39	D3
Castleknock Downs		39	C3
Castleknock Elms		39	D3
Castleknock Glade		39	D3
Castleknock Gra		39	C3
Castleknock Grn		39	D3
Castleknock Laurels		39	D3
Castleknock Lo		58	B1
Castleknock Meadows		39	C3
Castleknock Oaks		39	D3
Castleknock Pk		58	A1
Castleknock Parklands		40	A3
Castleknock Pines Lwr		40	A3
Castleknock Pines Upr		39	C3
Castleknock Ri		39	C3
Castleknock Rd		58	B1
Castleknock Sta		39	D2
Castleknock Vale		39	C3
Castleknock Vw		39	D3
Castleknock Village Cen		58	A1
Castleknock Wk		39	C3
Castleknock Way		39	C3
Castleknock Wd		39	D3
Castlelands 9		114	B1
Castlelands, The		95	D2
Castlelands Gro		114	B1
Castle Lawns		13	C1
Castle Lawns Est		92	B3
Castle Mkt off Drury St		124	C4
Castle Pk	Dublin 24	92	B3
Castle Pk	Black.	100	B3
Castle Pk	Clond.	80	B2
Castle Pk	Leix.	66	B2
Castle Pk	Swords	11	D1
Castle Pk Est		92	B3
Castlepark Rd		114	A2
Castle Riada Av		69	C2
Castle Riada Cres		69	C2
Castle Riada Dr		69	C3
Castle Riada Gro		69	C2
Castle Rd	Dublin 3	64	B2
Castle Rd	Lucan	69	C2
Castle Rosse		37	C3
Castlerosse Cres		37	C3
Castlerosse Dr		37	C3
Castlerosse Vw		37	C3
Castle Shop Cen		11	D1
Castleside Dr		95	D2
Castle St	Dublin 2	124	C3
Castle St	Bray	122	A1
Castle St	Dalkey	114	B2
Castle St Shop Cen		122	A1
Castle Ter		14	A2
Castletimon Av		45	D1
Castletimon Dr		45	D1
Castletimon Gdns		45	D1
Castletimon Grn		45	D1
Castletimon Pk		45	D1
Castletimon Rd		45	D1
Castletymon Ct		92	B3
Castleview	Dublin 5	46	A2
Castleview 3	Dublin 16	108	B1
Castle Vw	Carrick.	116	B2
Castleview Est		22	A2
Castleview Pk		13	D2
Castle Vw Rd		80	B2
Castle Vil 3		114	B2
Castlewood		25	D2
Castlewood Av		86	A2
Castlewood Cl off Castlewood Av		86	A2
Castlewood La		86	A2
Castlewood Pk		86	A2
Castlewood Pl		86	A2
Castlewood Ter		86	A2
Cathal Brugha St		125	D1
Cathedral La		75	D3
Cathedral St		125	D1
Cathedral Vw Ct			
off Cathedral Vw Wk		75	D3
Cathedral Vw Wk		75	D3
Catherines La off Church St Upr		124	B1
Catherine St off Ash St		124	A4
Cats Ladder 3		115	C1
Cavalry Row		75	C1
Cavendish Row off Parnell St		62	A3
Ceannchor Rd		54	C3
Ceannt Fort		74	B2
Cecil Av		63	D2
Cecilia St off Temple La S		124	C3
Cedar Av		91	D1
Cedar Brook Av		71	C3
Cedar Brook Pl		71	C3
Cedar Brook Wk		71	C3
Cedar Brook Way		71	C3
Cedar Ct	Dublin 6W	85	C3
Cedar Ct	Dunb.	22	B2
Cedar Ct	Lough.	118	B3
Cedar Dr	Dunb.	22	B2
Cedar Dr	Palm.	57	C3
Cedar Gro 1		38	A1
Cedar Hall off Prospect La		87	C3
Cedar Lo 6		106	B2
Cedarmount Rd		98	A3
Cedar Pk	Dublin 13	48	A1
Cedar Pk	Leix.	66	A2
Cedars, The 13	Abb.	119	C3
Cedars, The	D.L.	100	A3
Cedar Sq		99	C3
Cedar Wk		48	A2
Cedarwood Av		43	C1
Cedarwood Cl		43	C1
Cedarwood Grn		31	C3
Cedarwood Gro		43	C1
Cedarwood Pk		43	C1
Cedarwood Ri		43	C1
Cedarwood Rd		31	C3
Ceide Dun Eanna (Ennafort Dr)		47	C3
Ceide Gleannaluinn (Glenaulin Dr)		72	A1
Ceide Phairc An Bhailtini (Villa Park Dr)		60	A2
Celbridge Rd	Leix.	66	A2
Celbridge Rd	Lucan	67	D3
Celestine Av		77	D2
Celtic Pk Av		45	D3
Celtic Pk Rd		45	D3
Cenacle Gro		119	C3
Central Pk Business Pk		110	B3
Centre Pt Business Pk		81	D2
Century Business Pk		30	B3
Chalet Gdns		69	C1
Chalfont Av		13	D1
Chalfont Dr		13	D2
Chalfont Pl		13	D2
Chalfont Rd		13	D2
Chamber St		75	D3
Chancery La		124	C4
Chancery Pl		124	B2
Chancery St		124	B2
Chanel Av		46	B2
Chanel Gro		46	B1
Chanel Rd		46	A2
Chapel Av		77	D2
Chapelizod Bypass		72	A1
Chapelizod Ct		72	A1
Chapelizod Hill Rd		72	A1
Chapelizod Ind Est		72	B1
Chapelizod Rd Dublin 8		73	C1
Chapelizod Rd Dublin 20		73	C1
Chapel La	Dublin 1	124	C1
Chapel La	Swords	11	D1
Chapel Rd		19	C2
Charlemont		45	D3
Charlemont Av		101	D3
Charlemont Ct		86	A1
Charlemont Gdns off Charlemont St		76	A3
Charlemont Mall		86	A1
Charlemont Par		63	C3
Charlemont Pl		86	A1
Charlemont Rd		63	D2
Charlemont Sq off Charlemont St		76	A3
Charlemont St		76	A3
Charles La		62	B3
Charles St Gt		62	B3
Charles St W		124	B2
Charleston Av		86	A2
Charleston Rd		86	A2
Charlestown		30	B2
Charlestown Av		30	B3
Charlestown Ct		30	B2
Charlestown Dr		30	B2
Charlestown Grn		30	B2
Charlestown Pk		30	B2
Charlestown Way		30	B2
Charleville	Dublin 14	96	A3
Charleville	Dublin 16	94	A3
Charleville Av		63	C3
Charleville Mall		63	C3
Charleville Rd	Dublin 6	85	D2
Charleville Rd	Dublin 7	61	C2
Charleville Sq		94	B2
Charlotte Quay		77	C2
Charlotte Ter 2		115	C2
Charlotte Way		76	A3
Charlton Lawn		97	D2
Charnwood		122	A3
Charnwood Grn		38	A2
Chase, The		110	B2
Chatham Row off William St S		125	D4
Chatham St		125	D4
Chaworth Ter off Hanbury La		124	A3
Cheaters La off Redmonds Hill		76	A3
Cheeverstown Av		94	A3
Cheeverstown Rd		90	A3
Chelmsford La		86	B1
Chelmsford Rd		86	B1
Chelsea Gdns		65	C2
Cheltenham Pl off Portobello Br		86	A1
Cherbury Ct		98	B2
Cherbury Gdns		98	B2
Cherbury Ms		98	B2
Cherbury Pk Av		68	B2
Cherbury Pk Rd		68	B2
Cherries, The 1		108	A2
Cherries Rd		109	D2
Cherrington Cl		121	C3
Cherrington Dr		121	C3
Cherrington Rd		120	B3
Cherry Av	Carp.	38	B3
Cherry Av	Swords	10	B2
Cherry Ct	Dublin 6W	85	C3
Cherry Ct 2	Lough.	118	B3
Cherry Dr		38	B3
Cherryfield Av Dublin 6		86	B2
Cherryfield Av Dublin 12		83	D3
Cherryfield Cl		25	D3
Cherryfield Ct		25	C3
Cherryfield Dr		83	D3
Cherryfield Lawn		25	D3
Cherryfield Pk		25	D3
Cherryfield Rd		83	C3
Cherryfield Vw		25	C3
Cherryfield Wk		25	D2
Cherrygarth	Still.	98	B3
Cherry Garth	Swords	10	B2
Cherry Gro	Dublin 12	83	D3
Cherry Gro	Swords	10	B2
Cherry Lawn		39	C3
Cherry Lawns		68	A2
Cherrymount Cres		63	D1
Cherrymount Gro		63	D1
Cherrymount Pk		61	D2
Cherry Orchard Av		71	D3
Cherry Orchard Ct		71	D3
Cherry Orchard Cres		71	D3
Cherry Orchard Dr		71	D3
Cherry Orchard Grn		71	C2
Cherry Orchard Gro		71	D3
Cherry Orchard Ind Est		71	D1
Cherry Orchard Par 1		71	D3
Cherry Orchard Pk		71	D3
Cherry Orchard Sta		71	D3
Cherry Orchard Way off Cherry Orchard Av		71	D3
Cherry Pk	Carp.	38	B3
Cherry Pk	Swords	10	B2
Cherry Tree Dr		122	A3
Cherry Wd		118	B3
Cherrywood Av		80	A2
Cherrywood Business Pk		120	A1
Cherrywood Pk		118	B3
Cherrywood Rd		120	B1
Chester Downs		113	D1
Chesterfield Av Dublin 8		59	D3
Chesterfield Av Dublin 15		58	B1
Chesterfield Cl		58	B1
Chesterfield Copse		58	B1
Chesterfield Gro		58	B1
Chesterfield Pk		58	B1
Chesterfield Vw		58	B1
Chester Rd		86	A1
Chester Sq 8		114	A1
Chestnut Ct		45	D2
Chestnut Gro Dublin 16		108	B2
Chestnut Gro Dublin 24		91	D1
Chestnut Pk 2		111	D2
Chestnut Rd Dublin 12		82	A2
Chestnut Rd Still.		98	A2
Christ Ch Cath		124	C3
Christchurch Pl		124	B3
Church Av (Irishtown) Dublin 4		77	D3
Church Av (Rathmines) Dublin 6		86	A2
Church Av Dublin 8		74	B2
Church Av (Glasnevin) Dublin 9		44	A3
Church Av (Blanchardstown) Dublin 15		39	C2
Church Av Kill.		119	C3
Church Av 2 Port.		20	B3
Church Av N (Drumcondra)		62	B1
Church Ct		58	A1
Churchfields		96	A3
Church Gdns		86	A2
Churchgate Av		65	C2
Church Gates		123	C1
Church Gro		103	D2
Churchill Ms 10		114	B1
Churchill Ter		87	D1
Church Lands	Bray	122	A2
Churchlands	Sandy.	109	D3
Church La	Dublin 2 off College Grn		125	D3
Church La (Rathfarnham) Dublin 14		95	C2
Church La	Grey.	123	C2
Church La S off Kevin St Lwr		76	A3
Church Pk Av		85	C2
Church Pk Ct		85	C2
Church Pk Dr		85	C2
Church Pk Lawn		85	C2
Church Pk Vw		85	C2
Church Pk Way		85	C2
Church Rd Dublin 3		77	C1
Church Rd (Finglas) Dublin 11		42	B2
Church Rd Dublin 13		50	B2
Church Rd Bray		122	A2

Name	Page	Grid
Church Rd *Dalkey*	114	B2
Church Rd *Grey.*	123	C1
Church Rd *Kill.*	118	B1
Church Rd *Mala.*	14	A2
Church Rd *Mulh.*	26	B2
Church Rd *Swords*	11	C1
Church St *Dublin 7*	124	B2
Church St (Finglas) *Dublin 11*	42	B2
Church St (Howth) *Dublin 13*	52	B2
Church St E	77	C1
Church St Upr	124	B1
Church Ter *Dublin 7* off Church St	124	B2
Church Ter *7 Bray*	122	A1
Churchtown Av	96	B1
Churchtown Business Pk	96	A3
Churchtown Cl	96	B1
Churchtown Dr	96	B1
Churchtown Rd Lwr	96	B1
Churchtown Rd Upr	96	B1
Church Vw *1*	80	A3
Churchview Av	118	B1
Churchview Dr	118	B1
Churchview Pk	118	B1
Church Vw Rd	118	B2
Cianlea	8	A1
Cian Pk	62	B1
Cill Cais	103	D2
Cill Eanna	47	D3
Cill Manntan Pk *2*	122	A2
City Junct Business Pk	35	C2
Citylink Business Pk	82	B1
City Quay	125	F2
Claddagh Grn	71	D2
Claddagh Rd	71	D2
Clanawley Rd	64	B1
Clanboy Rd	46	A3
Clanbrassil Cl	85	D1
Clanbrassil St Lwr	75	D3
Clanbrassil St Upr	85	D1
Clancarthy Rd	64	A1
Clancy Av	42	B1
Clancy Rd	43	C1
Clandonagh Rd	46	A3
Clanhugh Rd	64	A1
Clanmahon Rd	46	A3
Clanmaurice Rd	46	A3
Clanmawr	121	D2
Clanmoyle Rd	64	A1
Clanranald Rd	46	A3
Clanree Rd	46	A3
Clanwilliam Pl	77	C3
Clarehall Shop Cen	35	C2
Clare La	125	E4
Claremont Av	43	C3
Claremont Ct	61	C1
Claremont Dr	43	D2
Claremont Gro *1*	119	C1
Claremont Pk (Pairc Clearmont) *Dublin 4*	78	A3
Claremont Rd *Dublin 13*	51	C1
Claremont Rd *Cabin.*	117	C1
Claremont Rd *Kill.*	119	C1
Claremont Vil	113	D1
Claremount Pines	117	C1
Claremount Ter *11*	122	B2
Clarence Mangan Rd	75	D3
Clarence St	101	C3
Clarendon Mkt off Chatham St	125	D4
Clarendon Row off Clarendon St	125	D4
Clarendon St	125	D4
Clare Rd	44	B3
Clare St	125	E4
Clareville Ct	61	D1
Clareville Gro	61	D1
Clareville Pk	61	D1
Clareville Rd	85	C2
Clarinda Manor	113	D1
Clarinda Pk E	113	D1
Clarinda Pk N	101	D3
Clarinda Pk W	113	D1
Clarke Ter	75	C3
Clarkeville Ter *1*	57	D3
Classons Br	96	B1
Claude Rd	62	A2
Cleggan Av	71	D2
Cleggan Pk	71	D2
Cleggan Rd (Bothar Cloiginn)	71	D2
Clifden Dr	71	D2
Clifden Rd	72	A2
Cliffords La	12	A1
Cliff Ter *1*	114	B1
Cliff Wk (Fingal Way)	53	D2
Clifton Av	100	B3
Clifton La	100	B3
Clifton Ms	86	A1
Clifton Pk	121	C1
Clifton Ter	100	B3
Cliftonville Rd	62	B1
Clinches Ct	63	C3
Clogher Rd	84	B1
Cloghran	17	C1
Cloister Av	99	D3
Cloister Grn	99	D3
Cloister Gro	99	D3
Cloister Pk	99	D3
Cloisters, The *Dublin 6W*	85	C3
Cloisters, The *Dublin 9*	45	C3
Cloister Sq	99	D3
Cloister Way	99	D3
Clonard Av	109	C2
Clonard Cl	109	C2
Clonard Dr	109	C2
Clonard Gro	109	C2
Clonard Lawn	109	C2
Clonard Pk	109	C2
Clonard Rd *Dublin 12*	84	A1
Clonard Rd *Dublin 16*	109	C2
Clonasleigh *2*	121	C2
Clondalkin Commercial Pk	70	B3
Clondalkin Enterprise Cen	70	A3
Clondalkin Sta	70	B3
Clonee Br	23	D3
Clonee Bypass	23	D3
Clonfadda Wd	98	B2
Clonfert Rd	84	B1
Clonkeen Ct	112	B3
Clonkeen Cres	112	B2
Clonkeen Dr	112	B2
Clonkeen Gro	112	B2
Clonkeen Lawn *1*	112	B3
Clonkeen Rd	112	A2
Clonlara Rd	78	A2
Clonlea	108	B2
Clonlea Wd *1*	108	B2
Clonliffe Av	62	B2
Clonliffe Gdns	62	B2
Clonliffe Rd	62	B2
Clonmacnoise Gro	84	B2
Clonmacnoise Rd	84	B2
Clonmel Rd	43	D1
Clonmel St	76	A3
Clonmore Rd *Dublin 3*	62	B3
Clonmore Rd *Still.*	98	A3
Clonmore Ter	62	B3
Clonrosse Ct off Elton Dr	47	D1
Clonrosse Dr	47	D1
Clonrosse Pk off Elton Dr	47	D1
Clonshaugh Business & Tech Pk	33	D3
Clonshaugh Cl	34	A2
Clonshaugh Ct *1*	34	A2
Clonshaugh Cres	34	A2
Clonshaugh Dr	34	B2
Clonshaugh Grn	34	B2
Clonshaugh Gro	34	B2
Clonshaugh Hts	34	A2
Clonshaugh Ind Est	34	A3
Clonshaugh Lawns	34	A2
Clonshaugh Meadow	34	A2
Clonshaugh Pk	34	A2
Clonshaugh Ri *2*	34	A2
Clonshaugh Rd	34	A3
Clonshaugh Wk	34	B2
Clonsilla Cl	39	C2
Clonsilla Pk	39	C2
Clonsilla Rd	38	B2
Clonskeagh Br	87	C3
Clonskeagh Dr	87	C3
Clonskeagh Rd *Dublin 6*	87	C2
Clonskeagh Rd *Dublin 14*	87	C3
Clonskeagh Sq	87	C3
Clontarf Castle off Castle Av	64	B2
Clontarf Golf Course	64	A1
Clontarf Pk	65	C2
Clontarf Prom	64	A2
Clontarf Rd	63	D2
Clontarf Rd Sta	63	D2
Clonturk Av	62	B1
Clonturk Gdns	62	B1
Clonturk Pk	62	B1
Cloonlara Cres off Cloonlara Rd	42	B3
Cloonlara Dr off Cloonlara Rd	42	B3
Cloonlara Rd	42	B3
Cloonmore Av	102	B2
Cloonmore Cl	102	B2
Cloonmore Cres	102	B2
Cloonmore Dr	102	A2
Cloonmore Gdns	102	B2
Cloonmore Grn	102	A2
Cloonmore Gro	102	B2
Cloonmore Lawn	102	A2
Cloonmore Pk	102	A2
Cloonmore Rd	102	B2
Close, The *Dublin 6W*	94	A2
Close, The *Dublin 9*	45	D1
Close, The (Ballinteer) *Dublin 16*	108	B3
Close, The (Ballyboden) *Dublin 16*	106	A2
Close, The (Kilnamanagh) *Dublin 24*	91	D2
Close, The (Tallaght) *4 Dublin 24*	104	A1
Close, The (Lutterell Hall) *Dunb.*	22	A2
Close, The *Gra M.*	68	B3
Close, The *Kins.*	12	A2
Close, The *8 Mala.*	15	C3
Close, The *Manor.*	25	C2
Close, The *Still.*	98	A2
Clover Hill Dr	72	A3
Cloverhill Ind Est	70	B3
Clover Hill Rd *Dublin 10*	72	A3
Cloverhill Rd *Clond.*	70	B3
Cloyne Rd	84	B1
Cluain Mhuire	113	D2
Cluain R'	69	D2
Club Rd	82	A2
Clune Rd	42	B1
Cluny Gro	113	D3
Cluny Pk	114	A3
Clyde La	87	C1
Clyde Rd	87	C1
Cnoc Aoibhean	67	C3
Coast Rd *Dublin 13*	37	D2
Coast Rd *Mala.*	14	B2
Coburg Pl	63	C3
Cois Coillte *3*	118	B3
Cois Na hAbhann	103	D1
Colbert's Fort	91	D3
Colberts Fort Cotts	91	D2
Coldcut Rd	70	B1
Coldwell St	113	C1
Colepark Av	72	A2
Colepark Dr	72	A2
Colepark Grn	72	B2
Colepark Rd	72	A2
Coleraine St	124	B1
Coliemore Rd	115	C2
Coliemore Vil *3*	115	C2
College Business & Tech Pk	27	C2
College Cres	94	A1
College Dr	94	A1
Collegefort	57	D1
College Gate	57	D1
College Grn	125	D3
College Gro	57	D1
College La	125	F3
College Pk *Dublin 6W*	94	A1
College Pk *Dublin 15*	58	A1
College Pk Av	109	C3
College Pk Cl	109	C3
College Pk Ct *1*	109	C3
College Pk Dr *2*	109	C3
College Pk Gro	109	C3
College Pk Way	109	C3
College Rd *Dublin 15*	58	A1
College Rd (Ballinteer) *Dublin 16*	107	D3
College St *Dublin 2*	125	D3
College St *Dublin 13*	37	D3
College Vw *1*	92	A3
Collegewood	57	D1
Colliers Av	86	B2
Collins Av	45	D3
Collins Av E	46	A3
Collins Av Extension	44	A1
Collins Av W	44	B2
Collins Ct *Dublin 9*	45	D3
Collins Ct *Black.* off Sweetmans Av	99	D2
Collins Dr	43	C1
Collins Grn	43	C1
Collins Pk	45	D3
Collinsview	43	C1
Collins Pl	43	C1
Collins Row	43	C2
Collinstown Business Pk	33	C1
Collinstown Cres *1*	70	A3
Collinstown Cross Ind Est	33	C1
Collinstown Gro	70	B3
Collinstown Rd	70	B2
Collins Wd	45	C2
Colthurst	69	D2
Colthurst Cl	69	D2
Colthurst Cres	69	D2
Colthurst Gdns	69	D2
Colthurst Grn	69	D2
Colthurst Ms	69	D2
Colthurst Pk	69	D2
Colthurst Ri	69	D2
Colthurst Rd	69	D2
Colthurst Way	69	D2
Comeragh Rd	83	D1
Commons Rd *Clond.*	80	A3
Commons Rd *Lough.*	120	B1
Commons St	125	F2
Con Colbert Rd (Bothar Coilbeard) *Dublin 8*	74	A2
Con Colbert Rd (Bothar Coilbeard) *Dublin 10*	73	D2
Congress Gdns *10*	114	A1
Congress Hall	22	A3
Congress Pk	22	A3
Connaught St	61	D2
Connaught Ter off Rathgar Rd	85	D3
Connolly Av *Dublin 8*	74	A2
Connolly Av *Mala.*	19	D1
Connolly Cres	19	D1
Connolly Gdns	74	A2
Connolly Sta	125	F1
Conor Clune Rd	59	D1
Conquer Hill Rd	65	C3
Conquer Hill Ter	65	C2
Constellation Rd	33	C2
Constitution Hill	124	B1
Convent Av *Dublin 3*	63	C2
Convent Av *Bray*	122	B2
Convent Ct *1*	110	B1
Convent La *Dublin 14*	95	C3
Convent La *Port.*	21	D1
Convent Lawns	72	A2
Convent Rd *Black.*	99	D2
Convent Rd *Clond.*	80	B3
Convent Rd *Dalkey*	114	B2
Convent Rd *D.L.*	101	D3
Convent Vw *12 Bray*	122	B2
Convent Vw *Clond.*	80	B3
Convent Vw Cotts *Dublin 7*	60	A1
Convent Vw Cotts *Clond.*	80	A3
Conway Ct off Macken St	77	C2
Conyngham Rd	74	A1
Cookstown Est Rd	91	C2
Cookstown Ind Est	91	C3
Cookstown Rd	90	B2
Cookstown Way	91	C3
Cook St	124	B3
Coolamber Ct *2*	94	A3
Coolamber Pk	94	A3

Name	Page	Grid
Coolatree Cl	45	D2
Coolatree Pk	45	C2
Coolatree Rd	45	D2
Cooldrinagh La	67	C3
Cooldrinagh Ter	67	C2
Cooleen Av	45	C1
Coolevin	118	B2
Coolevin La		
off Long La	75	D3
Cooley Rd	83	D1
Coolgariff Rd	45	C2
Coolgreena Cl	45	D2
Coolgreena Rd	45	D2
Coolkill	109	D3
Coolmine Boul	38	B2
Coolmine Cl	38	B2
Coolmine Cotts	26	B3
Coolmine Ct	38	B2
Coolmine Grn	38	B2
Coolmine Ind Est	38	B2
Coolmine Lawn	38	B2
Coolmine Ms 1	38	B2
Coolmine Pk	38	B2
Coolmine Rd	38	B3
Coolmine Wds	38	B2
Coolnevaun	110	B1
Coolock Av	46	B1
Coolock Cl	46	B1
Coolock Dr	46	B1
Coolock Grn	46	B1
Coolock Gro	46	B1
Coolock Ind Est	47	C1
Coolock La	33	C3
Coolock Village	46	B2
Coolrua Dr	45	C1
Coombe, The	124	A4
Copeland Av	63	D1
Copeland Gro	63	D1
Cope St	125	D3
Copper All	124	C3
Coppice, The	57	C3
Coppinger Cl	99	C3
Coppinger Glade	99	C3
Coppinger Row		
off William St S	125	D4
Coppinger Wk	99	C3
Coppinger Wd	99	C3
Coppins, The	116	B1
Corballis Row		
off Kevin St Upr	124	B4
Corbawn Av	121	D1
Corbawn Cl	121	D2
Corbawn Ct	121	D2
Corbawn Dale	121	D2
Corbawn Dr	121	D2
Corbawn Glade	121	D2
Corbawn Gro	121	D2
Corbawn La	121	C2
Corbawn Lawn	121	C2
Corbawn Wd	121	C2
Corcaill	20	B1
Corduff Av	27	D3
Corduff Cl	27	D3
Corduff Cotts	39	C1
Corduff Cres	27	D3
Corduff Gdns	27	D3
Corduff Gro	27	C3
Corduff Pk	27	C3
Corduff Pl	27	D3
Corduff Way	27	D3
Corkagh Vw	80	A3
Cork Hill	124	C3
Cork St	75	C3
Cormac Ter	95	C1
Cornelscourt	112	A3
Cornelscourt Hill Rd	117	C1
Corn Ex Pl		
off George's Quay	125	E2
Cornmarket	124	B3
Corporation St	125	E1
Corrib Rd	84	B3
Corrig Av	113	D1
Corrig Cl		
off Lugaquilla Av	92	B1
Corrig Pk	113	D1
Corrig Rd Dalkey	114	B2
Corrig Rd D.L.	113	D1
Corrig Rd Still.	110	A2
Corryberg	94	A2
Cottage Pl		
off Portland Pl	62	A2
Coulson Av	85	D3
Coultry Av	32	B3
Coultry Cres	32	A3
Coultry Dr	32	A3
Coultry Gdns	32	A3
Coultry Gro	32	B3
Coultry Lawn	32	B3
Coultry Pk	32	B3
Coultry Rd	32	A3
Coultry Way	32	A3
Coundon Ct	118	B2
Court, The Dublin 3		
off Clontarf Rd	64	A2
Court, The Dublin 5	48	A3
Court, The Dublin 6W	94	A2
Court, The Dublin 9	45	C3
Court, The Dublin 13	50	A1
Court, The Dublin 16	108	B2
Court, The (Cookstown)		
Dublin 24	91	C2
Court, The (Kilnamanagh)		
Dublin 24	91	D1
Court, The (Lutterell Hall)		
Dunb.	22	A2
Court, The (Plunkett Hall)		
Dunb.	22	A1
Court, The (Ballyowen)		
Lucan	69	D2
Court, The 7 Mala.	15	C3
Court, The Mulh.	26	A2
Court, The Swords	9	C1
Courthill Dr	22	A2
Courtlands	118	A1
Courtyard, The		
Dublin 14	95	D2
Courtyard, The Cool.	38	A3
Courtyard, The 6 Fox.	111	D2
Courtyard, The 1 Mala.	15	C3
Cove, The 1	13	D1
Cowbooter La	53	C2
Cowley Pl	62	A2
Cow Parlour	75	C3
Cowper Downs	86	A3
Cowper Dr	86	B3
Cowper Gdns	86	B3
Cowper Rd	86	A3
Cowper St	61	C3
Cowper Village	86	A3
Crag Av	80	B1
Crag Av Business Pk	80	B1
Crag Av Ind Cen	80	B1
Crag Cres	71	C3
Crag Ter	80	B1
Craigford Av	46	A3
Craigford Dr	46	A3
Craiglands 4	115	C2
Craigmore Gdns	100	A2
Crampton Bldgs		
off Temple Bar	125	D3
Crampton Ct	124	C3
Crampton Quay	125	D2
Crampton Rd	77	D3
Crane La	124	C3
Crane St	75	C2
Cranfield Pl	77	D3
Cranford Ct	88	A3
Cranmer La	77	C3
Crannagh	87	C3
Crannagh Castle	95	C2
Crannagh Ct	95	C2
Crannagh Gro	95	D2
Crannagh Pk	95	D2
Crannagh Rd	95	C2
Crannagh Way	95	D2
Crannoge Rd	31	D3
Crannogue Cl	31	D3
Crannogue Rd	31	D3
Crawford Av	62	A2
Creighton St	125	F3
Cremona Rd	72	A2
Cremore Av	43	D3
Cremore Cres	43	D3
Cremore Dr	43	D3
Cremore Hts		
off Ballygall Rd E	43	D2
Cremore Lawn	43	D3
Cremore Pk	43	D3
Cremore Rd	43	D3
Cremorne	94	A3
Crescent, The Dublin 3	63	D2
Crescent, The (Donnybrook)		
Dublin 4	87	C2
Crescent, The (Beaumont)		
Dublin 9	45	C2
Crescent, The (Whitehall)		
Dublin 9	45	C3
Crescent, The		
Dublin 13	50	A1
Crescent, The (Ballinteer)		
Dublin 16	108	B3
Crescent, The (Ballyboden)		
Dublin 16	106	A2
Crescent, The		
Dublin 24	104	A1
Crescent, The (Cookstown)		
Dublin 24	91	C2
Crescent, The (Kilnamanagh)		
Dublin 24	91	D1
Crescent, The (Lutterell Hall)		
Dunb.	22	A2
Crescent, The Gra M.	12	A3
Crescent, The Kins.	12	A3
Crescent, The Lucan	67	D3
Crescent, The 5 Mala.	15	C3
Crescent, The 3 Swords	11	D1
Crescent, The (Seatown Pk)		
Swords	9	C1
Crescent Dr	94	A1
Crescent Gdns	63	C3
Crescent Pl	63	D2
Crescent Vil	62	A1
Crestfield Av	44	B2
Crestfield Cl	44	B2
Crestfield Dr	44	B2
Crestfield Pk		
off Crestfield Cl	44	B2
Crinan Strand	77	C1
Crinken Glen	120	B3
Crinken La	120	B3
Croaghpatrick Rd	60	A2
Crofton Av	101	C3
Crofton Rd	101	C2
Crofton Ter	101	C2
Croftwood Cres	71	D3
Croftwood Dr	71	D3
Croftwood Gdns	71	D3
Croftwood Grn	72	A3
Croftwood Gro	71	D3
Croftwood Pk	72	A3
Croke Pk Ind Est	62	B3
Croker La	75	C2
Cromcastle Av	46	A1
Cromcastle Dr	46	A1
Cromcastle Grn	46	A1
Cromcastle Pk	46	A1
Cromcastle Rd	46	A1
Cromlech Ct	31	D3
Cromlech Flds	121	C1
Cromwells Fort Rd	83	C2
Cromwells Quarters	74	B2
Cross & Passion Coll	45	C3
Cross Av Boot.	99	C1
Cross Av D.L.	101	C3
Crossbeg Ind Est	82	A3
Cross Guns Br	61	D2
Cross Kevin St	76	A3
Crosslands Ind Est	82	A3
Crosstrees	53	C2
Crosthwaite Pk E	113	D1
Crosthwaite Pk S	113	D1
Crosthwaite Pk W	113	D1
Crosthwaite Ter	101	C3
Crotty Av	83	D2
Crown All		
off Temple Bar	125	D3
Crow St	125	D3
Croydon Gdns	63	C1
Croydon Grn	63	C2
Croydon Pk Av	63	C1
Croydon Ter	63	C1
Cruiserath Business Pk	27	D1
Crumlin Pk	84	A1
Crumlin Rd	84	A1
Crumlin Shop Cen	74	B3
Cuala Gro	122	B3
Cuala Rd Dublin 7	61	C2
Cuala Rd Bray	122	B3
Cuckoo La	124	B2
Cuffe La	76	A3
Cuffe St	76	A3
Cullenswood Gdns	86	B2
Cullenswood Pk	86	B2
Culmore Pk	71	D1
Culmore Rd	71	D1
Cul Na Greine	103	D1
Cumberland Rd	76	B3
Cumberland St	101	C3
Cumberland St N	62	A3
Cumberland St S	125	F4
Cunningham Dr	114	B3
Cunningham Rd	114	B2
Curlew Rd	83	D1
Curragh Av 3	26	B1
Curragh Cres 1	27	C1
Curragh Dr 2	27	C1
Curragh Grn 1	26	B1
Curragh Hall	26	B1
Curragh La 4	26	B1
Curragh Ms 2	26	B1
Curragh Rd 4	27	C1
Curved St		
off Eustace St	124	C3
Curzon St	76	A3
Cushlawn Pk	103	C3
Custom Ho	125	E2
Custom Ho Quay	125	E2
Cymric Rd	78	A2
Cypress Av 3	106	B2
Cypress Ct	118	B3
Cypress Downs	94	A2
Cypress Dr	94	A2
Cypress Garth	94	A2
Cypress Gro N	94	A2
Cypress Gro Rd	94	A2
Cypress Gro S	94	A2
Cypress Lawn	94	A2
Cypress Pk	94	A2
Cypress Rd	98	A2

D

Name	Page	Grid
Dakota Av	33	C2
Dalcassian Downs	61	D2
Dale, The (Cookstown)		
Dublin 24	91	C2
Dale, The (Kilnamanagh)		
Dublin 24	91	D1
Dale, The Dunb.	22	A1
Dale, The Manor.	25	C2
Dale Cl 1	110	A1
Dale Dr	98	A3
Dalepark Rd	103	D2
Dale Rd	98	A3
Dale Tree Av	105	C3
Dale Tree Cres	105	C3
Dale Tree Dr	105	C3
Dale Tree Gro	105	C3
Dale Tree Pk	105	C3
Dale Tree Rd	105	C3
Dale Tree Vw	105	C3
Dale Vw	118	B2
Dale Vw Pk 3	118	B2
Dale Vw Rd	8	A1
Dalkey	114	B1
Dalkey Av	114	B3
Dalkey Ct	114	B2
Dalkey Gro	114	B2
Dalkey Pk	114	B2
Dalkey Rock	114	B3
Dalkey Sound	115	C2
Dalkey Sta	114	B2
Dal Riada	15	C3
Damastown Cl	26	A2
Damastown Ct	26	A1
Damastown Grn	25	D1
Damastown Way	26	A2
Dame Ct	125	D3
Dame La	124	C3
Dame St	124	C3
Dane Rd	31	D3
Danes Ct	65	D2
Danesfort	64	B2
Daneswell Rd	62	A1
Dangan Av	84	A3
Dangan Dr	84	A3
Dangan Pk	84	A3
Danieli Dr	46	B3
Danieli Rd	46	B3
Daniel St	75	D3
Dargan Ct 13	122	B2
Dargle Dr	107	D1
Dargle Hts	106	A1
Dargle Lo 1	106	A1
Dargle Rd Dublin 9	62	A2
Dargle Rd Black.	111	D1
Dargle Valley	107	D1
Dargle Vw	108	A1
Dargle Wd	106	A1
Darley Cotts 3	122	A2
Darleys Ter	75	C3
Darley St	85	C3
Darling Est	59	D1

Name	Page	Grid
Dartmouth Ho Ind Est	72	B3
Dartmouth La	86	B1
Dartmouth Pl	86	A1
Dartmouth Rd	86	A1
Dartmouth Sq	86	B1
Dartmouth Ter	86	A1
off Dartmouth Ter		
Dartry Cotts	96	A1
Dartry Pk	86	A3
Dartry Rd	86	A3
David Pk	62	A2
David Rd	62	A2
Davis Pl *off*		
Thomas Davis St S	124	B4
Davitt Pl	118	B2
Davitt Rd *Dublin 12*	74	A3
Davitt Rd *Bray*	122	A2
Dawson Ct *Dublin 2*		
off Stephen St	124	C4
Dawson Ct *Black.*	99	C2
Dawson La	125	E4
Dawson St	125	D4
Deans Ct 1	112	A2
Deans Gra	112	A2
Deansgrange		
Business Pk	112	A2
Dean's Gra Rd	112	A1
Deanstown Av	41	D2
Deanstown Dr	42	A2
Deanstown Grn	42	A2
Deanstown Pk	42	A2
Deanstown Rd	42	A2
Dean St	124	B4
Dean Swift Grn	43	D2
Dean Swift Rd	43	D2
Dean Swift Sq		
off Swifts All	124	B3
De Burgh Rd	74	B1
Decies Rd	72	A2
De Courcy Sq	61	D1
Deerhaven Av	25	D1
Deerhaven Cl	25	D1
Deerhaven Cres	25	D1
Deerhaven Grn	25	D2
Deerhaven Pk	25	D1
Deerhaven Vw	25	D1
Deerhaven Wk	25	D2
Deerpark Av *Dublin 15*	58	B1
Deerpark Av *Kilt.*	103	C3
Deerpark Cl *Dublin 15*	58	B1
Deerpark Cl *Kilt.*	103	D3
Deerpark Dr *Dublin 15*	58	B1
Deerpark Dr *Kilt.*	103	D3
Deerpark Grn 9	103	D3
Deerpark Lawn	58	B1
Deerpark Pl	103	D3
Deerpark Ri	103	D3
Deerpark Rd *Dublin 15*	58	B1
Deerpark Rd *Kilt.*		
Deerpark Rd *Still.*	98	A2
Deerpark Ter 10	103	D3
Deerpark Way	103	D3
Delaford Av	105	D1
Delaford Dr	105	D1
Delaford Gro	105	D1
Delaford Lawn	105	D1
Delaford Pk	105	D1
Delbrook Manor	109	C2
Delbrook Pk	109	C2
Delhurst	24	B3
Delhurst Av	24	B3
Delhurst Ct 1	25	C3
Delhurst Gro 1	24	B3
Delhurst Ms 2	25	C3
Dell, The	108	A2
Del Val Av	49	C2
Del Val Ct	49	C2
Delville Rd	43	D2
Delvin Rd	61	C2
Delwood Cl	39	C3
Delwood Dr	39	C3
Delwood Gro	38	B3
Delwood Lawn	38	B3
Delwood Pk	39	C3
Delwood Rd	39	C3
Delwood Wk	39	C3
Demesne	64	B1
Denmark St Gt	62	A3
Denville Ct	118	B2
Denzille La	125	F4
Denzille Pl		
off Denzille La	125	F4
Department of Defence		
Dublin 7		
off Infirmary Rd	74	B1
Department of Defence		
Dublin 9		
off St. Mobhi Rd	62	A1
Dermot O'Hurley Av	77	D2
Derravaragh Rd	84	B3
Derry Dr	84	A2
Derrynane Gdns	77	D2
Derrynane Par	62	A2
Derry Pk	84	A2
Derry Rd	84	A2
De Selby	102	A2
De Selby Cl	102	A2
De Selby Ct	102	A2
De Selby Cres	102	A2
De Selby Downs	102	A2
De Selby Dr	102	A2
De Selby Grn	102	A2
De Selby La 2	102	A2
De Selby Lawns	102	A2
De Selby Ri 1	102	A2
De Selby Rd	102	A2
Desmond Av	101	C3
Desmond Cotts 4	114	B3
Desmond St	75	D3
Devenish Rd	84	B2
Deverell Pl	125	E1
Deverys La	61	D2
De Vesci Ter	101	C3
Devitt Vil 11	114	A1
Devon Cl 6	112	B1
Devoy Rd	74	A3
Dewberry Pk	21	C1
Digges La		
off Stephen St	124	C4
Digges St	76	A3
Digges St Lwr		
off Cuffe St	76	A3
Dingle, The	57	C3
Dingle Rd	60	B2
Dispensary La		
Dublin 14	95	C3
Dispensary La 1 *Lucan*	68	A1
Distillery La	66	B1
Distillery Rd	62	B2
Distributor Rd	30	B3
Diswellstown Rd	38	A3
Dixon Vil 12	114	A1
Docklands		
Innovation Pk	63	D3
Dock Pl S		
off Dock St S	77	C2
Dock St S	77	C2
Dodder Av	104	B2
Dodderbank	86	B3
Dodder Ct	104	B2
Dodder Cres	104	B2
Dodder Dale	95	C2
Dodder Grn	104	B2
Dodder Lawn	104	B2
Dodder Pk Dr	95	D1
Dodder Pk Gro	95	D1
Dodder Pk Rd	95	D1
Dodder Ter	77	D2
Doddervale	96	A1
D'Olier St	125	D2
Dollymount Av	65	D2
Dollymount Gro	65	C2
Dollymount Pk	65	D2
Dollymount Ri	65	D2
Dolmen Ct	31	D3
Dolphin Av	75	C3
Dolphin Mkt		
off Dolphin's Barn St	75	C3
Dolphin Rd	74	B3
Dolphin's Barn	75	C3
Dolphin's Barn St	75	C3
Dominican Conv	60	A1
Dominick La	124	C1
Dominick Pl	124	C1
Dominick St	101	C3
Dominick St Lwr	124	C1
Dominick St Upr	61	D3
Domville Dr	94	A2
Domville Gro 2	119	C3
Domville Rd	94	A2
Donaghmede Av	48	B1
Donaghmede Dr	48	B1
Donaghmede Pk	48	B1
Donaghmede Rd	48	A1
Donaghmede		
Shop Cen	48	A1
Donard Rd	83	D1
Donelan Av	74	B2
Donnybrook Castle Ct	87	D2
Donnybrook Cl	87	D3
Donnybrook Grn	87	D3
Donnybrook Manor	87	C2
Donnybrook Rd	87	C2
Donnycarney Rd	45	D3
Donnycastle	87	D2
Donomore Av	102	B2
Donomore Cres	103	C2
Donomore Grn	102	B2
Donomore Pk	103	C2
Donore Av	75	C3
Donore Rd	75	C3
Donore Ter		
off Brown St S	75	C3
Donovan La		
off Clanbrassil		
St Lwr	75	D3
Doonamana Rd	118	A1
Doonanore Pk	118	A1
Doon Av	61	C3
Doon Ct	31	D3
Doonsalla Dr	118	A1
Doonsalla Pk	118	A1
Doris St	77	C2
Dornden Pk	88	B3
Dorney Ct	121	C2
Dorset La	62	A3
Dorset Pl		
off Dorset St Lwr	62	A3
Dorset St Lwr	62	A3
Dorset St Upr	62	A3
Dowkers La	75	D3
Dowland Rd	83	D2
Dowling's Ct		
off Lombard St E	125	F2
Dowling's Ct S		
off Lombard St E	125	F2
Downpatrick Rd	84	B1
Dowth Av	61	C2
Doyle's La	65	D2
Drapier Grn	43	D2
Drapier Rd	43	D2
Drayton Cl	100	B3
Drimnagh Castle	83	C1
Drimnagh Rd	83	D1
Drinagh Abbey	116	A2
Drinaghmore	116	A1
Drinagh More Av	116	A2
Drinagh More Cl 2	116	A2
Drinagh More Cl 3	116	A2
Drive, The (Ballinteer)		
Dublin 16	108	B2
Drive, The (Ballyboden)		
Dublin 16	106	B1
Drive, The *Dublin 24*		
Dunb.	104	A1
Drive, The *Gra M.*	68	B3
Drive, The *Kins.*	12	A2
Drive, The *Manor.*	25	C2
Drive, The *Mulh.*	26	A2
Drive, The *Swords*	9	C1
Droim Na Coille Ct 4	69	D2
Dromard Rd	83	D1
Dromawling Rd	45	D2
Dromcarra Av	102	B1
Dromcarra Dr	102	B1
Dromcarra Grn	102	B1
Dromcarra Gro	102	B2
Dromdawn Av	45	C2
Dromeen Av	45	D2
Dromheath Av	26	B2
Dromheath Dr	26	B2
Dromheath Gdns	26	B2
Dromheath Gro	26	B2
Dromheath Pk	26	B2
Dromlee Cres	45	D2
Dromnanane Pk	45	D2
Dromnanane Rd	45	D2
Dromore Rd	84	A1
Druid Ct	31	D3
Druid's Valley	118	A3
Drumahill	109	D1
Drumalee Av		
off Drumalee Rd	61	C3
Drumalee Ct		
off Drumalee Rd	61	C3
Drumalee Dr		
off Drumalee Rd	61	C3
Drumalee Gro		
off Drumalee Rd	61	C3
Drumalee Pk	61	C3
Drumalee Rd	61	C3
Drumcairn Av	90	B3
Drumcairn Dr	90	B3
Drumcairn Gdns	90	B3
Drumcairn Pk	90	B3
Drumcliffe Dr	60	B2
Drumcliffe Rd	60	B2
Drumcondra Pk	62	B2
Drumcondra Rd Lwr	62	A2
Drumcondra Rd Upr	62	B1
Drumcondra Sta	62	B2
Drumfinn Av	71	D1
Drumfinn Pk	72	A2
Drumfinn Rd (Bothar		
Drom Finn)	72	A2
Drumkeen Manor	113	C3
Drummartin Cl	97	D3
Drummartin Cres 1	97	D3
Drummartin Link Rd, The		
Dublin 14	109	D1
Drummartin Link Rd, The		
Dublin 16	109	D1
Drummartin Pk	109	D1
Drummartin Rd	97	D3
Drummartin Ter	97	D3
Drummond Pl		
off Mount Drummond		
Av	85	D1
Drumnigh Rd	36	B1
Drumnigh Wd	36	B1
Druncondra Br	62	B1
Drury St	124	C4
Drynam Cl 1	12	A3
Drynam Ct	11	D2
Drynam Cres	12	A3
Drynam Dr	12	A3
Drynam Glen 3	12	B3
Drynam Grn 4	12	B3
Drynam Gro	12	A3
Drynam Pl	12	A3
Drynam Ri	12	A3
Drynam Rd	11	D1
Drynam Sq	12	A3
Drynam Vw 2	12	B3
Drynam Wk 2	12	A3
Drynam Way 3	12	A3
Drysdale Cl	104	A2
Dubber Cross	30	B2
Dublin City Uni	44	A2
Dublin Corporation Food Mkt		
off St. Michan's St	124	C1
Dublin Ind Est	43	C3
Dublin Port Tunnel	63	D3
Dublin Rd *Dublin 13*	49	C2
Dublin Rd *Dunb.*	22	B3
Dublin Rd *Mala.*	13	C3
Dublin Rd *Shank.*	120	B1
Dublin Rd *Swords*	17	C1
Dublin St *Dublin 13*	37	D3
Dublin St *Swords*	11	C1
Dublin Zoo	60	A3
Dufferin Av	75	D3
Duggan Pl *off Rathmines*		
Rd Upr	86	A2
Duke La	125	D4
Duke La Lwr		
off Duke St	125	D3
Duke Row		
off North Circular Rd	62	B3
Duke St	125	D4
Dun Aengusa	103	D2
Dunamase	99	C1
Dún An Óir	103	D1
Dunard Av	60	B3
Dunard Ct	60	B2
Dunard Dr	60	B2
Dunard Pk	60	B3
Dunard Rd	60	B3
Dunard Wk	60	B3
Dunawley Av	80	A1
Dunawley Dr	80	A1
Dunawley Gro	80	A1
Dunawley Way	80	A1
Dunbo Ter		
off Church St	52	B2
Dunboy	116	B2
Dunboyne Business Pk	22	A1
Dunboyne Castle	22	A3
Dunbur Ter 8	122	A1

Name	Page	Grid
Duncairn Av	122	A1
Duncairn Ter	122	A1
Duncarrig	51	C2
Dundaniel Rd	45	D1
Dundela Av	114	A1
Dundela Cres	114	A1
Dundela Haven	114	A1
Dundela Pk	114	A1
Dundrum Business Pk	97	C1
Dundrum Bypass	109	C1
Dundrum Castle	108	B1
Dundrum Gate Apartments 4	108	B1
Dundrum Rd	96	B1
Dundrum Shop Cen	96	B3
Dundrum Wd	108	B1
Dunedin Ct 7	112	B1
Dunedin Dr 8	112	B1
Dunedin Pk	112	B1
Dunedin Ter	112	B1
Dun Emer Dr	109	C1
Dun Emer Pk	109	C1
Dun Emer Rd	109	C1
Dunes, The	21	C3
Dungar Ter off Northumberland Av	101	D3
Dungriffan Rd	53	C3
Dun Laoghaire Ind Est	112	B2
Dun Laoghaire Sta	101	D2
Dunleary Hill	101	C3
Dunleary Rd	101	C2
Dunluce Rd	64	B1
Dunmanus Rd	60	B2
Dunmore Gro	91	D1
Dunmore Lawn	91	D1
Dunmore Pk	91	D1
Dunne St	62	B3
Dunree Pk	47	C1
Dunsandle Ct	58	A1
Dunsandle Gro	58	A1
Dunseverick Rd	64	B1
Dunsink Av	42	A2
Dunsink Dr	42	A2
Dunsink Gdns	42	B2
Dunsink Grn	42	A2
Dunsink La	41	C2
Dunsink Observatory	41	C2
Dunsink Pk	42	A2
Dunsink Rd	42	B2
Dunsoghly Av	41	D1
Dunsoghly Dr	41	D1
Dunsoghly Grn	41	D1
Dunstaffnage Hall Apartments 2	111	C1
Dunville Av	86	A2
Dunville Ter off Mountpleasant Av Upr	86	A1
Durham Pl 8	113	D1
Durham Rd	88	A1
Durrow Rd	84	B2
Dursey Row 5	39	D1
Dwyer Pk	122	A1

E

Name	Page	Grid
Eagle Hill	99	D2
Eagle Hill Av	85	C3
Eagle Ter 2	97	C3
Eaglewood 1	113	C3
Earl Pl	125	D1
Earls Ct	60	B2
Earlscourt Ind Est	96	A3
Earlsfort	69	D3
Earlsfort Av	69	D3
Earlsfort Cl	69	D3
Earlsfort Ct	69	D2
Earlsfort Dr	69	D3
Earlsfort Gdns	69	D2
Earlsfort Grn	69	D3
Earlsfort La	69	D3
Earlsfort Lawn	69	D2
Earlsfort Mans off Adelaide Rd	76	A3
Earlsfort Meadows	69	D2
Earlsfort Pk	69	D2
Earlsfort Ri	69	D3
Earlsfort Rd	69	D3
Earlsfort Ter	76	A3
Earlsfort Vale	69	D3
Earlsfort Vw	69	D3
Earlsfort Way	69	D3
Earl St N	125	D1
Earl St S	124	A4
Eastern Breakwater	78	B2
East Link	77	D2
Eastmoreland La	77	C3
Eastmoreland Pl	77	C3
East Oil Jetty	78	B2
East Pt Business Pk	63	D3
East Rd	77	D1
East Wall Rd	63	C2
Eastwood Cl	41	D2
Eastwood Cres	41	D2
Eastwood Pk	42	A2
Eaton Brae Dublin 14	96	A1
Eaton Brae Shank.	121	C2
Eaton Ct	122	B3
Eaton Pl	100	A2
Eaton Rd	85	C3
Eaton Sq Dublin 6W	85	C3
Eaton Sq Black.	100	A2
Eaton Wd Av	121	C2
Eaton Wd Ct	121	C2
Eaton Wd Grn	121	C2
Eaton Wd Gro	121	C2
Ebenezer Ter	75	C3
Eblana Av	101	D3
Eblana Vil off Grand Canal St Lwr	77	C2
Eccles Ct off Eccles Pl	62	A3
Eccles Pl	62	A3
Eccles St	62	A3
Echlin St	75	C2
Eden Av	107	D1
Edenbrook Ct 1	95	C3
Edenbrook Dr	94	B3
Edenbrook Pk	94	B3
Eden Ct	107	D1
Eden Cres	107	D1
Eden Gro	107	D1
Edenmore Av	47	C2
Edenmore Cres	47	D2
Edenmore Dr	47	D2
Edenmore Gdns	47	D2
Edenmore Grn	47	D2
Edenmore Gro	47	D2
Edenmore Pk	47	C2
Eden Pk	113	D1
Eden Pk Av	109	D1
Eden Pk Dr	97	D3
Eden Pk Rd	97	D3
Eden Quay	125	D2
Eden Rd Lwr	113	D1
Eden Rd Upr	113	D1
Eden Ter	113	D1
Edenvale Rd	86	B2
Eden Vil 3	113	D1
Edgewood Lawns	27	C3
Edmondsbury Ct 1	69	C1
Edmondstown	106	B3
Edmondstown Grn	106	B2
Edmondstown Pk	106	B2
Edmondstown Rd	106	B3
Edward Rd	122	B2
Edwards Ct	106	B2
Edwin Ct 5	114	A2
Effra Rd	85	D2
Eglington Rd	122	A1
Eglinton Ct	87	C2
Eglinton Pk Dublin 4	87	C2
Eglinton Pk D.L.	113	C1
Eglinton Rd	87	C2
Eglinton Sq	87	C2
Eglinton Ter Dublin 4	87	C2
Eglinton Ter Dublin 14	97	C3
Elderberry	68	A3
Elderwood Rd	57	C3
Eldon Ter off South Circular Rd	75	C3
Elgin Rd	87	C1
Elizabeth St	62	B2
Elkwood	94	A3
Ellenfield Rd	45	C2
Ellensborough	103	D3
Ellensborough Av	103	D3
Ellensborough Cl	103	D3
Ellensborough Copse	103	D3
Ellensborough Ct	103	D3
Ellensborough Cres	103	D3
Ellensborough Dale	103	D3
Ellensborough Downs	103	D3
Ellensborough Gra	103	D3
Ellensborough Grn	103	D3
Ellensborough Gro	103	D3
Ellensborough La	103	D3
Ellensborough Lo	103	D3
Ellensborough Meadows	103	D3
Ellensborough Pk	103	D3
Ellensborough Ri	103	D3
Ellensborough Vw	103	D3
Ellensborough Wk	103	D3
Ellesmere 1	110	B2
Ellesmere Av	61	C3
Ellis Quay	75	C1
Ellis St off Benburb St	75	C1
Elmbrook	69	C2
Elmbrook Cres	69	C2
Elmbrook Lawn	69	C2
Elmbrook Wk	69	C2
Elmcastle Cl	92	A2
Elmcastle Ct	92	A2
Elmcastle Dr	92	A2
Elmcastle Grn	92	A2
Elmcastle Pk	92	A2
Elmcastle Wk	92	A2
Elm Cl	69	C3
Elm Ct Jobs.	102	A2
Elm Ct Lucan	69	C3
Elmdale Cl	71	D2
Elmdale Cres	71	D2
Elmdale Dr	71	D2
Elmdale Pk	71	C2
Elm Dene	69	C3
Elm Dr Jobs.	102	A2
Elm Dr Lucan	69	C3
Elmfield Av	36	A3
Elmfield Cl 1	36	A3
Elmfield Ct 4	36	A3
Elmfield Cres	36	A3
Elmfield Dr 2	36	A3
Elmfield Grn	36	A3
Elmfield Gro	36	A3
Elmfield Ind Est	80	B1
Elmfield Lawn	36	A3
Elmfield Pk off Elmfield Av	36	A3
Elmfield Ri	36	A3
Elmfield Vale 3	36	A3
Elmfield Wk	36	A3
Elmfield Way	36	A3
Elm Gro	68	B3
Elm Gro Black.	99	D3
Elm Gro Jobs.	102	A2
Elm Gro Lucan	69	C3
Elm Gro Cotts off Blackhorse Av	60	A2
Elmgrove Ter 9	122	A1
Elm Mt Av	45	D3
Elm Mt Cl	45	D3
Elm Mt Ct	46	A3
Elm Mt Cres	45	D2
Elm Mt Dr	45	D3
Elm Mt Gro	45	D2
Elm Mt Hts	45	D2
Elm Mt Lawn	45	D2
Elm Mt Pk	45	D2
Elm Mt Ri	45	D2
Elm Mt Rd	45	D3
Elm Mt Vw	45	D3
Elm Pk	88	A2
Elmpark Av	86	B1
Elmpark Ter	85	C3
Elm Rd Dublin 9	45	D3
Elm Rd Dublin 12	82	A2
Elms, The Dublin 4	88	A3
Elms, The 14 Abb.	119	C3
Elms, The Black.	99	C2
Elms, The Dunb.	22	B2
Elms, The Shank.	121	C3
Elm Vale	69	C3
Elm Way Dublin 16	108	A2
Elm Way Lucan	69	C3
Elm Wd	69	C3
Elmwood Av Lwr	86	B1
Elmwood Av Upr off Elmwood Av Lwr	86	B2
Elmwood Cl	25	C3
Elmwood Ct 8	8	A1
Elmwood Dr	8	A1
Elmwood Pk	8	A1
Elmwood Rd	8	A1
Elner Ct	21	C1
Elton Ct Dublin 13 off Elton Dr	47	D1
Elton Ct Dunb.	22	B2
Elton Ct D.L.	114	B1
Elton Ct Leix.	66	A2
Elton Dr Dublin 13	47	D1
Elton Dr Dunb.	22	B2
Elton Gro	22	B2
Elton Pk Dublin 13	47	D1
Elton Pk D.L.	114	A1
Elton Wk off Elton Dr	47	D1
Ely Cres	104	B3
Ely Dr	104	B3
Ely Grn 1	104	B3
Ely Gro	104	B3
Ely Manor	104	B3
Ely Pl	76	B3
Ely Pl Upr off Ely Pl	76	B3
Ely Vw	104	B3
Embassy Lawn	87	C3
Emerald Cotts	77	C3
Emerald Pl off Sheriff St Lwr	77	C1
Emerald Sq	75	C3
Emerald St	77	C1
Emily Pl off Sheriff St Lwr	76	B1
Emmet Ct	73	D3
Emmet Rd	73	D2
Emmet Sq	99	C1
Emmet St Dublin 1	62	B3
Emmet St (Haroldscross) Dublin 6	85	D1
Emmet St 1 Sally.	113	D2
Emor St	75	D3
Emorville Av	75	D3
Emorville Sq off South Circular Rd	75	C3
Empress Pl	62	B3
Enaville Rd	63	C2
Engine All	124	A4
Ennafort Av (Ascal Dun Eanna)	47	C3
Ennafort Ct	47	C3
Ennafort Dr (Ceide Dun Eanna)	47	C3
Ennafort Gro	47	C3
Ennafort Pk	47	C3
Ennafort Rd	47	C3
Ennel Av	47	C2
Ennel Ct 3	119	C3
Ennel Dr	47	C2
Ennel Pk	47	C2
Ennis Gro	77	D3
Enniskerry Rd	61	D2
Erne Pl	77	C2
Erne Pl Little	125	F3
Erne St Lwr	77	C2
Erne St Upr	77	C2
Erne Ter Front off Erne St Upr	77	C2
Erne Ter Rere off Erne St Upr	77	C2
Errigal Gdns	83	D1
Errigal Rd	83	D1
Erris Rd	61	C2
Erskine Av	123	D3
Esker Dr	68	A2
Esker La (north) Lucan	69	C1
Esker La (south) Lucan	69	C2
Esker Lawns	68	B1
Esker Lo	69	C2
Esker Lo Av	69	C2
Esker Lo Cl	69	C2
Esker Lo Vw	69	C2
Esker Manor	68	B2
Esker Meadow	69	C2
Esker Meadow Cl	69	C2
Esker Meadow Ct	69	C2
Esker Meadow Grn	69	C2
Esker Meadow Gro	69	C2
Esker Meadow Lawn	69	C2
Esker Meadow Ri	69	C2
Esker Meadow Vw	69	C2
Esker Pk	69	C2
Esker Pines	69	C1
Esker Rd	68	B2
Esker S	68	B3
Esker Wds Ct	69	C2
Esker Wds Dr	69	C2
Esker Wds Gro	69	C2
Esker Wds Ri	69	C2
Esker Wds Vw	69	C2

Esker Wds Wk	69	C2
Esmond Av	63	C2
Esplanade Ter 14	122	B2
Esposito Rd	83	D2
Essex Quay	124	C3
Essex St E	124	C3
Essex St W	124	C3
Estate Av	88	B3
Estate Cotts	77	C3
Estuary Ct	9	C1
Estuary Pk	13	C2
Estuary Roundabout	9	C1
Estuary Row	14	A1
Estuary Wk	13	C2
Eugene St	75	C3
Eustace St	124	C3
Everton Av	61	C3
Evora Cres	52	B2
Evora Pk	52	B2
Evora Ter		
off St. Lawrence Rd	52	B2
Ewington La	75	C3
Excalibur Dr	123	D1
Exchange Ct		
off Dame St	124	C3
Exchange St Lwr	124	C3
Exchange St Upr		
off Lord Edward St	124	C3
Exchequer St	124	C3

F

Faber Gro 3	112	B1
Fade St	124	C3
Fairbrook Lawn	95	C3
Fairfield Av	63	C3
Fairfield Pk Dublin 6	85	D3
Fairfield Pk Grey.	123	C1
Fairfield Rd (Glasnevin)	62	A1
Fairgreen Ct 10	122	A1
Fairgreen Ter 11	122	A1
Fair Haven 1	14	A2
Fairlawn Pk		
off Fairlawn Rd	42	B2
Fairlawn Rd	42	B2
Fairlawns	114	A2
Fairview	63	C2
Fairview Av (Irishtown)	77	D2
Fairview Av Lwr	63	C2
Fairview Av Upr	63	C2
Fairview Grn	63	C2
Fairview Lawn	118	A3
Fairview Pas		
off Fairview Strand	63	C2
Fairview Strand	63	C2
Fairview Ter	63	C2
Fairways	94	B2
Fairways Av	43	C2
Fairways Grn	43	C2
Fairways Gro	43	C2
Fairways Pk	43	C2
Fairy Hill	111	D1
Faith Av	63	C3
Falcarragh Rd	44	B2
Falls Rd	120	B1
Farmhill Dr	97	C2
Farmhill Pk	97	D3
Farmhill Rd	97	C2
Farmleigh Av	111	C1
Farmleigh Cl	111	C1
Farmleigh Pk	111	C1
Farney Pk	78	A3
Farnham Cres	42	B2
Farnham Dr	42	B2
Farrenboley Cotts	96	B1
Farrenboley Pk	96	B1
Father Colohan Ter 4	122	A2
Father Matthew Br	124	A3
Fatima Mans	74	B3
Fatima Ter	122	A1
Faughart Rd	84	B2
Faussagh Av	60	B1
Faussagh Rd	61	C2
Feltrim	19	C1
Feltrim Hall	11	D2
Feltrim Ind Pk	12	A2
Feltrim Rd	12	B3
Fenian St	125	E4
Ferguson Rd	62	A1
Fergus Rd	95	C3
Ferncourt Av	104	B3
Ferncourt Cl	104	B3
Ferncourt Cres 2	104	B3
Ferncourt Dr 3	104	B3

Ferncourt Grn	104	B3
Ferncourt Pk	104	B3
Ferncourt Vw	104	B3
Ferndale Dublin 24	103	D1
Ferndale Manor.	25	D2
Ferndale Av	43	C2
Ferndale Glen	120	B3
Ferndale Hill	120	A3
Ferndale Rd Dublin 11	43	C2
Ferndale Rd Shank.	120	B3
Fernhill Av	93	D1
Fernhill Pk	93	D1
Fernhill Rd	93	D1
Fernleigh	56	A1
Fernleigh Cl	38	A3
Fernleigh Ct	56	A1
Fernleigh Dale	56	A1
Fernleigh Dr	38	A3
Fernleigh Grn	56	A1
Fernleigh Gro	56	A1
Fernleigh Pk	56	A1
Fernleigh Pl 3	56	A1
Fernleigh Vw	56	A1
Ferns Rd	84	B2
Fernvale Dr	83	D1
Fernwood Av	91	C3
Fernwood Cl	103	C1
Fernwood Ct	91	C3
Fernwood Lawn	91	C3
Fernwood Way	103	C1
Ferrard Rd	85	D3
Ferrycarrig Av	34	B3
Ferrycarrig Dr	34	B3
Ferrycarrig Grn 2	34	B3
Ferrycarrig Pk	34	B3
Ferrycarrig Rd	34	B3
Ferrymans Crossing	77	C1
Fertullagh Rd	61	C2
Fettercairn Rd	90	A3
Fey Yerra 1	111	C2
Fforester	69	C2
Fforester Cl	69	C2
Fforester Ct	69	C2
Fforester Lawn	69	C2
Fforester Pk	69	C2
Fforester Wk	69	C2
Fforester Way	69	C2
Field Av	83	D2
Fields Ter		
off Ranelagh Rd	86	B1
Finches Ind Pk	83	C1
Findlater Pl		
off Parnell St	62	B3
Findlaters St	74	B1
Findlater St 14	114	A1
Fingal Pl	61	C3
Fingal St	75	C3
Finglas Business Cen	30	B3
Finglas Business Pk	43	C3
Finglas Pk	43	C3
Finglas Pl	42	B2
Finglas Rd	43	C2
Finglas Rd Old	43	D3
Finglas Shop Cen	42	B1
Finglaswood Rd	42	A1
Finlay Sq	98	A2
Finnsgreen	68	A3
Finnsgrove	68	A3
Finnstown Fairways	68	A3
Finn St	61	C3
Finnsvale	68	A3
Finnsview	68	A3
Finsbury Pk	96	B3
Firgrove 1	119	C3
Firhouse Rd Dublin 16	93	D3
Firhouse Rd Dublin 24	93	D3
Firhouse Rd W	103	D3
First Av Dublin 1	77	C1
First Av (Inchicore)		
Dublin 10	73	C2
First Av Dublin 24	91	C2
Fishamble St	124	B3
Fitzgerald Pk 2	113	C3
Fitzgerald St	85	D1
Fitzgibbon La	62	B3
Fitzgibbon St	62	B3
Fitzmaurice Rd	43	D2
Fitzroy Av	62	A2
Fitzwilliam Ct		
off Pembroke St Upr	76	B3
Fitzwilliam La	76	B3
Fitzwilliam Pl	76	B3
Fitzwilliam Quay	77	D2
Fitzwilliam Sq E	76	B3

Fitzwilliam Sq N	76	B3
Fitzwilliam Sq S	76	B3
Fitzwilliam Sq W	76	B3
Fitzwilliam St		
(Ringsend)	77	D2
Fitzwilliam St Lwr	76	B3
Fitzwilliam St Upr	76	B3
Fleet St	125	D2
Fleming Pl	77	C3
Fleming Rd	62	A1
Flemings La		
off Haddington Rd	77	C3
Flemingstown Pk	96	B2
Fleurville	99	D3
Floraville Av	80	B2
Floraville Dr	81	C3
Floraville Est	81	C2
Floraville Lawn	81	C2
Florence Rd	122	A1
Florence St		
off Lennox St	76	A3
Florence Ter 2	122	B1
Florence Vil 12	122	A1
Flower Gro	113	D3
Foley St	125	E1
Fontenoy St	61	D3
Fontenoy Ter	122	B2
Fonthill Abbey 2	95	C3
Fonthill Ct 3	95	C3
Fonthill Pk	95	C3
Fonthill Retail Pk	70	A1
Fonthill Rd Dublin 14	95	C3
Fonthill Rd Clond.	70	A1
Fonthill Rd S	80	B3
Forbes La	75	C2
Forbes St	77	C2
Forest Av Dublin 24	10	B2
Forest Av Swords	10	B2
Forest Boul	10	A2
Forest Cl	92	A1
Forest Ct	10	B2
Forest Cres	10	B2
Forest Dale	10	B2
Forest Dr Dublin 24	92	A1
Forest Dr Swords	10	B2
Forest Flds Rd	10	B2
Forest Grn Dublin 24	92	A1
Forest Grn Swords	10	B2
Forest Gro	10	A2
Forest Lawn	92	A1
Forest Pk Dublin 24	92	A1
Forest Pk Leix.	66	A2
Forest Pk Swords	10	B2
Forest Rd	10	A3
Forest Vw 1	10	B2
Forest Wk	10	B2
Forest Way 2	10	B2
Forestwood Av	32	A3
Forestwood Cl	32	A3
Fortfield Av	94	B1
Fortfield Ct	94	B1
Fortfield Dr	94	B2
Fortfield Gdns	86	A3
Fortfield Gro	94	B1
Fortfield Pk	94	B2
Fortfield Rd	94	B1
Fortfield Ter	86	A3
Forth Rd	63	D3
Fortlawn	38	A1
Fortlawn Av	38	A1
Fortlawn Dr	38	A1
Fortlawns	114	A3
Fortunestown Rd	102	B2
Fortview Av	65	C3
Fosterbrook	98	B1
Foster Cotts		
off Phibsborough Rd	61	D3
Foster Pl S	125	D3
Fosters, The	98	A2
Fosters Av	98	A2
Foster Ter	62	B3
Fountain Pl	124	A2
Fountain Rd	74	B1
Four Cts		
(Courts of Justice)	124	B2
Fourth Av Dublin 1	77	C1
Fourth Av Dublin 24	91	C3
Fownes St	125	D2
Foxborough Av	69	C3
Foxborough Cl	69	C3
Foxborough Cres	69	C3
Foxborough Downes	69	C3
Foxborough Dr	69	C3
Foxborough Gdns	69	D3
Foxborough Glen	69	D3

Foxborough Grn	69	D3
Foxborough Gro	69	D3
Foxborough Hts	69	D3
Foxborough Hill	69	C3
Foxborough La	69	D3
Foxborough Meadows	69	C3
Foxborough Pk	69	C3
Foxborough Pl	69	C3
Foxborough Ri	69	C3
Foxborough Row	69	D3
Foxborough Wk	69	C3
Foxborough Way	69	C3
Foxdene Dr	70	A3
Foxdene Gdns	70	A2
Foxdene Grn	69	D3
Foxdene Gro	70	A2
Foxdene Pk	70	A2
Foxes Gro	121	C2
Foxfield	68	A3
Foxfield Av	48	A2
Foxfield Cres	48	B2
Foxfield Dr	48	B2
Foxfield Grn	48	B2
Foxfield Gro	48	A2
Foxfield Hts	48	A2
Foxfield Lawn	48	B2
Foxfield Pk	48	B2
Foxfield Rd	48	A2
Foxfield St. John	48	B2
Foxford	69	D2
Foxhill Av	47	D1
Foxhill Cl	35	D3
Foxhill Ct	47	D1
Foxhill Cres	47	D1
Foxhill Dr	47	D1
Foxhill Grn	35	D3
Foxhill Gro	35	D3
Foxhill Lawn	47	D1
Foxhill Pk	47	D1
Foxhill Way	47	D1
Foxpark	68	A3
Foxrock	111	D3
Foxrock Av	111	D2
Foxrock Cl	112	A2
Foxrock Ct	111	D2
Foxrock Cres	112	A2
Foxrock Grn	112	A2
Foxrock Gro	112	A2
Foxrock Manor	111	C2
Foxrock Mt 1	111	D2
Foxrock Pk	111	D2
Foxrock Wd	112	A2
Foxs La	48	B3
Foxwood Lucan	68	A3
Foxwood Swords	11	D1
Foyle Rd	63	C2
Francis St	124	B3
Frankfort	96	B2
Frankfort Av	85	D2
Frankfort Ct	85	D3
Frankfort Pk	96	B2
Frascati Pk	99	D2
Frascati Rd	99	D2
Frascati Shop Cen	99	D2
Frederick Ct		
off Hardwicke St	62	A3
Frederick La	125	E4
Frederick La N	62	A3
Frederick St N	62	A3
Frederick St S	125	E4
Frenchmans La		
off Gardiner St Lwr	125	E1
Friarsland Av	97	C2
Friarsland Rd	97	C2
Friar's Wk 8	80	B2
Friary Av	124	A2
Friel Av	72	A3
Fumbally La	75	D3
Furry Pk Ct	64	B1
Furry Pk Ind Est	32	B2
Furry Pk Rd	64	B1
Furze Rd Dublin 8	58	B2
Furze Rd Sandy.	110	A3

G

Gables, The 4	111	D3
Gaelic St	63	C3
Gainsborough Av	13	C2

Gainsborough Cl **3**	13	C2
Gainsborough Ct	12	B2
Gainsborough Cres	12	B2
Gainsborough Downs	12	B2
Gainsborough Grn	12	B2
Gainsborough Lawn	12	B2
Gainsborough Pk	12	B2
Gairdini Sheinleasa	44	A1
Gallaun Rd	31	D3
Galloping Grn **3**	111	C2
Galmoy Rd	61	C2
Galtrim Pk	122	A1
Galtrim Rd	122	A2
Galtymore Cl	73	D3
Galtymore Dr	74	A3
Galtymore Pk	83	D1
Galtymore Rd	74	A3
Gandon Cl	85	D1
Gandon Ms	68	B1
Garden Croath	99	D3
Garden La	124	A4
Gardiner La	62	B3
Gardiner Row	62	A3
Gardiner's Pl	62	A3
Gardiner St Lwr	62	B3
Gardiner St Mid	62	A3
Gardiner St Upr	62	A3
Gardini Lein		
(Lein Gdns)	47	D3
Gardini Phairc An Bhailtini		
(Villa Park Gdns)	60	A2
Garnish Sq **3**	39	D1
Garrynisk Cl	91	D2
Garrynisk Est	91	D2
Garrynure	86	B3
Garryowen Rd	72	B2
Gartan Av	62	A2
Gartan Ct	9	D1
Gartan Dr	9	D1
Garth, The *Dublin 24*	91	D1
Garth, The (Cookstown)		
Dublin 24	91	C2
Garville Av	85	D3
Garville Av Upr	85	D3
Garville Rd	85	D3
Gas Yd La	14	A2
Gaybrook Lawns	13	C2
Gaywood Ind Est	26	B1
Geoffrey Keating Rd		
off O'Curry Rd	75	D3
George's Av	99	D2
George's Hill	124	B2
George's La	124	A1
George's Pl *Dublin 1*	62	A3
George's Pl *Black.*	99	D2
George's Pl *D.L.*	101	C3
George's Quay	125	E2
George's St Lwr	101	D3
George's St Upr	101	D3
Georgian Hamlet	37	D3
Georgian Village	58	A1
Geraldine St	61	D3
Geraldine Ter	86	B3
Geraldstown Wds	32	A3
Geraldstown Wds		
Apartments **1**	32	A3
Gerald St	77	C2
Gilbert Rd	75	D3
Gilford Av	88	A1
Gilford Ct	88	A1
Gilford Dr	88	A1
Gilford Pk	88	A1
Gilford Rd	88	A1
Giltspur Brook	122	A3
Glade, The *Dublin 16*	108	B2
Glade, The (Cookstown)		
Dublin 24	91	C2
Glade, The *Palm.*	57	C3
Glandore Rd	113	C1
Glandore Rd	45	C3
Glasanaon Ct		
off Glasanaon Pk	43	C2
Glasanaon Pk	43	C2
Glasanaon Rd	43	C1
Glasaree Rd	43	C1
Glasilawn Av	43	D2
Glasilawn Rd	43	C3
Glasmeen Rd	43	C3
Glasmore Pk	8	A1

Glasnamana Pl	43	C2
Glasnamana Rd	43	C3
Glasnevin Av	43	C1
Glasnevin Br	61	D1
Glasnevin		
Business Pk	42	A3
Glasnevin Ct	43	C3
Glasnevin Downs	43	C3
Glasnevin Dr	43	D2
Glasnevin Hill	44	A3
Glasnevin Pk	43	D1
Glasnevin Wds	43	C3
Glasson Ct	96	B1
Glasthule Bldgs **15**	114	A1
Glasthule Rd	114	A1
Glaunsharoon	87	C2
Gleann Na Ri	118	A3
Gleann Na Smol		
Dublin 24	103	D1
Gleann Na Smol *D.L.*	103	D1
Glebe, The	68	B2
Glebe Vw	42	B1
Gledswood Av	97	C1
Gledswood Cl	97	C1
Gledswood Dr	97	C1
Gledswood Pk	97	C1
Glen, The (Ballinteer)		
Dublin 16	108	B3
Glen, The (Ballyboden)		
Dublin 16	106	B1
Glen, The **14** *D.L.*	113	D1
Glen, The *Lou.V.*	66	A1
Glenaan Rd	44	B2
Glen Abbey Complex	91	D2
Glenabbey Rd	98	A3
Glenageary Av	113	D2
Glenageary Ct	113	D2
Glenageary Hall	114	A2
Glenageary Lo	113	D2
Glenageary Office Pk	113	C2
Glenageary Pk	113	D2
Glenageary Rd Lwr	113	D1
Glenageary Rd Upr	113	C1
Glenageary Sta	113	D1
Glenageary Wds	113	C1
Glenalbyn Rd	111	C1
Glenalua Hts	119	C1
Glenalua Rd	119	C1
Glenalua Ter	119	C1
Glenamuck Rd	117	C2
Glenanne	84	B3
Glenard Av *Dublin 7*	61	C3
Glenard Av *Bray*	122	B2
Glenarm Av	62	B2
Glenarm Sq	62	A2
Glenarriff Rd	59	D1
Glenart Av	99	C3
Glenaulin	58	A3
Glenaulin Dr		
(Ceide Glennaluinn)	72	A1
Glenaulin Grn	71	D1
Glenaulin Pk		
(Pairc Gleannaluinn)	58	A3
Glenaulin Rd	71	D1
Glen Av	117	C1
Glenavon Pk	118	B3
Glenavy Pk	84	B3
Glenayle Rd	47	D1
Glenayr Rd	95	D1
Glenbeigh Pk	60	B3
Glenbeigh Rd	60	B3
Glenbourne Gro	116	A1
Glenbower Pk	96	B3
Glenbrook Gro	95	C3
Glenbrook Rd	41	D3
Glencairn	110	B3
Glencarr Ct **4**	119	C3
Glencarrig	51	C1
Glencarrig Ct	104	B2
Glencarrig Dr	104	B2
Glencarrig Grn	104	B2
Glencarr Lawn	119	C3
Glencar Rd	60	B3
Glen Cl	117	D1
Glencloy Rd	44	B2
Glencorp Rd	45	C2
Glencourt Est	122	A3
Glen Dale *Cabin.*	117	C1
Glendale *Leix.*	66	B1
Glendale Dr	122	A3
Glendale Meadows	67	C1
Glendale Pk	94	A1
Glendalough Rd	62	A1
Glendhu Pk	41	D3
Glendhu Rd	41	D3

Glendoher Av	107	C1
Glendoher Cl	106	B1
Glendoher Dr	107	C1
Glendoher Pk	107	C1
Glendoher Rd	106	B1
Glendoo Cl		
off Lugaquilla Av	92	B1
Glendown Av	93	D1
Glendown Cl		
off Glendown Gro	93	D1
Glendown Ct	93	D1
Glendown Cres	93	D1
Glendown Grn		
off Glendown Gro	93	D1
Glendown Gro	93	D1
Glendown Lawn	94	A1
Glendown Pk	93	D1
Glendown Rd	93	D2
Glen Dr	117	D1
Glen Druid	121	C1
Glendun Rd	44	B2
Glenealy Downs	25	D2
Glenealy Rd	85	C1
Glen Ellan Cl	8	B1
Glen Ellan Dr	8	B1
Glen Ellan Cres	8	B1
Glenfarne Rd	47	C1
Glenfield Av	70	A1
Glenfield Cl	70	A1
Glenfield Dr	70	A1
Glenfield Gro	70	A1
Glenfield Pk	70	A1
Glengara Cl **4**	113	D1
Glengara Pk	113	D1
Glengariff Par	62	A2
Glen Garth	117	C1
Glen Gro	117	D1
Glenhill Av	43	C2
Glenhill Ct	43	C2
Glenhill Dr	42	B2
Glenhill Gro	43	C2
Glenhill Pk	42	B2
Glenhill Vil		
off Glenhill Pk	42	B2
Glen Lawn Dr	117	C1
Glenlyon Cres	105	C2
Glenlyon Gro	105	C2
Glenlyon Pk	105	C2
Glenmalure Pk	74	B3
Glenmalure Sq	86	B3
Glenmaroon Pk	71	D1
Glenmaroon Rd	71	D1
Glenmore Ct	107	C2
Glenmore Pk	107	C2
Glenmore Rd	60	B3
Glen Na Smol	122	A3
Glenomena Gro	98	A1
Glenomena Pk	88	A3
Glenpark Cl	57	C3
Glenpark Dr	57	C3
Glenpark Rd	57	C3
Glenshane Cl	102	A1
Glenshane Cres	102	A1
Glenshane Gdns	102	A1
Glenshane Grn	102	A1
Glenshane Gro	102	B1
Glenshane Lawns	102	A1
Glenshane Pk	102	A1
Glenshesk Rd	45	C2
Glenside Vil **2**	57	D3
Glen Ter **16**	114	A1
Glenties Dr	42	A2
Glenties Pk	42	A2
Glentow Rd	44	B2
Glentworth Pk	35	D3
Glenvale	69	C3
Glenvara Pk	105	C2
Glenvar Pk	99	C2
Glenview	113	D3
Glenview Dr **4**	104	B1
Glenview Ind Est	74	A3
Glenview Lawn	93	C3
Glenview Lawns	93	C3
Glenview Pk	92	B3
Glenville Av	39	C2
Glenville Ct	38	B3
Glenville Dr	38	B2
Glenville Garth	38	B2
Glenville Grn	39	C2
Glenville Gro	39	C2
Glenville Ind Est	98	A2
Glenville Lawn	38	B3
Glenville Rd	38	B3
Glenville Way	39	C2
Glen Wk	117	C1

Glenwood Rd	47	C1
Glin Av	34	B3
Glin Cres	34	B3
Glin Dr	34	B3
Glin Glen	34	B3
Glin Gro	34	B3
Glin Pk	34	B3
Glin Rd	34	B3
Gloucester La *off Sean*		
McDermott St Lwr	62	B3
Gloucester Pl	62	B3
Gloucester Pl Lwr	62	B3
Gloucester Pl N	62	B3
Gloucester Pl Upr		
off Gloucester Pl	62	B3
Gloucester St S	125	F2
Glovers All	125	D4
Goatstown Av	97	C2
Goatstown Rd	97	D2
Golden Br	73	D2
Goldenbridge Av	74	A3
Goldenbridge Gdns	74	A3
Goldenbridge Ter		
off Connolly Av	74	A3
Golden La	124	C4
Goldsmith St	61	D3
Goldsmith Ter **13**	122	A1
Golf La	111	D3
Golf Links Rd	21	C3
Gordon Av	112	A3
Gordon Pl		
off Richmond St S	76	A3
Gordon St	77	C2
Gorsefield Ct	47	C2
Gortbeg Av		
off Gortbeg Rd	42	B3
Gortbeg Dr		
off Gortbeg Rd	42	B3
Gortbeg Pk		
off Gortbeg Rd	42	B3
Gortbeg Rd	42	B3
Gortmore Av	42	B3
Gortmore Dr	42	B3
Gortmore Pk		
off Gortmore Rd	42	B3
Gortmore Rd	42	B3
Gort Na Mona Dr	112	A3
Gosworth Pk	114	A2
Government Bldgs	125	E4
Gowrie Pk	113	C1
Gracefield Av	47	C3
Gracefield Ct	46	B3
Gracefield Rd	46	B3
Grace O'Malley Dr	52	B2
Grace O'Malley Rd	52	B2
Grace Pk Av	62	B1
Grace Pk Ct	45	C2
Grace Pk Gdns	62	B1
Grace Pk Hts	45	C2
Grace Pk Meadows	45	D3
Grace Pk Rd	62	B1
Grace Pk Ter	63	C1
Grafton St	125	D4
Graham Ct	62	A3
Graigue Ct	31	D2
Granard Br	39	D2
Granby La	62	A3
Granby Pl	124	C1
Granby Row	62	A3
Grand Canal Bk		
Dublin 8	75	C2
Grand Canal Bk		
(Ranelagh) *Dublin 8*	86	A1
Grand Canal		
Business Cen	73	C3
Grand Canal Harbour		
off James's St	74	B2
Grand Canal Pl N	75	C2
Grand Canal Quay	75	C2
Grand Canal St Lwr	77	C2
Grand Canal St Upr	77	C2
Grand Canal Vw	74	A3
Grand Par	86	A1
Grange, The	112	B2
Grange Abbey Cres	36	B3
Grange Abbey Dr	36	B3
Grange Abbey Gro	36	B3
Grange Abbey Rd	36	B3
Grange Av	37	C3
Grange Brook	107	C2
Grangebrook Av	107	C2
Grangebrook Cl	107	C2
Grangebrook Pk	107	C2
Grangebrook Vale	107	C2
Grange Cl *Dublin 13*	49	C1

Name	Page	Grid
Grange Cl Sally.	113	C3
Grange Cotts 3 Black.	111	C1
Grange Cotts 1 Deans Gra	112	A1
Grange Ct	107	D2
Grange Cres	112	B2
Grange Downs	95	D3
Grange Dr	49	C1
Grangefield	108	B3
Grangegorman Lwr	124	A1
Grangegorman Upr	61	C3
Grange Gro 2	112	A1
Grange Hall	108	B3
Grange Lo Av	36	B3
Grange Manor	68	B3
Grange Manor Av	107	D1
Grange Manor Cl	107	D1
Grange Manor Dr	107	D1
Grange Manor Gro	107	D1
Grange Manor Rd	107	D1
Grangemore	36	A3
Grangemore Av	36	A3
Grangemore Cl	36	A3
Grangemore Cres	36	A3
Grangemore Dr	36	A3
Grangemore Gro	36	A3
Grangemore Lawn	36	A3
Grangemore Pk	36	A3
Grangemore Rd	36	A3
Grange Par	49	C1
Grange Pk Dublin 13	37	C3
Grange Pk Dublin 14	95	C3
Grange Pk Corn.	112	A2
Grange Pk Av	48	A2
Grange Pk Cl	48	A2
Grange Pk Cres	48	A2
Grange Pk Dr	48	A2
Grange Pk Grn	48	A2
Grange Pk Gro	48	A2
Grange Pk Par	48	A2
Grange Pk Ri	48	A2
Grange Pk Rd	48	A2
Grange Pk Wk	48	A2
Grange Ri	37	C3
Grange Rd Dublin 13	48	A3
Grange Rd Dublin 14	95	C2
Grange Rd Dublin 16	95	C3
Grange Rd Bald.	36	B3
Grange Way	49	C1
Grange Wd Dublin 16	108	A2
Grangewood D.L.	112	B2
Granitefield	113	C3
Granite Hall 5	113	D1
Granite Pl	87	D1
Granite Ter off Inchicore Ter S	73	D2
Grantham Pl	76	A3
Grantham St	76	A3
Grants Row	77	C2
Granville Cl	118	A1
Granville Cres	118	A1
Granville Pk	111	D1
Granville Rd Cabin.	118	A1
Granville Rd Deans Gra	111	D1
Grattan Br	76	A1
Grattan Ct E off Grattan St	77	C2
Grattan Cres	73	D2
Grattan Hall	36	A3
Grattan Lo	36	A3
Grattan Par	62	A2
Grattan Pl off Grattan St	77	C2
Grattan St	77	C2
Gray Sq	124	A4
Gray St	124	A4
Great Clarence Pl off North Circular Rd	61	D3
Great Western Av	61	D3
Great Western Sq	61	D3
Great Western Vil	61	D3
Greek St	124	B2
Green, The Dublin 9	45	D1
Green, The (Ballinteer) Dublin 16	108	B2
Green, The (Ballyboden) Dublin 16	106	A1
Green, The Dublin 24	91	D1
Green, The Dunb.	22	A1
Green, The Kins.	12	A3
Green, The Mala.	14	A2
Green, The (Robswall) 2 Mala.	15	C3
Green, The Manor.	25	C2
Green, The Mulh.	26	A2
Green, The Swords	9	C1
Greenacre	93	D3
Greencastle Av	46	B1
Greencastle Cres	34	B3
Greencastle Dr	34	B3
Greencastle Par	47	C1
Greencastle Pk	34	B3
Greencastle Rd	34	B3
Greendale Av	48	B2
Greendale Rd	48	B2
Greendale Shop Cen	48	B2
Greenfield Cres	87	D3
Greenfield Manor	87	D3
Greenfield Pk Dublin 4	87	D3
Greenfield Pk Dublin 24	105	C2
Greenfield Rd Dublin 13	50	B1
Greenfield Rd Still.	98	B2
Greenfort Av	70	A1
Greenfort Cl	70	A1
Greenfort Cres	70	A1
Greenfort Dr	70	A1
Greenfort Gdns	70	B1
Greenfort Lawns	70	B1
Greenfort Pk	70	A1
Greenhills Business Cen	92	B2
Greenhills Business Pk	92	B3
Greenhills Ind Est	83	C3
Greenhills Rd Dublin 12	82	B3
Greenhills Rd Dublin 24	92	B2
Green Isle Business Pk	90	A1
Green Isle Ct 1	90	A1
Greenlands	109	D2
Greenlands, The	95	D2
Green La	66	A2
Greenlawns 1	34	B3
Greenlea Av	94	B1
Greenlea Dr	94	B1
Greenlea Gro	94	B1
Greenlea Pk	94	B1
Greenlea Rd	94	B1
Greenmount Av	85	D1
Greenmount Ct off Greenmount Av	85	D1
Greenmount La	85	D1
Greenmount Lawns	85	D1
Greenmount Rd	85	D1
Greenmount Sq off Greenmount La	85	D1
Grenore Ter off Grattan St	77	C2
Green Pk	96	A1
Greenridge Ct	39	C1
Green Rd	99	C2
Green Rd, The	115	C2
Green St	124	B1
Green St E	77	C1
Green St Little	124	B2
Greentrees Dr	93	D1
Greentrees Pk	83	D3
Greentrees Rd	83	D3
Greenville Av	75	D3
Greenville Rd	100	A3
Greenville Ter	75	D3
Greenwich Ct	86	A2
Greenwood Av	35	D3
Greenwood Cl	35	D3
Greenwood Ct	35	D3
Greenwood Dr	35	D3
Greenwood Lawn off Greenwood Dr	35	D3
Greenwood Pk 2	35	D3
Greenwood Wk	35	D3
Greenwood Way	35	D3
Grenville La	62	A3
Grenville St	62	A3
Greygates	98	B2
Greyhound Racing Stadium	85	D1
Greys La	53	C3
Greystones Sta	123	D2
Greythorn Pk	113	C3
Griffeen	69	C3
Griffeen Av	69	D3
Griffeen Glen Av	68	B3
Griffeen Glen Boul	69	C3
Griffeen Glen Chase	68	B3
Griffeen Glen Ct	69	C3
Griffeen Glen Cres	68	B3
Griffeen Glen Dale	68	B3
Griffeen Glen Dene	68	B3
Griffeen Glen Dr	69	C3
Griffeen Glen Grn	68	B3
Griffeen Glen Gro	69	C3
Griffeen Glen Lawn	68	B3
Griffeen Glen Rd (east) Lucan	69	C3
Griffeen Glen Rd (west) Lucan	68	B3
Griffeen Glen Vale	69	C3
Griffeen Glen Vw	68	B3
Griffeen Glen Way	69	C3
Griffeen Rd	69	C3
Griffeen Way	69	C2
Griffith Av Dublin 9	44	B3
Griffith Av Dublin 11	43	D3
Griffith Br	74	A3
Griffith Cl	43	C3
Griffith Ct	63	C1
Griffith Downs	44	B3
Griffith Dr	43	C3
Griffith Lawns	44	A3
Griffith Par	43	C3
Griffith Rd	43	C2
Griffith Sq off Wesley Pl	75	D3
Griffith Sq S off South Circular Rd	75	C3
Griffith Wk	63	C1
Grosvenor Av	122	B2
Grosvenor Ct Dublin 3	64	B1
Grosvenor Ct Dublin 6W	94	A1
Grosvenor Lo	85	D2
Grosvenor Pk	85	D2
Grosvenor Pl	85	D2
Grosvenor Rd	85	D2
Grosvenor Sq	85	D1
Grosvenor Ter 5 Dalkey	115	C2
Grosvenor Ter D.L.	101	C3
Grosvenor Vil	85	D2
Grotto Av	99	C1
Grotto Pl	98	B1
Grove, The Dublin 5	48	A3
Grove, The Dublin 9	45	C3
Grove, The (Ballinteer) Dublin 16	108	B2
Grove, The (Meadow Mt) Dublin 16	108	A1
Grove, The Dublin 24	104	A1
Grove, The (Cookstown) Dublin 24	91	C2
Grove, The (Kilnamanagh) Dublin 24	91	C2
Grove, The (Lutterell Hall) Dunb.	22	A1
Grove, The Gra M.	68	B3
Grove, The Kins.	12	A3
Grove, The Lou.V.	66	A2
Grove Av Dublin 6 off Grove Rd	85	D1
Grove Av (Finglas) Dublin 11	43	C1
Grove Av Black.	99	C2
Grove Av Mala.	14	B2
Grove Ct 1	10	A1
Grove Ho Gdns	99	C3
Grove Ind Est	30	B1
Grove La	35	D3
Grove Lawn Black.	99	C3
Grove Lawn Mala.	14	B2
Grove Pk Dublin 6	85	D1
Grove Pk Dublin 13	35	D3
Grove Pk Av	43	C1
Grove Pk Cres	43	D1
Grove Pk Dr	43	C1
Grove Pk Rd	43	C1
Grove Rd (Rathmines) Dublin 6	85	D1
Grove Rd (Finglas) Dublin 11	43	C1
Grove Rd (Blanchardstown) Dublin 15	38	B2
Grove Rd Mala.	14	A2
Grove Wd	43	C1
Guild St	77	C1
Guilford Ter	121	C2
Guinness Brewery	75	C2
Guinness Enterprise Cen	75	C2
Gulistan Cotts	75	C2
Gulistan Pl	86	A1
Gulistan Ter	86	A1
Gurteen Av	72	A2
Gurteen Pk	72	A2
Gurteen Rd	72	A1

H

Name	Page	Grid
Hacketsland	121	C1
Haddington Lawns	114	A2
Haddington Pk 6	114	A2
Haddington Pl	77	C3
Haddington Rd	77	C3
Haddinton Ter	101	D3
Haddon Pk off Seaview Av N	64	A2
Haddon Rd	64	C1
Hadleigh Ct	40	A3
Hadleigh Grn	40	A3
Hadleigh Pk	40	A3
Hagans Ct	76	B3
Haigh Ter	101	D3
Hainault Dr	117	C1
Hainault Gro	117	C1
Hainault Lawn	117	C1
Hainault Pk	116	B1
Hainault Rd	111	D3
Halliday Rd	75	C1
Halliday Sq	75	C1
Halston St	124	B1
Hamilton Ct 1	22	B2
Hamilton Hall	22	B3
Hamilton St	75	C3
Hammond La	124	A2
Hammond St	75	D3
Hampstead Av	44	A2
Hampstead Ct	44	A2
Hampstead Pk	44	A3
Hampton Ct	65	C1
Hampton Cres	98	B1
Hampton Grn	60	B2
Hampton Hermitage & Theresian Trust	63	C1
Hampton Pk	98	B2
Hanbury La Dublin 8	124	A3
Hanbury La Lucan	68	A1
Hannaville Pk	85	C3
Hanover La	124	B4
Hanover Quay	77	C2
Hanover Sq W off Hanover La	124	B4
Hanover St E	125	F3
Hanover St W off Ash St	124	A4
Hansfield	25	C2
Hansfield Rd	24	B2
Ha'penny Br	76	A1
Harbour Ct off Marlborough St	76	A1
Harbour Cres	114	B2
Harbourmaster Pl	125	F1
Harbour Rd Dublin 13	52	B1
Harbour Rd Dalkey	114	B1
Harbour Rd D.L.	101	C2
Harbour Ter	101	C2
Harbour Vw off St. Lawrence Rd	53	C2
Harcourt Grn	76	A3
Harcourt La off Harcourt Rd	76	A3
Harcourt Rd	76	A3
Harcourt St	76	A3
Harcourt Ter	76	A3
Harcourt Ter La	76	B3
Hardbeck Av	83	C2
Hardiman Rd	62	A1
Hardwicke Pl	62	A3
Hardwicke St	62	A3
Harelawn Av	70	B2
Harelawn Cres	70	B2
Harelawn Dr	70	B1
Harelawn Grn	70	B2
Harelawn Gro	70	B1
Harelawn Pk	70	B2
Harlech Cres	97	D2
Harlech Downs	97	D2
Harlech Gro	97	D2
Harlech Vil	97	D2
Harman St	75	C3
Harmonstown Rd	47	C3
Harmonstown Sta	47	C3

Name	Page	Grid
Harmony Av	87	C2
Harmony Row	77	C2
Harold Rd	75	C1
Harolds Cross Rd	85	D1
Harold's Gra Rd	108	A3
Haroldville Av	75	C3
Harrington St	76	A3
Harrison Row	85	D3
Harry St	125	D4
Hartstown Rd	25	D3
Harty Av	83	D2
Harty Ct	83	D2
Harty Pl	75	D3
Harvard	97	D2
Hastings St	77	D2
Hastings Ter 17	114	A1
Hatch La	76	A3
Hatch Pl		
off Hatch La	76	A3
Hatch St Lwr	76	A3
Hatch St Upr	76	A3
Havelock Pl		
off Bath Av	77	D3
Havelock Sq E	77	D3
Havelock Sq N	77	D3
Havelock Sq S	77	D3
Havelock Sq W	77	D3
Havelock Ter		
off Bath Av	77	D3
Haven, The Dublin 9	44	A3
Haven, The Mala.	13	D1
Haven Vw 2	13	D1
Haverty Rd	63	D2
Hawkins La	123	C3
Hawkins St	125	E2
Hawthorn Av	63	C3
Hawthorn Dr	108	B1
Hawthorn Lawn	40	A3
Hawthorn Lo	40	A3
Hawthorn Manor 1	99	D3
Hawthorn Pk	11	C2
Hawthorn Rd	81	D2
Hawthorns, The 15	119	C3
Hawthorns Rd	109	D2
Hawthorn Ter	63	C3
Haydens Cl	68	B3
Haydens Grn	68	B3
Hayden's La	68	A3
Hayden Sq	98	A2
Haydens Wk	68	B3
Haymarket	124	A2
Hayworth Dr	24	B3
Hayworth Vw	24	B3
Hazel Av	110	A1
Hazelbrook Ct	85	C3
Hazelbrook Dr	84	B3
Hazelbrook Pk	92	B2
Hazelbrook Rd	84	B3
Hazelbury Grn	25	C1
Hazelbury Pk	25	C2
Hazel Ct 6	20	B3
Hazelcroft Gdns		
off Hazelcroft Rd	42	B2
Hazelcroft Pk		
off Hazelcroft Rd	42	B2
Hazelcroft Rd	42	B2
Hazeldene	87	D2
Hazelgrove Jobs.	102	B2
Hazel Gro Port.	20	B3
Hazelgrove Ct	102	B2
Hazel Lawn (Blanchardstown)		
Dublin 15	39	C2
Hazel Lawn 5 D.L.	113	C2
Hazel Pk	84	B3
Hazel Rd	45	D3
Hazel Vil	110	A1
Hazelwood	121	C2
Hazelwood Av	25	D3
Hazelwood Cl	80	A3
Hazelwood Ct Dublin 5	46	A1
Hazelwood Ct Clons.	25	D3
Hazelwood Cres Clond.	80	A3
Hazelwood Cres Clons.	25	D3
Hazelwood Dr	46	A2
Hazelwood Grn	25	D3
Hazelwood Gro	46	A2
Hazelwood La	80	A3
Hazelwood Pk	46	A2
Hazelwood Vw	80	A3
Headford Gro	96	A3
Healthfield Rd	85	D3
Healy St		
off Rutland Pl N	62	B3
Heaney Av	71	D3
Heany Av	115	C2
Heath, The Dublin 6W	94	A2
Heath, The Dublin 24	91	C2
Heath Cres	59	D1
Heather Cl	108	A2
Heather Dr	108	A2
Heather Gdns	21	D1
Heather Gro Dublin 16	108	A2
Heather Gro Palm.	71	C1
Heather Lawn	108	A2
Heather Pk	108	A2
Heather Rd Dublin 16	108	A2
Heather Rd Sandy.	110	A3
Heather Vw Av	103	D2
Heather Vw Cl	103	D2
Heather Vw Dr	103	D2
Heather Vw Lawn	103	D2
Heather Vw Pk	103	D2
Heather Vw Rd	103	D2
Heathervue	123	C2
Heather Wk	21	D1
Heathfield	100	B3
Heath Gro	60	A1
Hedgerows, The	111	D3
Heidelberg	97	D2
Heights, The Dublin 16	108	B3
Heights, The Kins.	12	A3
Heights, The Mala.	14	B3
Hellers Copse	99	C3
Hendrick La		
off Benburb St	75	C1
Hendrick Pl	75	C1
Hendrick St	124	A2
Henley Ct	96	B2
Henley Pk	96	B2
Henley Vil	96	B2
Henrietta La	61	D3
Henrietta Pl	124	B1
Henrietta St	124	B1
Henry Pl	125	D1
Henry Rd	72	A3
Henry St	125	D1
Herbert Av	88	B3
Herbert Cotts	87	C1
Herbert Hill	109	C1
Herbert La	77	C3
Herberton Dr	74	B3
Herberton Pk	74	B3
Herberton Rd Dublin 8	74	B3
Herberton Rd		
Dublin 12	74	B3
Herbert Pk	87	C1
Herbert Pl	77	C3
Herbert Rd Dublin 4	77	D3
Herbert Rd (Blanchardstown)		
Dublin 15	39	D2
Herbert St	76	B3
Hermitage Av	107	D1
Hermitage Cl	107	D1
Hermitage Ct	107	D1
Hermitage Cres	69	D1
Hermitage Downs	107	D1
Hermitage Dr	107	D1
Hermitage Gdn	69	D1
Hermitage Grn	69	D1
Hermitage Gro	107	D1
Hermitage Lawn	107	D1
Hermitage Manor	69	D1
Hermitage Pk		
Dublin 16	107	D1
Hermitage Pk Lucan	69	D1
Hermitage Pl	69	D1
Hermitage Rd	69	D1
Hermitage Valley	69	D1
Hermitage Vw	107	D1
Hermitage Way	69	D1
Heuston Sta	74	B1
Hewardine Ter		
off Killarney St	62	B3
Heytesbury La	87	C1
Heytesbury Pl		
off Long La	75	D3
Heytesbury St	76	A3
Hibernian Av	63	C3
Hibernian Ind Est	92	A3
Highfield Av	107	D2
Highfield Cl	11	C1
Highfield Ct	85	D3
Highfield Cres	11	C1
Highfield Downs	11	C1
Highfield Dr	107	D2
Highfield Grn	11	C1
Highfield Gro	86	A3
Highfield Lawn	11	C1
Highfield Pk Dublin 14	96	B2
Highfield Pk Leix.	66	A2
Highfield Rd	85	D3
Highland Av	117	C1
Highland Gro	117	C1
Highland Lawn	117	C1
Highland Vw	117	C1
High Pk	45	C3
Highridge Grn	110	A1
High St Dublin 8	124	B3
High St Dublin 24	91	D3
Highthorn Pk	113	C1
Highthorn Wds 3	113	C1
Hill, The Dublin 16	108	B3
Hill, The Black.	101	C3
Hill, The Mala.	14	A3
Hill, The 6 Mulh.	26	A3
Hill, The Still.	99	C3
Hillbrook Wds	38	A1
Hill Cotts 1	119	D1
Hill Ct	21	C1
Hillcourt Pk	113	D2
Hillcourt Rd	113	D2
Hillcrest Dublin 6W	94	A3
Hillcrest Lucan	68	A2
Hillcrest (Mooretown) 1		
Swords	13	C1
Hillcrest Av	68	A2
Hillcrest Ct	68	A2
Hillcrest Ter	68	A2
Hillcrest Grn	68	A2
Hillcrest Gro	68	A2
Hillcrest Hts	68	A2
Hillcrest Lawns	68	A2
Hillcrest Pk Dublin 11	43	D1
Hillcrest Pk Lucan	68	A2
Hillcrest Rd	68	A2
Hillcrest Vw	68	A2
Hillcrest Wk	68	A2
Hillcrest Way	68	A2
Hill Dr	14	A3
Hillsbrook Av	83	D3
Hillsbrook Cres	83	D3
Hillsbrook Dr	84	A3
Hillsbrook Gro	83	D3
Hillside Dalkey	114	B2
Hillside Grey.	123	C2
Hillside Dr	95	D2
Hillside Pk	106	B1
Hillside Rd	123	D2
Hillside Vw	49	C2
Hill St	62	A3
Hilltop Lawn	120	B3
Hilltop Shop Cen	47	D2
Hilltown	10	A2
Hilltown Cl	10	B1
Hilltown Ct 4	10	B1
Hilltown Grn 5	10	B1
Hilltown Gro	10	B1
Hilltown Lawn	10	B1
Hilltown Pk	10	B1
Hilltown Rd	10	B1
Hilltown Way	10	B1
Hill Vw	108	A1
Hillview Cotts 3	112	B3
Hillview Dr	112	B3
Hillview Glade 2	108	A1
Hillview Gro	108	A1
Hillview Lawn	112	B3
Hilton Gdns	108	B2
Hoeys Ct		
off Castle St	124	C3
Hogan Av	77	C2
Hogan Pl	77	C2
Hole In The		
Wall Rd, The	36	A3
Hole in Wall Rd, The	36	A2
Holles Row	76	B2
Holles St	125	F4
Hollows, The 7	68	A2
Holly Av	110	A2
Hollybank Av	86	B2
Hollybank Rd	62	A1
Hollybrook Ct		
off Hollybrook Rd	64	A2
Hollybrook Ct Dr	64	A2
Hollybrook Gro	63	D2
Hollybrook Pk	64	A2
Hollybrook Rd	64	A2
Holly Ct	118	B3
Holly Pk	121	C2
Holly Pk Av	111	D1
Holly Rd Dublin 9	63	D1
Holly Rd Dublin 12	81	D2
Hollyville Lawn	57	C3
Hollywood Dr	97	D3
Hollywood Pk	97	D3
Holmston Av	113	D1
Holmwood	117	D2
Holycross Av	62	B2
Holy Cross Coll	62	B2
Holyrood Pk		
off Sandymount Av	88	A1
Holywell	109	D1
Holywell Av	48	A1
Holywell Cres	48	A1
Holywell Rd	48	A1
Home Fm Pk	62	B1
Home Fm Rd	44	A3
Homelawn Av	104	B1
Homelawn Dr	104	B1
Homelawn Gdns	104	B1
Homelawn Rd	104	B1
Homelawn Vil	104	A1
Homeleigh	56	B1
Home Vil	87	C1
Homeville	86	A2
Homeville, The 1	105	C1
Homeville Ct 4	105	C1
Honey Pk 8	113	C2
Hope Av	63	C3
Hope St	77	C2
Hopkins Sq	98	A2
Horseman's Row		
off Parnell St	62	A3
Horton Ct	95	C1
Hotel Yd	125	D2
House of Retreat	73	D3
House of St. John		
of God	111	C1
Howard St	77	C2
Howth Castle	51	D2
Howth Golf Course	51	D3
Howth Junct	48	B1
Howth Rd Dublin 3	63	D1
Howth Rd Dublin 5	47	C3
Howth Rd (Howth)		
Dublin 13	51	D1
Howth Sta	52	B1
Howth Vw Pk	48	A1
H.S. Reilly Br	42	A3
Huband Br	77	C3
Huband Rd	83	C1
Hudson Rd	114	A1
Hughes Rd E	83	D2
Hughes Rd N	83	D2
Hughes Rd S	83	D2
Hume Av	81	D1
Hume Cen	72	A3
Hume St	76	B3
Hunters Av	105	C3
Hunters Ct	105	C3
Hunters Cres	105	C3
Hunters Grn	105	C3
Hunters Gro	105	C3
Hunters Hill	105	C3
Hunters La	105	C3
Hunters Meadow	105	C3
Hunters Par	105	C3
Hunters Pl	105	C3
Hunters Rd	105	C3
Hunter's Run	25	D1
Hunter's Run The Cl	25	D1
Hunter's Run The Dr	25	D1
Hunter's Run The Glade	25	D1
Hunter's Run The Gro	25	C1
Hunter's Run The Pk	25	D2
Hunter's Run The Ri	25	D1
Hunter's Run The Vw	25	D1
Hunter's Run The Way	25	D1
Hunters Wk	105	C3
Hunters Way	105	C3
Huntstown Av	25	D2
Huntstown Cl	26	A3
Huntstown Ct	25	D2
Huntstown Dr	25	D2
Huntstown Glen	25	D2
Huntstown Grn	26	A3
Huntstown Gro	26	A3
Huntstown Lawn	26	A3
Huntstown Pk	26	A3
Huntstown Ri	26	A3
Huntstown Rd	26	A3
Huntstown Way	26	A3
Huntstown Wd	25	D2
Huxley Cres	75	C3

Hyacinth St	63	C3
Hyde Pk *Dublin 6W*	94	B2
Hyde Pk *D.L.*	114	B3
Hyde Pk Av	99	C2
Hyde Pk Gdns	99	C2
Hyde Rd	114	B1
Hyde Sq	98	A1

I		
I.D.A. Ind Cen	61	C3
I.D.A. Small Ind Cen	33	D3
Idrone Av	105	D1
Idrone Cl	106	D1
Idrone Dr	105	D1
Idrone Pk	105	D1
Idrone Ter	99	D2
ILAC Cen	76	A1
Imaal Rd	61	C2
Inagh Ct	119	C3
Inagh Rd	72	A2
Inbhir Ide	13	D2
Inbhir Ide Cl	13	D1
Inbhir Ide Dr	13	D1
Inchicore Par	73	D2
Inchicore Rd	74	A2
Inchicore Sq	73	D2
Inchicore Ter N	73	D2
Inchicore Ter S	73	D2
Infirmary Rd	74	B1
Inglewood	38	A1
Inglewood Cl	25	D3
Inglewood Cres	25	D3
Inglewood Dr	38	A1
Inglewood Rd	38	A1
Ingram Rd	75	D3
Inis Fail	103	D2
Innisfallen Par	62	A2
Innishmaan Rd	44	B2
Innismore	83	D2
Inns Quay	124	B2
Invermore Gro		
off Carraroe Av	48	A1
Inverness Rd	63	C2
Inver Rd	60	B2
Iona Cres	62	A1
Iona Dr	62	A2
Iona Pk	62	A2
Iona Rd	61	D2
Iona Vil	62	A1
Iris Gro	98	A2
Irishtown Rd	77	D2
Irvine Cres		
off Church Rd	77	C1
Irvine Ter	77	C1
Irwin Ct	74	B2
Irwin St	74	B2
Island St	75	C1
Island Vw *Dublin 5*	49	C2
Island Vw *Mala.*	14	B2
Island Vil		
off Hogan Av	77	C2
Isolda Rd	78	A2
Ivar St	75	C1
Iveagh Bldgs		
off Kevin St Upr	75	D3
Iveagh Gdns	84	A1
Iveleary Rd	44	B2
Iveragh Ct	77	D3
Iveragh Rd	44	B2

J		
James Connolly Pk	80	B1
James Connolly Sq	122	A1
James Joyce Ct	49	C2
James Larkin Rd		
Dublin 3	89	C1
James Larkin Rd		
Dublin 5	48	A3
James McCormack		
Gdns	50	A1
James Pl E	76	B3
James's Gate		
off James's St	74	B2
James's St	74	B2
James's St E	76	B3
James's Ter **6**	14	A2
James St N	63	C3
Jamestown Av	73	C3
Jamestown		
Business Pk	82	B1
Jamestown Ind Est	73	C3
Jamestown Rd (Inchicore)		
Dublin 8	73	C3

Jamestown Rd (Finglas)		
Dublin 11	42	B1
Jamestown Sq	73	C3
Janelle Shop Cen	42	B2
Jane Ville		
off Tivoli Rd	101	C3
Jerome Connor Pl		
off Sullivan St	74	B1
Jervis La Lwr	124	C2
Jervis La Upr	124	C1
Jervis St	124	C1
Jetty Rd	78	B1
Jobstown	102	B2
Jobstown Rd	102	A2
John Dillon St	124	B4
John F. Kennedy Av	82	A1
John F. Kennedy Dr	82	B1
John F. Kennedy		
Ind Est	82	A1
John F. Kennedy Pk	82	A1
John F. Kennedy Rd	82	A1
John McCormack Av	83	D2
Johnsbridge	68	B3
Johnsbridge Av	68	B3
Johnsbridge Cl	68	B3
Johnsbridge Grn	68	B3
Johnsbridge Gro	68	B3
Johnsbridge Meadows	68	B3
Johnsbridge Pk	68	B3
Johnsbridge Wk	68	B3
Johns La W	124	A3
Johnsons Ct		
off Grafton St	125	D4
Johnsons Pl		
off King St S	125	D4
Johnstown Av	113	C3
Johnstown Ct	113	C3
Johnstown Gro	113	C3
Johnstown La	113	C3
Johnstown Pk		
Dublin 11	43	D2
Johnstown Pk *Corn.*	113	C3
Johnstown Rd	113	A1
John St S	124	A4
John St W	124	A3
Jones's Rd	62	B2
Jones Ter **15**	122	B2
Josephine Av		
off Leo St	62	A3
Joshua La		
off Dawson St	125	D4
Joyce Av	116	B1
Joyce Rd	62	A1
Joyce Way	81	D1
Joy St		
off Barrow St	77	C2
Jugback Cres	8	A1

K		
KCR Ind Est	84	B3
Keadeen Av	92	B1
Kearns Pl	74	B1
Keeper Rd	74	B3
Kells Rd	84	B3
Kelly's Av	101	C3
Kellys Row	62	A3
Kellystown Rd	108	A3
Kelston Av	111	D2
Kelston Dr	111	D2
Kelston Hall **9**	111	D2
Kelston Pk	111	C2
Kelston Vw **10**	111	D2
Kelvin Cl	21	C1
Kempton Av	59	D1
Kempton Ct	59	D1
Kempton Grn	59	C1
Kempton Gro	59	D1
Kempton Heath	59	D1
Kempton Lawn	59	D1
Kempton Pk	59	D1
Kempton Ri	59	D1
Kempton Vw	59	D1
Kempton Way	59	D1
Kenah Hill	119	C3
Kenilworth La	85	D2
Kenilworth Pk	85	D2
Kenilworth Rd	85	D2
Kenilworth Sq E	85	D2
Kenilworth Sq N	85	D2
Kenilworth Sq S	85	D2
Kenilworth Sq W	85	D2
Kenmare Par		
off Dorset St Lwr	62	A2
Kennedy Pk **2**	122	A3

Kennelsfort Grn	71	C1
Kennelsfort Rd	71	C1
Kennelsfort Rd Lwr	57	D3
Kennelsfort Rd Upr	71	C1
Kennington Cl	93	C2
Kennington Cres	93	C2
Kennington Lawn	93	D2
Kennington Rd	93	C2
Kentfield	121	C1
Keogh Sq	73	D2
Kerlogue Rd	78	A2
Kerrymount Av	116	B1
Kerrymount Cl **1**	117	C1
Kerrymount Grn	117	C1
Kerrymount Mall	117	C1
Kerrymount Ri	117	C1
Kettles La	11	D3
Kevanagh Av	72	A3
Kevin St Lwr	76	A3
Kevin St Upr	124	B4
Kew Pk	67	D3
Kew Pk Av	67	D3
Kew Pk Cres	67	D3
Kickam Rd	74	A2
Kilakea Cl		
off Tibradden Dr	92	B1
Kilakea Dr		
off Tibradden Dr	92	B1
Kilbarrack Av	49	C2
Kilbarrack Gdns	49	C2
Kilbarrack Gro	48	B2
Kilbarrack Ind Est	48	B1
Kilbarrack Par	48	A1
Kilbarrack Rd	48	A1
Kilbarrack Shop Cen	48	A1
Kilbarrack Sta	48	A2
Kilbarrack Way	48	B1
Kilbarron Av	45	D1
Kilbarron Dr	45	D1
Kilbarron Pk	45	D1
Kilbarron Rd	45	D1
Kilbegnet Cl	114	B2
Kilbogget Gro	118	A2
Kilbogget Vil **1**	118	A1
Kilbride Rd	64	B1
Kilbrina	22	A2
Kilcarrig Av	90	B3
Kilcarrig Cl	90	B3
Kilcarrig Cres	90	B3
Kilcarrig La	90	B3
Kilclare Av	102	B1
Kilclare Cres	102	B1
Kilclare Dr	102	B1
Kilclare Gdns	102	B1
Kilcolman Ct **7**	114	A2
Kilcross Av	109	D3
Kilcross Cl **2**	109	D3
Kilcross Ct	109	C3
Kilcross Cres	109	C3
Kilcross Dr	109	C3
Kilcross Gro	109	C3
Kilcross Lawn	109	D3
Kilcross Pk	109	D3
Kilcross Rd	109	D3
Kilcross Sq	109	D3
Kilcross Way **1**	109	D3
Kildare Pk	84	A1
Kildare Rd	84	B1
Kildare St	125	E4
Kildonan Av	42	A1
Kildonan Dr	42	A1
Kildonan Rd	42	A1
Kilfenora Dr	36	A3
Kilfenora Rd	84	B2
Kilgobbin Rd	110	A3
Kilkieran Ct	60	B1
Kilkieran Rd	60	B1
Kill Abbey	112	A1
Killakee Av	104	B2
Killakee Ct	104	B2
Killakee Gdns	104	B2
Killakee Grn	104	B2
Killakee Gro	104	B2
Killakee Lawns	104	B2
Killakee Pk	104	B2
Killakee Ri	104	B2
Killakee Vw	104	B2
Killakee Wk	104	B2
Killakee Way	104	B2
Killala Rd	60	B2
Killan Rd	77	C1
Killarney Av	62	B3
Killarney Par	62	A2
Killarney St	62	B3
Killarney Vil **5**	122	A2

Killary Gro		
off Ardara Av	48	A1
Kill Av	112	B1
Killeen	13	C2
Killeen Av	13	C2
Killeen Ct **2**	13	C2
Killeen Cres	13	C2
Killeen Ms	14	A2
Killeen Pk	13	C2
Killeen Rd *Dublin 6*	86	A2
Killeen Rd *Dublin 10*	82	A1
Killeen Rd *Dublin 12*	82	A1
Killeen Ter	14	A2
Killester Av	64	B3
Killester Ct	46	B3
Killester Pk	46	B3
Killester Sta	64	B1
Killinarden Est	102	B2
Killinarden Hts	103	C2
Killinarden Rd	102	B2
Killinardin		
Enterprise Pk	103	C2
Killincarrick Rd	123	D2
Killincarrig Manor	123	C3
Killiney	119	D1
Killiney Av	118	B2
Killiney Cen	113	D3
Killiney Ct **5**	119	C3
Killiney Gate	119	C2
Killiney Gro	114	A3
Killiney Heath	119	C2
Killiney Hill Pk	114	B3
Killiney Hill Rd	119	C1
Killiney Oaks **6**	119	C3
Killiney Rd	114	A2
Killiney Sta	119	D2
Killiney Ter **2**	114	B1
Killiney Twrs **8**	114	A1
Killiney Vw	114	A1
Killininny Cotts	104	B2
Killininny Ct		
Apartments **1**	104	B2
Killininny Rd	104	B2
Kill La	112	A2
Kill O' The Gra	112	B1
Kilmacud Av	110	A1
Kilmacud Pk	98	A3
Kilmacud Rd Upr		
Dublin 14	97	D3
Kilmacud Rd Upr *Still.*	110	A1
Kilmainham Br	74	A2
Kilmainham La	74	A2
Kilmantain Pl **6**	122	A2
Kilmartin Cres	90	B3
Kilmartin Dr	90	A3
Kilmartin Gdns	90	A3
Kilmartin Pk	90	A3
Kilmashogue Br	107	D3
Kilmashogue Cl		
off Kilmashogue Dr	92	B1
Kilmashogue Dr	92	B1
Kilmashogue Gro	92	B1
Kilmore Av *Dublin 5*	46	A1
Kilmore Av *Kill.*	119	C2
Kilmore Cl	46	A1
Kilmore Cres	46	A1
Kilmore Dr	46	A1
Kilmore Rd	46	A2
Kilmorony Cl	48	A1
Kilnamanagh Rd	83	C2
Kilnamarragh		
Shop Cen	92	A2
Kilohan Gro	93	C1
Kilrock Rd	53	C2
Kilshane Rd *Dublin 11*	41	D2
Kilshane Rd *Kilsh.*	28	B1
Kiltalown	102	B3
Kiltalown Av	102	A2
Kiltalown Cl	102	A2
Kiltalown Ct	102	A2
Kiltalown Cres	102	A2
Kiltalown Dr	102	A2
Kiltalown Grn	102	A2
Kiltalown Hts	102	A2
Kiltalown Pk	102	A2
Kiltalown Rd	102	A2
Kiltalown Vw	102	A2
Kiltalown Wk	102	A2
Kiltalown Way	102	A2

162

Kilteragh Dr 116 B1
Kilteragh Pines 3 111 D3
Kilteragh Rd 117 C1
Kiltipper Av 104 A2
Kiltipper Cl 104 A2
Kiltipper Dr 104 A2
Kiltipper Gate 3 103 D3
Kiltipper Ri 1 103 D3
Kiltipper Rd 103 D3
Kiltipper Vw 2 103 D3
Kiltipper Way 103 D2
Kiltuck Pk 2 121 C3
Kilvere 94 B2
Kilworth Rd 73 D3
Kimberley Rd 123 D1
Kimmage Ct 84 B3
Kimmage Gro 85 C3
Kimmage Rd Lwr 85 C2
Kimmage Rd W 84 A3
Kinahan St 74 B1
Kincora Av 64 A2
Kincora Ct 65 C2
Kincora Dr 64 B2
Kincora Gro 64 B2
Kincora Pk 64 B2
Kincora Rd 64 B2
King Edward Ct 7 122 A2
Kingram La 76 B3
Kings Av 63 C3
Kings Hall Dublin 20 72 B1
Kings Hall 2 Swords 12 A2
Kings Inns St 124 C1
Kingsland Par 86 A1
Kingsland Pk Av 76 A3
Kingsmill Rd 122 B1
Kingston 108 B3
Kingston Av 108 B3
Kingston Cl 108 B3
Kingston Ct 107 C1
Kingston Cres 108 B3
Kingston Dr 108 B3
Kingston Grn 108 B3
Kingston Gro 108 B3
Kingston Hts 108 B3
Kingston Lawn 108 B3
Kingston Pk 108 B3
Kingston Ri 108 B3
Kingston Vw 108 B3
Kingston Wk 108 B3
King St N 124 B1
King St S 125 D4
Kingswood Av 91 D1
Kingswood Castle 81 D3
Kingswood Dr 91 D1
Kingswood Vw 91 C1
Kinlen Rd 123 C3
Kinsaley 19 C2
Kinsaley Br 19 D2
Kinsaley Business Pk 19 D2
Kinsaley La 19 D2
Kinsaley Research Cen 19 C3
Kinsealy Ct 12 B2
Kinsealy Downs 12 B3
Kinvara Av 59 D1
Kinvara Dr 59 D1
Kinvara Gro 59 D1
Kinvara Pk 59 D1
Kinvara Rd 59 D1
Kippure Av 92 B1
Kippure Pk 42 A3
Kirkfield 1 38 A2
Kirkpatrick Av 38 B3
Kirkpatrick Dr 38 B3
Kirkwood 88 A1
Kirwan St 75 C1
Kirwan St Cotts
  off Kirwan St 61 C3
Kitestown Rd 53 C3
Knapton Ct
  off Vesey Pl 101 C3
Knapton Lawn 101 C3
Knapton Rd 101 C3
Knights Br 64 B2
Knights Wd 33 C3
Knockaire 106 A1
Knockaulin 66 A2
Knockcullen 94 A3
Knockcullen Dr 94 A3
Knockcullen Lawn 94 A3

Knockcullen Pk 94 A3
Knockcullen Ri 106 A1
Knockdara 14 B3
Knockfield Grn 105 D1
Knockfield Manor 105 D1
Knocklyon 106 A1
Knocklyon Av 93 D3
Knocklyon Cl 105 D1
Knocklyon Ct 105 D1
Knocklyon Cres 105 C2
Knocklyon Dr 94 A3
Knocklyon Gate
  Apartments 1 105 C2
Knocklyon Grn 105 D1
Knocklyon Gro 105 D1
Knocklyon Hts 105 D1
Knocklyon Hill 105 C2
Knocklyon Ms 93 D3
Knocklyon Pk 105 D1
Knocklyon Rd 106 A1
Knockmaroon Hill 58 A3
Knockmaroon Rd 58 A3
Knockmeenagh La 81 C3
Knockmeenagh Rd 80 B3
Knockmitten Cl 81 D1
Knockmitten La 81 D1
Knockmitten La N 81 D1
Knockmore Av 102 B2
Knockmore Cres 102 B2
Knockmore Dr 102 B2
Knockmore Gdns 102 B2
Knockmore Grn 102 B2
Knockmore Gro 102 B2
Knockmore Pk 102 B2
Knock-na-Cree Gro 115 C3
Knock-na-Cree Pk 114 B3
Knock-na-Cree Rd 114 B3
Knocknarea Av 84 A1
Knocknarea Rd 83 D1
Knocknashee 97 D3
Knock Riada 72 B1
Knocksinna 111 D2
Knocksinna Ct 8 111 D2
Knocksinna Cres 111 D2
Knocksinna Gro 4 111 D2
Knocksinna Pk 111 D2
Knowth Ct 31 D3
Kor Dev Pk 82 B1
Kyber Rd 59 D3
Kyle-Clare Rd 78 A2
Kylemore Av 72 A3
Kylemore Dr 72 B3
Kylemore Pk Ind Est 72 B3
Kylemore Pk N 72 A3
Kylemore Pk S 72 B3
Kylemore Pk W 72 B3
Kylemore Rd Dublin 10 72 B2
Kylemore Rd Dublin 12 72 B3
Kylemore Rd Dublin 20 72 A1

L

Laburnum Rd 87 C3
Laburnum Wk 57 C3
Lad La 76 B3
Lady's Well Rd 26 B2
Lagan Rd 42 B3
Lakelands, The 95 C2
Lakelands Av 110 A1
Lakelands Cl 110 A1
Lakelands Cres 110 A1
Lakelands Dr 110 A1
Lakelands Gro 110 A1
Lakelands Lawn 110 A1
Lakelands Pk 95 C1
Lakelands Rd 110 A1
Lakeshore Dr 11 D2
Lakeview Dr 11 D2
Lally Rd 73 C2
Lambay Cl 119 C3
Lambay Ct 15 C2
Lambay Dr 119 C3
Lambay Rd 44 A3
Lambourne Village 64 B2
Lambourne Wd 117 D2
Lambs Ct
  off James's St 74 B2
Landen Rd 72 B3
Landscape Av 96 A2
Landscape Cres 96 A2
Landscape Gdns 96 A2
Landscape Pk 96 A2
Landscape Rd 96 A2
Landys Ind Est 94 A3
Lanesborough Av 30 B2

Lanesborough Dr 31 C2
Lanesborough Gdns 30 B2
Lanesborough Gro 31 C2
Lanesborough Rd 30 B2
Lanesborough Ter 30 B2
Lanesborough Vw 30 B3
Lanesville 112 B1
Langrishe Pl
  off Summerhill 62 B3
Lanndale Lawns 91 C3
Lansdowne Gdns
  off Shelbourne Rd 77 D3
Lansdowne Hall
  off Tritonville Rd 77 D3
Lansdowne La 77 D3
Lansdowne Pk
  Dublin 4 77 C3
Lansdowne Pk
  Dublin 16 94 A3
Lansdowne Rd 77 C3
Lansdowne Rd
  Stadium 77 D3
Lansdowne Rd Sta 77 D3
Lansdowne Ter
  off Serpentine Av 87 D1
Lansdowne Valley Cres
  off Kilworth Rd 83 D1
Lansdowne Valley Rd 83 C1
Lansdowne Village 77 D3
Lansdown Valley Pk 73 D3
Laracor Gdns 48 A1
Laragh 119 C2
Laragh Cl
  off Laragh Cl 48 A1
Laragh Gro 48 A1
Larch Dr 4 106 B2
Larchfield Dublin 14 96 B2
Larchfield Dunb. 22 B3
Larchfield Pk 97 C2
Larchfield Rd 97 C2
Larch Gro 86 B2
Larkfield 69 D1
Larkfield Av
  Dublin 6W 85 C2
Larkfield Av Lucan 69 D2
Larkfield Cl 69 D1
Larkfield Ct 69 D2
Larkfield Gdns 85 C2
Larkfield Grn 69 D1
Larkfield Gro
  Dublin 6W 85 C3
Larkfield Gro (Ballyowen)
  Lucan 69 D1
Larkfield Pk 85 C2
Larkfield Pl 69 D2
Larkfield Ri 69 D1
Larkfield Vw 69 D1
Larkfield Way 69 D1
Larkhill Rd 44 A2
Latchford Cl 24 B2
Latchford Grn 25 C2
Latchford Pk 25 C2
Latchford Sq 25 C2
Latchford Ter 25 C2
La Touche Cl 123 D2
La Touche Ct 108 A2
La Touche Dr 73 C3
La Touche Pk 123 C3
La Touche Pl 123 C3
La Touche Rd Dublin 12 83 C1
La Touche Rd Grey. 123 C3
Lauderdale Est 122 A3
Lauderdale Ter 3 122 A3
Lauders La 50 B1
Laundry La 85 D2
Laurel Av Dublin 14 96 B3
Laurel Av Lough. 118 B3
Laurel Ct 39 C3
Laurel Dr 96 B3
Laurel Hill 6 113 D1
Laurel Lo Rd 39 D3
Laurel Pk 80 B2
Laurel Rd 96 B3
Laurels, The Dublin 6W 85 C3
Laurels, The Dublin 14 96 B3
Laurelton 95 D1
Laurence Brook 72 B1
Laurleen 111 C2
Lavarna Gro 94 B1
Lavarna Rd 84 B3
Laverna Av 39 C3
Laverna Dale 39 C3
Laverna Gro 39 C3
Laverna Way 57 C1
Lavery Av 71 D3

Lavista Av (Killester)
  Dublin 5 64 B1
La Vista Av Dublin 13 51 C3
Lawn, The Dublin 11 42 B1
Lawn, The (Ballinteer)
  Dublin 16 108 B2
Lawn, The (Ballyboden)
  Dublin 16 106 A1
Lawn, The (Cookstown)
  Dublin 24 91 C2
Lawn, The Kins. 12 A2
Lawnswood Pk 111 C1
Lawson Spinney 13 C2
Lawson Ter 18 114 A1
Lea Cres 88 A1
Leahys Ter 78 A3
Lea Rd 88 A1
Le Bas Ter
  off Leinster Rd W 85 D2
Le Broquay Av 72 A3
Lee Rd 61 C1
Leeson Cl 76 B3
Leeson La 76 B3
Leeson Pk 86 B1
Leeson Pk Av 86 B1
Leeson Pl 76 B3
Leeson St Br 76 B3
Leeson St Lwr 76 B3
Leeson St Upr 86 B1
Leeson Village 86 B1
Le Fanu Dr 72 A3
Le Fanu Rd 72 A2
Lehaunstown Rd 117 D3
Leicester Av 85 D2
Leighlin Rd 84 B2
Lein Gdns
  (Gardini Lein) 47 D3
Lein Pk 47 C2
Lein Rd 47 C2
Leinster Av 63 C3
Leinster La
  off Leinster St S 125 E4
Leinster Lawn 97 C1
Leinster Mkt
  off D'Olier St 125 D2
Leinster Pl 85 D2
Leinster Rd 85 D2
Leinster Rd W 85 D2
Leinster Sq 86 A2
Leinster St E 63 C3
Leinster St N 61 D2
Leinster St S 125 E4
Leinster Ter 2 80 B2
Leitrim Pl off
  Grand Canal St Upr 77 C3
Leixlip Pk 66 A2
Leixlip Rd 67 D3
Leix Rd 61 C2
Leland Pl 77 C1
Lemon St 125 D4
Lennox Pl 86 A1
Lennox St 76 A3
Lentisk Lawn 48 A1
Leo Av
  off Leo St 62 A3
Leopardstown Av 111 C3
Leopardstown Ct 2 110 B2
Leopardstown Dr 111 C2
Leopardstown Gdns 111 C2
Leopardstown Gro 111 C2
Leopardstown Hts 110 A3
Leopardstown Lawn 2 111 C2
Leopardstown Oaks 111 C2
Leopardstown Office Pk 110 B2
Leopardstown Pk 111 C2
Leopardstown Retail Pk 110 B3
Leopardstown Ri 110 B3
Leopardstown Rd 110 B3
Leopardstown Valley 116 A1
Leo St 62 A3
Leslie Av 115 C2
Leslies Bldgs 61 D3
Leukos Rd 78 A2
Le Vere Ter 85 D1
Liberty La 76 A3
Library Rd D.L. 101 C3
Library Rd Shank. 120 B2
Liffey Cl 69 D2
Liffey Ct 69 D2
Liffey Cres 69 D2
Liffey Dale 69 D2
Liffey Dockyard 77 D1
Liffey Downs 1 69 D1
Liffey Dr 69 D2

Name	Page	Grid
iffey Gdns	69	D2
iffey Glen 2	69	D2
iffey Grn	69	D2
iffey Hall	69	D2
iffey Lawn	70	A1
iffey Pk	69	D2
iffey Pl 3	69	D2
iffey Ri	69	D2
iffey Rd	69	D2
iffey Row	69	D1
iffey St	73	C2
iffey St Lwr	125	D2
iffey St Upr	125	D2
iffey St W *off Benburb St*	75	C1
iffey Vale	69	D2
iffey Valley Ave	69	D2
iffey Valley Pk	69	D2
iffey Vw	69	D2
iffey Vw Apts 2	66	B2
iffey Wk	70	A1
iffey Way	69	D2
iffey Wd	69	D2
imekiln Av	93	C1
imekiln Cl	93	D1
imekiln Dr	93	D1
imekiln Gro	83	D3
imekiln La	93	C1
imekiln Pk	93	D1
imekiln Rd	93	C1
imelawn Pk	38	A2
imelawn Pk Ct	38	A2
imelawn Pk Glade	38	A2
imelawn Pk Grn	38	A2
imelawn Pk Hill	38	A2
imelawn Pk Ri	38	A2
imelawn Pk Wd	38	A2
imes Rd	109	D2
ime St	77	C2
imetree Av	21	C1
imewood Av	47	D1
imewood Pk	47	D1
imewood Rd	47	D1
incoln La	124	A2
incoln Pl	125	E4
inden	99	C3
inden Gro	99	C3
inden Lea Pk	110	B1
inden Vale	99	D3
indsay Rd	61	D2
inenhall Par	124	B1
inenhall Ter	124	B1
ink Rd	114	A1
inks, The	20	B3
innetfields	24	B2
innetfields Av	24	B2
innetfields Cl	24	B2
innetfields Ct	24	B2
innetfields Dr	24	B2
innetfields Pk	24	B2
innetfields Ri	24	B2
innetfields Sq	24	B2
innetfields Vw	24	B2
innetfields Wk	24	B2
ios Cian	8	A1
ios Na Sidhe	103	D2
isburn St	124	B1
iscannor Rd	60	B1
iscanor 1	115	C1
iscarne	70	B2
iscarne Gdns	70	B2
isle Rd	83	D2
ismore Rd	84	B2
issadel Av	74	A3
issadel Ct	84	A1
issadel Cres	12	B1
issadel Dr	84	A1
issadel Gro	12	B2
issadel Pk	12	B2
issadel Rd	84	A1
issadel Wd	12	B2
issenfield	86	A1
issen Hall Av 4	9	C1
issen Hall Cl 5	9	C1
issen Hall Dr	9	D1
issen Hall Pk 1	9	D1
itten La	125	D2
ittle Britain St	124	B1
ittle Meadow 5	112	B3
ittlepace	25	C1
ittlepace Cl	25	C1
ittlepace Ct	25	C1
ittlepace Cres	25	C1
ittlepace Dr	25	C1
ittlepace Gallops	25	C1
Littlepace Meadow	25	C1
Littlepace Pk	25	C1
Littlepace Rd	25	C1
Littlepace Vw	25	C1
Littlepace Wk	25	C1
Littlepace Way	25	C1
Littlepace Wds	25	C1
Little Strand St	124	B2
Llewellyn Cl	108	A1
Llewellyn Ct	108	A1
Llewellyn Gro	108	A1
Llewellyn Lawn	108	A1
Llewellyn Pk	108	A1
Llewellyn Way	108	A1
Lock Rd	68	A3
Lodge, The	113	D1
Loftus La	124	C1
Lohunda Cres	38	A2
Lohunda Dale	38	A2
Lohunda Downs	38	A2
Lohunda Dr	38	A2
Lohunda Gro	38	A2
Lohunda Pk	25	D3
Lohunda Rd	38	A2
Lombard St E	125	F2
Lombard St E	125	F3
Lombard St W	75	D3
Lomond Av	63	C2
London Br	77	D3
Londonbridge Dr *off Londonbridge Rd*	77	D3
Londonbridge Rd	77	D3
Longdale Ter	44	A1
Longford La *off Longford St Gt*	124	C4
Longford Pl	101	C3
Longford St Gt	124	C4
Longford St Little	124	C4
Longford Ter	100	B3
Longlands	11	D1
Long La *Dublin 7*	62	A3
Long La (Tenter Flds) *Dublin 8*	75	D3
Long La Gro	75	D3
Longmeadow	117	D1
Longmeadow Gro	113	C3
Long Mile Rd	82	B2
Longs Pl	75	C2
Longwood Av	75	D3
Longwood Pk	95	D3
Lorcan Av	45	C1
Lorcan Cres	45	C1
Lorcan Dr	45	C1
Lorcan Grn	45	D1
Lorcan Gro	45	C1
Lorcan O'Toole Pk	84	A3
Lorcan Pk	45	C1
Lorcan Rd	45	C1
Lorcan Vil	45	D1
Lord Edward St	124	C3
Lordello Rd	120	B3
Lord's Wk	60	A2
Loreto Av *Dublin 14*	95	D3
Loreto Av *Dalkey*	115	C2
Loreto Ct	95	D3
Loreto Cres	95	D3
Loreto Gra	122	A3
Loreto Pk	95	D3
Loreto Rd	75	C3
Loreto Row	95	D3
Loreto Ter	95	D3
Loretto Av 2	122	B2
Loretto Ter 3	122	B2
Loretto Vil 4	122	B2
Lorne Ter *off Brookfield Rd*	74	B2
Lotts	125	D2
Lough Conn Av	72	A1
Lough Conn Dr	72	A1
Lough Conn Rd (Bothar Loch Con)	72	A1
Lough Conn Ter	72	A1
Lough Derg Rd	47	D2
Loughlinstown	120	B1
Loughlinstown Dr	118	B3
Loughlinstown Ind Est	118	B3
Loughlinstown Pk	118	B3
Loughlinstown Wd	118	B3
Loughsallagh Br	23	C3
Lourdes Rd	75	C3
Louvain	97	D2
Louvain Glade	97	D2
Love La E	77	D3
Lower Dodder Rd	95	D1
Lower Glen Rd	58	A3
Lower Kilmacud Rd *Dublin 14*	97	D3
Lower Kilmacud Rd *Still.*	98	A3
Lower Rd *Dublin 20*	57	D2
Lower Rd *Shank.*	121	C3
Luby Rd	74	A2
Lucan	68	B1
Lucan Br	68	B1
Lucan Bypass	68	B2
Lucan Hts	68	B1
Lucan Rd *Dublin 20*	69	D1
Lucan Rd *Lucan*	69	D1
Lucan Rd *Palm.*	57	C3
Lucan Shop Cen	68	A2
Ludford Dr	108	B1
Ludford Pk	108	B1
Ludford Rd	108	B1
Lugaquilla Av	92	B1
Luke St	125	E2
Lullymore Ter	75	C3
Lurgan St	124	B1
Lutterell Hall	22	A1
Luttrell Pk	38	B3
Luttrell Pk Cl	38	B3
Luttrell Pk Cres	56	B1
Luttrell Pk Dr	38	B3
Luttrell Pk Grn	38	B3
Luttrell Pk Gro	38	B3
Luttrell Pk La	38	B3
Luttrell Pk Vw	38	B3
Luttrellstown Av	56	B1
Luttrellstown Beeches	56	B1
Luttrellstown Chase	56	A1
Luttrellstown Cl	56	B1
Luttrellstown Ct	56	B1
Luttrellstown Dale	56	A1
Luttrellstown Dr	56	B1
Luttrellstown Glade	56	B1
Luttrellstown Grn	56	B1
Luttrellstown Gro	56	B1
Luttrellstown Heath	56	B1
Luttrellstown Hts	56	B1
Luttrellstown Lawn	56	B1
Luttrellstown Oaks	56	B1
Luttrellstown Pk	56	B1
Luttrellstown Pl	56	B1
Luttrellstown Ri	56	B1
Luttrellstown Thicket	56	B1
Luttrellstown Vw	56	B1
Luttrellstown Wk	56	B1
Luttrellstown Way	56	B1
Luttrellstown Wd	57	C1
Lynchs La	72	B2
Lynchs Pl	61	D3
Lyndon Gate	60	A2
Lynwood	109	C1

M

Name	Page	Grid
M50 Business Pk	92	A1
Mabbot La	125	E1
Mabel St	62	A2
Macartney Br	76	B3
McAuley Av	47	C2
McAuley Dr	47	C2
McAuley Pk	47	C2
McAuley Rd	47	C2
McCabe Vil	98	B1
McCarthy's Bldgs *off Cabra Rd*	61	D2
McCreadie's La	13	D2
McDowell Av	74	B2
McGrane Ct 3	109	C1
McKee Av	30	B3
McKee Barracks	60	B3
McKee Dr	60	B3
McKee Pk	60	B3
McKee Rd	42	B1
McKelvey Av	30	A3
McKelvey Rd	30	B3
Macken St	77	C2
Macken Vil	77	C2
Mackies Pl	76	B3
Mackintosh Pk	112	B3
McMahon St	75	D3
McMorrough Rd	85	C3
Macroom Av	34	A3
Macroom Rd	34	B3
Madden's La	118	A3
Madeleine Ter	73	D2
Madison Rd	74	B3
Magenis Pl	125	F3
Magennis Sq *off Pearse St*	125	F3
Magenta Cres	33	C3
Magenta Hall	45	C1
Magenta Pl	113	D1
Mageough Home	86	A3
Mahers Pl *off Macken St*	77	C2
Maiden Row	72	B1
Main Rd	92	A3
Main Rd Tallaght	92	B3
Main St (Raheny) *Dublin 5*	47	D3
Main St (Finglas) *Dublin 11*	42	B1
Main St (Baldoyle) *Dublin 13*	37	D3
Main St (Howth) *Dublin 13*	53	C2
Main St (Dundrum) *Dublin 14*	96	B3
Main St (Rathfarnham) *Dublin 14*	95	C2
Main St *Dublin 20*	72	B1
Main St *Dublin 24*	92	A3
Main St *Black.*	99	D2
Main St *Bray*	122	A2
Main St *Clond.*	80	B2
Main St *Dunb.*	22	A2
Main St *Leix.*	66	B2
Main St *Lucan*	68	A1
Main St *Mala.*	14	A2
Main St *Swords*	11	C1
Malachi Rd	75	C1
Malahide Rd *Dublin 3*	63	D2
Malahide Rd *Dublin 5*	46	A3
Malahide Rd *Dublin 17*	47	C1
Malahide Rd *Balg.*	35	D1
Malahide Rd *Swords*	11	D1
Malahide Roundabout	11	D1
Malahide Sta	14	A2
Malborough Ct 9	114	A2
Mall, The *Dublin 15*	38	B2
Mall, The *Leix.*	66	B2
Mall, The *Lucan*	68	A1
Mall, The *Mala.*	14	A2
Mallin Av	75	C3
Malone Gdns	77	D2
Malpas Pl *off Malpas St*	75	D3
Malpas St	75	D3
Malpas Ter *off Malpas St*	75	D3
Maltings, The	122	A1
Mander's Ter *off Ranelagh Rd*	86	B1
Mangerton Rd	83	C1
Mannix Rd	62	A1
Manor Av *Dublin 6W*	94	B1
Manor Av *Grey.*	123	C3
Manor Cl	108	A2
Manor Cres	25	C2
Manor Dr	36	A3
Manorfields	25	C2
Manor Grn	107	D2
Manor Heath	108	A1
Manor Pk (Ballinteer) *Dublin 16*	107	D2
Manor Pk *Dublin 20*	71	D1
Manor Pl	75	C1
Manor Ri	108	A2
Manor Rd	71	D1
Manor St	61	C3
Mansion Ho	125	D4
Mantua Pk	9	C1
Maolbuille Rd	44	A2
Mapas Av	114	A2
Mapas Rd	114	B2
Maple Av *Castle.*	39	C3
Maple Av *Still.*	110	A3
Maple Cl	39	C3
Maple Dr *Dublin 6W*	85	C3
Maple Dr *Castle.*	39	C3
Maple Dr *Dunb.*	22	B2
Maple Glen	39	C3
Maple Grn	39	C3
Maple Gro	39	C3
Maple Lawn	39	C3
Maple Manor	118	A1

Maple Rd 87 C3
Maples, The
  Dublin 14 97 C1
Maples, The D.L. 100 A3
Maples Rd 109 D2
Maplewood Av 103 C1
Maplewood Cl 103 C1
Maplewood Ct 103 C1
Maplewood Dr 103 C1
Maplewood Grn 103 C1
Maplewood Lawn 103 C1
Maplewood Pk 103 C1
Maplewood Rd 102 B1
Maplewood Way 103 C1
Maquay Br 77 C3
Maretimo Gdns E 100 A2
Maretimo Gdns W
  off Newtown Av 100 A2
Maretimo Pl
  off Newtown Av 100 A2
Maretimo Rd
  off Newtown Av 100 A2
Maretimo Vil
  off Newtown Av 99 D2
Marewood Cres 31 D3
Marewood Dr 31 D3
Marewood Gro 31 D3
Marfield Cl 5 103 D3
Marfield Ct 6 103 D3
Marfield Cres 8 103 D3
Marfield Grn 103 D3
Marfield Gro 7 103 D3
Marfield Lawn 4 103 D3
Marfield Pl 103 D3
Margaret Pl 77 D2
Marguerite Rd 62 A1
Marian Cres 94 B3
Marian Dr 94 B2
Marian Gro 94 B3
Marian Pk Dublin 12 49 C1
Marian Pk (Rathfarnham)
  Dublin 14 94 B3
Marian Pk Black. 111 D1
Marian Rd 94 B3
Marie Vil 5 122 B2
Marigold Av 35 C3
Marigold Ct 4 35 C3
Marigold Cres 5 35 C3
Marigold Gro 6 35 C3
Marigold Pk 7 35 C3
Marina Village 14 A1
Marine Av 114 A1
Marine Ct 114 A1
Marine Dr 78 A3
Marine Par 114 A1
Marine Rd 101 D3
Mariners Cove 53 C3
Mariner's Port 77 C1
Marine Ter 9 Bray 122 B1
Marine Ter D.L. 101 D3
Marine Ter Grey. 123 D1
Marino Av 63 D1
Marino Av E 119 D2
Marino Av W 119 C2
Marino Grn 63 D1
Marino Inst of Ed 63 C1
Marino Mart 63 D2
Marino Pk 63 C2
Marino Pk Av 63 C2
Marion Vil 75 C2
Market Sq 8 122 A2
Market St S 75 C2
Marks All W 124 B4
Marks La 125 F3
Mark St 125 F3
Marlay Vw 108 A3
Marlborough Ms 60 B3
Marlborough Pk 2 113 D2
Marlborough Pl 125 E1
Marlborough Rd (Donnybrook)
  Dublin 4 86 B2
Marlborough Rd
  Dublin 7 60 B3
Marlborough Rd
  G'geary 114 A2
Marlborough St 125 D1
Marlborough Ter 10 122 B1
Marley Av 107 D1
Marley Cl 108 A1

Marley Ct N 108 A1
Marley Ct S 108 A1
Marley Dr 107 D1
Marley Gro 107 D1
Marley Lawn 107 D1
Marley Ri 107 D1
Marley Vil 1 107 D1
Marley Wk 107 D1
Marlfield 117 D1
Marne Vil 61 D3
Marrowbone La 75 C3
Marrowbone La Cl 75 C2
Marshalsea La 75 C2
Marsham Ct 110 A1
Martello Av 101 D3
Martello Ct 21 C1
Martello Ms 88 B2
Martello Ter Boot. 99 C1
Martello Ter 1 Bray 122 B1
Martello Vw 78 A3
Martello Wd 88 B1
Martin Savage Pk 41 C3
Martin Savage Rd 59 D2
Martins Row 58 B3
Martin St 86 A1
Mart La 112 A3
Maryfield Av 46 A2
Maryfield Coll 45 C3
Maryfield Cres 46 A2
Maryfield Dr 46 A2
Maryland 3 121 C2
Mary's Abbey 124 B2
Mary St 124 B2
Mary St Little 124 B2
Maryville Rd 47 C3
Mask Av (Ascal Measc) 46 B2
Mask Cres 46 B2
Mask Dr 46 B2
Mask Grn 46 B2
Mask Rd 46 B2
Mastersons La
  off Charlemont St 76 A3
Mather Rd N 98 A2
Mather Rd S 98 A2
Maunsell Pl
  off Mountjoy St 62 A3
Maxwell Rd 86 A2
Maxwell St 75 C3
Mayberry Pk 91 D2
Mayberry Rd 91 D2
Mayfair 14 B2
Mayfield 95 D1
Mayfield Rd (Terenure)
  Dublin 6W 85 C3
Mayfield Rd (Kilmainham)
  Dublin 8 74 B3
Mayfield Ter
  Dublin 16 108 B2
Mayfield Ter 4 Bray 122 A3
May La 124 A2
Mayne Br 37 D2
Mayne Rd 36 B1
Mayola Ct 96 B2
Mayor St Lwr 77 C1
Mayor St Upr 77 D1
May St 62 B2
Mayville Ter 1 115 C2
Maywood Av 48 A3
Maywood Cl 48 A3
Maywood Cres 48 A3
Maywood Dr 48 A3
Maywood Gro 48 A3
Maywood La 48 A3
Maywood Pk 48 A3
Maywood Rd 48 A3
Meades Ter 77 C2
Meadow, The
  Dublin 16 108 B2
Meadow, The Mala. 15 C3
Meadow Av 2 108 B1
Meadowbank 95 D1
Meadowbrook Av 49 D1
Meadowbrook Lawn 49 D1
Meadowbrook Pk 49 D1
Meadow Cl
  Dublin 16 108 A1
Meadow Cl Black. 111 D1
Meadow Copse 25 D2
Meadow Ct 1 118 B3
Meadow Dale 1 25 D2
Meadow Downs 25 D3
Meadow Dr 25 D2
Meadow Grn 25 D3
Meadow Gro 108 A1

Meadow Mt 108 A1
Meadow Pk 108 A1
Meadow Pk Av 96 A3
Meadows, The
  Dublin 5 47 C3
Meadows, The
  Dunb. 22 A3
Meadows E, The 91 C2
Meadows W, The 91 C2
Meadow Vale 112 B3
Meadow Vw
  Dublin 14 108 A1
Meadow Vw Dunb. 22 A2
Meadow Vil 1 108 A1
Meadow Way 25 D2
Meakstown Cotts 30 B2
Meath Pl Dublin 8 124 A4
Meath Pl Bray 122 B1
Meath Rd 122 B2
Meath Sq
  off Gray St 124 A4
Meath St 124 A3
Meehan Sq 98 A1
Meetinghouse La
  off Mary's Abbey 124 C2
Mellifont Av 101 D3
Mellowes Av 42 A1
Mellowes Ct 42 B1
Mellowes Cres 42 B1
Mellowes Pk 42 A1
Mellowes Rd 42 A1
Mellows Br 124 A2
Melrose Av 63 C2
Melrose Pk 12 A3
Melville Cl 31 C3
Melville Ct 30 B3
Melville Cres 30 B3
Melville Dr 30 B3
Melville Grn 30 B3
Melville Gro 31 C3
Melville Pk 30 B3
Melville Ter 30 B3
Melville Vw 30 B3
Melville Way 30 B3
Melvin Rd 85 C3
Memorial Rd 125 E2
Mercer St Lwr 124 C4
Mercer St Upr 76 A3
Merchamp 65 C2
Merchants Quay 124 B3
Merchants Rd 77 D1
Meretimo Vil 26 122 B2
Meridianpoint 123 D2
Merlyn Dr 88 A2
Merlyn Pk 88 A2
Merlyn Rd 88 A2
Merrion Cres 88 B3
Merrion Gro 98 B1
Merrion Pk 98 B2
Merrion Pl 125 E4
Merrion Rd 87 D1
Merrion Row 125 E4
Merrion Shop Cen 88 A2
Merrion Sq E 125 F4
Merrion Sq N 125 F4
Merrion Sq S 125 F4
Merrion Sq W 125 E4
Merrion Strand 88 B2
Merrion St Lwr
  off Clare St 125 E4
Merrion St Upr 76 B3
Merrion Vw Av 88 A2
Merrion Village 88 A2
Merrywell Ind Est 82 A3
Merton Av 75 C3
Merton Cres 86 B3
Merton Dr 86 B2
Merton Rd 86 B3
Merton Wk 86 B3
Merville Av Dublin 3 63 C2
Merville Av Still. 110 B1
Merville Rd 110 B1
Mespil Rd 76 B3
Mews, The Dublin 3 64 B2
Mews, The (Dollymount)
  Dublin 3 65 D2
Mews, The 6 Mala. 15 C3
Michael Collins Pk 80 A1
Middle Ill 64 B1
Milesian Av 12 A2
Milesian Ct 12 A2
Milesian Gro 12 A2
Milesian Lawn 12 A2
Milford 13 C1
Military Cem 60 A2

Military Rd (Rathmines)
  Dublin 6 86 A1
Military Rd (Kilmainham)
  Dublin 8 74 B2
Military Rd (Phoenix Pk)
  Dublin 8 73 C1
Military Rd Kill. 119 C2
Millbourne Av 62 A1
Millbrook Av 47 D1
Millbrook Ct 74 B2
Millbrook Dr 48 A1
Millbrook Gro 47 D1
Millbrook Lawns 104 A1
Millbrook Rd 47 D1
Millbrook Village
  off Prospect La 87 C3
Mill Cen 80 B1
Millennium Br 76 A1
Millennium
  Business Pk 28 B2
Millfarm 22 B2
Millgate Dr 93 D1
Mill La Dublin 8
  off Newmarket 75 D3
Mill La Dublin 15 41 C3
Mill La Dublin 20 57 D3
Mill La Leix. 66 B2
Mill La Lough. 121 C1
Mill La Business Pk 67 C2
Millmount Av 62 A1
Millmount Gro 96 B3
Millmount Pl 62 B1
Millmount Ter
  (Drumcondra) Dublin 9
  off Millmount Av 62 B1
Millmount Ter (Dundrum)
  Dublin 14
  off Millmount Gro 96 B1
Millmount Vil 62 A1
Mill Pk 80 A2
Mill Pond
  Apartments, The 4 80 B2
Mill Rd 39 D2
Millstead 39 D2
Millstream Rd 67 D3
Mill St 75 D3
Milltown Av 86 B3
Milltown Br Rd 86 B3
Milltown Dr 96 A2
Milltown Gro 96 A2
Milltown Hill
  off Milltown Rd 86 B3
Milltown Path 86 B3
Milltown Rd 86 B3
Millview Cl 1 13 C2
Millview Ct 13 C2
Millview Lawns 13 C2
Millview Rd 13 C2
Millwood Pk 47 D1
Millwood Vil 47 D1
Milton Ter 14 122 A1
Milward Ter 16 122 B2
Misery Hill 77 C2
Moatfield Av 47 C1
Moatfield Pk 47 C1
Moatfield Rd 47 C1
Moatview Av 34 B3
Moatview Ct 34 B2
Moatview Dr 34 B2
Moatview Gdns 34 B3
Moeran Rd 83 D2
Moira Rd 75 C1
Moland Pl
  off Talbot St 125 E1
Molesworth Pl
  off Molesworth St 125 E4
Molesworth St 125 E4
Molyneux Yd 124 A3
Monalea Dr 105 C1
Monalea Gro 105 C1
Monalea Pk 105 C1
Monalea Wd 105 C1
Monaloe Av 117 D1
Monaloe Ct 1 117 D1
Monaloe Cres 2 112 B3
Monaloe Dr 112 B3
Monaloe Pk 112 B3
Monaloe Pk Rd 112 B3
Monaloe Way 112 B3
Monarch Ind Est 91 D3
Monasterboice Rd 84 A1
Monastery Cres 81 C2
Monastery Dr 81 C2
Monastery Gate 81 D2
Monastery Gate Av 81 C2

Monastery Gate Cl	81	D2
Monastery Gate Copse	81	C2
Monastery Gate Grn	81	C2
Monastery Gate Lawns	81	D2
Monastery Gate Vil	81	C2
Monastery Heath	81	C2
Monastery Heath Av	81	C2
Monastery Heath Ct	81	C2
Monastery Heath Grn	81	C2
Monastery Heath Sq	81	C2
Monastery Hts 1	81	C2
Monastery Pk	80	B2
Monastery Ri	80	B2
Monastery Rd	80	B2
Monastery Shop Cen	81	C2
Monastery Wk	81	C2
Monck Pl	61	D3
Monksfield	81	C2
Monksfield Ct	81	C1
Monksfield Downs	81	C1
Monksfield Gro	81	C2
Monksfield Hts	81	C2
Monksfield Lawn	81	C1
Monksfield Meadows	81	C2
Monksfield Wk	81	C2
Monks Meadow	15	D3
Monkstown Av	112	B1
Monkstown Cres	100	B3
Monkstown Fm	112	B1
Monkstown Gate	101	C3
Monkstown Gro	112	B1
Monkstown Rd	100	A2
Monkstown Sq 4	112	B1
Monkstown Valley	100	B3
Montague Ct off Protestant Row	76	A3
Montague La	76	A3
Montague Pl off Montague La	76	A3
Montague St	76	A3
Montebello Ter 17	122	B2
Monte Vella	114	B2
Montgommery Vw	12	A1
Montone Business Pk	74	B1
Montpelier Dr	74	B1
Montpelier Gdns	74	B1
Montpelier Hill	74	B1
Montpelier Par	100	A3
Montpelier Pk	75	C1
Montpelier Pl	75	C1
Montpelier Vw	102	B2
Montrose Av	45	D2
Montrose Cl	45	D2
Montrose Ct	45	D2
Montrose Cres	46	A1
Montrose Dr	45	D1
Montrose Gro	45	D2
Montrose Pk	45	D2
Moorefield	118	B2
Moore La	125	D1
Moore's Cotts 4	111	D1
Moore St	125	D1
Mooretown Av	8	B1
Mooretown Gro 3	8	B1
Mooretown Pk 4	8	B1
Mooretown Rd	8	B1
Moorfield	70	A3
Moorfield Av	70	B3
Moorfield Cl 2	70	B3
Moorfield Dr	70	B3
Moorfield Grn	70	B3
Moorfield Lawns	70	B3
Moorings, The	14	B2
Moreen Av	109	D2
Moreen Lawn 3	109	D3
Moreen Pk	109	D3
Moreen Rd	109	D3
Moreen Wk	109	D3
Morehampton La	87	C1
Morehampton Rd	87	C1
Morehampton Sq	86	B1
Morehampton Ter	87	C1
Morgan Pl off Inns Quay	124	B2
Morning Star Av	124	A1
Morning Star Rd	75	C3
Mornington Av	114	B1
Mornington Gro	46	B2
Mornington Rd	86	B2
Morrogh Ter	63	C1
Moss St	125	E2
Mountain Pk	104	A1

Mountain Vw	120	B3
Mountain Vw Apartments 5	122	A3
Mountain Vw Av off Harolds Cross Rd	85	D2
Mountain Vw Cotts Dublin 6	86	B2
Mountain Vw Cotts Castle.	56	B1
Mountain Vw Dr	96	A3
Mountain Vw Pk Dublin 14	96	A3
Mountainview Pk Grey.	123	C1
Mountain Vw Rd Dublin 6	86	B2
Mountain Vw Rd 1 Kill.	119	C2
Mountain Vil 2	119	C2
Mount Albany	111	D1
Mount Albion Rd	96	A3
Mount Albion Ter 1	96	A3
Mount Alton	105	D1
Mount Alton Ct	105	D1
Mount Andrew	69	D1
Mount Andrew Av	56	A3
Mount Andrew Cl	56	A3
Mount Andrew Ct	69	D1
Mount Andrew Dale	56	A3
Mount Andrew Gro	56	A3
Mount Andrew Ri	56	A3
Mount Annville	98	A3
Mount Annville Conv	97	D3
Mount Annville Lawn	97	D3
Mount Annville Pk	98	A3
Mount Annville Rd	97	D3
Mount Annville Wd	98	A3
Mount Argus Cl	85	C2
Mount Argus Ct	85	C2
Mount Argus Cres	85	C2
Mount Argus Grn	85	C2
Mount Argus Gro	85	C2
Mount Argus Pk	85	C2
Mount Argus Rd	85	C2
Mount Argus Ter	85	C2
Mount Argus Vw	85	C2
Mount Argus Way	85	C2
Mount Auburn 1	114	A3
Mount Bellew Cres 1	69	D2
Mount Bellew Grn 2	69	C2
Mount Bellew Ri 1	69	C2
Mount Bellew Way	69	C2
Mount Brown	74	B2
Mount Carmel Av	97	C3
Mount Carmel Pk	105	C1
Mount Carmel Rd	97	C2
Mount Dillon Ct	46	B2
Mountdown Dr	93	D1
Mountdown Pk	93	D1
Mountdown Rd	93	D1
Mount Drinan Av	12	A3
Mount Drinan Cres	12	A3
Mount Drinan Gro 5	12	A3
Mount Drinan Lawn 1	12	B3
Mount Drinan Pk	12	A3
Mount Drinan Wk	12	A3
Mount Drummond Av	85	D1
Mount Drummond Sq	85	D1
Mount Eagle Grn	110	A3
Mount Eagle Gro	110	A3
Mount Eagle Lawn	110	A3
Mount Eagle Pk	110	A3
Mount Eagle Ri	110	A3
Mount Eagle Vw	110	A3
Mount Eagle Way	110	A3
Mount Eden Rd	87	C2
Mountfield	14	A3
Mount Gandon	68	A1
Mount Harold Ter	85	D2
Mounthaven	123	C1
Mount Jerome Cem	85	C1
Mountjoy Cotts	62	A2
Mountjoy Par off North Circular Rd	62	B3
Mountjoy Pl	62	B3
Mountjoy Prison	62	A2
Mountjoy Prison Cotts off Cowley Pl	62	A2
Mountjoy Sq E	62	B3
Mountjoy Sq N	62	A3
Mountjoy Sq S	62	A3
Mountjoy Sq W	62	A3
Mountjoy St	61	D3
Mountjoy St Mid	61	D3
Mount Merrion Av	98	B2

Mount Norris Vil 18	122	B2
Mount Olive Gro	48	A1
Mount Olive Pk	48	A1
Mount Olive Rd	48	A1
Mountpleasant Av Lwr	86	A1
Mountpleasant Av Upr	86	A1
Mountpleasant Bldgs	86	A1
Mountpleasant Par off Mountpleasant Pl	86	A1
Mountpleasant Pl	86	A1
Mountpleasant Sq	86	A1
Mount Prospect Av	65	C2
Mount Prospect Dr	65	C1
Mount Prospect Gro	65	D1
Mount Prospect Lawns	65	C2
Mount Prospect Pk	65	C2
Mount Sackville Conv	58	A2
Mount Salus Rd	115	C3
Mountsandel	117	C2
Mount Sandford	87	C2
Mount Shannon Rd	74	B3
Mount St Cres	77	C1
Mount St Lwr	77	C2
Mount St Upr	76	B3
Mount Symon	25	D3
Mount Symon Cl	25	C3
Mount Symon Cres	25	C3
Mount Symon Dale	25	C3
Mount Symon Dr	25	D3
Mount Symon Grn	25	C3
Mount Symon Ri	25	C3
Mount Tallant Av	85	C3
Mount Tallant Ter off Harolds Cross Rd	85	D1
Mount Temple Rd	75	C1
Mount Town Lwr	113	C1
Mounttown Rd 4	113	C1
Mount Town Rd Upr	101	C3
Mount Vw Rd	38	A1
Mount Wd	113	C2
Mourne Rd	74	B3
Moyclare Av	49	D1
Moyclare Cl	49	D1
Moyclare Dr	49	D1
Moyclare Gdns	50	A1
Moyclare Pk	49	D1
Moyclare Rd	49	D1
Moy Elta Rd	63	C3
Moy Glas Av	69	C3
Moy Glas Chase	69	C3
Moy Glas Cl	69	C3
Moy Glas Ct	69	C3
Moy Glas Dale	69	C3
Moy Glas Dene	69	C3
Moy Glas Dr	69	C3
Moy Glas Glen	69	C3
Moy Glas Gro	69	C3
Moy Glas Grn	69	C3
Moy Glas Lawn	69	C3
Moy Glas Pk	69	C3
Moy Glas Rd	69	C3
Moy Glas Vale	69	C3
Moy Glas Vw	69	C3
Moy Glas Way	69	C3
Moy Glas Wd	69	C3
Moyle Cres	80	B2
Moyle Rd	60	B1
Moyne Rd	86	B2
Moynihan Ct	92	B3
Moyville	106	B2
Moyville Lawns	106	B1
Muckross Av	83	D3
Muckross Cres	83	D3
Muckross Dr	84	A3
Muckross Grn	84	A3
Muckross Gro	83	D3
Muckross Par off Killarney Par	62	A2
Muckross Pk	83	D3
Muirfield Dr	83	C1
Mulberry Cres	57	C1
Mulberry Dr	57	C1
Mulberry Pk	57	C1
Mulcahy Keane Est	83	C3
Muldowney Ct	14	B2
Mulgrave St	101	D3
Mulgrave Ter	113	D1
Mulhuddart Wd	26	A2
Mullinastill Rd	120	B1
Mulroy Rd	61	C1
Mulvey Pk	97	C2
Munster St	61	D2
Munster Ter 3	114	B1

Murphystown Rd	110	A3
Murrays Cotts off Sarsfield Rd	73	D2
Murtagh Rd	75	C1
Muskerry Rd	72	B2
Mygan Business Pk	30	B3
Mygan Pk Ind Est	30	B3
Myra Cotts	74	A2
Myra Manor	19	D1
Myrtle Av 16	113	D1
Myrtle Gro	110	B1
Myrtle Pk	113	D1

N

Naas Rd Dublin 12	82	A2
Naas Rd Dublin 22	81	D2
Naas Rd Business Pk	83	C1
Naas Rd Ind Pk	83	C1
Nangor Cres 1	80	A2
Nangor Rd Dublin 12	81	C1
Nangor Rd Clond.	80	A2
Nangor Rd Business Cen	81	D1
Nanikin Av	47	D3
Nash St	73	C3
Nashville Pk	53	C2
Nashville Rd	53	C2
Nassau Pl	125	E4
Nassau St	125	D3
National Mus	125	E4
National Museum, Collins Barracks	75	C1
National Transport Mus	51	D2
Naul Rd	16	B1
Navan Rd Dublin 7	59	D1
Navan Rd Dublin 15	40	A3
Navan Rd (Blanchardstown) Dublin 15	26	B3
Navan Rd Dunb.	22	A2
Navan Rd Mulh.	25	D1
Neagh Rd	85	C3
Neillstown Av	70	B3
Neillstown Cres	70	B3
Neillstown Dr	70	B2
Neillstown Gdns	70	B3
Neillstown Pk	70	B3
Neilstown Cotts 2	80	B1
Neilstown Rd	70	B2
Neilstown Shop Cen	70	A3
Neilstown Village Ct 1	70	B3
Nelson St	62	A3
Nephin Rd	60	A2
Neptune Ter 4	114	B1
Nerano Rd	115	C2
Nerneys Ct	62	A3
Neville Rd	86	A3
Nevinstown La	11	C3
New Bawn Dr	104	A1
New Bawn Pk	104	A1
New Bride St	76	A3
Newbridge Av	77	D3
Newbridge Dr	77	D3
New Brighton Ter 9	122	A2
Newbrook Av	48	B1
Newbrook Rd	48	B1
Newbury Av	34	A3
Newbury Dr	34	A3
Newbury Gro	34	A3
Newbury Lawns	34	A3
Newbury Pk	34	A3
Newbury Ter 1	34	A3
Newcastle Rd	68	A2
New Ch St	124	A1
Newcomen Av	63	C3
Newcomen Br	63	C3
Newcomen Ct off North Strand Rd	63	C3
Newcourt	9	C1
Newcourt Av	122	B3
Newcourt Business Pk	30	A1
Newcourt Ms 3	9	C1
Newcourt Rd	122	B3
Newcourt Vil 6	122	B3
New Gra Rd Dublin 7	61	C2
New Gra Rd Black.	111	D1
Newgrove Av	78	A3
New Gro Est	36	B3
Newhall Ct	102	A2

Name	Page	Grid
New Ireland Rd	74	B3
Newlands Av	81	C3
Newlands Business Cen	80	B3
Newlands Dr	80	B3
Newlands Manor	90	A1
Newlands Manor Ct	90	A1
Newlands Manor Dr	90	A1
Newlands Manor Fairway	90	A1
Newlands Manor Grn	90	A1
Newlands Manor Pk	90	A1
Newlands Pk	80	B3
Newlands Retail Cen	80	B3
Newlands Rd *Clond.*	80	B3
Newlands Rd *Lucan*	68	B1
New Lisburn St *off Coleraine St*	124	B1
New Lucan Rd	56	B3
Newmarket	75	D3
Newmarket St	75	D3
New Nangor Rd	80	A1
New Pk Lo 7	111	D2
New Pk Rd	111	D1
Newport St	75	C2
New Rd (Inchicore) *Dublin 8*	73	C3
New Rd *Dublin 13*	53	C3
New Rd *Clond.*	80	B2
New Rd *Grey.*	123	C1
New Rd 1 *Swords*	11	D1
New Rd, The *Dublin 11*	28	B3
New Row S	75	D3
New Row Sq	124	B4
New St	14	A2
New St Gdns	75	D3
New St S	75	D3
Newtown Av *Dublin 17*	35	C3
Newtown Av *Black.*	100	A2
Newtown Cotts	47	C1
Newtown Dr	47	C1
Newtown Glendale	66	B1
Newtown Ind Est	35	C3
Newtown Pk *Dublin 17*	35	C3
Newtown Pk *Dublin 24*	92	B3
Newtown Pk *Black.*	111	D1
Newtown Pk *Leix.*	66	B1
Newtownpark Av	99	D3
Newtown Pk Ct 5	111	D1
Newtown Rd	35	C3
Newtown Vil	100	A2
New Vale	120	B2
New Vale Cotts	120	B3
New Vale Cres	120	B2
New Wapping St	77	C1
Niall St	61	C3
Nicholas Av *off Church St*	124	B1
Nicholas Pl *off Patrick St*	124	B4
Nicholas St	124	B4
Ninth Lock Rd	80	B2
Nore Rd	60	B1
Norfolk Mkt *off Parnell St*	62	A3
Norfolk Rd	61	D2
Norseman Pl	75	C1
North Av	98	A2
Northbrook Av	86	B1
Northbrook Av Lwr *off North Strand Rd*	63	C3
Northbrook Av Upr	63	C3
Northbrook La	86	B1
Northbrook Rd	86	A1
Northbrook Ter	63	C3
Northbrook Vil *off Northbrook Rd*	86	A1
Northbrook Wk	86	B1
North Circular Rd *Dublin 1*	62	A3
North Circular Rd *Dublin 7*	62	A2
Northcote Av	101	C3
Northcote Pl	101	C3
North Dublin Docklands	78	A1
Northern Cl	34	B2
Northern Cross Business Pk	30	A3
North Gt Clarence St	62	B3
North Gt Georges St	62	A3
Northland Dr	43	C3
Northland Gro	43	C3
North Pk Business & Office Pk	30	A3
North Quay Extension	77	D1
North Rd *Dublin 8*	59	C1
North Rd *Dublin 11*	30	A1
North Rd Number 1	78	A1
Northside Shop Cen	34	A3
North Strand Rd *Dublin 1*	63	C3
North Strand Rd *Dublin 3*	63	C3
North St	9	C1
North St Business Pk	9	C1
Northumberland Av	101	D3
Northumberland Rd	101	D3
Northumberland Pl *off Northumberland Av*	101	D3
Northumberland Rd	77	C3
North Wall Quay	77	C1
Northway Est	30	A3
North W Business Pk	28	A1
Nortons Av	61	D3
Norwood	119	C3
Norwood Pk	86	B2
Nottingham St	63	C3
Novara Av	122	A1
Novara Ms 15	122	A1
Novara Pk 10	122	A2
Novara Ter 11	122	A2
Nugent Rd	96	A3
Nurney Lawn	36	A3
Nurseries, The 4 *B'brack*	119	C2
Nurseries, The *Mulh.*	26	B2
Nurseries, The *Swords*	10	B2
Nutgrove Av (Ascal An Charrain Chno)	95	D3
Nutgrove Cres	96	A3
Nutgrove Enterprise Pk	96	A3
Nutgrove Office Pk	96	A3
Nutgrove Pk	97	C1
Nutgrove Shop Cen	96	A3
Nutgrove Way	96	A3
Nutley Av	87	D2
Nutley La	88	A3
Nutley Pk	88	A3
Nutley Rd	87	D2
Nutley Sq	87	D3

O

Name	Page	Grid
Oak Apple Grn	85	D3
Oak Av	33	C3
Oak Cl	81	D1
Oak Ct	33	C3
Oakcourt Av	71	D1
Oakcourt Cl	71	D1
Oakcourt Dr	71	D1
Oakcourt Gro	71	D1
Oakcourt Lawn	71	D1
Oakcourt Lawns	71	D1
Oakcourt Pk	71	D1
Oak Cres	33	C2
Oakdale Cl	105	C3
Oakdale Cres	104	B3
Oakdale Dr *Dublin 24*	105	C3
Oakdale Dr *Corn.*	113	C3
Oakdale Gro	105	C3
Oakdale Pk	104	B3
Oakdale Rd	104	B3
Oak Dene	114	A3
Oakdown Rd	96	A3
Oak Downs	80	A3
Oak Dr *Dublin 9*	33	C3
Oak Dr *Dublin 12*	81	D2
Oakfield	80	B1
Oakfield Ind Est	80	B1
Oakfield Pl	75	D3
Oak Grn	33	C3
Oak Gro	33	C3
Oaklands	123	C2
Oaklands Av	11	D1
Oaklands Cres	86	D1
Oaklands Dr *Dublin 4*	87	D1
Oaklands Dr *Dublin 6*	86	A1
Oaklands Pk *Dublin 4*	87	D1
Oaklands Pk *Swords*	11	D1
Oaklands Ter *Dublin 4* *off Serpentine Av*	87	D1
Oaklands Ter *Dublin 6*	85	D3
Oak Lawn *Dublin 9*	33	C3
Oak Lawn *Dublin 15*	39	D3
Oak Lawn *Castle.*	40	A3
Oaklawn *Leix.*	66	A2
Oaklawn Cl	66	A2
Oaklawn W	66	A1
Oakley Gro	99	D3
Oakley Pk *Dublin 3*	65	C2
Oakley Pk *Black.*	99	D3
Oakley Rd	86	B1
Oak Lo	58	A1
Oak Pk Av	45	C1
Oak Pk Cl	45	C1
Oak Pk Dr	33	C3
Oak Pk Gro	33	C3
Oak Ri *Dublin 9*	33	C3
Oak Ri *Clond.*	80	A3
Oak Rd *Dublin 9*	63	D1
Oak Rd *Dublin 12*	81	D2
Oak Rd Business Pk	81	D1
Oaks, The *Dublin 3*	65	D2
Oaks, The *Dublin 16*	108	B2
Oaks, The (Cookstown) *Dublin 24*	91	C2
Oaks, The 16 *Abb.*	119	C3
Oaks, The 5 *Lough.*	118	B3
Oaks, The (Hilltown) *Swords*	10	B2
Oakton Ct	118	B2
Oakton Dr	118	B2
Oakton Grn 2	118	B2
Oakton Pk	118	B2
Oaktree Av	39	C3
Oaktree Dr	39	C3
Oaktree Grn	39	C3
Oaktree Gro	39	C3
Oaktree Lawn	39	C3
Oaktree Rd	110	B2
Oak Vw	33	C3
Oakview Av	25	D3
Oakview Cl	25	D3
Oakview Ct	25	D3
Oakview Dr	25	D3
Oakview Gro 1	25	D3
Oakview Lawn	25	D3
Oakview Ri	25	D3
Oakview Wk	25	D3
Oakview Way	25	D3
Oak Way	80	A3
Oakwood Av *Dublin 11*	43	C1
Oakwood Av *Swords*	11	C1
Oakwood Cl	31	C3
Oakwood Gro Est	80	A1
Oakwood Pk	31	C3
Oakwood Rd	31	C3
Oatfield Av	70	B2
Oatfield Cl	70	B2
Oatfield Cres	70	B2
Oatfield Dr	70	B2
Oatfield Gro	70	B2
Oatfield Lawn	70	B2
Oatfield Pk	70	B2
Obelisk Ct 6	111	D1
Obelisk Gro	99	D3
Obelisk Ri	111	D1
Obelisk Vw	111	C1
Obelisk Wk	99	D3
O'Brien Rd	83	D2
O'Brien's Inst	63	D1
O'Brien's Pl N	62	A1
O'Brien's Ter *off Prospect Rd*	61	D2
Observatory La *off Rathmines Rd Lwr*	86	A1
O'Byrne Rd	122	A3
O'Byrne Vil 7	122	A3
O'Carolan Rd	75	D3
Ocean Pier	78	A1
O'Connell Av	61	D3
O'Connell Br	76	A1
O'Connell Gdns	77	D3
O'Connell St Lwr	125	D1
O'Connell St Upr	125	D1
O'Curry Av	75	D3
O'Curry Rd	75	D3
O'Daly Rd	44	A3
Odd Lamp Rd	59	D2
O'Devaney Gdns	74	B1
O'Donnell Gdns 9	113	D1
O'Donoghue St	73	C3
O'Donovan Rd	75	D3
O'Donovan Rossa Br *off Winetavern St*	124	B3
O'Dwyer Rd	83	D2
Offaly Rd	61	C2
Offington Av	51	C1
Offington Ct	51	C2
Offington Dr	51	C2
Offington Lawn	51	C2
Offington Pk	51	C1
O'Hanlon's La	14	A2
O'Hogan Rd	73	C2
Olaf Rd	75	C1
Old Ballycullen Rd	105	C1
Oldbawn	104	A2
Old Bawn Av	103	D1
Old Bawn Cl	104	A2
Old Bawn Ct	104	A1
Old Bawn Dr	104	A1
Old Bawn Rd	103	D2
Old Bawn Ter 1	104	A1
Old Bawn Way	103	D1
Old Belgard Rd	91	C1
Old Belgard Rd Business Pk	91	C2
Oldbridge Cl	69	C3
Old Br Rd	94	A2
Oldbridge Wk	69	C3
Old Brighton Ter 12	122	A3
Old Cabra Rd	60	B2
Old Camden St *off Harcourt Rd*	76	A3
Old Castle Av	51	C3
Old Corduff Rd	39	C1
Old Cornmill Rd	67	D3
Old Co Glen	84	B1
Old Co Rd	84	A1
Oldcourt Av	104	B3
Oldcourt Cl	104	B2
Oldcourt Cotts	104	B2
Oldcourt Fm	104	B2
Oldcourt Lawn	104	A2
Oldcourt Lo	104	B2
Oldcourt Manor	104	B3
Oldcourt Rd	105	C3
Oldcourt Ter 8	122	A3
Oldcourt Vw	104	B2
Old Dublin Rd	98	B3
Old Dunleary	101	C3
Old Fairgreen	22	A2
Old Fm, The	97	D3
Old Golf Links, The	14	B2
Old Hill	66	A2
Old Hill, The	66	B1
Old Kilmainham	74	A2
Old Kilmainham Village	74	A2
Old Malahide Rd	46	B1
Old Mill Ct	75	D3
Old Mountpleasant *off Mountpleasant Pl*	86	A1
Old Naas Rd	82	B1
Old Orchard	94	A3
Old Quarry	114	B2
Old Rathmichael	120	A3
Old Rectory	68	B1
Old Rectory Pk	97	C2
Old Rd	20	A3
Old Sawmills Ind Est	83	C3
Old St	14	A2
Oldtower Cres	70	A1
Oldtown Av	44	A1
Oldtown Pk	44	A1
Oldtown Rd	44	A1
Old Yellow Walls Rd	13	C1
O'Leary Rd	74	A3
Olivemount Gro	97	C1
Olivemount Rd	97	C1
Oliver Bond St	124	A3
Oliver Plunkett Av (Irishtown) *Dublin 4*	77	D2
Oliver Plunkett Av *D.L.*	112	B1
Oliver Plunkett Rd	112	B1
Oliver Plunkett Sq 9	112	B1
Oliver Plunkett Ter 10	112	B1
Oliver Plunkett Vil 5	112	B1
Olney Cres	95	C2
Omac Business Cen	80	B2
Omni Pk	44	B1
Omni Pk Shop Cen	44	B1
O'Moore Rd	73	C2
O'Neachtain Rd	62	A1
O'Neill's Bldgs	76	A3
Ongar	24	B2
Ongar Pk	25	C3
Ontario Ter	86	A1
Onward Cl	21	C1
Onward Wk	21	C1

Name	Page	Grid
Ophaly Ct	97	C2
O'Quinn Av	74	B2
O'Rahilly Par		
off Moore St	125	D1
Oranmore Rd	71	D2
Orchard, The Dublin 3	63	C2
Orchard, The Dublin 5	46	B3
Orchard, The Dublin 6W	84	B3
Orchard, The 3 Dublin 13	35	D3
Orchard, The Black.	111	D1
Orchard, The 3 Cool.	38	B3
Orchard, The Palm.	57	C3
Orchard Av	38	A2
Orchard Cl	38	B2
Orchard Cotts 2	99	D3
Orchard Ct	38	B2
Orchard Grn	38	B2
Orchard Gro	38	B2
Orchard La Dublin 6	86	A1
Orchard La Black.	111	D1
Orchard Lawns	71	D2
Orchard Rd Dublin 3	63	C2
Orchard Rd Dublin 5	48	B3
Orchard Rd Dublin 6	86	A3
Orchard Rd Clond.	80	B2
Orchardston	94	B3
Orchardstown Av	94	B3
Orchardstown Dr	94	B3
Orchardstown Pk	94	B3
Orchardstown Vil	94	B3
Orchard Ter 9	122	A3
Orchardton 1	106	B1
Ordnance Survey Office	58	B2
Ordnance Survey Rd	58	B2
O'Reilly's Av	74	B2
Oriel Pl	63	C3
Oriel St Lwr	77	C1
Oriel St Upr	77	C1
Orlagh Av	105	D2
Orlagh Cl	106	A2
Orlagh Ct	105	D2
Orlagh Cres	105	D2
Orlagh Downs	106	A2
Orlagh Gra	106	A2
Orlagh Grn	105	D2
Orlagh Gro	105	D2
Orlagh Lawn	105	D2
Orlagh Lo	106	A2
Orlagh Meadows	106	A2
Orlagh Pk	105	D2
Orlagh Pines	105	D2
Orlagh Ri	106	A2
Orlagh Vw	106	A2
Orlagh Way	105	D2
Orlagh Wd	106	A2
Ormeau Dr	114	B2
Ormeau St		
off Gordon St	77	C2
Ormond Mkt Sq off Ormond Quay Upr	124	B2
Ormond Quay Lwr	124	C2
Ormond Quay Upr	124	B2
Ormond Rd N	62	B1
Ormond Rd S (Rathmines)	86	A2
Ormond Sq	124	B2
Ormond St	75	C3
O'Rourke Pk	113	C2
Orpen Cl	99	C3
Orpen Dale	99	C3
Orpen Grn	111	C1
Orpen Hill	111	C1
Orpen Ri	111	C1
Orwell Gdns	96	A1
Orwell Pk	96	A1
Orwell Pk Av	93	D2
Orwell Pk Cl	93	D2
Orwell Pk Cres	93	D2
Orwell Pk Dale	93	D2
Orwell Pk Dr	93	D2
Orwell Pk Glade	93	D2
Orwell Pk Glen	93	D2
Orwell Pk Grn	93	D2
Orwell Pk Gro	93	D2
Orwell Pk Hts	93	D2
Orwell Pk Lawns	93	D2
Orwell Pk Ri	93	D2
Orwell Pk Vw	93	D2
Orwell Pk Way	93	D2
Orwell Rd Dublin 6	85	D3
Orwell Rd Dublin 6W	93	D2
Orwell Rd Dublin 14	96	A1
Orwell Shop Cen	93	D2
Orwell Wds	96	A1
Oscar Sq	75	D3
Oscar Traynor Rd	34	A3
O'Shea's Cotts 3	117	D1
Osprey Av	93	C1
Osprey Dr	93	D2
Osprey Lawn	93	D1
Osprey Pk	93	C1
Osprey Rd	93	D2
Ossory Rd	63	C3
Ossory Sq	75	D3
Ostman Pl	61	C3
O'Sullivan Av	62	B2
Oswald Rd	78	A3
Otranto Pl	114	A1
Oulart	11	C2
Oulton Rd	64	B2
Our Ladys Cl	75	C2
Our Lady's Hospice	85	C1
Our Lady's Rd	75	C2
Oval, The	57	D3
Ovoca Rd	75	D3
Owendoher Haven	106	B1
Owendoher Lo	106	B1
Owendore Av	95	C2
Owendore Cres	95	C2
Owens Av	74	B2
Owenstown Pk	98	A2
Oxford Rd	86	A1
Oxford Ter Dublin 3 off Church Rd	77	C1
Oxford Ter Dublin 6 off Oxford Rd	86	A1
Oxmantown La off Blackhall Pl	75	C1
Oxmantown Rd	61	C3
Oxmantown Rd Lwr off Arbour Hill	75	C1
P		
Pace Av	25	C1
Pace Cres	25	C1
Pacelli Av	49	C2
Pace Rd	25	C1
Pace Vw	25	C1
Packenham	101	C3
Paddock, The Dalkey	59	C1
Paddocks, The Dalkey	114	B1
Paddocks, The Dunb.	22	A2
Pairc Baile Munna	43	D1
Pairc Clearmont (Claremont Pk)	78	A3
Pairc Gleannaluinn (Glenaulin Pk)	58	A3
Pairc Gleann Trasna	103	D3
Pakenham Rd	100	B3
Pakerton off Sloperton	101	C3
Palace St off Dame St	124	C3
Palmer Pk	107	C1
Palmers Av	71	C1
Palmers Cl	71	C1
Palmers Copse	71	C1
Palmers Ct	71	C1
Palmers Cres	71	C1
Palmers Dr	71	C1
Palmers Glade	71	C1
Palmers Gro	71	C1
Palmers Lawn	71	C1
Palmers Pk	71	C1
Palmers Rd	71	C1
Palmerston Av	71	D1
Palmerston Dr	57	D3
Palmerston Gdns	86	A3
Palmerston Gro	87	C3
Palmerston La	86	A3
Palmerston Pk Dublin 6	86	A3
Palmerston Pk Palm.	71	C1
Palmerston Pl	61	D3
Palmerston Rd	86	A3
Palmerston Vil	86	A3
Palmerstown Av	71	C1
Palmerstown Cl	71	C1
Palmerstown Ct	71	C1
Palmerstown Dr	57	D3
Palmerstown Grn	71	C1
Palmerstown Hts	71	C1
Palmerstown Lawn	71	C1
Palmerstown Manor	71	C1
Palmers Wk	71	C1
Palms, The	97	D2
Paradise Pl	62	A3
Parc Na Silla Av	120	B1
Parc Na Silla Cl	120	B1
Parc Na Silla La	120	B1
Parc Na Silla Ri	120	B1
Park, The Dublin 9	45	D2
Park, The Dublin 24	104	B1
Park, The (Greenhills) Dublin 24	91	D1
Park, The (Lutterell Hall) Dunb.	22	A1
Park, The Gra M.	68	B3
Park, The Kins.	12	A2
Park, The Lou.V.	66	A1
Park, The Mala.	15	C3
Park Av Dublin 4	88	A1
Park Av Dublin 15	57	D1
Park Av Dublin 16	95	C3
Park Av Deans Gra	112	A2
Park Av (Hilltown) Swords	10	B1
Park Av Will.	107	C1
Park Cl	113	D2
Park Ct	113	D2
Park Cres Dublin 8	60	A2
Park Cres Dublin 12	84	A3
Park Dr Dublin 6	86	B2
Park Dr Cabin.	117	C1
Park Dr Av	39	D3
Park Dr Cl	39	D3
Park Dr Ct	39	D3
Park Dr Cres	39	D3
Park Dr Grn	57	D1
Park Dr Gro	39	D3
Park Dr Lawn	39	D3
Parkgate Pl Business Cen	74	B1
Parkgate St	74	B1
Parkhill Av	91	D2
Parkhill Cl off Parkhill Ri	91	D2
Parkhill Ct	91	D2
Parkhill Dr	91	D2
Parkhill Grn	91	D2
Parkhill Lawn off Parkhill Rd	91	D2
Parkhill Ri	91	D2
Parkhill Rd	91	D2
Parkhill Way	92	D1
Parklands	39	D3
Parklands, The	95	C3
Parklands Av	104	B2
Parklands Ct	104	B2
Parklands Dr	104	B3
Parklands Rd	105	C2
Parklands Vw	104	B2
Park La Dublin 4	88	A1
Park La Dublin 20	72	B1
Park La E	125	E3
Park Lawn	65	D1
Park Lo	39	D3
Park Manor	57	C1
Parkmore Dr	94	B1
Parkmore Ind Est	82	B2
Park Pl off South Circular Rd	74	A1
Park Rd Dublin 7	59	D1
Park Rd D.L.	101	D3
Park Rd Sally.	113	D3
Park Shop Cen	61	C3
Park St	73	C2
Park Ter	124	A4
Parkvale Dublin 13	49	D1
Parkvale Dublin 16	109	C2
Parkview Dublin 7	60	B3
Park Vw Dublin 15	58	B1
Park Vw Clons.	38	A2
Park Vw Mala.	15	C3
Parkview Port.	21	C1
Parkview Swords	10	A1
Parkview Av (Haroldscross) Dublin 6	85	D2
Park Vw Av (Rathmines) Dublin 6	86	A2
Park Vw Lawns	80	A3
Park Vil Dublin 15	40	A3
Park Vil Black.	99	C3
Parkway Business Cen	82	A3
Park W Av Dublin 10	81	D1
Park W Av Dublin 22	81	D1
Park W Business Pk	71	D3
Park W Ind Pk	72	A3
Park W Rd	71	D3
Parkwood Av	104	A2
Parkwood Gro	104	A2
Parkwood Lawn	104	A2
Parkwood Rd 2	104	A2
Parliament Row off Fleet St	125	D3
Parliament St	124	C3
Parnell Av off Parnell Rd	85	D1
Parnell Cotts	14	A3
Parnell Ct	85	D1
Parnell Pl	62	A3
Parnell Rd Dublin 12	75	C3
Parnell Rd Bray	122	A1
Parnell Sq E	62	A3
Parnell Sq N	62	A3
Parnell Sq W	62	A3
Parnell St Dublin 1	124	C1
Parnell St Sally.	113	D2
Parochial Av 2	37	D3
Parslickstown Av	26	B2
Parslickstown Cl	26	B2
Parslickstown Ct	26	B2
Parslickstown Dr	26	B2
Parslickstown Gdns	26	A2
Parslickstown Grn	26	B2
Partridge Ter	73	C3
Patrician Pk 5	113	C1
Patrician Vil	99	C3
Patrick Doyle Rd	96	B1
Patricks Row off Carysfort Av	99	D2
Patrick St Dublin 8	124	B4
Patrick St D.L.	101	D3
Patrickswell Pl	42	B2
Patriotic Ter off Brookfield Rd	74	B2
Paul St	124	A2
Pavilion Rd	123	C2
Pavilions Shop Cen, The	11	D1
Pavillion Gate 1	117	C2
Pea Fld	99	C2
Pearse Av	113	C3
Pearse Brothers Pk	107	C1
Pearse Cl 9	113	C2
Pearse Dr	113	C2
Pearse Gdns	113	C2
Pearse Grn 10	113	C2
Pearse Gro off Great Clarence Pl	77	C2
Pearse Ho	125	F3
Pearse Pk	113	C2
Pearse Rd	113	C2
Pearse Sq	77	C2
Pearse Sta	125	F3
Pearse St Dublin 2	125	E3
Pearse St Sally.	113	C3
Pearse Vil	113	C3
Pear Tree Fld 4	111	C1
Pecks La	40	A3
Pembroke Cotts (Donnybrook) Dublin 4	87	C2
Pembroke Cotts (Ringsend) Dublin 4	77	D2
Pembroke Cotts (Dundrum) Dublin 14	97	C3
Pembroke Cotts Boot.	98	B1
Pembroke Gdns	77	C3
Pembroke La Dublin 2	76	B3
Pembroke La Dublin 4	77	C3
Pembroke Pk	87	C1
Pembroke Pl off Pembroke St Upr	76	B3
Pembroke Rd	77	C3
Pembroke Row	76	B3
Pembroke St	77	D2
Pembroke St Lwr	76	B3
Pembroke St Upr	76	B3
Penrose St	77	C2
Percy French Rd	83	D2
Percy La	77	C3
Percy Pl	77	C3
Peter Row	124	C4
Petersons Ct	125	F2
Peters Pl	76	A3
Peter St	124	C4
Petrie Rd	75	D3
Pheasant Run	25	D1
Pheasant Run The Dr	25	D1
Pheasant Run The Grn	25	D1

Name	Page	Grid
Pheasant Run The Gro	25	D1
Pheasant Run The Pk	25	D1
Phibsborough	61	D2
Phibsborough Av	61	D3
Phibsborough Pl	61	D3
Phibsborough Rd	61	D3
Philipsburgh Av	63	C2
Philipsburgh Ter	63	C1
Philomena Ter	77	D2
Phoenix Av	40	A3
Phoenix Ct *Dublin 7*		
off Cavalry Row	75	C1
Phoenix Ct *Dublin 15*	40	A3
Phoenix Dr	40	A3
Phoenix Gdns	40	A3
Phoenix Manor	60	B3
Phoenix Pl		
off Phoenix Av	40	A3
Phoenix St *Dublin 7*	124	A2
Phoenix St *Dublin 10*	73	C2
Phoenix Ter	99	C1
Pigeon Ho Rd	77	D2
Pig La	62	B3
Piles Bldgs		
off Golden La	124	C4
Piles Ter		
off Sandwith St Upr	125	F3
Pilot Vw	114	B1
Pimlico	124	A4
Pimlico Sq		
off The Coombe	124	A4
Pim St	75	C2
Pine Av	111	D3
Pinebrook	25	D2
Pinebrook Av	46	A3
Pinebrook Cl	25	D2
Pinebrook Cres		
off Pinebrook Av	46	A2
Pinebrook Downs	25	D2
Pinebrook Glen	25	D2
Pinebrook Gro		
off Pinebrook Rd	46	A3
Pinebrook Hts	25	D2
Pinebrook Lawn	26	A3
Pinebrook Ri	46	A3
Pinebrook Rd	46	A3
Pinebrook Vale	25	D2
Pinebrook Vw	25	D2
Pinebrook Way	25	D2
Pine Copse Rd	108	B1
Pine Ct *Black.*	111	D1
Pine Ct *Port.*	21	C2
Pine Gro	94	A3
Pine Gro Pk	8	A1
Pine Gro Rd	8	A1
Pine Haven	99	C1
Pine Hurst	60	B2
Pine Lawn *Dublin 24*	104	A1
Pine Lawn *Black.*	111	D1
Pine Rd	78	A2
Pines, The *Dublin 5*	46	B3
Pines, The **2**		
Dublin 14	109	D1
Pines, The *Dublin 16*	108	A3
Pinetree Cres	91	D2
Pinetree Gro	91	D2
Pine Valley Av	108	A3
Pine Valley Dr	108	A3
Pine Valley Gro	108	A3
Pine Valley Pk	108	A3
Pine Valley Way	108	A3
Pineview Av	103	D2
Pineview Dr	103	D2
Pineview Gro	103	D2
Pineview Lawn	103	D2
Pineview Pk	104	A2
Pineview Ri	103	D2
Pineview Rd	103	D2
Pinewood	118	B2
Pinewood Av	43	D1
Pinewood Cl	122	A3
Pinewood Ct	26	A3
Pinewood Cres	43	D1
Pinewood Dr	43	D1
Pinewood Grn	43	D1
Pinewood Gro	43	D1
Pinewood Pk	94	B3
Pinewoods	80	A3
Pinewood Vil	43	D1

Name	Page	Grid
Pinnockhill		
Roundabout	11	C2
Plato Business Pk	26	A1
Plaza Shop Cen, The	11	D1
Pleasants La	76	A3
Pleasants Pl	76	A3
Pleasants St	76	A3
Plums Rd	109	D2
Plunkett Av *Dublin 11*	30	A3
Plunkett Av *Fox.*	111	D3
Plunkett Cres	30	A3
Plunkett Dr	30	A3
Plunkett Grn	30	A3
Plunkett Gro	30	A3
Plunkett Rd	42	A1
Poddle Pk	84	B3
Polo Rd	60	A3
Poolbeg St	125	E2
Poole St	124	A4
Poplar Row	63	C2
Poplars, The	100	A3
Poppintree Ind Est	31	C3
Poppintree Pk La W	31	C3
Porters Av	38	B2
Portersfield	38	B2
Porters Rd	38	A2
Porterstown Rd	38	A2
Portland Cl	62	B3
Portland Pl	62	A2
Portland Rd	123	D3
Portland Rd N	123	C3
Portland Row	62	B3
Portland St N	62	B3
Portmahon Dr	74	B3
Portmarnock Av **2**	21	C2
Portmarnock Br	20	B3
Portmarnock Cres	21	C1
Portmarnock Dr	21	C1
Portmarnock Gro	21	C1
Portmarnock Pk	21	C1
Portmarnock Ri	21	C2
Portmarnock Sta	20	A3
Portmarnock Wk	21	C1
Portobello Br	86	A1
Portobello Harbour	86	A1
Portobello Pl	86	A1
Portobello Rd	85	D1
Portobello Sq *off*		
Clanbrassil St Upr	85	D1
Portside Business Cen	63	D3
Port Side Ct	63	C3
Potato Mkt		
off Green St Little	124	B2
Pottery Rd	112	B3
Pound St	66	B2
Powers Ct		
off Warrington Pl	77	C3
Powers Sq		
off John Dillon St	124	B4
Prebend St	124	B1
Preston St	62	B3
Price's La *Dublin 2*	125	D2
Prices La *Dublin 6*	86	A1
Priestfield Cotts	75	C3
Priestfield Dr *off*		
South Circular Rd	75	C3
Priestfield Ter *off*		
South Circular Rd	75	C3
Primrose Av	61	D3
Primrose Gro	35	C3
Primrose Hill	101	C3
Primrose La	68	A1
Primrose St	61	D3
Prince Arthur Ter	86	A2
Prince of Wales Ter		
Dublin 4	87	D1
Prince Of Wales Ter **16**		
Bray	122	A1
Princes St N	125	D2
Princes St S	125	F2
Princeton	97	D2
Priorswood Rd	34	B3
Priory, The *Dublin 7*	60	A1
Priory, The *Dublin 16*	107	D1
Priory, The **4** *Mala.*	14	A2
Priory Av	99	C2
Priory Ct **1**	107	D2
Priory Dr	98	B3
Priory E	60	A1
Priory Gro	98	B3
Priory Hall	98	B3
Priory N	60	A1
Priory Rd	85	C2
Priory W	60	A1

Name	Page	Grid
Proby Pk	114	A2
Probys La	124	C2
Proby Sq	99	D3
Promenade Rd	64	A3
Prospect Av *Dublin 9*	61	D1
Prospect Av *Dublin 16*	106	B2
Prospect Cem	61	D1
Prospect Ct	106	B3
Prospect Dr	106	B2
Prospect Glen	106	B3
Prospect Gro	106	B2
Prospect Heath	106	B2
Prospect Hts	106	B3
Prospect La	87	C3
Prospect Lawn	117	C1
Prospect Meadows	106	B2
Prospect Rd	61	D2
Prospect Sq	61	D1
Prospect Ter (Sandymount)		
off Beach Rd	78	A3
Prospect Vw	106	B2
Prospect Way	61	D1
Protestant Row	76	A3
Prouds La	125	D4
Prussia St	61	C3
Purley Pk	21	C1
Purser Gdns	86	A2
Putland Rd	122	A3
Putland Vil **10**	122	A3

Q

Name	Page	Grid
Quarry Dr	83	D3
Quarryfield Ct	81	C3
Quarry Rd (Cabra)		
Dublin 7	61	C2
Quarry Rd *Grey.*	123	C3
Queens Pk	100	A3
Queens Rd	101	D3
Queen St	124	A2
Quinns La	76	B3
Quinn's Rd	121	C3
Quinsborough Rd	122	A1

R

Name	Page	Grid
Racecourse Shop Cen	37	C3
Radlett Gro	21	C1
Rafters Av	84	A1
Rafters La	84	A1
Rafters Rd	84	A1
Raglan La	87	C1
Raglan Rd	87	C1
Raheen Av	102	B1
Raheen Cl	102	B1
Raheen Ct	102	B1
Raheen Cres	102	B1
Raheen Dr *Dublin 10*	72	A3
Raheen Dr *Dublin 24*	102	B1
Raheen Lawn	122	B3
Raheen Pk *Dublin 10*	72	A3
Raheen Pk *Dublin 24*	102	B1
Raheen Pk *Bray*	122	B3
Raheen Rd	102	B1
Raheny Pk	48	A3
Raheny Rd	47	D2
Raheny Sta	47	D3
Railway Av *Dublin 8*		
off Tyrconnell Rd	73	D3
Railway Av (Inchicore)		
Dublin 8	73	C3
Railway Av *Dublin 13*	50	A1
Railway Av **3** *Mala.*	14	A2
Railway Cotts		
off Serpentine Av	87	D1
Railway Ct **2**	14	A2
Railway Ms	36	B3
Railway Rd *Dublin 13*	37	C3
Railway Rd **5** *Dalkey*	114	B2
Railway St	125	E1
Railway Ter		
off Grattan St	77	C2
Rainsford Av	75	C2
Rainsford La **3**	119	C2
Rainsford St	75	C2
Ralahine	118	B2
Raleigh Sq	84	A1
Ralph Sq **1**	66	B2
Ramillies Rd	72	B2
Ramleh Cl	87	C3
Ramleh Pk	87	C3
Ramleh Vil	86	B3
Ramor Pk	39	C2
Ranelagh Av	86	B1
Ranelagh Rd	86	A1

Name	Page	Grid
Raphoe Rd	84	A1
Rathbeal Ct **1**	8	B1
Rathbeale Cres	8	B1
Rathbeale Ri	11	C1
Rathdown Av	95	C1
Rathdown Cl	123	C1
Rathdown Ct	85	C3
Rathdown Cres	95	C1
Rathdown Dr	95	C1
Rathdown Gro **6**	109	D2
Rathdown Pk	95	C1
Rathdown Rd	61	D3
Rathdown Sq	61	C3
Rathdown Ter **7**	109	D2
Rathdown Vil	95	C1
Rathdrum Rd	85	C1
Rathfarnam Gate	95	C2
Rathfarnham Castle	95	C2
Rathfarnham Mill	95	C2
Rathfarnham Pk	95	C1
Rathfarnham Rd		
Dublin 6W	95	C1
Rathfarnham Rd		
Dublin 14	95	C1
Rathfarnham		
Shop Cen	94	B2
Rathfarnham Wd	95	D2
Rathgar Av	85	D2
Rathgar Pk	85	D3
Rathgar Rd	85	D3
Rathingle Rd	10	B2
Rathland Rd		
(Bothar Raitleann)	84	B3
Rathlin Rd	44	A3
Rathlyon	105	C2
Rathlyon Pk	105	C2
Rathmichael	120	A2
Rathmichael Dales	120	A2
Rathmichael Haven	120	A2
Rathmichael Hill	120	A2
Rathmichael La	120	A2
Rathmichael Manor	120	B1
Rathmichael Pk	121	C2
Rathmichael Wds	121	C2
Rathmines Av	86	A2
Rathmines Rd Lwr	86	A1
Rathmines Rd Upr	86	A2
Rathmintan Cl **3**	102	A2
Rathmintan Ct	102	A2
Rathmintan Cres	102	A2
Rathmore Av	110	A1
Rathmore Pk	48	A3
Rath Row	125	E2
Rathsallagh Av	121	C1
Rathsallagh Br	121	C1
Rathsallagh Dr	121	C2
Rathsallagh Gro	121	C1
Rathsallagh Pk	121	C1
Rathvale Av	47	C1
Rathvale Dr	47	C1
Rathvale Gro		
off Rathvale Av	47	C1
Rathvale Pk	47	C1
Rathvilly Dr	42	A2
Rathvilly Pk	42	A2
Rathvilly Rd	42	A2
Ratoath Av		
(Ascal Ratabhachta)	41	D2
Ratoath Dr	41	D1
Ratoath Est	60	A1
Ratoath Rd *Dublin 7*	60	B2
Ratoath Rd *Dublin 11*	41	D2
Ratra Rd	59	D1
Ravensdale Cl	84	B3
Ravensdale Pk	84	B3
Ravensdale Rd	63	D3
Ravens Rock Rd	110	A2
Ravenswell Rd	122	A1
Ravenswood	25	C2
Ravenswood Av	25	C3
Ravenswood Cres	25	C3
Ravenswood Dr	25	C3
Ravenswood Grn	25	C3
Ravenswood Lawn	25	C3
Ravenswood Ri	25	C2
Ravenswood Rd	25	C3
Ravenswood Vw	25	C3
Raymond St	75	D3
Redberry	68	A3
Red Brick Ter **3**	99	D3
Redcourt Oaks	65	D2
Red Cow Business Pk	82	A2
Red Cow Cotts **3**	57	D3
Red Cow La	124	A1

Name	Page	Grid
Redesdale Cres	98	A3
Redesdale Rd	98	A3
Redfern Av	21	C1
Redmonds Hill	76	A3
Redwood Av	92	A2
Redwood Cl		
off Redwood Av	92	A2
Redwood Ct		
Dublin 14	96	A2
Redwood Ct Dublin 24		
off Parkhill Rd	91	D2
Redwood Dr	91	D2
Redwood Gro	99	C2
Redwood Hts		
off Redwood Pk	92	A2
Redwood Lawn	91	D2
Redwood Pk	92	A2
Redwood Ri		
off Redwood Pk	92	A2
Redwood Vw		
off Redwood Av	92	A2
Redwood Wk	91	D2
Reginald Sq		
off Gray St	124	A4
Reginald St	124	A4
Rehoboth Av	75	C3
Rehoboth Pl	75	C3
Reillys Av off		
Dolphin's Barn St	75	C3
Reuben Av	74	B3
Reuben St	75	C3
Rialto Br	74	B3
Rialto Bldgs		
off Rialto Cotts	74	B3
Rialto Cotts	74	B3
Rialto Dr	74	B3
Rialto St	74	B3
Ribh Av	47	C3
Ribh Rd	47	C3
Richelieu Pk	88	A2
Richmond	111	D1
Richmond Av	100	B3
Richmond Av N	63	C2
Richmond Av S	86	B3
Richmond Cotts		
Dublin 1	62	B3
Richmond Cotts		
(Inchicore)		
Dublin 8	74	A2
Richmond Cotts N		
off Richmond Cotts	62	B3
Richmond Ct	96	B1
Richmond Cres	62	B3
Richmond Est	63	C2
Richmond Grn	100	B3
Richmond Gro	100	B3
Richmond Hill		
Dublin 6	86	A1
Richmond Hill Black.	100	B3
Richmond La		
off Russell St	62	B3
Richmond Ms	86	A1
Richmond Par	62	B3
Richmond Pk	100	B3
Richmond Pl	86	A1
Richmond Pl S		
off Richmond St S	86	A1
Richmond Rd	62	B3
Richmond Row	86	A1
Richmond Row S		
off Richmond St S	76	A3
Richmond St N	62	B3
Richmond St S	76	A3
Richmond Ter 19	122	B2
Richview Office Pk	87	C3
Richview Pk	86	B3
Ridgeford		
Apartments	109	C1
Ridge Hill	119	C3
Ridgewood Av	10	A2
Ridgewood Cl	10	A2
Ridgewood Ct	10	A2
Ridgewood Grn	10	A3
Ridgewood Pk	10	A2
Ridgewood Pl	10	A2
Ridgewood Sq	10	A2
Ringsend Br	77	D2
Ringsend Pk	77	D2
Ringsend Rd	77	C2
Ring St	73	C3
Ring Ter	73	D3
Rise, The (Drumcondra)		
Dublin 9	44	A3
Rise, The (Ballinteer)		
Dublin 16	108	B3
Rise, The (Ballyboden)		
Dublin 16	106	B2
Rise, The (Cookstown)		
Dublin 24	91	C2
Rise, The		
(Kilnamanagh)		
Dublin 24	91	D1
Rise, The Dalkey	114	B2
Rise, The Kins.	12	A2
Rise, The Leix.	66	A1
Rise, The Mala.	14	A2
Rise, The (Robswall) 3		
Mala.	15	C3
Rise, The Manor.	25	C3
Rise, The Still.	98	B2
River Cl 2	121	C1
River Ct 1	22	B3
Riverdale	66	B2
River Forest	66	B1
River Gdns	44	A3
River La	121	C1
River Rd Dublin 11	41	D3
River Rd Dublin 15	41	D3
Riversdale	109	C1
Riversdale Av		
Dublin 6	95	D1
Riversdale Av Clond.	80	B1
Riversdale Av Palm.	57	C3
Riversdale Ct	57	C3
Riversdale Cres	80	B1
Riversdale Dr	80	B1
Riversdale Grn		
Dublin 6W	84	B3
Riversdale Gro Palm.	57	C3
Riversdale Ind Est	82	B1
Riversdale Pk Clond.	80	B1
Riversdale Pk Palm.	57	C3
Riversdale Rd	80	B1
Riverside 3	80	B1
Riverside Av	34	A3
Riverside Cotts	94	B2
Riverside Cres	34	A3
Riverside Dr Dublin 14	95	D2
Riverside Dr Dublin 17	34	A3
Riverside Dr Palm.	57	C3
Riverside Gro	34	A3
Riverside Pk	34	A3
Riverside Rd	34	A3
Riverside Wk	87	C3
Riverston Abbey	60	A1
River Valley Av	11	C1
River Valley Cl	10	B1
River Valley Ct	10	B1
River Valley Dr	10	B1
River Valley Gro	10	B2
River Valley Hts	10	B1
River Valley Lawn	11	C2
River Valley Pk	10	B2
River Valley Rd	10	B1
River Valley Rd	10	B1
River Valley Vw	10	B1
River Valley Way	10	B1
Riverview Dublin 24	104	A2
Riverview Palm.	57	D3
Riverview		
Business Cen	81	D1
Riverview Ct	72	B1
Riverwood Chase	38	A3
Riverwood Cl	38	B3
Riverwood Copse	38	A3
Riverwood Ct	38	B3
Riverwood Cres	56	B1
Riverwood Dale	38	B3
Riverwood Dene	38	A3
Riverwood Dr	38	A3
Riverwood Gdns	56	B1
Riverwood Glebe	56	A1
Riverwood Glen	38	B3
Riverwood Grn	38	B3
Riverwood Gro	38	B3
Riverwood Heath	38	A3
Riverwood Lawn	38	B3
Riverwood Pk	56	A1
Riverwood Pl	56	A1
Riverwood Rd	38	B3
Riverwood Ter	38	A3
Riverwood Vale	38	B3
Riverwood Vw	38	B3
Riverwood Way	38	B3
Road, The	25	D2
Road Number 1	78	A1
Road Number 2	78	A1
Road Number 3	78	A1
Robert Emmet Br	85	D1
Robert Pl		
off Clonliffe Rd	62	B2
Robert St Dublin 3		
off Clonliffe Rd	62	B2
Robert St Dublin 8	75	C2
Robinhood		
Business Pk	82	A2
Robinhood Ind Est	82	B2
Robinhood Rd	82	B2
Robinsons Ct	124	A4
Robin Vil	57	D3
Robswall	15	C3
Rochestown Av	113	C3
Rochestown Pk	113	C3
Rochfort Av	69	D2
Rochfort Cl	69	D2
Rochfort Cres	69	D3
Rochfort Downs	69	D2
Rochfort Grn	69	D2
Rochfort Pk	69	D2
Rochfort Way	69	D3
Rockfield Dublin 14	109	C1
Rockfield Lucan	68	A3
Rockfield Av	93	D1
Rockfield Cl	38	B3
Rockfield Dr		
Dublin 12	84	A3
Rock Fld Dr Clond.	80	B3
Rockfield Dr Cool.	38	B3
Rockfield Pk	38	B2
Rockford Pk	100	A3
Rockfort Av	115	C2
Rock Hill	99	D2
Rockingham Av	66	A1
Rockingham Grn	66	A1
Rockingham Gro	66	A1
Rocklands 2	115	C1
Rock Lo	114	A3
Rock Rd	88	B3
Rockville Cres	100	A3
Rockville Dr	100	A3
Rockville Pk	100	A3
Rockville Rd	100	A3
Rockwood	68	A3
Rocwood	111	C2
Roebuck Av	98	B2
Roebuck Castle	97	D1
Roebuck Downs	97	C2
Roebuck Dr	83	D3
Roebuck Hall	97	D2
Roebuck Rd	97	C1
Roger's La	76	B3
Rollins Ct 7	113	C2
Rollins Vil	113	C2
Ronanstown	70	A3
Roncalli Rd	49	C2
Rookery, The	106	A1
Rooske Ct	22	A3
Rooske Rd	22	A3
Rope Wk Pl	77	D2
Rory O'Connor Pk	112	B1
Rory O'More Br	75	C1
Rosapenna Dr	36	A3
Rosary Gdns E	101	C3
Rosary Gdns W	101	C3
Rosary Rd	75	C3
Rosary Ter	77	D2
Rosbeg Ct	49	C2
Rosbank	104	A1
Rosedale (Hartstown)		
Clons.	24	B2
Rosedale Dunb.	22	A2
Rosedale Dr	24	B2
Rose Glen Av	48	B2
Rose Glen Rd	48	A2
Rosehaven 1	38	B3
Rosehill 7	111	D1
Roselawn	69	C1
Roselawn Av	39	C2
Roselawn Cl	39	C2
Roselawn Ct	39	D2
Roselawn Cres	39	C2
Roselawn Dr Bray	122	A3
Roselawn Dr Castle.	39	C2
Roselawn Glade	39	C2
Roselawn Gro	39	C2
Roselawn Pk	122	A3
Roselawn Rd	39	C2
Roselawn Vw	39	C2
Roselawn Wk	39	C2
Roselawn Way	39	D2
Rosemount	96	B2
Rosemount Av	46	B3
Rosemount		
Business Pk	28	B3
Rosemount Ct		
Dublin 14	97	C3
Rosemount Ct Boot.	98	B1
Rosemount Cres	97	C1
Rosemount Pk	97	C2
Rosemount Pk Rd	28	A3
Rosemount Rd	61	D3
Rosemount Ter	98	B1
Rose Pk	112	B1
Rosevale Ct		
off Brookwood Glen	47	C3
Rosevale Mans	47	C3
Rosewood Gro	69	D3
Rosmeen Gdns	101	D3
Rosmeen Pk	113	D1
Rossecourt Av 2	69	D3
Rossecourt Grn 6	69	D3
Rossecourt Gro 1	69	D3
Rossecourt La 5	69	D3
Rossecourt Ri	69	D3
Rossecourt Sq 4	69	D3
Rossecourt Ter 7	69	D3
Rossecourt Way 3	69	D3
Rossfield Av	90	A3
Rossfield Cres	90	A3
Rossfield Dr	90	A3
Rossfield Gdns	102	A1
Rossfield Grn	102	A1
Rossfield Gro	102	A1
Rossfield Pk	90	A3
Rossfield Way	102	A1
Rosslyn 13	122	A2
Rosslyn Ct	122	A2
Rosslyn Gro 14	122	A2
Rossmore Av		
Dublin 6W	93	D2
Rossmore Av		
Dublin 10	72	A2
Rossmore Cl	93	D3
Rossmore Cres	93	D2
Rossmore Dr		
Dublin 6W	93	D2
Rossmore Dr		
Dublin 10	72	A1
Rossmore Gro	93	D2
Rossmore Lawns	93	D2
Rossmore Pk	93	D3
Rossmore Rd		
Dublin 6W	93	D2
Rossmore Rd		
Dublin 10	72	A1
Ross St	124	B4
Ross St	60	B3
Ross Vw	57	D3
Rostrevor Rd	95	D1
Rostrevor Ter	95	D1
Rothe Abbey	74	A3
Rowan Av	110	A2
Rowanbyrn	100	A3
Rowan Hall		
off Prospect La	87	C3
Rowan Pk Av	100	A3
Rowans, The 17	119	C3
Rowans Rd	109	D2
Rowlagh Av	70	A2
Rowlagh Cres	70	A2
Rowlagh Gdns	70	A2
Rowlagh Grn	70	A2
Roxboro Cl	114	A3
Royal Canal Bk	61	D3
Royal Canal Ter	61	D3
Royal Hosp (Museum of		
Modern Art)	74	B2
Royal Liver Retail Pk	82	B1
Royal Marine Ter 3	122	B1
Royal Oak	33	C3
Royal Ter		
off Inverness Rd	63	C2
Royal Ter E	113	D1
Royal Ter La 9	113	C1
Royal Ter N 10	113	D1
Royal Ter W	113	D1
Royse Rd	61	D2
Royston	84	A3
Ruby Hall	112	B2
Rugby Rd	86	A1

Rugby Vil
 off Rugby Rd 86 A1
Rugged La 56 A1
Rushbrook 39 C2
Rushbrook Av 93 C2
Rushbrook Ct 93 D2
Rushbrook Dr 93 D2
Rushbrook Gro 93 D2
Rushbrook Pk 93 D2
Rushbrook Vw 93 C2
Rushbrook Way 93 D2
Rusheeney 25 C2
Rusheeney Av 25 D2
Rusheeney Cl 25 C2
Rusheeney Ct 25 D2
Rusheeney Cres 25 D2
Rusheeney Grn 25 D2
Rusheeney Gro 25 D2
Rusheeney Manor 25 C2
Rusheeney Pk 25 C2
Rusheeney Vw 25 D2
Rusheeney Way 25 D2
Rus-in-Urbe Ter 11 113 D1
Russell Av Dublin 3 62 A2
Russell Av Jobs. 102 A1
Russell Av E 63 C3
Russell Cl 102 A1
Russell Ct 102 A1
Russell Cres 102 A1
Russell Downs 102 A1
Russell Dr 102 A1
Russell Grn 102 A1
Russell Gro 102 A1
Russell La 102 A1
Russell Lawns 102 A1
Russell Meadows 102 A1
Russell Pl 102 A1
Russell Ri 102 A1
Russell St 62 B3
Russell Vw 102 A1
Russell Wk 102 A1
Rutland Av 85 C1
Rutland Gro 85 C1
Rutland Pl
 off Clontarf Rd 64 B3
Rutland Pl N 62 B3
Rutland Pl W 62 A3
Rutland St Lwr 62 B3
Rutledges Ter 75 C3
Ryders Row
 off Parnell St 76 A1
Ryecroft 122 A2
Ryemont Abbey 66 A1
Rye River 66 B1
Rye River Av 66 B2
Rye River Cl 66 B2
Rye River Ct 66 B2
Rye River Cres 66 B2
Rye River Gdns 66 B2
Rye River Gro 66 B2
Rye River Mall 66 B2
Rye River Pk 66 B2
Ryevale Lawns 66 B1

S

Sackville Av 62 B3
Sackville Gdns 62 B3
Sackville La
 off O'Connell St Lwr 125 D1
Sackville Pl 125 D2
Saddlers Av 26 B3
Saddlers Cl 26 B3
Saddlers Cres 26 B3
Saddlers Dr 1 26 B3
Saddlers Glade 26 B3
Saddlers Gro 26 B3
Saddlers Lawn 26 B3
St. Agnes Pk 84 A2
St. Agnes Rd 84 A2
St. Aidan's Dr 97 D2
St. Aidan's Pk 63 D2
St. Aidan's Pk Av 63 D2
St. Aidan's Pk Rd 63 D2
St. Aidan's Ter 20 122 A1
St. Alban's Pk 88 B2
St. Alban's Rd 75 D3
St. Alphonsus Av 62 B2
St. Alphonsus Rd 62 A2

St. Andoens Ter
 off Cook St 124 B3
St. Andrews 69 C1
St. Andrews Dr 69 D1
St. Andrews Fairway 69 D1
St. Andrews Grn 69 D1
St. Andrew's Gro 14 A2
St. Andrew's La
 off Trinity St 125 D3
St. Andrews Pk 8 A1
St. Andrew's St 125 D3
St. Andrews Wd 69 D1
St. Annes 84 A3
St. Anne's Av 47 D3
St. Anne's Dr 47 D3
St. Anne's Pk 121 C3
St. Annes Rd 75 C3
St. Anne's Rd N 62 A2
St. Anne's Sq 99 D2
St. Anne's Ter 47 D3
St. Ann's Sq 5 20 B3
St. Ann's Sq Lwr 4 20 B3
St. Anthony's Av 80 B3
St. Anthony's
 Business Pk 81 D2
St. Anthony's Cres 83 C3
St. Anthony's Pl
 off Temple St N 62 A3
St. Anthony's Rd 74 B3
St. Aongus Cres 92 B2
St. Aongus Grn 92 B2
St. Aongus Gro 92 B2
St. Aongus Lawn 92 B2
St. Aongus Rd 92 B2
St. Assam's Av 48 A3
St. Assam's Dr 48 A3
St. Assam's Pk 48 A2
St. Assam's Rd E 48 A3
St. Assam's Rd W 48 A3
St. Attracta Rd 61 C2
St. Aubyn's Ct 9 119 C3
St. Audoens Ter
 off School Ho La W 124 B3
St. Augustine's Pk 111 D1
St. Augustine St 124 A3
St. Barnabas Gdns 63 C3
St. Begnet's Vil 114 B2
St. Brendan's Av 46 B2
St. Brendan's Cotts 77 D2
St. Brendan's Cres 93 C1
St. Brendan's Dr 46 B2
St. Brendan's Pk 47 C2
St. Brendan's Ter
 Dublin 5 46 B1
St. Brendan's Ter D.L.
 off Library Rd 101 C3
St. Bricin's Pk 75 C1
St. Bridget's Av 63 C3
St. Bridget's Dr 83 C3
St. Brigid's Av 3 20 B3
St. Brigids Ch Rd 111 C1
St. Brigid's Cotts
 (Blanchardstown)
 Dublin 15 39 D2
St. Brigids Cotts
 Clond. 81 C3
St. Brigid's Ct
 off St. Brigid's Dr 46 B3
St. Brigid's Cres 46 B2
St. Brigid's Dr
 Dublin 5 46 B3
St. Brigid's Dr Clond. 80 B3
St. Brigids Flats 87 C3
St. Brigids Gdns 77 C1
St. Brigids Grn 46 B3
St. Brigids Gro 46 B3
St. Brigids Lawn 46 B3
St. Brigid's Pk
 (Blanchardstown)
 Dublin 15 39 D2
St. Brigid's Pk 1 Clond. 80 B3
St. Brigid's Pk Corn. 112 A3
St. Brigid's Rd
 Dublin 5 46 B2
St. Brigid's Rd Clond. 80 B3
St. Brigid's Rd Lwr 62 A2
St. Brigid's Rd Upr 62 A2
St. Brigids Shop Mall 46 B2
St. Brigid's Ter 21 122 A1
St. Broc's Cotts 87 C2
Saintbury Av 119 C2
St. Canice's Pk 43 D2
St. Canice's Rd 43 D2
St. Catherine's Av 75 C3
St. Catherine's La W 124 A3

St. Catherine's Pk
 Dalkey 114 A2
St. Catherine's Pk D.L. 114 A1
St. Catherine's Rd 114 A2
St. Clare's Av off
 Harolds Cross Rd 85 D1
St. Clare's Home 43 D2
St. Clare's Ter off Mount
 Drummond Av 85 D1
St. Clement's Rd 62 A2
St. Colmcilles Ct 1 11 C1
St. Colmcille's Way 105 C2
St. Columbanus Av 96 B1
St. Columbanus Pl 96 B1
St. Columbanus Rd 96 B1
St. Columbas Hts 11 C1
St. Columbas Ri 11 C1
St. Columba's Rd 83 C3
St. Columba's Rd Lwr 62 A2
St. Columba's Rd Upr 62 A2
St. Columcille's Cres 2 11 D1
St. Columcille's Ter 22 122 A1
St. Columcills Pk 11 D1
St. Conleth's Rd 83 C3
St. Cronan's Av 8 A1
St. Cronan's Cl 1 10 B1
St. Cronan's Ct 8 A1
St. Cronan's Gro 8 A1
St. Cronan's Lawn 8 A1
St. Cronan's Rd 23 122 A1
St. Cronan's Vw 2 10 B1
St. Cronan's Way 3 10 B1
St. Davids 46 A3
St. Davids Pk 46 A3
St. David's Ter Dublin 7
 off Blackhorse Av 60 B3
St. David's Ter
 (Glasnevin)
 Dublin 9 44 A3
St. Davids Wd 44 A3
St. Declan Rd 63 C1
St. Declan Ter 63 D1
St. Dominic's Av 104 A1
St. Dominic's Cen 104 A1
St. Dominic's Ct 3 104 A1
St. Dominic's Rd 104 A1
St. Dominic's Ter 104 A1
St. Donagh's Cres 48 A1
St. Donagh's Pk 48 B1
St. Donagh's Rd 48 A1
St. Eithne Rd 61 C2
St. Elizabeth's Ct off
 North Circular Rd 61 C3
St. Enda's Dr 95 C3
St. Enda's Pk 95 C3
St. Enda's Rd 85 C3
St. Finbar's Cl 93 C1
St. Finbar's Rd 60 B1
St. Finian's 68 B2
St. Finian's Av 68 B2
St. Finian's Cl 68 B2
St. Finian's Cres 68 B2
St. Finian's Gro 68 B2
St. Fintan Rd 61 C2
St. Fintan's Cres 51 C3
St. Fintan's Gro 51 C3
St. Fintan's Pk
 Dublin 13 51 C3
St. Fintan's Pk Black. 112 A1
St. Fintan's Rd 51 C3
St. Fintan's Ter 4 57 D3
St. Fintan's Vil 112 A1
St. Fintan Ter 61 C1
St. Gabriel's 118 A1
St. Gabriels Ct 65 D2
St. Gabriel's Rd 65 D2
St. Gall Gdns N 96 B1
St. Gall Gdns S 96 B1
St. Gatien Ct 107 C1
St. Gatien Rd 2 107 C1
St. George's Av
 Dublin 3 62 B2
St. George's Av Kill. 119 C1
St. Gerard's Rd 83 C3
St. Helena's Dr 42 B2
St. Helena's Rd 42 B2
St. Helen's 114 A1
St. Helen's Rd 98 B1
St. Helens Wd 98 B2
St. Ignatius Av 62 A2
St. Ignatius Rd 62 A2
St. Ita's Rd 62 A1
St. Ive's 14 A2
St. James Pl 73 D2

St. James's Av
 Dublin 3 62 B2
St. James's Av
 Dublin 8 75 C2
St. James's Pl
 off Tyrconnell Rd 73 D3
St. James's Rd 83 C3
St. James's Ter 75 C3
St. James's Wk 74 B3
St. Jarlath Rd 61 C2
St. Johns 88 A2
St. John's Av Dublin 8
 off John St S 124 A4
St. John's Av Clond. 80 A3
St. John's Cl 80 A3
St. John's Ct Dublin 3 64 A1
St. Johns Ct Dublin 5 46 A1
St. John's Ct Clond. 80 A3
St. John's Cres 80 A3
St. John's Dr 80 A3
St. John's Grn 80 A3
St. John's Lawn 80 A3
St. John's Pk Clond. 80 A3
St. John's Pk D.L. 101 C3
St. John's Pk W 80 A3
St. John's Rd
 Dublin 4 88 A1
St. John's Rd Clond. 80 A3
St. John's Rd W 74 A2
St. John St
 off Blackpitts 75 D3
St. Johns Wd Dublin 3 64 B2
St. John's Wd Clond. 80 A2
St. John's Wd W 80 A3
St. Joseph's Av
 Dublin 3 62 B2
St. Joseph's Av
 Dublin 9 62 A2
St. Joseph's Conv 85 C3
St. Josephs Ct 61 C3
St. Joseph's Gro 97 C3
St. Joseph's Par 62 A3
St. Joseph's Pl
 off Dorset St Upr 62 A3
St. Joseph's Rd
 Dublin 7 61 C3
St. Joseph's Rd
 Dublin 12 83 C3
St. Joseph's Sq
 off Vernon Av 65 C2
St. Joseph's St
 off Synnott Pl 62 A3
St. Joseph's Ter Dublin 1
 off North Circular
 Rd 62 B3
St. Joseph's Ter
 Dublin 3 63 C2
St. Kevins Av 86 A3
St. Kevins Gdns 86 A3
St. Kevin's Par 75 D3
St. Kevins Pk (Rathgar)
 Dublin 6 86 A3
St. Kevin's Pk Still. 110 A1
St. Kevin's Rd 85 D1
St. Kevin's Sq 122 A2
St. Kevin's Ter 15 122 A2
St. Kevin's Vil 113 C1
St. Killian's Av 82 B3
St. Killian's Pk 1 80 B2
St. Laurence Gro 72 B1
St. Laurence Rd 72 B1
St. Laurence's Mans 77 C1
St. Laurences Pk 98 B3
St. Laurence's Ter 24 122 A1
St. Laurence St N
 off Sheriff St Lwr 76 B1
St. Lawrence
 O'toole Av 1 20 B3
St. Lawrence Pl
 off Sheriff St Lwr 76 B1
St. Lawrence Rd (Clontarf)
 Dublin 3 64 A2
St. Lawrence Rd (Howth)
 Dublin 13 52 B2
St. Lawrences Ct 64 A2
St. Lawrence St
 off Sheriff St Lwr 76 B1
St. Lawrence Ter 53 C2
St. Lomans Rd 69 D1
St. Luke's Cres 96 B1
St. Maelruans Pk 104 A1
St. Magdalene Ter 77 D2
St. Malachy's Dr 83 C3
St. Malachy's Rd 62 A1

171

Entry	Page	Grid
St. Margaret's Av Dublin 5	48	B2
St. Margaret's Av Mala.	14	A2
St. Margaret's Av N off North Circular Rd	62	B3
St. Margaret's Business Pk	30	A3
St. Margaret's Cl 23	114	B1
St. Margaret's Ct 1	30	B3
St. Margaret's Halting Site	31	D2
St. Margaret's Pk	14	A2
St. Margaret's Rd Dublin 11	30	B3
St. Margaret's Rd B'mun	30	B2
St. Margaret's Rd Mala.	14	A2
St. Margaret's Ter	75	C3
St. Mark's Av	70	A1
St. Mark's Cres	70	A2
St. Mark's Dr	70	B2
St. Mark's Gdns	70	A2
St. Mark's Grn	70	A2
St. Mark's Gro	70	A2
St. Marnock's Av	20	B3
St. Martin's Dr	84	B3
St. Martin's Pk	84	B2
St. Mary's Av (Rathfarnham)	95	C2
St. Mary's Av N	62	A3
St. Mary's Av W	73	D2
St. Mary's Coll	86	A1
St. Mary's Cres	83	D1
St. Mary's Dr	83	D1
St. Mary's La	77	C3
St. Mary's Pk Dublin 12	83	D2
St. Mary's Pk Dublin 15	41	D2
St. Mary's Pk Leix.	66	B1
St. Mary's Pl off Main St	53	C2
St. Mary's Pl N	62	A3
St. Mary's Rd Dublin 3	63	C3
St. Mary's Rd Dublin 12	83	D2
St. Mary's Rd Dublin 13 off Main St	53	C2
St. Mary's Rd S	77	C3
St. Mary's St	101	C3
St. Mary's Ter Dublin 7	62	A3
St. Marys Ter 22 Bray	122	B2
St. Mary's Ter 1 Dunb.	22	A2
St. Mel's Av	93	C1
St. Michael's Est	74	A3
St. Michael's Hill	124	B3
St. Michael's La off High St	124	B3
St. Michael's Rd	62	A1
St. Michael's Ter	75	D3
St. Michan's St	124	B2
St. Mobhi Boithirin	44	A3
St. Mobhi Cl	44	A3
St. Mobhi Dr	62	A1
St. Mobhi Gro	62	A1
St. Mobhi Rd	62	A1
St. Mobhis Br	62	A1
St. Mochtas	38	B3
St. Mochtas Av	38	B2
St. Mochtas Chase	38	B2
St. Mochtas Dr	38	A3
St. Mochtas Grn	38	B3
St. Mochtas Gro	38	B2
St. Mochtas Lawn	38	A2
St. Mochtas Rd	38	A3
St. Mochtas Vale	38	B2
St. Nessan's Ter off Tuckett's La	52	B2
St. Nicholas Pl	124	B4
St. Oliver's Pk	71	C3
St. Pappin Grn	43	D2
St. Pappin Rd	43	D2
St. Patrick Av off North Strand Rd	63	C3
St. Patrick's Av 1 Clond.	80	A1
St. Patrick's Av 6 Dalkey	114	B2
St. Patrick's Av Port.	20	B3
St. Patrick's Cath	124	B4
St. Patrick's Cl Dublin 8	124	B4
St. Patrick's Cl 11 D.L.	112	B1
St. Patrick's Cotts	95	C3
St. Patrick's Cres	112	B1
St. Patrick's Nat Sch	62	B1
St. Patrick's Par	62	A2
St. Patrick's Pk (Blanchardstown) Dublin 15	39	C2
St. Patrick's Pk Clond.	80	A1
St. Patrick's Pk Dunb.	22	A2
St. Patrick's Rd Dublin 9	62	A2
St. Patrick's Rd Dublin 12	83	C3
St. Patrick's Rd Clond.	80	A1
St. Patrick's Rd Dalkey	114	B2
St. Patrick's Sq 1 Bray	122	A1
St. Patrick's Sq 7 Dalkey	114	B2
St. Patrick's Ter Dublin 1 off Russell St	62	B3
St. Patrick's Ter Dublin 3 off North Strand Rd	63	C3
St. Patrick's Ter Dublin 8	73	D2
St. Patrick's Ter 6 D.L.	113	C1
St. Patrick's Vil	77	D2
St. Paul's Ter 21	114	A1
St. Peters Av	61	D2
St. Peters Cl	61	D3
St. Peter's Cres	83	D3
St. Peter's Dr	83	D3
St. Peter's Pk	22	A2
St. Peter's Rd Dublin 7	61	D2
St. Peter's Rd Dublin 12	83	C3
St. Peter's Ter Dublin 13	52	B2
St. Peter's Ter 6 D.L.	114	A1
St. Philomena's Rd	61	D2
St. Ronan's Av	70	A3
St. Ronan's Cl	70	A3
St. Ronan's Cres	70	A2
St. Ronan's Dr	70	A2
St. Ronan's Gdns	70	A2
St. Ronan's Grn	70	A2
St. Ronan's Gro	70	A2
St. Ronan's Pk	70	A3
St. Ronan's Way	70	A3
St. Stephen's Grn	76	B3
St. Stephen's Grn N	125	D4
St. Stephen's Grn Pk	76	A3
St. Stephen's Grn Shop Cen	76	A2
St. Stephen's Grn S	76	A3
St. Stephen's Grn W	76	A3
St. Sylvester Vil	14	A3
St. Teresa's La	84	A3
St. Teresa's Pl off Prospect Av	61	D1
St. Teresa's Rd Dublin 9	61	D1
St. Teresa's Rd (Crumlin) Dublin 12	84	A3
St. Theresa Gdns	75	C3
St. Thomas' Mead	98	B2
St. Thomas' Rd (Tenter Flds) Dublin 8	75	D3
St. Thomas' Rd Still.	98	A2
St. Thomas's Av off Constitution Hill	124	B1
St. Vincent's Home	59	D1
St. Vincents Pk	100	A2
St. Vincents Rd	123	D2
St. Vincent St N	61	D3
St. Vincent St S (Tenter Flds)	75	D3
St. Vincent St W	73	D2
St. Werburghs	12	A1
Salamanca	97	D2
Sallowood Vw	32	B3
Sallyglen	113	D2
Sallymount Av	86	B1
Sallymount Gdns	86	B1
Sallynoggin	113	C2
Sallynoggin Pk	113	C2
Sallynoggin Rd	113	C2
Sally Pk	105	C1
Sally Pk Cl	105	C1
Sally's Br	85	C1
Salthill & Monkstown Sta	100	B2
Salzburg	97	D2
Sampsons La	124	C1
Sandford Av (Donnybrook) Dublin 4	87	C2
Sandford Av Dublin 8	75	C3
Sandford Cl	86	B2
Sandford Gdns Dublin 4	87	C2
Sandford Gdns Dublin 8 off Donore Av	75	C3
Sandford Rd	86	B2
Sandford Ter	86	B2
Sand Holes, The	57	D1
Sandon Cove	64	B2
Sandwith Pl	125	F3
Sandwith St Lwr	125	F3
Sandwith St Upr	125	F3
Sandycove Av E	114	B1
Sandycove Av W	114	A1
Sandycove Av E La	114	B1
Sandycove Glastule Sta	113	D1
Sandycove Rd	114	A1
Sandyford	109	D3
Sandyford Business Cen	110	A2
Sandyford Downs	109	D3
Sandyford Ind Est	110	A2
Sandyford Office Pk	110	B2
Sandyford Pk Dublin 16	109	D3
Sandyford Pk Leo.	110	B2
Sandyford Rd	109	C1
Sandyford Vw	109	C3
Sandyford Village	109	D3
Sandyhill Av	31	D3
Sandyhill Gdns	31	D3
Sandymount Av	87	D1
Sandymount Castle Dr	88	A1
Sandymount Castle Rd	88	A1
Sandymount Grn	78	A3
Sandymount Rd	78	A3
Sandymount Sta	88	A1
Sans Souci Pk	98	B1
Sans Souci Wd	122	A2
Santa Sabina Manor	51	C2
Santry Av	32	A3
Santry Av Ind Est	32	B3
Santry Business Pk	33	C2
Santry Cl	33	C3
Santry Ct	33	C3
Santry Hall Ind Est	44	B1
Santry Vil	33	C3
Sarah Curran Av	107	C1
Sarah Curran Rd 1	107	C1
Sarah Pl	74	A1
Sarsfield Ct	68	A1
Sarsfield Pk	68	B1
Sarsfield Quay	75	C1
Sarsfield Rd Dublin 8	73	D2
Sarsfield Rd Dublin 10	73	C2
Sarsfield St Dublin 7	61	D3
Sarsfield St Sally.	113	C2
Sarsfield St 4	68	A1
Sarto Lawn	49	C1
Sarto Ri	49	C1
Sarto Rd	49	C2
Saul Rd	84	B1
Saval Gro	114	A3
Saval Pk Cres	114	A3
Saval Pk Gdns	114	A2
Saval Pk Rd	114	A2
Scholarstown Pk	106	A2
Scholarstown Rd	106	A2
School Av	46	B3
Schoolhouse La	125	E4
School Ho La W	124	B1
School St	75	C2
Scotchstone Br	9	C1
Scott Pk	122	B3
Seabank Ct	114	A1
Seabrook Manor	20	A3
Seabury	88	B1
Seabury Av	13	C1
Seabury Cl	13	C1
Seabury Cl 5	13	C1
Seabury Cres	13	C2
Seabury Dale 3	13	C1
Seabury Downs	13	C2
Seabury Dr	13	C1
Seabury Gdns	12	B1
Seabury Glen	13	C1
Seabury Grn	13	C1
Seabury Gro 4	13	C2
Seabury Hts	12	B1
Seabury La	13	C2
Seabury Lawns 1	12	B1
Seabury Meadows	12	B1
Seabury Orchard	13	C1
Seabury Par	13	C1
Seabury Pk	12	B1
Seabury Pl	13	C2
Seabury Rd	13	C1
Seabury Vw	13	C1
Seabury Vw	12	B1
Seabury Wk	13	C2
Seabury Wd	12	B1
Seacliff Av	49	C1
Seacliff Dr	49	C1
Seacliff Rd	49	C1
Seacourt	65	C2
Seacrest	122	B2
Seafield	121	D1
Seafield Av Dublin 3	65	C2
Seafield Av Black.	100	B3
Seafield Cl	98	A1
Seafield Ct Dublin 13	50	A1
Seafield Ct Kill.	119	C3
Seafield Ct Mala.	14	A2
Seafield Cres	98	A1
Seafield Down	65	D2
Seafield Dr	98	A1
Seafield Gro	65	D2
Seafield Pk	98	B1
Seafield Rd Boot.	98	A1
Seafield Rd Kill.	119	C3
Seafield Rd E	65	C2
Seafield Rd W	64	B2
Seafield Ter 6	115	C2
Seafort Av	78	A3
Seafort Cotts off Seafort Av	78	A3
Seafort Gdns	78	A3
Seafort Vil off Seafort Av	78	A3
Seagrange Av	37	C3
Seagrange Dr	37	D3
Seagrange Rd	49	C1
Seamount Dr	14	B3
Seamount Gro	14	B3
Seamount Hts	14	B3
Seamount Pk	14	B3
Seamount Rd	14	B3
Seamount Vw	12	A1
Seamus Ennis Rd	42	B1
Sean Heuston Br	74	B1
Sean McDermott St Lwr	62	B3
Sean McDermott St Upr	125	D1
Sean More Rd	78	A3
Sean O'Casey La	62	B3
Seapark Dublin 3	65	C2
Seapark Mala.	14	B2
Seapark Dr	65	C2
Seapark Hill	14	B3
Seapark Rd	65	C2
Seapoint Av 1 Dublin 13	37	D3
Seapoint Av Black.	100	A2
Seapoint Ct 5 Dublin 13	37	D3
Seapoint Ct Bray	122	A1
Seapoint Rd	122	A1
Seapoint Sta	100	A2
Seapoint Ter 17	122	A1
Seapoint Vil 18	122	A1
Sea Rd	13	D1
Seatown Pk	9	C1
Seatown Rd	9	C1
Seatown Roundabout	9	C1
Seatown Ter	11	D1
Seatown Vil	9	C1
Seatown Wk	11	D1
Seatown W	9	C1
Seaview Av	63	C3
Seaview Av N	64	A2
Seaview Lawn	120	B1
Seaview Pk	120	B1
Sea Vw Ter Dublin 4	87	D2
Seaview Ter Dublin 13	53	C2
Seaview Wd	120	B1
Second Av Dublin 1	77	C1
Second Av (Cookstown) Dublin 24	91	C2

Name	Page	Grid
Sefton Grn	112	B2
Sefton Hall **11**	111	D2
Selskar Ter	86	A1
Serpentine Av	87	D1
Serpentine Pk	77	D3
Serpentine Rd	77	D3
Serpentine Ter	87	D1
Seskin Vw Av	104	A1
Seskin Vw Dr	104	A1
Seskin Vw Pk	104	A2
Seskin Vw Rd	104	A1
Seven Hos **12**	113	D1
Seven Oaks	44	B3
Seville Pl	63	C3
Seville Ter	62	B3
Seymour Rd	122	A1
Shamrock Cotts *off Shamrock Pl*	63	C3
Shamrock Pl	63	C3
Shamrock St *off Primrose St*	61	D3
Shamrock Ter	63	C3
Shamrock Vil	85	D2
Shanard Av	44	A1
Shanard Rd	44	A1
Shanboley Rd	45	C1
Shancastle Av	70	A1
Shancastle Cl	70	A1
Shancastle Cres	70	A1
Shancastle Dr	70	A1
Shancastle Lawns	70	A1
Shancastle Pk	56	A3
Shandon Cres	61	D2
Shandon Dr	61	D2
Shandon Gdns	61	C1
Shandon Pk *Dublin 7*	61	D2
Shandon Pk *Black.*	100	A2
Shandon Rd	61	D2
Shanganagh Cliffs	121	C1
Shanganagh Gro	121	C3
Shanganagh Rd	119	C3
Shanganagh Ter	119	C2
Shanganagh Vale	118	A2
Shanganagh Wd	121	C2
Shangan Av	44	B1
Shangan Cres	32	B3
Shangan Gdns	44	B1
Shangan Rd	62	A2
Shangan Grn	44	B1
Shangan Pk	44	B1
Shangan Rd	44	B1
Shanglas Rd	45	C1
Shanid Rd	85	C3
Shankill Business Cen	121	C2
Shankill Shop Cen	121	C2
Shankill Sta	121	C2
Shankill Vw **19**	122	A1
Shanliss Av	44	B1
Shanliss Dr	44	B1
Shanliss Gro	44	B1
Shanliss Pk	44	B1
Shanliss Rd	44	A1
Shanliss Wk	44	B1
Shanliss Way	44	B1
Shannon Ter	74	B2
Shanowen Av	44	A2
Shanowen Cres	44	B1
Shanowen Dr	44	B1
Shanowen Gro	44	A1
Shanowen Pk	44	A1
Shanowen Rd	44	B2
Shanowen Rd Ind Est	44	B2
Shanrath Rd	45	C1
Shantalla Av	45	C2
Shantalla Dr	45	C2
Shantalla Pk	45	C2
Shantalla Rd	45	C2
Shanvarna Rd	45	C1
Sharavogue	114	A2
Shaws La	77	D3
Shaw St	125	E3
Sheelin Av	119	C3
Sheelin Dr	119	C3
Sheelin Gro	119	C3
Sheelin Hill **8**	119	C3
Sheelin Wk	119	C3
Sheephill Av	27	D3
Sheephill Grn	27	D3
Sheephill Pk	27	D3
Sheepmoor Av	38	A1
Sheepmoor Cl	38	A1
Sheepmoor Cres	38	A1
Sheepmoor Gdns	38	A1
Sheepmoor Grn	38	A1
Sheepmoor Gro	38	A1
Sheepmoor Lawn	38	A1
Sheepmoor Way	38	A1
Shelbourne Av	77	D3
Shelbourne La	77	C3
Shelbourne Pk Greyhound Stadium	77	D2
Shelbourne Rd	77	D3
Shelerin Rd	38	A2
Shellysbanks Rd	78	B3
Shelmalier Rd	63	C3
Shelmartin Av	63	C2
Shelmartin Ter	63	C1
Shelton Dr	84	A3
Shelton Gdns	84	A3
Shelton Gro	84	A3
Shelton Pk	84	A3
Sheriff St Lwr	125	F1
Sheriff St Upr	77	D1
Sherkin Gdns	44	B3
Sherrard Av	62	A2
Sherrard St Lwr	62	A3
Sherrard St Upr	62	A3
Shielmartin Dr	51	C3
Shielmartin Pk	54	A2
Shielmartin Rd	54	A2
Ship St Gt	124	C3
Ship St Little	124	C3
Shrewsbury	88	A1
Shrewsbury Hall	121	C3
Shrewsbury Lawn	118	A1
Shrewsbury Pk	88	A1
Shrewsbury Rd *Dublin 4*	87	D2
Shrewsbury Rd *Shank.*	121	C3
Shrewsbury Wd	118	A1
Sibthorpe La	86	B1
Sidbury Ct **20**	122	B2
Sidmont Gdns	122	A2
Sidmonton Av	122	B2
Sidmonton Ct	122	B2
Sidmonton Gdns	122	B2
Sidmonton Pl **6**	122	B2
Sidmonton Rd *Bray*	122	B2
Sidmonton Rd *Grey.*	123	D1
Sidmonton Sq **7**	122	B2
Sigurd Rd	61	C3
Silchester Ct **13**	113	D1
Silchester Cres	113	D1
Silchester Pk	113	D1
Silchester Rd	113	D1
Silchester Wd **3**	113	D2
Silleachain La	67	C1
Silloge Av	43	D1
Silloge Gdns	44	A1
Silloge Rd	44	A1
Silverberry	68	B3
Silver Birches *Dublin 14*	97	C3
Silver Birches *Dunb.*	22	B2
Silver Birches Cl	22	B2
Silver Birches Cres	22	B2
Silverdale	68	A3
Silver Pines **3**	110	B2
Silverwood Dr *Dublin 6W off Templeville Dr*	94	A2
Silverwood Dr *Dublin 14*	94	B3
Silverwood Rd	94	B3
Simmon's Ct *off Simmonscourt Castle*	87	D1
Simmonscourt Av	87	D1
Simmonscourt Castle	87	D1
Simmonscourt Rd	87	D1
Simmonscourt Ter	87	D1
Simonscourt Sq	87	D1
Simonscourt Vw	87	D1
Sion Hill	99	C1
Sion Hill Av	85	C3
Sion Hill Ct	45	C3
Sion Hill Rd	45	C3
Sion Rd	113	D3
Sir Ivor Mall **1**	111	C3
Sir John Rogersons Quay	77	C1
Sitric Rd	75	C1
Skelligs Ct **1**	27	D3
Skellys La	45	D2
Skippers All	124	B3
Skreen Rd	60	A2
Slademore Av	35	C3
Slademore Cl	47	D1
Slademore Ct	35	C3
Slademore Dr	47	D1
Slade Row	75	C1
Slane Rd	84	B1
Slaney Cl	61	C1
Slaney Rd	61	C1
Slemish Rd	60	A2
Slievebloom Pk	83	D1
Slievebloom Rd	83	D1
Slievemore Rd	84	A1
Slievenamon Rd	74	A3
Slieve Rua Dr	98	A3
Sloan Ter **21**	122	B2
Sloperton	101	C3
Slopes, The	101	C3
Smithfield	124	A2
Smiths Vil	101	C3
Snowdrop Wk	35	C3
Snugborough Rd	27	D3
Snugborough Rd (extension)	38	B2
Somerby Rd	123	D2
Somerset St *off Doris St*	77	D2
Somerton	113	C2
Somerville Av	83	D2
Somerville Grn	83	D2
Somerville Pk	83	D2
Sommerton La	56	B2
Sommerville	96	B2
Sonesta	13	D1
Sorbonne	97	D2
Sorrel Dale	38	A2
Sorrel Dr	38	A2
Sorrel Heath	38	A2
Sorrento Cl **7**	115	C2
Sorrento Dr	114	B2
Sorrento Hts **1**	115	C3
Sorrento Lawn **9**	115	C2
Sorrento Ms **3**	115	C3
Sorrento Rd	114	B2
South Av	98	A3
South Bk Rd	78	A2
South Circular Rd	74	A1
South Co Business Pk	110	B3
Southdene	100	B3
South Docks Rd	77	D2
Southern Cross Av	74	A2
Southern Cross Route	108	A3
South Esplanade	122	B2
South Gt Georges St	124	C4
South Hill *Dublin 6*	86	A3
South Hill *Dublin 13*	51	C3
South Hill Av	98	B2
South Hill Pk	98	B2
South Lotts Rd	77	D3
South Pk	112	A3
South Pk Dr	112	A3
South Pk Number 4 *off Alexandra Rd*	78	B1
South Winds **11**	114	B1
Southwood Pk	99	C2
Spade Enterprise Cen	75	C1
Spafield Ter	87	D1
Spa Rd (Kilmainham) *Dublin 8*	73	D2
Spa Rd (Phoenix Pk) *Dublin 8*	60	A3
Spawell Br	94	A3
Spencer Dock	77	C1
Spencer St off *South Circular Rd*	75	C3
Spencer St N	63	C3
Spencer Vil	114	A1
Sperrin Rd	73	D3
Spiddal Pk	71	D2
Spiddal Rd	71	D2
Spire Vw Ct	85	D2
Spire Vw La	85	D2
Spitalfields	124	B4
Springfield Rd	47	C1
Springfield *Dublin 7*	60	A2
Springfield *Dublin 24*	91	C3
Springfield Av	94	B2
Springfield Cres	94	B2
Springfield Dr	94	B2
Springfield Pk *Dublin 6W*	94	B2
Springfield Pk *Deans Gra*	111	D3
Springfield Rd	94	B2
Spring Gdn La	125	E3
Spring Gdn St	63	C3
Springhill Av	112	A1
Springhill Cotts **3**	112	A1
Springhill Pk *Dalkey*	114	A2
Springhill Pk *Deans Gra*	112	A1
Springlawn	39	C1
Springlawn Cl	39	C1
Springlawn Ct	39	C2
Springlawn Dr	39	C2
Springlawn Grn	39	C2
Springlawn Hts	39	C1
Springlawn Rd	39	C1
Springvale	106	B2
Spruce Av	110	A2
Square, The *Dublin 4*	77	D2
Square, The *Dublin 6W*	85	C2
Square, The *Dublin 24*	103	D1
Square, The **3** *Lucan*	68	A1
Square Ind Complex, The	91	D3
Square Shop & Leisure Cen, The	103	D1
Stable La *Dublin 2 off Harcourt St*	76	A3
Stable La *Dublin 4 off Londonbridge Rd*	77	D3
Stables, The	98	B3
Stadium Business Pk	29	C3
Stamer St	76	A3
Stanford Grn	83	D2
Stanhope Cen	61	D3
Stanhope Grn	75	C1
Stannaway Av	84	A2
Stannaway Dr	84	B2
Stannaway Rd	84	A2
Stapolin Lawns	37	C3
Station Cl	80	B1
Stationcourt	38	B3
Stationcourt Pk	38	B3
Stationcourt Vw	38	B3
Stationcourt Way	38	B3
Station Rd *Dublin 5*	47	D3
Station Rd *Dublin 13*	50	A1
Station Rd *Clond.*	80	B1
Station Rd *Dunb.*	22	B2
Station Rd *D.L.*	114	A1
Station Rd *Kill.*	119	D2
Station Rd *Lou.V.*	66	A1
Station Rd *Port.*	20	A3
Station Rd **4** *Shank.*	121	C2
Station Rd Business Pk	70	B3
Station Vw **2**	38	B3
Station Way	36	B3
Steeples, The	73	C2
Steevens La	75	C2
Stella Av	44	A3
Stephens La	77	C3
Stephens Pl *off Stephens La*	77	C3
Stephens Rd	74	A3
Stephen St	124	C4
Stephen St Upr	124	C4
Stiles Ct, The *off The Stiles Rd*	64	A2
Stiles Rd, The	64	A2
Stillorgan Ct **2**	110	B1
Stillorgan Gro	111	C1
Stillorgan Heath	110	B1
Stillorgan Ind Est	109	D2
Stillorgan Pk	99	C3
Stillorgan Pk Av	99	C3
Stillorgan Rd *Dublin 4*	87	D2
Stillorgan Rd *Still.*	98	B2
Stillorgan Shop Cen	98	B3
Stillorgan Wd	110	A1
Stirling Pk	96	A1
Stirrup La *off Beresford St*	124	B1
Stockhole La	17	C1
Stocking La	106	A3
Stockton Ct	40	A3
Stockton Dr	58	A1
Stockton Grn	58	A1
Stockton Gro	58	A1
Stockton Lawn	40	A3
Stockton Pk	58	A1
Stonebridge	25	C3
Stonebridge Av	25	C3
Stonebridge Cl **1**	121	C3
Stonebridge Dr	25	C3

Name	Page	Grid
Stonebridge La 1	120	B2
Stonebridge Rd Clons.	25	C3
Stonebridge Rd Shank.	120	B2
Stonemasons Grn 2	108	A2
Stonemasons Way	108	A2
Stonepark Abbey	95	D3
Stonepark Ct	95	D3
Stonepark Dr	95	D3
Stonepark Grn	95	D3
Stonepark Orchard	95	D3
Stoneview Pl	101	D3
Stoneybatter	75	C1
Stoneylea Ter 1	122	A3
Stoney Rd Dublin 3 off East Wall Rd	63	C3
Stoney Rd (Dundrum) Dublin 14	97	C3
Store St	125	E1
Stormanstown Rd	43	D2
Stradbrook Cl	112	A1
Stradbrook Gdns	100	A3
Stradbrook Hill 4	112	A1
Stradbrook Lawn	100	A3
Stradbrook Pk	100	A3
Stradbrook Rd	100	A3
Stralem	25	C3
Strandmill Av	21	C3
Strandmill Pk 1	21	C3
Strandmill Rd	21	C3
Strand Rd (Sandymount) Dublin 4	78	A3
Strand Rd Dublin 13	51	C2
Strand Rd Bray	122	B1
Strand Rd Kill.	119	D2
Strand Rd Mala.	13	D1
Strand Rd Port.	20	B3
Strand St Dublin 4	77	D2
Strand St Mala.	14	A2
Strand St Gt	124	C2
Strandville Av E	64	C3
Strandville Av N	63	C3
Strandville Ho	64	C3
Strangford Gdns	63	C3
Strangford Rd E	63	C3
Strathmore Rd	119	C1
Streamstown La	119	C3
Streamville Ct 10	119	C3
Streamville Rd	48	A1
Suffolk St	125	D3
Sugarloaf Cres	122	A3
Sugarloaf Ter 12	122	A3
Suir Rd	74	A2
Sullivan St	74	B1
Summerfield (Blanchardstown) Dublin 15	39	C2
Summerfield 2 Dublin 24	104	A1
Summerfield Av	39	C2
Summerfield Cl (Blanchardstown) Dublin 15	39	C2
Summerfield Cl 8 Dalkey	114	B2
Summerfield Grn	39	C2
Summerfield Lawns	39	C2
Summerfield Meadows	39	C2
Summerfield Pk	39	C2
Summerfield Ri	39	C1
Summerhill	62	B3
Summerhill Par Dublin 1	62	B3
Summerhill Par D.L.	101	D3
Summerhill Pl	62	B3
Summerhill Rd	101	D3
Summer Pl	62	B3
Summerseat Ct	25	C1
Summer St N	62	B3
Summer St S	75	C2
Summerville	64	B2
Summerville Pk	86	A2
Sunbury Gdns	86	A3
Suncroft Av 2	21	C3
Suncroft Dr	102	A1
Suncroft Pk	102	A1
Sundale Av	102	A2
Sundale Cl	102	A2
Sundale Cres	102	A1
Sundale Grn	102	A1
Sundale Gro	102	A1
Sundale Hts	102	A1
Sundale Pk	102	A1
Sundale Rd	102	A1
Sundale Vil	102	A1
Sundale Wk	102	A1
Sundrive Pk	85	C2
Sundrive Rd	84	B1
Sundrive Shop Cen	85	C2
Sunnybank Ter	96	B3
Sunshine Ind Est	84	A1
Superquinn Shop Cen Dublin 12	83	C2
Superquinn Shop Cen Dublin 16	106	A1
Susan Ter	75	D3
Susanville Rd	62	B2
Sussex Rd	86	B1
Sussex St	101	D3
Sussex Ter Lwr off Mespil Rd	76	B3
Sussex Ter Upr off Leeson St Upr	76	B3
Sutton Ct	49	D1
Sutton Cross Shop Cen	50	B1
Sutton Downs	49	D2
Sutton Gro	49	D1
Sutton Lawns	49	D1
Sutton Pk	49	D1
Sutton Sta	50	A1
Swallowbrook	25	D1
Swallowbrook Cres	25	D1
Swallowbrook Pk	25	D1
Swallowbrook Vw	25	D1
Swan Pl off Morehampton Rd	87	C1
Swan Shop Cen	86	A2
Swans Nest Av	48	B1
Swans Nest Ct	48	B1
Swans Nest Rd	48	A1
Swanville Pl	86	A2
Swanward Business Cen	82	A3
Swanward Ct	85	C1
Swan Yd off Harry St	125	D4
Sweeneys Ter off Mill St	75	D3
Sweetbriar La	110	A1
Sweetmans Av	99	D2
Sweetmount Av	96	B3
Sweetmount Dr	96	B3
Sweetmount Pk	96	B3
Swiftbrook	102	A1
Swiftbrook Av	102	A1
Swiftbrook Cl	102	A1
Swiftbrook Dr	102	A1
Swiftbrook Pk	102	A1
Swifts All	124	A4
Swift's Gro	34	A2
Swifts Row off Ormond Quay Upr	124	B2
Swilly Rd	60	B2
Swords	12	A1
Swords Business Pk	9	D1
Swords Manor Av	8	A3
Swords Manor Ct 1	8	A3
Swords Manor Cres 2	8	A3
Swords Manor Dr 3	8	A3
Swords Manor Gro 6	8	A3
Swords Manor Vw 4	8	A3
Swords Manor Way 5	8	A3
Swords Rd Dublin 9	44	B3
Swords Rd Collins.	16	B3
Swords Rd Mala.	13	C2
Swords St	61	C3
Sybil Hill Av	47	C3
Sybil Hill Rd	47	C3
Sycamore Av Dublin 24	91	D1
Sycamore Av Cabin.	117	C1
Sycamore Av Castle.	39	C3
Sycamore Cl Dublin 24	91	D1
Sycamore Cl Cabin.	117	C1
Sycamore Cl 6	113	C2
Sycamore Cres Cabin.	117	C1
Sycamore Cres Still.	98	B2
Sycamore Dr 1 Dublin 16	108	B1
Sycamore Dr Dublin 24	92	A1
Sycamore Dr Cabin.	117	C1
Sycamore Dr Castle.	39	C3
Sycamore Grn	117	C1
Sycamore Gro Cabin.	117	C1
Sycamore Gro 3 Fox.	111	D2
Sycamore Lawn Cabin.	117	C1
Sycamore Lawn Castle.	39	C3
Sycamore Pk Dublin 11	31	C3
Sycamore Pk Dublin 24	92	A1
Sycamore Rd Castle.	39	C3
Sycamore Rd (Finglas) Dublin 11	31	C3
Sycamore Rd Dublin 12	82	A2
Sycamore Rd Dublin 16	108	B1
Sycamore Rd Still.	98	B2
Sycamores, The 18 Abb.	119	C3
Sycamores, The Mala.	14	B2
Sycamore St	124	C3
Sycamore Vw	39	C3
Sycamore Wk	117	C1
Sydenham Ms Bray	122	B2
Sydenham Ms D.L.	101	D3
Sydenham Rd (Sandymount) Dublin 4	87	D1
Sydenham Rd (Dundrum) Dublin 14	97	C3
Sydenham Vil Dublin 14	97	C3
Sydenham Vil 27 Bray	122	B2
Sydney Av	99	D2
Sydney Par Av	88	A2
Sydney Par Sta	88	A2
Sydney Ter	99	D2
Sykes La	85	D3
Sylvan Av	91	D1
Sylvan Cl	91	D1
Sylvan Dr	91	D1
Synge La	76	A3
Synge Pl	76	A3
Synge St	76	A3
Synnott Pl	62	A3
Synnott Row	62	A2

T

Name	Page	Grid
Tailor's Mkt	75	D2
Talbot Av	13	C2
Talbot Ct Dublin 15	39	D2
Talbot Ct 6 Mala.	13	C2
Talbot Downs	39	D2
Talbot La Dublin 1 off Talbot St	125	E1
Talbot La Kill.	114	A3
Talbot Lo	99	C3
Talbot Mem Br	76	B1
Talbot Pk	13	C2
Talbot Pl	125	F1
Talbot Rd 2 Kill.	119	C1
Talbot Rd Mala.	13	C2
Talbot St	125	E1
Tallaght Business Pk	103	C1
Tallaght Bypass	104	A1
Tallaght Enterprise Cen	91	A3
Tallaght Retail Cen	91	D3
Tallaght Rd	93	C3
Tallagt Rd	93	D3
Tamarisk Av	92	A1
Tamarisk Cl off Tamarisk Way	92	A1
Tamarisk Ct	92	A2
Tamarisk Dale off Tamarisk Dr	92	A1
Tamarisk Dr	92	A1
Tamarisk Gro off Tamarisk Pk	92	A2
Tamarisk Hts	92	A2
Tamarisk Lawn	92	A2
Tamarisk Pk	92	A2
Tamarisk Vw off Tamarisk Dr	92	A2
Tamarisk Wk off Tamarisk Dr	92	A1
Tamarisk Way	92	A1
Tandys La	68	A3
Taney Av	97	C3
Taney Cres	97	C3
Taney Dr	97	C3
Taney Gro	97	D3
Taney Lawn	97	C3
Taney Manor	97	C3
Taney Pk	97	C3
Taney Ri	97	C3
Taney Rd	97	C3
Tara Hill Cres	95	C3
Tara Hill Gro	95	C3
Tara Hill Rd	95	C3
Tara Lawn	48	A1
Tara St	125	E2
Tara St Sta	125	E2
Taylors Hill	108	A3
Taylor's La Dublin 8	75	C2
Taylor's La Dublin 16	106	B1
Temple Bar	125	D3
Temple Cotts	61	D3
Temple Ct Dublin 7	75	C1
Temple Ct Dublin 9	32	B2
Temple Cres	100	A2
Temple Gdns	86	A3
Temple Hill	100	A2
Temple La N	62	A3
Temple La S	124	C3
Temple Lawns	32	B2
Temple Manor	22	B1
Temple Manor Av	93	C1
Temple Manor Cl	93	C1
Temple Manor Ct	93	C1
Temple Manor Dr	93	C1
Temple Manor Gro	93	C1
Temple Manor Way	93	C1
Templemore Av	85	D3
Templeogue Lo	93	D2
Templeogue Rd	94	B2
Templeogue Wd	94	A2
Temple Pk	86	B3
Temple Pk Av	100	A3
Temple Pl	86	B1
Temple Rd Dublin 6	86	A3
Temple Rd Black.	99	D2
Templeroan	106	A1
Templeroan Av	106	A1
Templeroan Cl	106	A1
Templeroan Ct	106	A1
Templeroan Cres	106	A1
Templeroan Downs	106	B1
Templeroan Dr	106	A1
Templeroan Grn	106	A2
Templeroan Gro	106	A1
Templeroan Lo	106	A2
Templeroan Meadows	106	B1
Templeroan Ms	106	A1
Templeroan Pk	106	A1
Templeroan Vw	106	A1
Templeroan Way	106	A1
Temple Sq	86	A3
Temple St N	62	A3
Temple St W	75	C1
Temple Ter 10	115	C2
Templeview Av	35	D3
Templeview Cl	35	D3
Templeview Copse	35	D3
Templeview Ct	35	D3
Templeview Cres	35	D3
Templeview Downs	35	D3
Templeview Dr	36	A3
Templeview Grn	35	D3
Templeview Gro	35	D3
Templeview Lawn	35	D3
Templeview Pk	35	D3
Templeview Pl	35	D3
Templeview Ri	35	D3
Templeview Row	35	D3
Templeview Sq	35	D3
Templeview Vale 1	35	D3
Templeview Wk	36	A3
Templeview Way off Templeview Grn	36	A3
Temple Vil off Palmerston Rd	86	A2
Templeville Av	94	A2
Templeville Dr	94	A2
Templeville Pk	94	B2
Templeville Rd	93	D1
Terenure Coll	94	B1
Terenure Pk	85	C3
Terenure Pl	95	C1
Terenure Rd E	85	C3
Terenure Rd N	85	C3
Terenure Rd W	84	B3
Terminal Rd N	79	C1
Termon Ct 1	31	D3
Tetrarch Gro	22	B1
Texas La	13	D2
Thatch Rd, The	45	C2

174

Thicket, The 116 B1
Third Av Dublin 1 77 C1
Third Av Dublin 8
  off Dolphin's Barn 75 C3
Third Av (Cookstown)
  Dublin 24 91 C3
Thomas Ct 124 A4
Thomas Davis St S 124 B4
Thomas Davis St W 73 D3
Thomas La
  off O'Connell St Upr 125 D1
Thomas Moore Rd 83 C2
Thomas St E 77 D2
Thomas St W 75 C2
Thomastown Cres 11 113 C2
Thomastown Rd 113 D3
Thomond 121 C2
Thomond Rd 72 B2
Thormanby Lawns 53 C2
Thormanby Lo 53 D3
Thormanby Rd 53 C2
Thormanby Wds 53 C3
Thornbury Apartments 25 D1
Thorncastle St 77 D2
Thorncliffe 96 B1
Thorncliffe Pk 96 A1
Thorndale Av
  off Elm Mt Rd 46 A3
Thorndale Ct 45 C2
Thorndale Cres
  off Elm Mt Rd 46 A3
Thorndale Dr 44 A3
Thorndale Gro 44 A3
Thorndale Lawns
  off Elm Mt Rd 46 A3
Thorndale Pk
  off Elm Mt Rd 46 A3
Thornhill Rd 98 A3
Thornville Av 48 B2
Thornville Dr 48 B2
Thornville Pk 48 B2
Thornville Rd 48 B2
Thor Pl 75 C1
Three Rock Cl 92 B1
Three Rock Rd 110 A2
Thundercut All
  off Smithfield 124 A2
Tibradden Cl
  off Tibradden Dr 92 B1
Tibradden Dr 92 B1
Tibradden Gro
  off Tibradden Dr 92 B1
Ticknock Av 108 B3
Ticknock Dale 3 109 C3
Ticknock Gro 108 B3
Ticknock Hill 108 B3
Ticknock Pk 108 B3
Ticknock Way 108 B3
Timber Quay 78 A1
Tinkler's Path 58 B2
Tionscail Ind Est 11 D1
Tivoli 85 D2
Tivoli Cl 113 C1
Tivoli Rd 101 C3
Tivoli Ter E 101 C3
Tivoli Ter N 101 C3
Tivoli Ter S 101 C3
Tolka Cotts 43 C3
Tolka Est Rd 43 C3
Tolka Quay 77 D1
Tolka Quay Rd 78 B1
Tolka Rd 62 B2
Tolka Vale 43 C3
Tolka Valley
  Business Pk 42 B3
Tolka Valley Ind Est 42 B3
Tolka Valley Rd 42 A3
Tolka Vw Ter 43 C3
Tom Clarke Ho 63 C2
Tom Kelly Rd 86 A1
Tonduff Cl
  off Lugaquilla Av 92 B1
Tonguefield Rd 84 B2
Tonlegee Av 47 D1
Tonlegee Dr 47 C1
Tonlegee Rd 47 C1
Torca Rd 115 C3
Torlogh Gdns 63 C2
Torlogh Par 63 C1

Torquay Rd 111 C2
Torquay Wd 111 C2
Tory Sq 39 C1
Tourmakeady Rd 44 B2
Tower Av 85 D3
Tower Rd Dublin 15 58 A2
Tower Rd Clond. 80 B2
Tower Shop Cen 80 B2
Tower Vw Cotts 61 D1
Townsend St 125 E2
Townyard La 14 A2
Trafalgar La 100 A2
Trafalgar Rd 123 D1
Trafalgar Ter Black. 100 A2
Trafalgar Ter 4 Bray 122 B1
Tram Ter 65 C3
Tramway Cotts 61 D2
Tramway Ct
  off Station Rd 50 A1
Tramway Ter 88 A1
Tramway Vil 85 C3
Tranquility Gro 46 A1
Treepark Av 92 A2
Treepark Cl 92 A2
Treepark Dr 92 A2
Treepark Rd 92 A2
Trees Av 98 B3
Trees Rd Lwr 98 B3
Trees Rd Upr 98 A3
Tresilian 116 B1
Trevor Ter
  off Grattan St 77 C2
Trimbleston 97 D2
Trimleston Av 88 B3
Trimleston Dr 88 B3
Trimleston Gdns 88 B3
Trimleston Pk 88 B3
Trimleston Rd 98 B1
Trim Rd 45 D1
Trinity Coll 125 E3
Trinity Coll Enterprise
  Cen 77 C2
Trinity St 125 D3
Trinity Ter 63 C2
Tritonville Av 78 A3
Tritonville Ct 77 D3
Tritonville Cres 78 A3
Tritonville Rd 77 D3
Trosyrafon Ter 23 122 B2
Tryconnell Pk 73 D2
Tubbermore Av 11 115 C2
Tubbermore Rd 114 B2
Tuckett's La 52 B2
Tudor Ct 2 13 C1
Tudor Lawns 111 C3
Tudor Rd 86 B3
Tulip Ct 35 C3
Tullyvale 118 A3
Turnapin Cotts 33 D2
Turnapin Grn 33 C2
Turnapin Gro 33 D2
Turnapin La 33 C2
Turnberry 49 D1
Turnpike Rd 81 D2
Turret Rd 71 D1
Turrets, The 77 D3
Turrets Flats off
  Rathmines Rd Upr 86 A2
Tuscany Downs 47 D2
Tuscany Pk 49 D1
Tymon Cl 103 D2
Tymon Cres 103 D1
Tymon Gro 103 D1
Tymon Hts 104 B2
Tymon La 93 C2
Tymon Lawn 103 D2
Tymon N Av 92 B2
Tymon N Gdns 92 B3
Tymon N Grn 92 B2
Tymon N Gro 92 B2
Tymon N Lawn 92 B3
Tymon N Pk 92 B3
Tymon N Rd 92 B2
Tymonville Av 92 B2
Tymonville Ct 92 A2
Tymonville Cres 92 A2
Tymonville Dr 92 B2
Tymonville Gro 92 B2
Tymonville Pk 92 B2
Tymonville Rd 92 B2
Tynan Hall 91 D1
Tynan Hall Av 91 D1
Tynan Hall Gro 91 C1
Tynan Hall Pk 91 C1
Tyrconnell Rd 73 D3

Tyrconnell St 73 D3
Tyrconnell Vil
  off Grattan Cres 73 D2
Tyrone Pl 73 D3

U
Ullardmor 9 114 B2
Ulster St 61 D2
Ulster Ter 1 99 C3
Ulverton Cl 114 B1
Ulverton Ct 12 114 B1
Ulverton Rd 114 B1
University Coll
  Dublin 2 76 A3
University Coll
  Dublin 4 97 D1
University Coll
  (Sch of Nursing &
  Midwifery) Dublin 4 77 D3
Upper Cliff Rd 53 C2
Uppercross 69 D1
Uppercross Rd 74 B3
Upper Glen Rd 58 B3
Urney Gro 114 A3
U.S.A. Embassy
  (Residence) 59 C3
Ushers Island 75 C1
Ushers Quay 124 A2
Usher St 124 A2

V
Vale, The 57 C3
Valentia Par 62 A2
Valentia Rd 44 A3
Vale Vw Av 117 C1
Vale Vw Cl 117 C1
Valeview Cres 42 A2
Valeview Dr 42 A2
Valeview Gdns 42 A2
Vale Vw Gro 117 C1
Vale Vw Lawn 117 C1
Valley Pk Av 41 D2
Valley Pk Dr 41 D3
Valley Pk Rd 41 D3
Valley Vw 8 A1
Vauxhall Av 75 C3
Vavasour Sq 77 D3
Venetian Hall 46 B3
Ventry Dr 60 B1
Ventry Pk 60 B1
Ventry Rd 60 B1
Verbena Av Dublin 13 49 C2
Verbena Av Fox. 111 D3
Verbena Gro 49 C1
Verbena Lawns 49 C1
Verbena Pk 49 C1
Verdemont 38 B2
Vergemount
  off Clonskeagh Rd 87 C3
Vergemount Hall 87 C3
Vergemount Pk 87 C2
Vernon Av (Clontarf)
  Dublin 3 65 C2
Vernon Av Dublin 6
  off Frankfort Av 85 D2
Vernon Ct 65 C3
Vernon Dr 65 C1
Vernon Gdn 65 C2
Vernon Gro Dublin 3 65 C2
Vernon Gro (Rathgar)
  Dublin 6 86 A3
Vernon Heath 65 C1
Vernon Par
  off Clontarf Rd 64 A2
Vernon Pk 65 C2
Vernon Ri 65 C1
Vernon St 75 D3
Vernon Ter
  off Frankfort Av 86 A3
Veronica Ter 77 D2
Verschoyle Ct
  off Verschoyle Pl 77 C3
Verschoyle Pl 77 C3
Vesey Ms 101 C3
Vesey Pk 68 A2
Vesey Pl 101 C3
Vevay Cres 16 122 A2
Vevay Rd 122 A3
Vevay Vil 13 122 A3
Vicar St 124 A3
Vico Rd 119 D1
Victoria Av Dublin 4 87 C2
Victoria Av Bray 122 B2

Victoria Br 77 C2
Victoria Quay 75 C1
Victoria Rd (Clontarf)
  Dublin 3 64 A2
Victoria Rd (Terenure)
  Dublin 6 95 D1
Victoria Rd Dalkey 115 C2
Victoria Rd Grey. 123 C1
Victoria Rd Kill. 119 D1
Victoria St 75 D3
Victoria Ter Dublin 3
  off Clontarf Rd 65 C3
Victoria Ter Dublin 14 96 B3
Victoria Ter 10 Dalkey 114 B2
Victoria Vil Dublin 3 63 D2
Victoria Vil (Rathgar)
  Dublin 6 85 D3
View, The Dublin 16 108 B3
View, The Dublin 24 104 B1
View, The (Cookstown)
  Dublin 24 91 C2
View, The Mala. 15 C3
View, The Manor. 25 C2
Viking Pl
  off Arbour Hill 75 C1
Viking Rd 75 C1
Villa, The 12 A2
Villa Blanchard 39 D2
Village, The Dublin 5 48 A3
Village, The Dublin 9 44 B3
Village Cen 80 B2
Village Cen, The 5 68 A1
Village Ct 95 C2
Village Ct, The 6 68 A1
Village Gate, The 114 B2
Village Grn 92 A3
Village Hts 26 B3
Village Sq 104 A1
Villa Pk Av (Ascal Pairc An
  Bhailtini) 60 A2
Villa Pk Dr (Ceide Pairc An
  Bhailtini) 60 A2
Villa Pk Gdns (Gardini Pairc An
  Bhailtini) 60 A2
Villa Pk Rd (Bothar Pairc An
  Bhailtini) 60 A2
Villarea Pk 114 A1
Villiers Rd 86 A3
Vincent Ter 62 A1
Violet Hill Dr 43 C3
Violet Hill Pk 43 C3
Violet Hill Rd 43 C3
Virginia Dr
  off Virginia Pk 42 A2
Virginia Hts 91 C3
Virginia Pk 42 A2
Viscount Av 33 C2

W
Wad Br 44 A2
Wadelai Grn 44 A2
Wadelai Rd 43 D2
Wade's Av 47 D3
Wainsfort Av 94 A1
Wainsfort Cres 94 A1
Wainsfort Dr 84 A3
Wainsfort Gdns
  off Wainsfort Cres 94 A1
Wainsfort Gro 94 B1
Wainsfort Pk 94 A1
Wainsfort Rd 94 A1
Waldemar Ter 96 B3
Waldrons Br 96 A1
Walk, The Dublin 6W 94 A2
Walk, The Dublin 16 108 B3
Walk, The Dublin 24 104 A1
Walk, The Kins. 12 A3
Walk, The Lou.V. 66 A1
Walk, The Mala. 15 C3
Walk, The Manor. 25 C2
Walkinstown Av 83 C2
Walkinstown Cres 83 C2
Walkinstown Cross 83 C2
Walkinstown Dr 83 C2
Walkinstown Grn 83 C2
Walkinstown Mall 83 C2
Walkinstown Par 83 C2
Walkinstown Rd 83 C2
Walkinstown Rd (Bothar Chille
  Na Manac) 83 C2
Wallace Rd 83 D2
Walnut Av Dublin 9 44 B3
Walnut Av 1 Dublin 24 91 D1
Walnut Cl 91 D1

Walnut Ct	44	B3
Walnut Dr **2**	91	D1
Walnut Lawn	44	B3
Walnut Pk	44	B3
Walnut Ri	44	B3
Walnut Vw **5**	106	B2
Walsh Rd	44	A3
Waltersland Rd	110	B1
Waltham Ter	99	C2
Walworth Rd		
off Victoria St	85	D1
Warburton Ter **24**	122	B2
Wards Hill	75	D3
Warners La	76	B3
Warren, The	13	C2
Warren Av	56	B1
Warren Cl	56	B1
Warren Cres	56	B1
Warren Grn		
Dublin 13	50	A1
Warren Grn Carp.	56	B1
Warrenmount	75	D3
Warrenmount Pl	75	D3
Warrenpoint	64	A2
Warrenstown	27	C3
Warrenstown Cl	27	C3
Warrenstown Ct	27	C3
Warrenstown Downs	27	C3
Warrenstown Dr	27	C2
Warrenstown Garth	26	B3
Warrenstown Grn	27	C3
Warrenstown Gro	27	C3
Warrenstown Lawn	27	C3
Warrenstown Pk	27	C3
Warrenstown Pl	26	B3
Warrenstown Ri	27	C3
Warrenstown Row	27	C3
Warrenstown Vale	27	C3
Warrenstown Vw	26	B3
Warrenstown Wk	27	C3
Warrenstown Way	27	C3
Warren St	86	A1
Warrington La		
off Warrington Pl	77	C3
Warrington Pl	77	C3
Warwick Ter		
off Sallymount Av	86	B1
Wasdale Gro	95	D1
Wasdale Pk	95	C1
Washington La	94	B3
Washington Pk	94	B2
Washington St	75	D3
Watercourse	93	D2
Waterfall Av	62	B2
Waterfall Rd	47	D3
Watergate Est	103	D1
Waterloo Av	63	C3
Waterloo La	86	B1
Waterloo Rd	87	C1
Watermeadow Dr	103	D1
Watermeadow Pk	103	D1
Watermill Av	47	D3
Watermill Cl	104	A2
Watermill Dr	47	D3
Watermill Gro	104	A2
Watermill Lawn		
Dublin 5	48	A3
Watermill Lawn		
Dublin 24	104	A2
Watermill Rd	47	D3
Watermill Rd		
(Bothar An Easa)	47	D3
Waterside Av	12	A2
Waterside Cl	12	A2
Waterside Ct Port.	21	C1
Waterside Cres		
Swords	12	B2
Waterside Dr	12	A2
Waterside Grn	12	A2
Waterside Lawn	12	A2
Waterside Pk	12	A2
Waterside Ri **4**	12	A2
Waterside Rd **1**	12	A2
Waterside Wk	12	A2
Waterside Way **3**	12	A2
Waterstown Av	57	D3
Waterville Rd	27	D3
Waterville Row **1**	39	C1
Waterville Ter	39	D1
Watery La Clond.	80	B1
Watery La Swords	8	A1
Watling St	75	C2
Watson Av	118	B1
Watson Dr	118	B1

Watson Pk	118	B1
Watson Rd	118	B1
Watson's Est	118	B1
Waverley Av	63	C2
Waverley Business Pk	82	B1
Waverley Ter Dublin 6		
off Kenilworth Rd	85	D2
Waverley Ter **5** Bray	122	B1
Weatherwell Ind Est	70	B3
Weaver La off		
Phibsborough Rd	61	D3
Weavers Sq	75	D3
Weaver's St	75	D2
Wedgewood Est	109	D2
Weirview Dr	110	B1
Weldon's La **8**	37	D3
Wellesley Pl off		
North Circular Rd	62	B3
Wellfield Br	36	A2
Wellington Ct **17**	122	A2
Wellington La		
Dublin 4	87	C1
Wellington La		
Dublin 6W	93	D2
Wellington Monument 74		B1
Wellington Pk	93	D1
Wellington Pl		
(Donnybrook)	87	C1
Wellington Pl N	61	D3
Wellington Quay	124	C3
Wellington Rd		
Dublin 4	87	C1
Wellington Rd		
Dublin 6W	93	D2
Wellington Rd		
Dublin 8	74	A1
Wellington St	101	C3
Wellington St Lwr	62	A3
Wellington St Upr	61	D3
Wellmount Av	42	A2
Wellmount Cres	42	A2
Wellmount Dr	42	A2
Wellmount Grn	42	A2
Wellmount Par	42	A2
Wellmount Pk	42	A2
Wellmount Rd	42	A2
Wellpark Av	44	B3
Well Rd **2**	11	C1
Wellview Av	26	B1
Wellview Cres	26	B2
Wellview Grn	26	B1
Wellview Gro	26	B1
Wellview Pk	26	B2
Wendell Av	21	C1
Wentworth Ter		
off Hogan Pl	77	C2
Werburgh St	124	B3
Wesbury	110	B1
Wesley Hts	109	C2
Wesley Lawns	109	C2
Wesley Pl	75	D3
Wesley Rd	85	D3
Westbourne Lo	105	D1
Westbourne Rd	95	C1
Westbourne Ter **25**	122	A1
Westbrook	84	A3
Westbrook Rd	96	B2
Westbury	68	A3
Westbury Av	68	A2
Westbury Cl	68	A3
Westbury Dr	68	A2
Westbury Pk	68	A3
Westcourt		
off Basin St Upr	75	C2
Westcourt La	75	C2
Westend Village	38	B1
Western Ind Est	82	A2
Western Parkway		
Dublin 15	57	C1
Western Parkway		
Dublin 20	71	C1
Western Parkway		
Dublin 22	81	D3
Western Parkway		
Dublin 24	81	D3
Western Parkway		
Business Cen	82	B3
Western Parkway		
Business Pk	82	B3
Western Rd	75	C3
Western Way	61	D3
Westerton Ri **5**	108	B1
Westfield Av	67	C3
Westfield Pk	122	B2

Westfield Rd	85	C2
Westgate Business Pk	82	A3
Westhampton Pl	85	C3
Westhaven	25	D2
Westland Ct		
off Cumberland St S	125	F4
Westland Row	125	F3
Westlink Ind Est	72	B3
Westminster Ct **4**	116	B1
Westminster Lawns	111	C2
Westminster Pk	111	D2
Westminster Rd	111	D3
Westmoreland Pk	86	B1
Westmoreland St	125	D3
West Oil Jetty	78	B2
Weston Av	96	B3
Weston Cl Dublin 14	96	B3
Weston Cl Lucan	67	C3
Weston Ct	67	C3
Weston Cres	67	C3
Weston Dr	67	C3
Weston Grn	67	C3
Weston Gro	96	B3
Weston Hts	67	C3
Weston La	67	C3
Weston Lawn	67	C3
Weston Meadow	67	C3
Weston Pk Dublin 14	96	B3
Weston Pk Lucan	67	C3
Weston Rd	96	B3
Weston Ter	96	B3
Weston Way	67	C3
West Pk Dublin 5	47	C2
Westpark Dublin 24	104	A1
West Pk Dr	43	D3
Westpoint Business Pk	25	D1
Westpoint Ct		
Business Pk	82	B1
West Rd	63	C3
West Row	76	A1
West Ter	73	D2
Westview Ter **6**	122	B1
Westway	27	D3
Westway Cl	27	D3
Westway Gro	27	D3
Westway Lawns		
off Westway Gro	27	D3
Westway Pk	27	D3
Westway Ri	27	D3
Westway Vw	27	D3
Westwood Av	41	D2
Westwood Rd	41	D2
Wexford St	76	A3
Wharton Ter off		
Harolds Cross Rd	85	D1
Whately Pl	110	B1
Wheatfield	122	A3
Wheatfield Gro	21	C1
Wheatfield Rd		
Dublin 20	71	D1
Wheatfield Rd Port.	21	C1
Wheatfields Av	70	B2
Wheatfields Cl	70	B2
Wheatfields Ct	70	B2
Wheatfields Cres	70	B2
Wheatfields Dr	70	B2
Wheatfields Gro	70	B2
Wheatfields Pk	70	B2
Whitebank Rd	78	B2
Whitebarn Rd	96	A2
Whitebeam Av	87	C3
Whitebeam Rd	87	C3
Whitebeams Rd	109	D2
Whitebrook Pk	102	B1
Whitechapel Av	38	A1
Whitechapel Ct	38	A1
Whitechapel Cres	38	A1
Whitechapel Grn	38	A1
Whitechapel Lawn	38	A1
Whitechapel Pk	38	A1
Whitechapel Rd	38	A1
Whitechurch	107	C2
Whitechurch Abbey **7**	95	C3
Whitechurch Av	107	C2
Whitechurch Cl	107	C2
Whitechurch Ct	107	C2
Whitechurch Cres	107	C2
Whitechurch Dr	107	C2
Whitechurch Grn	107	C2
Whitechurch Gro	107	C2
Whitechurch Hill	107	C2
Whitechurch Lawn	107	C2
Whitechurch Pk	107	C2
Whitechurch Pines	95	C3
Whitechurch Pl	107	C2

Whitechurch Rd		
Dublin 14	95	C3
Whitechurch Rd		
Dublin 16	95	C3
Whitechurch Stream **5**	95	C3
Whitechurch Vw	107	C2
Whitechurch Wk	107	C2
Whitechurch Way	107	C2
Whitecliff	107	C1
Whitefriar Pl		
off Aungier St	124	C4
Whitefriar St	124	C4
White Hall	91	C1
Whitehall Cl	93	D1
Whitehall Gdns	84	A3
Whitehall Ms	111	D3
Whitton Pk	93	D1
Whitehall Rd		
(Rathfarnham)	96	A3
Whitehall Rd E	93	D1
Whitehall Rd W	93	D1
White Oak	97	C1
Whites La N	61	D3
Whites Rd	58	A2
Whitestown	26	B3
Whitestown Av	26	B3
Whitestown		
Business Pk	103	C2
Whitestown Cres	26	B3
Whitestown Dr		
Dublin 24	103	C1
Whitestown Dr Mulh.	26	A3
Whitestown Gdns	38	B1
Whitestown Grn	26	B3
Whitestown Gro	26	B3
Whitestown Pk	26	B3
Whitestown Rd	103	C1
Whitestown Wk	38	B1
Whitestown Way	103	D1
White's Vil	114	B2
Whitethorn	71	C2
Whitethorn Av	46	A2
Whitethorn Cl	45	D2
Whitethorn Cres		
Dublin 5	46	A2
Whitethorn Cres		
Dublin 10	71	C2
Whitethorn Dr	71	C2
Whitethorn Gdns	71	C2
Whitethorn Gro	46	A2
Whitethorn La		
off Thorncastle St	77	D2
Whitethorn Pk		
Dublin 5	46	A2
Whitethorn Pk		
Dublin 10	71	C2
Whitethorn Ri	46	A2
Whitethorn Rd		
Dublin 5	45	D2
Whitethorn Rd		
Dublin 14	87	C3
Whitethorn Wk **1** D.L.	112	B2
Whitethorn Wk **2** Fox.	111	D3
Whitethorn Way	71	C2
Whitshed Rd	123	C3
Whitton Rd	85	C3
Whitworth Av		
off Whitworth Pl	62	A2
Whitworth Pl	62	A2
Whitworth Rd Dublin 1		
off Seville Pl	63	C3
Whitworth Rd		
Dublin 9	61	D2
Whyteleaf Gro	36	A3
Wickham Way	109	C2
Wicklow La		
off Wicklow St	125	D3
Wicklow St	125	D3
Wigan Rd	62	A2
Wilderwood Gro	93	D2
Wilfield	88	A1
Wilfield Rd	88	A1
Wilfrid Rd	85	D2
Willbrook	107	C1
Willbrook Downs	107	C1
Willbrook Gro	95	C3
Willbrook Lawn	95	C3
Willbrook Pk	95	C3
Willbrook Rd	95	C3

Name		
Willbrook St	95	C3
Willfield Pk	88	A1
William's La		
off Princes St N	125	D2
William's Pk	86	A1
William's Pl S	75	D3
William's Pl Upr	62	A2
William's Row		
off Abbey St Mid	125	D2
William St N	62	B3
William St S	125	D4
Willie Nolan Rd	37	D3
Willington Av	93	D1
Willington Ct	93	D1
Willington Cres	93	D2
Willington Dr	93	D2
Willington Grn	93	D1
Willington Gro	93	D2
Willington Pk		
off Willington Gro	93	D2
Willmont Av	114	A1
Willow Av	80	A3
Willowbank		
Dublin 16	109	C1
Willow Bk *D.L.*	101	C3
Willowbank Dr	107	C1
Willowbank Pk	94	B3
Willow Business Pk	82	A1
Willow Ct	80	A3
Willow Dr	80	A3
Willowfield	88	A1
Willowfield Av	97	D2
Willowfield Pk	97	D2
Willow Gate	108	B1
Willow Gro *Clond.*	80	A3
Willow Gro *Corn.*	112	A3
Willow Gro **4** *D.L.*	113	C2
Willow Ms	88	B2
Willow Pk **5** *Fox.*	111	D2
Willow Pk *Dunb.*	22	B2
Willow Pk Av	43	D1
Willow Pk Cl	43	D1
Willow Pk Cres	43	C1
Willow Pk Dr	43	D1
Willow Pk Gro	43	D1
Willow Pk Lawn	43	D1
Willow Pk Rd	43	D1
Willow Pl	99	C1
Willow Rd *Dublin 12*	81	D1
Willow Rd *Dublin 16*	108	B1
Willows, The		
Dublin 11	61	C1
Willows, The **19** *Abb.*	119	C3
Willows, The *D.L.*	100	A3
Willows Ct	25	D3
Willows Dr	25	D3
Willows Grn	25	D3
Willows Rd	25	D3
Willow Ter		
off Rock Rd	99	C1
Willow Vale	118	B2
Willow Wd Cl	25	D3
Willow Wd Downs	25	D3
Willow Wd Grn	25	D3
Willow Wd Gro	25	D3
Willow Wd Lawn	25	D3
Willow Wd Pk	25	D3
Willow Wd Ri	25	D3
Willow Wd Vw	25	D3
Willow Wd Wk	25	D3
Willsborough Ind Est	33	D2
Willsbrook Av	69	C1
Willsbrook Cres	69	D1
Willsbrook Dr	69	C1
Willsbrook Gdns	69	C1
Willsbrook Grn	69	C1
Willsbrook Gro	69	C1
Willsbrook Pk	69	C1
Willsbrook Pl	69	C1
Willsbrook Rd	69	C2
Willsbrook Vw	69	C1
Willsbrook Way	69	C1
Wilson Cres	98	A2
Wilson Rd	98	A2
Wilsons Pl		
off Grants Row	77	C2
Wilton Pl	76	B3
Wilton Ter	76	B3
Windele Rd	62	A1
Windermere	25	C3
Windgate Ri	55	D2
Windgate Rd	53	C2
Windmill Av		
Dublin 12	84	A2
Windmill Av *Swords*	11	C1
Windmill Cres	84	A1
Windmill Lands	10	A1
Windmill La	125	F2
Windmill Pk	84	A2
Windmill Ri	11	C1
Windmill Rd	84	A2
Windrush	121	C2
Windsor Av	63	C2
Windsor Ct **12**	112	B1
Windsor Dr	112	B1
Windsor Ms **5**	14	A2
Windsor Pk	112	B1
Windsor Pl	76	B3
Windsor Rd	86	A2
Windsor Ter		
Dublin 8	85	D1
Windsor Ter *D.L.*	101	D3
Windsor Ter *Mala.*	14	A2
Windsor Vil	63	C2
Winetavern St	124	B3
Winton Av	85	D3
Winton Rd	86	B1
Wogans Fld	66	A2
Wolfe Tone Av	101	C3
Wolfe Tone Quay	75	C1
Wolfe Tone Sq E	122	A3
Wolfe Tone Sq Mid	122	A3
Wolfe Tone Sq N	122	A3
Wolfe Tone Sq S	122	A3
Wolfe Tone Sq W	122	A3
Wolfe Tone St	124	C1
Wolseley St	75	D3
Wolverton Glen	114	A2
Wood, The		
Dublin 24	104	A1
Wood, The *Shank.*	120	B3
Wood Avens	70	A3
Woodbank Av	41	D2
Woodbank Dr	41	D2
Woodberry *Castle.*	57	C1
Woodberry *Lucan*	68	A3
Woodbine Av	88	A3
Woodbine Cl	47	D1
Woodbine Dr	47	D2
Woodbine Pk		
Dublin 5	47	D2
Woodbine Pk *Boot.*	88	B3
Woodbine Rd		
Dublin 5	48	A1
Woodbine Rd *Boot.*	88	A3
Woodbrook Ct	38	A3
Woodbrook Cres	38	A3
Woodbrook Hall	38	A3
Woodbrook Lawn	122	A3
Woodbrook Pk		
Dublin 16	94	A3
Woodbrook Pk *Carp.*	38	A3
Woodbrook Sq	38	A3
Woodcliff Hts	53	C3
Wood Dale Cl	105	C2
Wood Dale Cres	105	C2
Wood Dale Dr	105	C2
Wood Dale Grn	105	C2
Wood Dale Gro	105	C2
Wood Dale Oak **2**	105	C2
Wood Dale Vw	105	C2
Woodfarm Av	71	D1
Woodfarm Dr	71	D1
Woodfield	106	A2
Woodfield Av	73	D2
Woodfield Pl		
off Woodfield Av	73	D2
Woodford	110	B2
Woodford Av	81	C2
Woodford Business Pk	33	C2
Woodford Cl	81	C2
Woodford Ct	81	C2
Woodford Cres	81	C1
Woodford Downs	81	C2
Woodford Dr	81	C2
Woodford Garth	81	C2
Woodford Gro	81	C2
Woodford Hts	81	C2
Woodford Hill	81	C2
Woodford Lawn	81	C2
Woodford Meadows	81	C1
Woodford Par	81	C1
Woodford Pk	81	C1
Woodford Pk Rd	81	C2
Woodford Ri	81	C2
Woodford Rd	81	C2
Woodford Ter	81	C2
Woodford Vw	81	C2
Woodford Vil	81	C2
Woodford Wk	81	C2
Woodford Way	81	C1
Woodhaven	86	B3
Woodhazel Cl	32	A3
Woodhazel Ter	32	A3
Woodlands *Dublin 6*	95	D1
Woodlands *Grey.*	123	D3
Woodlands **5** *Mulh.*	26	A3
Woodlands *Port.*	21	C2
Woodlands, The		
Dublin 14	95	D2
Woodlands Av *Corn.*	118	A1
Woodlands Av *Still.*	98	B3
Woodlands Ct	21	C2
Woodlands Dr *Corn.*	118	A1
Woodlands Dr *Still.*	98	B3
Woodlands Pk *Black.*	98	B2
Woodlands Pk *Corn.*	118	A1
Woodlands Rd	118	A1
Woodland Vil	86	B1
Woodlawn	33	C3
Woodlawn Av	33	D3
Woodlawn Cl	33	D3
Woodlawn Ct	33	D3
Woodlawn Cres		
Dublin 14	96	B2
Woodlawn Cres		
Dublin 17	33	D3
Woodlawn Dr	33	D3
Woodlawn Grn	33	D3
Woodlawn Gro		
Dublin 14	96	B2
Woodlawn Gro		
Dublin 17	33	D3
Woodlawn Ind Est	33	C1
Woodlawn Pk		
Dublin 14	96	B2
Woodlawn Pk		
Dublin 17	33	D3
Woodlawn Pk		
Dublin 24	105	C2
Woodlawn Pk **7** *D.L.*	101	C3
Woodlawn Pk Av	104	B1
Woodlawn Pk Dr	105	C1
Woodlawn Pk Gro	105	C1
Woodlawn Ri	33	D3
Woodlawn Ter	96	B3
Woodlawn Vw	33	D3
Woodlawn Wk	33	D3
Woodlawn Way	33	D3
Woodley Pk	109	D1
Woodley Rd	118	A1
Woodpark *Dublin 15*	39	D2
Woodpark *Dublin 16*	108	B2
Wood Quay	124	B3
Woodscape	68	A3
Woodside *Dublin 3*	65	C1
Woodside *Dublin 14*	95	D2
Woodside *Leix.*	66	A1
Woodside Dr	95	D2
Woodside Gro	95	D2
Woodstock Gdns	86	B2
Woodstock Pk	106	A1
Woodstown	105	C2
Woodstown Abbey	105	D2
Woodstown Av	105	C2
Woodstown Cl	105	D2
Woodstown Ct **3**	105	C2
Woodstown Dale	105	D2
Woodstown Dr	105	D2
Woodstown Gdns	105	D2
Woodstown Grn	105	D2
Woodstown Heath	105	C3
Woodstown Height	105	D3
Woodstown La	105	D3
Woodstown Lawn	105	C2
Woodstown Meadow	105	D2
Woodstown Par	105	D2
Woodstown Pk	105	C2
Woodstown Pl	105	D3
Woodstown Ri	105	D2
Woodstown Rd **2**	105	D2
Woodstown Vale	105	D3
Woodstown		
Village Cen	105	C2
Woodstown Wk **1**	105	D2
Woodstown Way	105	D3
Wood St	124	C4
Woodthorpe **4**	110	B1
Woodtown Pk	106	A3
Woodvale Av	38	A1
Woodvale Cres	38	A1
Woodvale Dr	38	A1
Woodvale Garth	38	A1
Woodvale Grn	26	A3
Woodvale Gro	38	A1
Woodvale Pk	26	A3
Woodvale Way	26	A3
Woodview *Black.*	99	C2
Woodview *Lucan*	67	D3
Woodview Cl	48	A1
Woodview Cotts	95	C2
Woodview Ct **5**	111	C1
Woodview Dr **14**	122	A3
Woodview Gro	39	C2
Woodview Hts	22	B3
Woodview Pk	48	A1
Woodville Av	69	C1
Woodville Cl	69	C1
Woodville Grn	69	C1
Woodville Gro	69	C1
Woodville Lawn	69	C1
Woodville Rd		
off Botanic Av	62	A1
Woodville Wk	69	C1
Wyattville Cl	118	B3
Wyattville Hill	118	B3
Wyattville Pk	118	B3
Wyattville Rd	118	B3
Wyckham Pk Rd	108	B1
Wynberg Pk	100	A3
Wyndham Pk	122	A1
Wynnefield Rd	86	A2
Wynnsward Dr	97	C1
Wynnsward Pk	97	C1
Wyteleaf Gro	36	A3
Wyvern Est	114	A3

X

Xavier Av	63	C3

Y

Yale	97	D2
Yankee Ter	99	D3
Yeates Way	71	D3
Yellow Meadows Av	81	C1
Yellow Meadows Dr	81	C1
Yellow Meadows Est	81	C1
Yellow Meadows Gro	81	C1
Yellow Meadows		
Lawn	81	C1
Yellow Meadows Pk	81	C1
Yellow Meadows Vale	81	C1
Yellow Rd	45	C2
Yellow Walls	13	D2
Yellow Walls Rd	13	D1
Yewland Ter	85	C3
York Av	86	A2
York Rd *Dublin 4*	77	D2
York Rd *Dublin 6*	86	A2
York Rd *D.L.*	101	C3
York St	124	C4
York Ter	101	C3

Z

Zion Rd	95	D1
Zoo Rd	74	B1